## DUE DATE

*Cambodia*

The publisher gratefully acknowledges the contribution provided by the General Endowment Fund of the Associates of the University of California Press.

# Cambodia

*A Shattered Society*

MARIE ALEXANDRINE MARTIN

*Translated by Mark W. McLeod*

*University of California Press*

BERKELEY    LOS ANGELES    LONDON

Originally published as *Le Mal cambodgien: histoire d'une société traditionnelle face à ses leaders politiques, 1946 –1987*
© 1989 Hachette, Paris; revised and updated for the English-language edition

University of California Press
Berkeley and Los Angeles, California

University of California Press, Ltd.
London, England

© 1994 by
The Regents of the University of California

*Library of Congress Cataloging-in-Publication Data*

Martin, Marie Alexandrine, 1932–
    [Mal cambodgien. English]
    Cambodia, a shattered society / Marie Alexandrine Martin :
translated by Mark W. McLeod.
        p.    cm.
    Includes bibliographical references and index.
    ISBN 0-520-07052-6 (alk. paper)
    1. Cambodia—History—20th century.   I. Title.
DS554.7.M37     1994
959.604—dc20                                          93-31837
                                                      CIP

Printed in the United States of America
9    8    7    6    5    4    3    2    1

The paper used in this publication meets the minimum requirements of
American National Standard for Information Sciences—Permanence of
Paper for Printed Library Materials, ANSI Z39.48-1984. ♾

*To the Khmer peasants*

As always, the women and children are the ones who suffer
most. . . . The abandonment of Angkor . . . is practically
nothing compared to the sufferings of the Khmer people.
The most important thing is to save the people, not the
monuments; for the moment, these can wait.

Bernard Philippe Groslier to Peter White (1981)

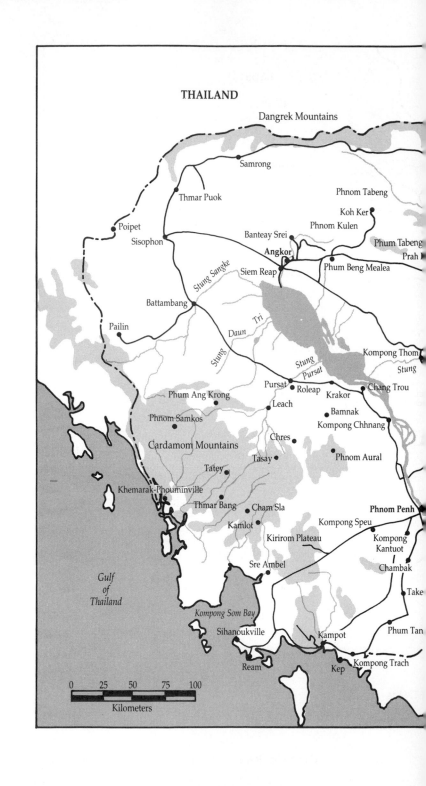

LAOS

Labansiek (plantation)

Bo Kheo

Labansiek

Lomphat

Stung Treng

River

Sambor

Poste Deshayes

Kratié

Senmonorom

O Raing

mcar
daung

Mekong

Camp Le Rolland

Poste Gatille

Snoul

ng    Chup

Mimot

VIETNAM

Prey Veng

N

Svay Rieng

River

ETNAM

- · - · —  Territorial borders

~~~~~  Waterways

————  Roads and trails

░░░░  Mountains

Cambodia: Relief and Principal Communication Routes

General Map of Indochina

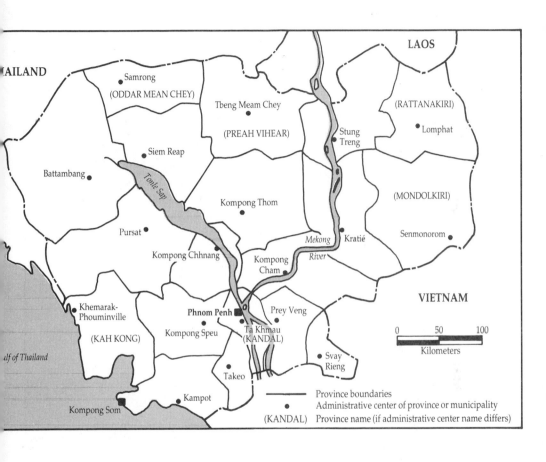

Administrative Map of Cambodia

# Contents

# Preface to the English-language Edition

Five years have passed since the publication of *Le Mal cambodgien* in France, years that have marked a diplomatic turning point in the evolution of the Khmer conflict and witnessed changes in the internal situation as well.

A revision of the book has thus proved necessary. It was facilitated by three one-month stays in Cambodia during November–December 1990, November–December 1991, and March–April 1993, which permitted me to verify, insofar as possible, the accounts gathered among Cambodian refugees along the Khmer-Thai border. This on-the-spot observation allowed me to add a chapter on daily life and continuing social changes under the state of Cambodia and to add a complement on the political negotiations that led to the signature and implementation of the 23 October 1991 peace treaty. The last pages summarize the political data for the year 1992 (additional data up to mid-September 1993 will be found in the chronology) and give an appreciation of the future.

## NOTE ON TRANSLITERATION

There is no standard romanization of the Cambodian language. The spelling of geographical names is the one found on maps. I respected the usual spelling of common words and expressions; for less common ones I adopted a free transcription that is as phonetically accurate as possible, that is,

*u* pronounced *oo*
*ea* as in *hear*
*ch* as *tia* in *Tiananmen*.

# Foreword

I, who am in no way a specialist on Cambodia, owe to Marie Martin the honor of introducing this book. But anyone, specialist or not, can appreciate its exceptional richness. No explanation of the text is necessary.

This book is also the fruit of an itinerary that began in the 1960s, somewhere near Phnom Penh or Pursat while Asia was exploding, an itinerary of patient and obstinate attention, strewn with outbursts of rage or distress, which are the opposite sides of hope. It is this itinerary, in many respects exemplary in social-science research, that deserves our attention.

We can do many things with tragedies; one course is to run from them. I cast no stone at anyone in this regard. Each of us knows the truly tragic process that has linked the destiny of the peoples of continental Southeast Asia; and the Cambodians have had more than their share in this drama. As in other cases so implacably recurrent throughout the world, researchers who depart with a flower in their notebooks discover what is, too often, the modern history of the third world—or rather simply history, for humankind is all "one single large mat," as they say in Madagascar. Civilians taken hostage, peasants displaced and piled up in the ultimate refuge of the camps, large-scale massacres, systematic torture, destruction of rural areas that had long been enriched by rural populations who left the best of themselves there; the murderous jargon of strategy and power politics, the din of tanks, the explosion of arms, the loss of meaning.

There was nothing that particularly destined Marie Martin, known for her work in ethnobotany, to move from the study of cardamom to that of strategy. If she did, it is because in the course of her long familiarity with Cambodia's society she witnessed, powerless, its destruction under contradictory pressures; she watched violence infiltrate throughout, observed the heavy clouds of international politics explode there in monstrous conflagrations. She herself also had, and with her, world opinion had, to witness this living nightmare: millions of cadavers piled up in mass graves that have been discovered year after year since 1979, for which the first task was a body count—apparently disputed, so great is the human need for classification.

Marie Martin could have fled from all that. As much as temperament, fate was at work. Hers pushed her to confront this dangerous question: What happened in Cambodia? What happened in Cambodia, with its ancient civilization, in Cambodia where, during these same 1970s Vietnamese armor and infantry massively occupied the frontier "sanctuaries," American bombers spread out over the countryside, and guerrillas circulated through the forest, and with an infinitely graceful gesture peasant women offered water to any passer-by. Bullets from armed men later disfigured the mythical versions of these living women, the *apsara* of Angkor, although they were immobile and made of stone.

This question stuck with her. She turned the ethnographer's powers of observation that inspired her *Introduction à l'ethnobotanique du Cambodge* and the perspective of classical ethnography toward an unusual subject: toward statistics of populations displaced and bombardments, acronyms of political factions, commentaries by diplomats, and testimony from refugees. But in this movement, which took her outside her familiar communities, which compelled her work to a kind of forced exile, the ethnographer of the Khmer world remained present.

That presence is what gives the book its full value, the product of a particular encounter between an individual itinerary and history, here a narrative of extraordinary ferocity. History as James Joyce defines it—"a nightmare from which I try to awaken"—has rarely fit the facts as it does in Cambodia.

In order to unravel this horrible tangle, a perception larger than that of classical ethnography was necessary; equally necessary was a viewpoint different from that of a political scientist, "foreign relations" expert, or specialized journalist, no matter how distinguished. A mind accustomed to the countryside or the camps as well as the capitals was needed; a mind capable of perceiving the external logic but also the internal causes and the relations between the two; disposed to go beyond the events in the narrow sense and to take a broader view of the "long term"; resolved not to limit itself to the viewpoint of a single one of the actors or systems of action in question, on pain of falling into one of the partial and therefore ideological explanations that the Cambodian tragedy unfortunately often receives. This tragedy deserves better, if one may be so bold. Therein lies the remarkable effort of this book.

That the work constitutes a document of exceptional interest does not make it a more reassuring one; this is why, from the perspective of the drama that it records, its approach is so realistic. What is written so convincingly here is harsh for human conscience: there are historical circumstances in which actors in conflict *are nevertheless on common ground in negation and death,* in which we search in vain to find out who, in the final analysis, was "right." We are unlikely to call out in regard to Cambodia, "Bien creusé vieille taupe" (well dug, old mole), from Marx's famous expression.

We must not scan this book for the soothing appearance of justice like Venus come from her bath; we cannot hope for a victor. In a certain sense, only the vanquished are to be found, including the world powers that confronted one another indirectly on Cambodian soil: the United States of America, China, the USSR, and also the Democratic Republic of Vietnam, so heavily present earlier in the conflict and still, at the time this text was written, bogged down in a so-called lightning war—which in fact contributed positive conditions for self-liberation—during a costly and often detested occupation for almost ten years.

At the head of the list of vanquished, I would obviously be inclined, as would Marie Martin, to place the Khmer people, a martyred people. But the Khmer people also produced the Pol Pots, the Ieng Sarys, the Khieu Samphans, the barely adolescent *yothea* who, under their leaders' direction, used methodical and murderous obstinacy in applying Bertolt Brecht's sorrowful aphorism: "If something about a country is wrong, you have to change the people and choose another one"—this same Khmer people, imbued among other interacting factors with a concept of hierarchy (*neak chuo,* knowing one's place) that worked both to help make Cambodia so peaceful and to make the Khmer revolution so terrible when "the children were in power," through an astonishing and terrible structural reversal. We are reminded of the "social drama" of ethnologist Victor Turner, for whom all crises reveal "a limited zone of transparency in the normally opaque surface of daily life."

Beyond its enduring contribution to our knowledge of the Cambodian question, this remarkable documentary survey keeps before us with implicit but uncommon clarity the reminder that neither cultures nor societies nor states are individuals who think; actors emerge and relations take shape among them, independent of each actor yet not therefore "objective," relations that chance and unfolding events embitter to the point of atrocity, beyond the understanding of anyone at the time; history has no meaning, and peace is a fragile glimmer that we must always and everywhere protect. After this book, no one should be able to make Cambodia a "pawn in their game"; no one should be able to cast the first stone or even to reach for one—but that is a long story.

Jean-François Baré
Paris, May 1988

# Acknowledgments

This book is a work that I would rather have seen written by Khmers. I thank them for their warm aid. Most of the politicians and intellectuals who bore witness asked to remain anonymous for personal and family safety, and I have respected their wish, while regretting that I could not acknowledge their help. The contribution from the peasants living as refugees in the border camps or abroad is no less considerable. I am grateful to Khmer political leaders for having welcomed me in their country between 1965 and 1975 and for having answered certain questions.

Without access to Khmer refugee camps in Thailand and to frontier settlements controlled by Thai authorities, many points would have remained obscure; I am in their debt for certain facilities.

The Centre national de la recherche scientifique de Paris and Georges Condominas—who was for many years my research director—made this study possible, even if the hazards of the economic crisis forced me in these last years to finance all my own fieldwork.

Charles Meyer cast a critical eye on chapters four and five; I thank him equally for having placed documents at my disposal. I express my gratitude to Peter White, editor of *National Geographic Magazine*, who supplied me with personal notes necessary for writing the epigraph.

Finally, my affectionate recognition goes to Gilles for his precious documentary aid and moral support, and to Annie, who proofread the entire text with her usual critical sense and generosity.

# Introduction: A Country Blessed by the Gods

Geographically situated between India and China and bearing their cultural imprints, Cambodia is the most original of the Indochinese peninsula's four countries.[1] A vast plain bordered on three sides by mountains and by the sea to the southwest, Cambodia is blessed with a tropical monsoon climate. There we observe a unique phenomenon, the seasonal reversal of the water flow: during the rainy season, the Mekong, originating in Tibet and swollen by melted snow, discharges its excess water upon reaching Phnom Penh, sending it northward where it accumulates in the immense lake of Tonle Sap, whose waters yield enormous catches of fish each year. With a catch of ocean fish as well, Cambodia ranks among the richest fishing countries in the world.

In 1970, few minorities inhabited this linguistically and culturally homogeneous land: 85 to 95 percent of the inhabitants spoke Khmer and followed the Buddha's teachings. This tolerant religion adapted well to the multitude of spirits who, along with the rains, rule Khmer life. There were no homeless people. Everyone owned a building, a villa, an apartment, a beautiful wooden house, a straw hut, or a hovel. Health, education, and, to a lesser degree, water policy were national priorities.

One-third the size of France, with woodlands covering 70 percent of its territory, Cambodia was considered an underdeveloped country but its seven million inhabitants had no care for tomorrow. Everyone—including the poor—had enough to eat.[2]

Cambodia is the heir of two magnificent empires, Funan (in the Mekong delta) and then Angkor, which knew how to control the waters.[3] The country emerged unharmed from decolonization, in marked contrast to the contiguous countries of Vietnam and Laos, where civil war raged side by side with the struggle against the foreigner. For a while, the sovereign head of state

1

was able to keep his country at peace. Townspeople found their calling in the bureaucracy, which they entered with as much righteousness as faith, as one enters a new religion. A few bold ones entered the liberal professions or took up small-scale commerce. Many worked in the service sector. The peasant farmed his paddy or the alluvial soil along the riverbanks. The mountain peoples (Khmers of the west, minorities of the northwest) followed slash-and-burn cultivation of rice.

Undocumented numbers of Chinese and Sino-Khmers in Cambodia enjoyed enormous profits by using every possible opportunity: the country's natural wealth, the credulity and needs of improvident cultivators to whom they lent money at usurious rates of interest, most townspeople's lack of enterprising spirit and business sense. Industrious, enterprising, intelligent, gifted in business, and hardworking, the Chinese and Sino-Khmers seldom smiled. But the Khmers needed them, accepted them, and some even went so far as marriage with them. They were allowed to have their own schools and to honor their spirits each year, which led to a superb celebration, as important for the Chinese community as the incomparable Water Festival for the Khmers.[4]

The Vietnamese kept to themselves, as did the approximately seventy thousand Muslims (Chams and Malays), the presence of whom was not troublesome. People were wary of the Vietnamese, and mixed unions were rare. Nevertheless, four hundred fifty thousand Vietnamese—fishing folk and artisans—inhabited the Khmer kingdom.[5]

The Khmers, on the contrary, smiled. In all circumstances, they gave an interlocutor the impression of complete agreement. The French took this smile as a sign of acquiescence and showed a certain paternalism tinted with condescension, being convinced of the superiority of their civilization though many of them had never bothered to visit Angkor.

As in Thailand, the fourth peninsular state, life was good. But in Cambodia the West had left its mark on little beyond Phnom Penh and the two seaside resorts, Sihanoukville and Kep. The Western presence remained, in the official use of the French language, in the villas inhabited by Westerners and the local bourgeoisie and in the typically French products available: wine, Camembert, and luxury goods brought in by ships five or six times a year to the country's only port, Sihanoukville, also known as Kompong Som. The women still wore the traditional skirt, the *sâmpot*; a light bodice hugged the bust and revealed a neck and shoulders that were often perfect. The children were beautiful, the men sometimes frivolous but discreet. The capital, shaded and attractive, nonchalant and silent, cast skyward the varnished rooftops of its royal palace. The jingling of the pedicabs' handbells prevailed over the honking of horns. The Cambodians had as yet little contact with dollars, limited by Prince Sihanouk's rejection of American aid in 1963.

In short, for Westerners the country breathed ease, well-being, understanding, and beauty, giving them also a feeling of the exotic. This sensation started with arrival at Pochentong airport, where new arrivals—above all the French—immediately began to feel better than at home.

A paradise! This is how foreigners described Cambodia up to the beginning of 1970; they saw it as a country of agreeable abandon. But for this, they had to remain impervious to politics and to the functioning of Khmer society—just as the Khmers did, and the French succeeded marvelously. In return, foreigners could live happily, passing dreamy weekends on the white sands and among the coconut trees of Sihanoukville or on the calcareous Kep islands.

This Eden was certainly not just a backdrop. It was a kind of puzzle, from which each person chose a particular piece of happiness, not necessarily identical to that of his neighbor. But peace reigned, a peace that certainly grew very fragile during the last years of the royal government; nevertheless, at the time, the seven million inhabitants shared in it.

Then, in less than ten years, the country experienced giant American bombers, illiterate Khmer Rouge killers, and an increasingly brutal colonization by a neighboring country.

These events remain enigmatic for Westerners, preoccupied above all with geopolitics. Stripped of all social context, the behavior of the leaders and its consequences cause dissatisfaction and discomfort among foreigners accustomed to rationalizing and with scant concern for the influence of society on events.

This book recounts the life of the Khmer people for several decades based on my experience as an anthropologist, on accounts given by peasants, political actors, and intellectuals, and on official documents. I have tried to examine these different sources, despite the difficulty inherent in maintaining exacting standards in the study of societies, placing as little of myself as possible in the work, yet without pretending to lack an opinion. The whole does not constitute an exhaustive study but rather an internal approach to what is conventionally termed "the Cambodian problem." If the examination of certain social facts is unpleasant, it concerns the entire society and is not aimed at particular individuals. Of historical events still poorly known, I have kept only the broad lines useful for understanding current events; similarly, I have summarized the geopolitical factors likely to help us visualize the future.

During the more than ten years since the monstrous Khmer Rouge revolution ended—without, however, bringing peace back to Cambodia—I

have conversed with Khmers of diverse social origins and ideological affili-
ations in refugee camps in Thailand, on the Khmer-Thai border, and in
France. Drawn to everything that constitutes the identity of populations, I
noticed with distress the inhibiting role played by certain behaviors and
conceptions specific to the Khmers. I hoped to see them evolve in a modern
world that is pitiless with those who cannot adapt themselves to it. Tradition
has been a barrier to collective reflection on the part of the Khmer elite.
Confronted by such inertia, I took up the pen.

# Part One

## PEACEFUL CAMBODIA

En ce temps-là j'étais crédule
Un mot m'était promission
Et je prenais les campanules
Pour les fleurs de la passion.

Louis Aragon, "L'Étrangère"

# 1  A Conservative Society

Despite historical vicissitudes, Khmer society seems to be unchanged by the centuries. From the smiling *apsara* of Angkor to the graceful peasant women of today, the silhouette is not notably different. Buddhism, established at the end of the thirteenth century, is still the national religion, and spirits retain a prominent role. Khmer remains the official language, and rice cultivation constitutes the main activity of the majority of the inhabitants. In 1970 the people still had recourse to the sovereign (who had become head of state) to seek justice. The province remains the supreme administrative division, even if it has changed dimensions. Respect for hierarchy is omnipresent. The love of grandeur that characterized the kings of Angkor manifests itself today in individuals, townspeople above all, constantly preoccupied with showing off their wealth, with surpassing their neighbors in everything.

Nevertheless, a distinction must be made between the peasantry—including the modest strata of the cities—and prosperous townspeople, well-off financially, intellectually, politically, or working in the public sector.

## THE MODEST NEEDS OF THE COMMON PEOPLE

Water is so important in Cambodia that the territory is called *teuk-dey* or "water-earth." The notion of native soil, *srok*, goes back to ancient times.[1] The word appears in the inscriptions carved into the steles of Angkor's temples. It is the natal *srok* and the parents' name that give status to a peasant.

Until 1970 rural inhabitants made up more than 85 percent of the Cambodian population.[2] Aside from peasants in exceptionally dry zones in northern Preah Vihear and Oddar Mean Chey provinces, whose poor soil and scant supplies of fish provide few sources of protein except for reptiles

7

and frogs, Khmers generally had enough of the two main components of their diet: rice and fresh or dried fish. Of course the vagaries of the climate affected the harvest. On the whole, however, people knew that they did not have to think about tomorrow: "We grew rice and, at mealtime, we went and caught a fish from a stream or nearby pool; we did not have to worry about tomorrow . . . , we were not used to foresight," an intellectual of peasant origins explains.[3]

This material abundance hardly gave the Khmers reason to provide for the future. They needed think only about the rains and, even in this regard, relied on the spirits or the king and were confident that things would work out. They took life easily, confident of their continued good fortune. The highland people of the west (Cardamom Mountains) toiled more in clearing the dense, humid forest, and in some places little fishing was possible. They bought essential foodstuffs with money earned from the obligatory and difficult harvesting of forest products that the state purchased from them. Despite difficult conditions (humidity, cold, isolation), they were hardly more provident than their neighbors of the plain. A little dried fish or crab paste with the addition of leaves picked in fallow land sufficed; sometimes they had only vegetable products and an egg from time to time.

Living from day to day, peasants who grew rice were content with a single crop,[4] which allowed them a great deal of leisure time. When it was not the growing season, they made tools and devices for fishing and added to their income by gathering and selling firewood and growing corn. At the market, women sold vegetable-fiber mats, cakes, and *num bâncok*, a Cambodian vermicelli covered with aromatic herbal sauce, to the inhabitants of the village or neighborhood. The most tiring tasks were carried out in the morning: work in the rice fields (plowing, harrowing, and sowing were done almost exclusively by men; replanting, weeding, and harvesting by all), gardening, collecting firewood, and fishing.

Slow to work but uncomplaining about the difficulty of a task for which their solid physique prepared him, peasants could still lounge about and take a daily nap after chores were done. In the hottest hours of the day villages lay silent, without activity. They came to life when classes were dismissed and work began on the day's second and last meal at around five o'clock. At nightfall came the sound of the same pestle in the rice mortar that had announced the awakening of the village at dawn. Indeed, the women chose the cool times of day for husking rice.

At the evening gatherings old men recounted tales, an episode from the *Ramayana*, or events they themselves had experienced. Their lives were composed of this succession of daily acts enlivened at day's end by cultural or historical evocations or by a bit of music from an orchestra made up of rice growers. All were in good spirits, despite their cares. Although the Cambodians did not suffer from malnutrition—or at worst, only from poor diets—some rural inhabitants who were heavily in debt found themselves in critical straits in the 1960s.

To treat illness villagers had recourse to medicinal plants, the most common of which everyone recognized and used. Traditional practitioners looked after the difficult cases; they excelled at curing skin diseases and certain emotional problems but had no remedy against trachoma, venereal diseases, cholera, and other serious illness.

On festival days at the pagoda or when they honored popular deities (particularly during the biannual festival of the soil spirits), people bustled about preparing foods and offerings for the monks and the supernatural powers. On these days, chickens were killed or sometimes a pig, alcohol was consumed, and there was much talk.

After the destitution of the preceding centuries, the social services begun by the French protectorate at the end of the nineteenth century gave the peasants relative tranquility. The peasants represented no danger for the colonial and royal authorities. They were even grateful to those who had brought them peace. In the words of a Khmer intellectual, the peasants "are class, candor, loyalty. Leaders haven't known how to take advantage of that."

## A RELENTLESS EDUCATION

Among the minority of Cambodia's inhabitants who lived in the cities there existed several strata. Pedicab drivers, domestic workers, small merchants, and office workers had a standard of living that was not much higher than that of the peasants. The Cambodian bourgeoisie, who were the high- and mid-level bureaucrats, included intellectuals with or without degrees and bureaucrats with rather elevated positions but no university diplomas. "An intellectual was someone who had undertaken studies that were or were not recognized by a diploma. In my parents' day, it was the *brevet*." Many of them came from the well-to-do peasantry but denied their backgrounds as soon as they attained public office. Honest bureaucrats found it difficult to live in a dignified manner, particularly in terms of dressing properly, one of the essential components of Khmer dignity.[5] Next to this "thinking" bourgeoisie was a "commercial" bourgeoisie mainly composed of Chinese, Sino-Khmers of Chinese culture, and a limited number of Khmers. Finally, there was the royal family and several high dignitaries, the ones who held real power.

A city dweller's daily routines differed little from the peasant's: most bureaucrats and small shopkeepers observed the Chinese soup break and the coffee break. The bureaucrats' uninterrupted schedule (seven A.M. until two P.M.) did not interfere with the ritual of the nap. With Khmer religious, royal, and national holidays added to French holidays, the city dweller had a schedule that was as comfortable as the peasant's. Businessmen alone sometimes worked while others rested. The Vietnamese and Chinese communities took only a three days' holiday for the New Year's Festival, and the latter celebrated the traditional festival of the Chinese spirits in splendid fashion. After two o'clock in the afternoon the cities usually resembled sleepy market towns and the capital an attractive European provincial town.

In the city the impact of education was much more visible. Boun Chan Mul, among the first Khmers to speak out in favor of independence, had a clear-sighted view of the behavior of his urban compatriots: irresolute, egotistical, equally lacking in generosity and a sense of solidarity, destroying what was meant for others if they could not have it themselves, animated by a spirit of vengeance that included the family of the target of their criticism, endlessly discussing details without ever moving on to essentials.[6] But how can this behavior be explained?

According to custom, Khmer children receive a strict education based on a morality inspired by Buddhist principles and recorded for the most part in treatises, the *chbap*, during the sixteenth and seventeenth centuries and unchanged since then. Other treatises, similarly inspired, were composed in the nineteenth century.[7] Nobody—neither neighboring countries nor colonizer—is responsible for this situation. The Khmers remain in charge of their children's traditional education.[8]

Under the French protectorate, most young people knew only this form of education. Even where primary schools existed, the weight of the family was always stronger. Only two secondary institutions were in operation when the French left in 1955; if France sinned, it was by a shortage and not an excess of education. France expanded the "pagoda schools," which were purely the creation of Khmers and in which Khmer lay teachers or monks taught. Before and after independence, the *chbap* formed the basic texts in secondary schools for the hours devoted to Khmer language and literature.

The texts used most are *The Treatise on the Morality of Girls*; *The Treatise on the Morality of Men* and its more pragmatic version, *The Treatise of the Poet Kram Ngoy*; *The Treatise of Ancient Sayings*; *The Treatise on the Heritage*; and *The Treatise on the Glorious Tradition*: "Oh, my children! Guard and conserve your parents' heritage with care so that it may long remain at your service." Its precepts are good in theory, but rigidly taught, they harm the individual and ultimately the society. "The fires within [troubles in a household] should not be taken outside and stirred up. Likewise, others' bad feelings should not be brought into the household."

Nor, in fact, are the good points of others to be retained; only the familial unit counts. Young children simply learn to perform the Buddhist greeting, the *sâmpeah*. Aside from this requirement, they can do anything, even strike their mother. Later, they may be beaten if they show themselves inflexible in educational matters, which parents take very seriously. Teaching begins when children are about six years of age. Generally the father educates the boys, the mother the girls. The teacher is expected to contribute to the moral virtues of the youngsters. "You should protect the family against all harm, that is, do not destroy the tradition that your parents pass on to you, do not try to oppose their advice, do not make them miserable on your account."[9]

As in many Asian countries, respect for elders and for hierarchy remains sacrosanct. In Cambodia this principle is rigorously applied. Members of the Chinese community abroad continue to venerate their ancestors, but personal initiatives remain the prerogative of everyone, even the very young. In the Khmer milieu, the *bâng*, or "elder," is automatically right. "Elder" means not only older persons but also those younger who have knowledge, power, wealth, or influence with "people in high places." The wife calls her husband *bâng* even if he is younger than she is. The younger-elder opposition thus expresses an entire hierarchical system.

> In the traditions of Khmer moral training, to protest against a parent's decision, to criticize one's boss or spiritual master, to rebel against a husband is inadmissible. It is understandable how such a mentality can lead to an abuse of power but also how dangerous a lack of wisdom or scruples can be, for once the link of confidence is broken, the divorce is irreparable, and the authority is forever rejected.

Younger persons must keep quiet. And adolescents have no chance to express themselves, much less to argue. It is not surprising if later they allow themselves to be trampled by an "elder" who is in the wrong or less competent than they are, if they remain defenseless in the face of a national tragedy or prefer to let a foreigner speak or act in their place. The taboos and personal rivalries are such that individuals will discuss social, political, and cultural problems more or less freely with a foreigner but remain mute with their compatriots.

The primary social rule may be stated as follows: be discreet, unobtrusive, keep to your station, that is, be a *nêak cuo*, "someone who knows his place." Men and women show a great deal of reserve or modesty. Young girls, more restrained than boys, have to make themselves forgotten, even to avoid making the floor creak when walking at home: "In Phnom Penh, if I made the slightest noise when walking, my mother said: 'Why do you have to stand out like that? Only whores want to be noticed.' When I settled in France, I had carpeting installed throughout the apartment," explains a young bourgeois woman from Phnom Penh. The fact that the group takes care of its members deprives individuals of all desire to struggle when they feel the need to do so. They may experience inclinations but have not learned to go further. Now, in the late twentieth century, young Khmers contest this absence of role, this place assigned by society: "Children no longer accept that their parents' authority should last a lifetime. The child no longer wants his father's power to be absolute. He wants to be allowed to discuss things, make judgments, and express his opinion if necessary."[10]

Nevertheless, on the whole, a monolithic hierarchy establishes itself inside the family, the village, the city, the entire country, a hierarchy founded not on each person's individual merits but on age and influence, on the prestige derived from a diploma. An intellectual explains:

> When I studied in Paris, nobody knew that I was enrolled in a doctoral program; they looked down on me. Just before the defense of my thesis, I announced it. The students belonging to the Union des étudiants khmers de France [see chapter 5] did not believe it. They checked the bulletin boards at the Sorbonne, and when they saw my name there, they became very friendly.

This prestige explains the peasants' desire to see their children pursue studies; obtaining a diploma opens the door to positions more respected than that of growing rice. It demonstrates in any case the acquisition of learning and thus brings respect, although learning and diplomas do not go hand-in-hand. In the 1960s children raised in the Khmer tradition, as most were, found themselves torn between their parents, before whom they could not display their knowledge, and their teachers, most of whom were French on the secondary level, who taught them to use reason. They were nonetheless conscious of being the descendants of the builders of Angkor, the heirs of an ancient and prestigious civilization. Prince Youtevong observes: "Despite centuries of suffering, reverses, and unparalleled difficulties, the Khmer still remains dazzled by his glorious past and does not—alas!—realize the very real distance between himself and other peoples. His arrogance as a civilized people remains intact."[11] Even so, the Khmers lack self-confidence, sensitive as they are to the decline of their country during the last several centuries, and ignorant as they are of their history.

Before independence, Khmer students learned mainly from their French teachers about "our ancestors the Gauls. . . . There were also several courses on Annam, Cambodia, India, and so forth, but as insignificant complementary subjects. Even the Cambodian language was taught to us by a French-man." After independence, several history teachers gave priority to Cam-bodia.[12] Others continued without changing anything. The Khmers themselves were not particularly interested to find out about it. They do not read. It is striking to observe that apartments inhabited by Khmers living in France (not to mention those elsewhere) are often empty of printed matter: there are few bookcases and hardly any books. In a transit camp in Thailand, a Khmer teacher of peasant origins notes:

> The Khmers find any pretext to avoid taking French or English courses. The Americans had to threaten them with refusing to con-sider their cases before they became more diligent in their English lessons. . . . In contrast to the Chinese or Vietnamese, who attend school and use the camp's libraries, Khmers prefer the video room; they don't try to educate themselves. In any case, they don't rec-ognize anything foreign to their customs. Before they leave for a third country, we try to explain what an airplane is and how to be-have on one, for most of them haven't ever seen one up close. But as far as I can tell, this does no good; they obstinately hold on to what they think and to what they don't know.[13]

In this particular case, the teacher's problems probably stem from the fact that he is a Khmer. In point of fact, after the troubles and tragedies that they have endured, for which certain of their compatriots can be blamed, Khmers are wary of one another.

As a result of this undemanding education, Khmer intellectuals have serious lacunae; they excel in the sciences and disciplines that require memorization, such as law, but they do not know the name of the king or in which century Angkor Wat was built (and yet take credit for it) and have never visited it. The *Treatise for the Peoples* stipulates, "If you know work and business and remember them without forgetting anything, you can become a high-ranking official, for you have a good memory." Further, "The Khmer child's constraining education denies the youth the possibility of decision making, even of all initiative. The Khmer, an excellent follower, needs a leader or a guide."[14] For his part, Sam Sok writes: "Our society's common behavior and habits, by crushing the individual and throttling initiative, generate a permanent psychosis of fear, a lack of self-confidence, and flight before responsibilities. They encourage a snail-like reflex, with each person drawing back inside his shell for security."[15] A young woman adds: "Nothing is explained to a child. Unlike the young Westerner, he never goes through the 'why' stage; if he makes a mistake, he receives a spanking but never an explanation. . . . Psychology is nonexistent among the Cambodians. A mother does not try to understand the internal problems that motivated her infant's act but rather the external reasons that might have provoked it."

In a remarkable and courageous thesis, Tith Huon, a former policeman of peasant origins, analyzed aspects of Cambodian society, particularly the traditional education:

> In Cambodia, importance is given to recitation rather than to reflection and to the diploma rather than to learning. For centuries, obtaining a diploma—of whatever kind—was considered the guarantee of receiving an administrative position. For a young Cambodian, learning means memorization. These well-grounded and widespread habits explain in large measure the absence of a critical sense so characteristic of Cambodians, even intellectuals.[16]

A consequence of this lack of cultural interest is that Khmers in groups have other Khmers as their main subject of conversation. They quickly move to scandalmongering, backstabbing, and calumny, and these lead to disputes and the impossibility of uniting. Moreover, Khmers recognize quality only in those whom they are bound by tradition to respect—an "elder" may lose his way or compromise himself, but all will be forgiven. Others have no right to make a mistake or even to change.

This behavior, fraught with consequences in the present crisis, is a manifestation of the Khmers' impetuous nature. "Cambodians are not rational; they are passionate, and they let hatred blind them." This hatred goes as far as the denial of scientific facts: Khmers refuse to admit that Vietnamese, the language of their hereditary enemy, belongs to the same family as Cambodian, the Mon-Khmer language family.[17]

Khmers knowingly and obstinately cling to a false statement, for the second rule of Khmer *savoir-vivre* is to avoid loss of face. This trait is widespread in Southeast Asia to varying degrees, but nothing—neither knowledge nor the coming of the modern world—attenuates it in Cambodia. To avoid loss of face means to persist in one's errors. Khmers do this with a great deal of elegance, concealing their feelings behind the facade of a charming smile directed at their interlocutor, Khmer or foreigner.[18] It does not fool Khmers, for it manifests a social rule they learned during youth, the second part of which is not to cause others to lose face.[19] "We smile to conceal our timidity, our shame, our misfortunes, and also out of respect for our interlocutor." An impassive face implies an immense self-restraint, the counterpart of which—explosion—may be violent though rare. However, we must not conclude that Khmers are violent by nature, as is sometimes said. Aside from the fact that such a statement is meaningless, traditional Cambodia had few tragedies. Except for scattered individual cases, murderous acts involved piracy, which sometimes raged cruelly when the sovereign's authority weakened or an enemy attacked. Even the practice of eating an enemy's liver to appropriate his strength, which Westerners discovered to their horror in the late 1960s, was not specifically Khmer but existed beyond Cambodia's borders. But "the Cambodian likes to be flattered," a Khmer explains. "You can get anything you want this way; it's a question of pride. But if you offend him in some way, he can no longer control himself and may kill you." Another describes this behavior as "a kind of madness that takes control, similar to the phenomenon of *amok* among the Malays. We call it *areak coan*, 'to be possessed.'" Indeed, Khmers easily become extremists once they forget social constraints. Further, once they assume power—when they can do whatever they wish—they do not try to get along with others: they purge or physically eliminate anyone who gets in their way.

For the Westerner, a disconcerting consequence of this second rule of Khmer *savoir-vivre* shows up in the varying answers that an educated Khmer can give to the same question after an interval of a day or two. Often an answer depends on the context in which the conversation takes place: he responds with what he believes the other wishes to hear in such a circumstance, for he wants to avoid conflict. The foreigner often perceives this courteous and disinterested gesture as a lie, whereas Khmers easily decipher the answer. Sometimes the Khmer interlocutor supplies only a part of the answer, and his various remarks converge toward a final point. Still other cases—although rarely—involve disinclination or lack of interest in explaining; he is caught off guard and saves face by saying anything that comes to mind. From this point of view, the peasant displays more straightforwardness in saying "I don't know" to a Khmer superior or a foreigner, for he has still not learned the city's artfulness. Moreover, he also feels respectful fear for the hierarchy and does not want to suffer the reprisals that an inappropriate reply would bring.

Therefore, in a way, Khmers are never wrong. If the foreigner presses an opposing viewpoint, he will make lasting enemies, for they are deeply vindictive. Unpredictable reactions may result when such an occurrence causes an old dispute to reemerge.

Khmer parents have so often repeated to children that they must be right in all circumstances and superior to others that, when they grow up, they naturally become arrogant. To match one's neighbor, one must have everything he or she has. Here is the origin of the envious side of the Khmer character, the jealousy expressed by a fleeting glimmer in the eyes, a barely perceivable change of tone, a slight change of gesture if one gives more of something—a gift or compliment—to one person than to another. Khmers keep this sense of frustration from childhood: excluded from the adults' discussions, youngsters tend to develop an inferiority complex that "can manifest itself by contempt for others, isolation, boastfulness about alleged abilities in order to try to place oneself on the same level as others."[20]

A guest is usually pampered in the city as well as in the countryside; one has to show that one has the means to treat a guest properly. The peasant and the poor city dweller add a dish to their ordinary fare. The better-off Khmer's table overflows with provisions. Before 1975 feasts given at home or in restaurants were on such a grand scale as to shock people of modest means. Today, this practice continues in Paris, where weddings are sometimes celebrated with lavish displays that shock non-Khmers who are aware of the great difficulties inside Cambodia and in the border settlements controlled by the opponents. The scarcity and famine under which they lived during the Khmer Rouge's regime has made a handful of Khmers stop to reflect; those people now live simply. Others do not try to regain the standing they had enjoyed in Phnom Penh but merely to preserve appearances vis-à-vis their compatriots. The same hierarchy, based on external signs of wealth, remains. They retain the same taste for luxury in cars. Cambodians used to prefer the Mercedes 220 S, a mark of respect and esteem. Nor has this changed: in France refugees buy first a television and then a car. As a result of this quasi-general trait, pamphlets printed to announce meetings or artistic events—which, for financial reasons, generally take place in the suburbs—give all the necessary directions for motorists but do not inform pedestrians of the metro stations and subsequent bus routes that they will need to take. And yet the concept of the hearth, of a warm and welcoming home, is unknown to them.

> The Westerner has a taste and a sense of comfort of which the Asian is ignorant. . . . The Cambodian is as ambitious as anyone else; he wants honors and wealth. But he does not employ this wealth in the same way others do. He does not think of his wealth from the point of view of comfort. His conception of material prosperity does not have the same material base the Westerner's has. The Cambodian paradise is inhabited by ravishing goddesses loaded with gold and precious stones . . . , but it is never a matter of material comfort.[21]

Indeed, in accordance with a tradition established in recent centuries, Cambodia apparently had no Khmer furnishings—only Chinese ones. In former times, wealthy Khmers lived in beautiful airy wooden houses but spurned them for concrete apartments or villas that the French introduced. At the end of the monarchy and under the republic the pinnacle of stylishness was to own a formica table and oilcloth armchairs, which were signs of modernity. Khmers did not invest in trinkets that they rarely had occasion to display and that represented no social prestige in the eyes of their compatriots. Banquets took place in the garden or at a restaurant.

This concern for social standing and the particular form of hierarchy described above results in a virtually exclusive focus on couples and children and on aged parents. Disinterested behavior is rare. Everything is paid for or kept on account; one never forgets to return it. Poverty may force peasants to economize, but they are generous and share with a foreigner things they consider luxuries: a bunch of bananas, a rare medicinal plant, or just a richer bowl of soup than the usual one. It was the kindness of rural inhabitants, still to be found among the modest people of the capital and other urban centers in 1970, that earned Cambodia its reputation as a paradise. Such spontaneity was less evident in the towns, perhaps because of the demands implicit in rising to a new and ostentatious social status.

This relentless tradition allows no exceptions. Perhaps of proven value in ancient times, it now constitutes a hindrance to all change, all progress in the modern era. It reproduces individuals who are incapable of questioning ossifying customs.

> We belong to the kind of "blocked society" that freezes in a kind of blind self-satisfaction and sees everything new as heresy, even if the new ideas may bring positive and progressive elements. It is the reign of archaism, the domination of the past, with all its injustices, social inequalities, fanaticism, and intolerance, particularly in the political class.[22]

It is noteworthy that, during the annual demonstrations of 7 January against the Vietnamese occupation, the Khmers of France voiced slogans in favor of "their country," of "Cambodia," but never in favor of "their compatriots" who live there. No placard mentioned them. The self-centered education that they have received lacks gentleness, despite the famous Khmer smile. Thus, a Buddhist monk states: "The Khmers are *slot-slap*, 'kind while being killed,' that is, they remain passive to the point of letting someone walk all over them. However, they are gentle only in appearance; they kill one another; this is not Buddhist." Hierarchical relations have such harshness that Khmer society is not a pleasant community in which to live.

These characteristics fade somewhat in the countryside, where the majority of the people live on an equal footing, aside from several notables and learned men (monks, traditional healers, teachers). Townspeople often do not bother to hide their contempt for others; since they consider themselves "superiors," they can do as they please.

Nevertheless, some individuals, of their own accord or because of contact with foreigners, acquire a different mentality. They speak their minds without restraint. Society cannot accept them without being forced to question itself and thus considers them abnormal, *chkuot*.

Perhaps the Khmers' behavior represents a reaction to centuries of suffering (from forced labor in royal corvées until the end of the nineteenth century; from civil wars and foreign occupation; from a protectorate desired by traditional elders and rejected by young people) with an egotistical need to live in peace, far from national problems, away from the cares of one's neighbor. This explanation may account for a lack of generosity toward their fellow citizens. But generosity still exists among the peasants, which leads us to believe that the affluent have gradually lost it. Moreover, this behavior does not mark the individual alone; the entire society remains closed. It is impenetrable and not easy to understand. According to ancient writings, the brilliance of the empire of Funan (from the beginning of the first millennium) radiated throughout Southeast Asia. The states that succeeded it—Chenla and above all the glorious Angkor—were open to foreign influences: kings as well as their subjects welcomed Indian influences, particularly in religion and art. They were capable of liberating themselves from foreign cultural constraints, adapting Indian art to their own talents in order to reveal something specifically Khmer—the genius of Angkor. In the modern era, while the country tried to develop itself, to open itself to foreign countries, change in the arts has come only in architecture, thanks to the talent of two people, Vann Molyvann and Lu Ban Hap, who were responsible for several modern projects. Classical dance has shown no sign of evolution since Westerners first learned of it; all the movements are codified and unchanged in quality or expression. Courtesy and the smile so much appreciated by Westerners do not correspond to an opening but rather to a protective veneer and a desire to be respected. The powerful Angkorian society did not reject foreigners or fear contacts; it benefited from them. On the contrary, does not the present inscrutable society offer evidence of weakness, of fragility that began in the fifteenth century and from which the Khmers have yet to liberate themselves?

## BUDDHISM AND THE OCCULT POWERS

We must not suppose that Buddhism guides Khmers in their material lives. The official religion only superimposed itself on a deeply ingrained popular religion, the belief in supernatural forces. After seven centuries of implantation, the Buddhism known as the Lesser Vehicle or Theravada has not succeeded in supplanting the spirits: like the other traditional traits, they impregnate the Khmers' whole life.

At the pagoda worshipers resolve problems regarding the future life, for the next reincarnation will take into account merits acquired through offerings to the Buddha and the monks, through gifts for ceremonies and for erecting new buildings in the monasteries, and finally through offerings made to the deceased. These are so many merits for the one who gives. In this sense, Buddhism has an economic function, for a portion of the peasantry's resources flows to the pagoda. But on an ethical level, Khmers completely transform this function, giving the offerings an element of materialism: the more spent on the pagoda, the more merit for the giver. However, venerable Yos Hut said: "Several factors must be considered. For example, the *intention* of the donor . . . and the *provenance* of the gifts. . . . A very tiny gift can produce great 'merit' if it is given with a pure intention, with the spirit of detachment, of love, of compassion."[23] Some Khmers believe that certain monks accentuated this distortion of Buddhism by soliciting offerings not only for deceased family members but for future deaths as well.

The practice of Buddhism does not imply many demands, even if it is governed by ten rules, some of which strongly resemble Christianity's commandments. Yet Buddhism appears much more tolerant. There is no special sacrament to become a believer; individuals do as they wish, guided mainly by concern for the future life. As Christians do, Khmer Buddhists kill in time of war, sometimes with cruelty. They can be just as ungrateful as the crocodile in the fairy tale if it proves useful; they are envious and jealous because of their education.[24] To define oneself as a Khmer by the fact of being a Buddhist, as some leaders presently do, amounts to presenting Buddhism as the axis of Khmer society, to the exclusion of the rules described above. Many other peoples in Asia practice Theravada—Laotians, Thais, Burmese, Ceylonese—yet they could not therefore be considered Khmers. That Buddhism has the same positive influence on these peoples cannot be denied. The question has been clearly stated: "Was not the Khmer Rouge's greatest error their failure to foresee the violence of which Khmers without religion are capable?"[25] Lifting the restraint imposed by the traditional education has a reverse side—the risk of violent explosions. It is obvious that the peaceful atmosphere of the pagodas has a calming effect on the people, but this is not enough to give them an identity.

To say that the faithful followers of Theravada settle automatically into fatalism is not a sufficient explanation in Cambodia or elsewhere. As stated above, Cambodian tradition determined quasi-definitively the place of each person in the community. Perhaps, although Buddhism's admirable principles underlie Khmer education, the authorities reinforced its moral tone and made the "younger-elder" obligation of respect—widespread in Southeast

Asia—a sui generis obligation, without taking individuals into account for fear that their sense of worth and initiative might make them forces for change. If the well-to-do were to avoid seeing their privileges endangered, a sufficiently strict education, maintained without fail, was necessary. Cambodian society went one step further: it used Buddhism to reinforce the advantages of mandarins[26] because, according to the Khmers, offerings give the donors merits in proportion to their size. This amounts to a perversion of Buddhist truth. Furthermore, the belief that, on earth, one receives what one deserves does not incite the faithful to rebel, particularly a people as conservative as the Khmers. The former member of the Democratic party Sim Var, who did not mince words, blamed an erroneous interpretation of Buddhism for the inertia of his compatriots in the face of the Khmer Rouge phenomenon:

> The Khmers on earth believe that they committed many transgressions in their past lives and that they can do nothing to alter their present condition. . . . The peoples of the whole world condemned the Khmer Rouge as murderers, but most Cambodians did not say a word. From this, I conclude that they are a dying people.[27]

In their material lives, Khmers place their fates in the hands of supernatural and occult powers—*nêak ta*, spirits of all sorts, malefic beings, and the influence of the stars—that dictate their behavior. Even beneficent spirits can punish if one does not give them the reverence they deserve. Consequently, Khmers are careful to avoid displeasing them. Adults will let a holy day pass without going to the pagoda but will not fail to offer candles and incense with prayers before beginning work in the rice field.[28] They do not enter a forest without sharing their first meal with the spirit who lives there. They will not cut a big tree without invoking the spirit who inhabits it in order to give it time to find another abode. They do not begin important forest gathering (cardamom, eagle-wood) without carrying out an elaborate propitiatory ceremony.[29] Each year they honor the *areak* responsible for certain diseases. They do not forget to render homage to the *mé nieng phteah* who protects the house. In short, any large or unusually shaped object is considered to be the abode of a spirit in whose good graces it is important to remain.

In 1970 urban inhabitants still practiced some of the rites, although they were ignorant of others that had fallen into disuse for obvious reasons: urbanization removed fields and forests from their surroundings, thus eliminating agrarian rituals and offerings to the spirits of the trees as well. Nonetheless, people continued to fear the *priey* and *mday daeum*, supernatural beings who kill children.[30] Astrology remained as powerful in

Phnom Penh as in the most remote villages. Sihanouk and the royal family consulted the palace astrologers before going anywhere; for a trip to the forest or a visit to relatives in a faraway village, peasants left on the auspicious day chosen by the oracle.

Thus religion is an important force in Khmers' daily lives. Buddhism, the religion that was revealed to them, with its terrestrial permanence through the clergy, determines their behavior toward ancestral spirits and toward future lives that they themselves would help to realize. The acts of occult supernatural powers that constantly influence the Khmers' daily lives are beyond human control; people can only attempt to attenuate their effects.

## MISAPPROPRIATION AND CORRUPTION, A PRECOLONIAL HERITAGE

Economic constraints and the constant necessity to show off go hand-in-hand with the acquisition of power and wealth, which are often obtained in a manner deemed inappropriate by the West. Princes in ancient Cambodia benefited from certain privileges. High officials received no salary but were allowed to draw off some of the wealth of the lands that they administered.

Two documents reveal the atmosphere in which the population lived at the time that the French arrived. In 1874 Étienne Aymonnier, a well-known specialist on the Khmers, wrote a critical report on the king, the royal family, and the mandarins.[31] The extravagant expenses of King Norodom, necessary to assure his prestige (despite his famous avarice), the unpopularity and the debauches of the princes who lived on presents, the exploitation of the people by the mandarins—nothing was missing from this long (thirty-four handwritten pages) description that included several hard-hitting sentences: "All the mandarins judge and plunder as soon as they have an official stamp, a seal. . . . All their numerous subordinates follow the example given by the great ones. Repression is nonexistent. . . . Cambodians themselves say that money is necessary for any trial; he who has sufficient money is assured of impunity." This report, written to facilitate passage of an administrative reform, may be considered biased yet stood side by side with letters of protest to the French resident, complaining about the intrigues of the king and mandarins.[32] The parallel is easy to draw for those who knew the excesses of the Khmer Republic (1970–75) or the influence peddling under the monarchical regime that preceded it. These "childlike, arrogant, and timorous people," as Aymonnier described them, have retained a certain naivete, a great pride, and live in fear of doing something that the "higher-ups" will condemn.

In 1875 Jean Moura, a historian sympathetic to the Khmers, noted: "At this moment, the plague of the country is the countless number of officials or mandarins who have titles but no specific function and who fleece the people in an outrageous fashion. They should be reduced to what is strictly necessary and should be remunerated, and new laws should be made to punish misappropriation."[33]

France attempted to put an end to the practice of personal levies by reorganizing the administration. Ordinances proclaimed in 1877 provided for monthly allowances to mandarins. But the latter continued to tap the state's coffers, all the more so in that their pay, diverted by high Khmer officials, was not regular. Tith Huon explains:

> The flaws of the royal administration led the protectorate's authorities to envision reforms, which came up against a silent resistance by the king and the mandarins. This partially explains the convention of 1884, which was imposed on the king and took the administration of his country from him and placed it under the authority of the protectorate. The 1884 convention aroused a general insurrection that presented numerous difficulties in the path of its implementation. But the French government achieved complete control of the country by around 1892, and, henceforth, the protectorate gradually pursued its reorganization of the Cambodian administration.[34]

Before taking up contemporary history, we should point out that Norodom Sihanouk, who became king in 1941, put an end to this line of corrupt and debauched princes who had lived at the expense of the people since Ang Duong died in 1860. But he was unable to impose the same rule on his entourage or on the administrators.

It is thus not surprising to note that in modern times Khmers' relations to the state should resemble patron-client bonds. Civil servants regard the state as a foster father. Considering public property as their own, they developed the habit of helping themselves to office supplies. Well-off peasants tried to avoid paying back loans made them by the state and even sought to get as much of the state's money as possible. This practice contributed to the failure of the Office royal de coopération (OROC) that Prince Sihanouk had created to help poor peasants.

The Khmers do not want to acknowledge the fact that a part of the state's budget is obtained by collecting taxes and that plundering the administration or avoiding repayment of a loan amounts to imposing more taxes on the population. Sim Var realized to his cost his compatriots' lack of civic spirit:

> The first time I ran in an election—for the constituent assembly—I was shut out because I referred to what I had seen in France. During a campaign meeting, people asked: "What do you think of the increase in taxes?" I replied: "If you want your country to be inde-

pendent, you have to pay taxes. Independence is a continuous action, so taxes increase each year." I then understood that people were not ready for independence.

Bribes were the rule in Cambodia. As the Cambodian proverb suggests—the opening of a (shirt) pocket faces up (and not down)—everyone expected something: a percentage of the profit from contracts that he helped to win; a cut of the official currency that he exchanged on the black market for personal profit; interest on bank funds that he increased. An individual risked becoming corrupted without even knowing it, as a minister who refused all compromise explains: he had accepted an invitation to dinner that was to be followed by a stop at a house of pleasure. The corrupter was waiting to pay the bill! Vietnamese and Chinese purchased naturalization in order to accede to one of the potentially lucrative posts from which Prince Sihanouk had excluded foreigners.[35] Customs officers were envied and involved in scandals even in the sixties. They held what Khmers called "fat" positions (among them policeman and minister) that were awarded to the highest bidders by influential power brokers. On a more modest scale, provincial administrators imitated their urban colleagues. In 1965 peasants were obliged to purchase civil documents for ten to twenty riels, depending on locality.[36] They had absolutely no recourse although, in theory, they could state their case to the chief of state during the biannual meetings of the People's Congress in Phnom Penh. But peasants could scarcely take the risk of exposing themselves to reprisals after returning to the village. Only rarely did they refuse to comply with the hierarchy.

Khmers have their own understanding of the country's financial resources. Bogged down in a traditional hierarchy, they are not trained to argue with superiors. Relying as they do on the "god-king," they believe in the omnipotence of those who govern them, in their ability to bring forth a miraculous surge of money, foodstuffs, or elements (rain) when needed.[37] Those who took refuge in the West, confronted with material difficulties, maintain the same attitude toward foreigners: Europeans should never have financial problems, particularly if they are civil servants, for a public servant never lacks money. Overwhelming burdens of patronage similar to European feudal practices becloud all levels of Cambodian administrative and social life.

## LEGITIMACY BY DIVINE ROYALTY

Angkor left a deep mark on the country's political organization. Since the beginning of the ninth century when the Shivaite *devaraja* (king of the gods) cult was established on nearby Mount Kulen, people venerated the kings, invested with divine power in the fashion of the Indian universal monarchs, who reigned over Khmer soil. This tradition endured for twelve centuries. If Buddhism replaced the Brahmanism of former times, a sacred aureole still adorns the master of the country. He obtains power because of his many merits: "The concept of *neak mean bonn* [he who has merits] allows the legitimization of any power in place, be it of divine or popular origin . . . ; [it is] closely linked with the notion of *bonn* that is inherent in the destiny of each person. [Thus,] royal power is necessarily personal power."[38] The title, moreover, has little importance: king or head of state having abdicated the throne, the main thing is that he be recognized as having received special powers. Until 1970, except for several thousand educated Khmers, the majority of the population—including the bourgeoisie, anxious to conserve its privileges by giving allegiance—venerated Prince Sihanouk as an authentic representative of the ancestral power. Did he not preside each year at the ceremony of the sacred furrow that marked, in the country, the beginning of agricultural labors? Did people not seek his help in case of drought? Like Indra, he was considered the dispenser of rain.

Sihanouk, wanting to bring a bit of well-being to the population, distributed not rain but bolts of cloth bearing the emblem of his party, a gift that many city dwellers, seeing it as nothing but an instrument of propaganda, challenged as useless. He had understood—and this is the important point—that belief in the divine power of the king, which was weakening in the cities, remained steadfast in the rural environment. Consequently, as much to learn of the material condition of his citizens as to bolster his popularity, Sihanouk made frequent trips to the provinces to inaugurate all new projects, thus maintaining contact with the common people.[39] Furthermore, he often traveled by helicopter, and peasants thus saw a king, sent by heaven to their villages to make life-giving water spring from a new pump. Royal line, religion, and water were reunited by the Master of the Earth, who came to spread his blessings and incidentally to strengthen popular beliefs.[40] Water and earth meant rice and thus life.

We now better understand the unchallenged power of the royal delegates under the post-Angkorian monarchy. We can also gauge the depth of the peasants' stupefaction and fear when, on 18 March 1970 Sihanouk was removed from the country's official politics by General Lon Nol and his soldiers. The troubles that followed were to be expected: in the absence of a divine king, decent life was no longer possible. This loss also explains the feeble impact of the Khmer Republic in the countryside and, by contrast, the people's sympathetic response, from 1970 to 1975, to the Front uni national du Cambodge (national united front of Cambodia, or FUNC), a political movement created by Prince Sihanouk that united Khmer Rouge and Sihanouk's supporters.

City dwellers hostile to Sihanouk understood the new situation a little late. Once the battle was engaged, everyone realized that it could be won only with the support of the dethroned sovereign. This is undoubtedly one of the reasons why, beginning in 1973, the republicans asked Sihanouk— exiled in Peking—to return to Phnom Penh. It is probably also for this reason that in 1979 Son Sann offered him the presidency (which he refused) of the nationalist movement that Son Sann had just created: the Front national de libération du peuple khmer (Khmer people's national liberation front, or FNLPK). And it was to have some credibility in the eyes of his compatriots that the adventurer André Ouk Thol, a Cambodian who is a naturalized Frenchman, set himself up in 1979 along the Khmer-Thai border under the name of Prince Suryavong. He thus succeeded in assembling around himself a starving population, in whose name he requested rice that he then sold to benefit himself and several assistants. When the fraud was discovered in 1980, the false prince disappeared from the border.

Thus there existed a gap between urbanites and rural inhabitants. The latter, in the majority, were ignorant of political machines and voted according to outmoded values. And those sincere people among the former, the smaller group, found it difficult to express new ideas and to establish them as guiding principles if they did not have the endorsement of the monarch.

## THE IMPORTANCE OF WOMEN AND THE CLANS

In 1955 Sihanouk gave women the right to vote. However, their social and political importance was a reality prior to this, even if political power formally belonged to men. The latest research on Khmer kinship confirms the eminent role of women, directly and through the intermediary of an older brother.[41] Traditionally, the uterine uncle intervened in important familial decisions and marriages, and he received part of an inheritance. Even today, a woman has a privileged place. When she marries, she keeps her maiden name. She governs the household, raises the children, and holds the purse strings, an important role in Southeast Asia. The *Treatise of the Father's Advice* insists on this point: "Wealth is maintained thanks to the wife, who knows how to preserve it." Khmers need to accumulate wealth and to show it off. Wealth is displayed chiefly in the form of jewels that the wife wears everyday, even when she goes to the market: large gleaming diamonds, precious stones, including magnificent sapphires produced in the country but also emeralds from Afghanistan, and twenty-four carat gold. As for silver, while Khmers like it in bars, women rarely adorn themselves with it, as a silver ring is of little value. But what a profusion of gold, diamonds, and precious stones! An observer can easily estimate the prosperity of a man by looking at the neck, ears, wrists, and hands of his wife. Even a peasant makes a point (albeit modest) of giving his wife these outward signs of wealth: earrings, gold chains, and—rarely, for they interfere with work in house and field—rings. In the countryside, a young girl would never go out with her girlfriends without adorning herself with a gold chain, borrowed from her mother or another female relative; she would rather stay home than go without wearing any jewelry. Perhaps as a consequence of the centuries of incessant wars suffered by the kingdom that forced people to flee on short notice, families took along a little sack containing the household's fortune. Whatever its origin, this practice reveals how trusting husbands are of their wives as well as the high social position of the woman. In France, even the most impoverished Cambodian women own at least one expensive ring and sometimes a mink coat after several years of work. They rarely abandon their traditional Khmer values.

Furthermore, a Khmer woman has great influence over her husband. Skillful in the art of pleasing and charming, she often gives him no rest until he accedes to her desires. Firm and smiling, she bends his will. If her husband is an influential man, even at a modest level, she builds a clientele for herself, a practice described by the Cambodian proverb: "If you are a colonel, your wife is a general." Many are the commercial and state transactions that go through her. As Sok Vanny points out, she "will find in intrigues an opening and a liberty that she was not allowed to enjoy as an adolescent."[42] She then becomes formidable, the more so if her husband has a high position, for her assistance to the wives of subordinates or to her own friends—which allows her to affirm her individuality—is not free.

Sometimes a whole family works together, more or less openly. There is no shortage of examples from the 1960s, and they created rancor in the urban milieu. When this occurs, a family "clan," through its men or women, stands in the way of everyone who attempts to act independently, who tries to deprive it of an opportunity to enrich itself or to exert its power.[43] The wife enjoys a recognized authority as a woman. In an interesting article, Jacques Népote studies filiation in Cambodia and shows that a Khmer man wanting to assert his authority has no choice but to assume the leadership of a clan. As a child, the Khmer was subordinate to his mother. When he marries, he depends on his wife's lineage, insofar as he respects the rules of marriage by marrying into a lineage superior to his own and living with his parents-in-law. The result is that, at home, the Khmer man is rarely in a position of strength.[44] In this context, becoming a *kru*, by acquiring knowledge or power—more or less licit—gives him a certain social status. This is the origin of the clans, the formation and upholding of which may generate violence.

KHMERITUDE

Speaking of the society set in its ancient structures, Sam Sok refers to the unchanging Khmer character and behavior that results:

> Gentle, affable, timid but concealing contention and bitterness, reticent in discussion and preferring the fait accompli; fiercely proud of the past but little informed of the views of non-Khmers; open to new ideas but conservative in regard to all of his surroundings; easily enthusiastic but impatient; witty; refined but appreciative of cheap humor and of feasting.[45]

This agreeable summary reveals the Khmers' potentials. While they remain crushed by a tradition that should be reconsidered, they nonetheless possess outstanding qualities.

With exemplary dignity, they recount past and present misfortunes without self-pity, wearing a smile that disconcerts Westerners who listen to atrocious but true accounts that would be unbearable on other lips. The principle of not bothering others applies with particular force here, and listeners appreciate it. Dignity also means dressing properly and taking one or two showers each day: Khmers stay as clean and neat as they can. Entering well-kept villages or the capital's elegant center was particularly pleasant when the visitor had just left the Chinese quarter. Europeans always appreciated the well-mannered Cambodians with whom they worked. But some of them did not realize that their own slovenliness could shock the indigenous people, just as they did not realize the negative impact of their verbal torrents in the face of Khmers' courtesy and reserve.

Fiercely independent, Khmers do not respond to threats against their personal freedom. They are willing to act if one gives them freedom of action, treats them with consideration, and shows them as much patience and courtesy as they display to the outsider. Toward strangers they react according to tradition; if obliged to show hospitality, they nevertheless do not put themselves out for others. Doctor Pannetier, always well-disposed toward the Khmers, notes: "Just as he shows an extreme discretion vis-à-vis other people, he does not allow anyone to enter his house. . . . Knowing in advance of the visit of a guest, he prefers to build a shelter, a little *sala* . . . a communal house for travelers that Cambodians build in great numbers throughout the countryside in order to avoid receiving people in their homes."[46] And Auguste Pavie explains the Khmer's attitude toward work:

> The Cambodian recognizes as his superior only the European. . . .
> One must not expect him to serve with good grace under a Siamese,
> Chinese, or Annamese boss, even for a light task. He will submit if
> he has no choice and will give only an insignificant effort, which

causes him to be called lazy, spineless, and so on. But alongside his own superiors or with Europeans, he will show his worth.[47]

Khmers like to be justly appreciated for their talents. The Americans' unthinking disdain shocked them. Conversely, the French, who were generally less distant, encountered no major problems in working with them during or after the protectorate.

Proud and sometimes arrogant, Khmers do not accept unsolicited aid from a stranger. It is thus futile to insist; they will only feel humiliated. Conversely, they can vow eternal gratitude for a service rendered them. In France, those who help them or support them in their present difficulties know how deep and even disproportionate the resulting attachment is. Likewise, the outsider once "admitted" cannot commit faux pas; one must grant any request and never criticize. However, if one questions their reputation or that of their country, the Khmers—in other respects so thoughtful—act like tyrants and, from one day to the next, change their excessive praise into unjust and even calumnious criticism. One must not express unpleasant truths.

Khmers possess qualities that allow them to change with the modern era. Those exiled in France have shown their capacity to adapt: the adults behave almost exactly as they did in Cambodia; the adolescents adjust, more or less; children, for their part, react differently according to their origins. For example, sons and daughters of peasants who continue to receive a Cambodian education at home have some difficulty in following French education. Others, raised by parents familiar with French customs, show an open-mindedness equal to that of their French counterparts. They need only to have had a French education from at least the first year of junior high school onward for them to be receptive to the scientific, literary, and philosophical values that are taught them. Conscientious and thirsty for knowledge after the long, intellectually empty Khmer Rouge period, they are often at the head of their classes and show a great deal of initiative. They have critical minds to match. If their parents motivate them to practice the Khmer language at home, speak to them of Cambodia, put good books summarizing its history at their disposal, and show them the necessity of respect for the ancestors, the virtues of the smile and of perseverance, as adults they could well be precious auxiliaries or leaders in education, the economy, and politics in a Cambodia once again free and sovereign.

# 2 The Colonial Heritage

From the ninth century until the middle of the fifteenth the Khmers reigned in Angkor. After the Siamese invested and captured the city in 1431, the Khmer kings established their capitals in several successive locations: Srey Santhor, Lovêk, Phnom Penh, and Oudong. Norodom I (1860–1904) reigned at Oudong when the first treaty with France was signed in 1863. In the same year he had Phnom Penh laid out; it has been the country's capital ever since.

## THE ESTABLISHMENT OF THE PROTECTORATE

The negligence of the Khmer monarchs had brought the country to the brink of ultimate catastrophe: the disappearance of Cambodia as a political and territorial entity. The first attempt at a Franco-Cambodian rapprochement was undertaken by a Khmer king who sought to save his kingdom from disaster. For several centuries of wars over succession, Cambodia was unable to defend its borders effectively. The Khmers' Siamese and Vietnamese neighbors had numerous opportunities to encroach upon Cambodian territory, which had become for them an object of rivalry.[1] Thus, the sovereign looked now to Siam, now to Vietnam as a means of anchoring the legitimacy of his power. In the nineteenth century the two invaders wanted to seize Phnom Penh: "One thing troubled them above all. Each of them wanted to have Phnom Penh and the Four-Arms region, the heart of the kingdom and its most strategic point. Without the Four-Arms, peace would have been signed with Cambodia divided up between Siam and Cochin China, and that would have been the end of the Khmer people."[2] The Khmers rebelled in 1837–1839 and succeeded in hampering the Vietnamese plans for imposing their laws and customs. The revolt became a general one in 1840–1841.[3] To defeat the invaders, King Ang Duong (1841–1860) was nevertheless compelled to accept the aid of Siam—which had placed him on the throne—in five long years of warfare. In 1845, however, he was unable to escape from double tutelage but did succeed in avoiding the partition of his country by its two protectors. Cambodia then experienced a period of internal peace, which allowed the king to reorganize the country.

But the truce was apparently a short one. In 1853 Ang Duong called upon a foreign power to stave off the Vietnamese menace. He chose France, a country unrepresented in the region except for large Catholic missions led by Monsignor Miche. The first letter Ang Duong addressed to the French emperor Napoleon III is not to be found in the archives. Jean Moura summarized the proposals that the Khmer sovereign intended to make to France:

> To disclose his grievances, his complaints with regard to his two fear-some neighbors; to declare his incapacity to obtain justice through his own means; finally, to announce his decision to place himself under the protection of France, to which he would cede, by treaty, the Cambodian territories that the Annamese had seized and never returned, even though no act of transfer had even taken place be-tween the two states.[4]

There is no proof that Ang Duong intended to cede these occupied provinces to France; in the diplomatic correspondence the French envoy, de Montigny, mentioned only the island of Kah Doot.[5]

The first attempt to arrange a Franco-Khmer meeting failed, for the Siamese, informed by the French envoy himself, opposed it. In November 1856 Ang Duong addressed a second letter to Napoleon III.[6] In this letter Ang Duong asserted his claim to the Cambodian provinces occupied by the Vietnamese. The Khmer monarch died in 1860, his request unfulfilled. There is no trace of any subsequent written claim by the Khmer sovereigns regarding this question until 1948, during Sihanouk's reign.

When Norodom I acceded to the throne in 1860, the regional political map had changed: France had just established itself in the Mekong delta and wanted a Cambodia freed of all foreign interference. The French presence in Cochin China removed the danger from the Vietnamese side, but the menace from the north remained. Norodom, caught up in palace quarrels and absorbed in his harem, proved incapable of reconquering the lands occupied by the Siamese (the provinces of Sisophon, Battambang, Siem Reap, Mlou Prey, and Tonle Rpou) and of throwing off the yoke of Siamese suzerainty.

"It was only on the day that we set foot in Cochin China that a negotiation with or concerning Cambodia began to appear opportune," a contemporary diplomatic letter reads.[7] Until then, Paris had recognized Siamese overlordship in Cambodia. But in 1862 the policy changed; Admiral Bonard, in charge of Saigon and other conquered territories in Cochin China, received full powers to negotiate with Cambodia, a problem that had previously been under the jurisdiction of the French consul at Bangkok. In August 1863 Bonard's successor, Admiral de la Grandière, proceeded to Phnom Penh to work out a treaty that raised objections from the Siamese. To Siam's protests the admiral replied: "The king of Cambodia now asks for the protection of His Majesty the Emperor, and France will no doubt consent to grant him this protectorate in order to avoid being compelled by circumstances to seize a kingdom whose complete independence is incompatible with our interests in Cochin China."[8]

De la Grandière—who does not seem to have been troubled by scruples—was probably telling the truth when he specified that the treaty was signed at Norodom's request, even though Norodom, undoubtedly fearing reprisals, wrote to the Siamese minister of war the day after signing to complain that France had forced the treaty on him: "I cannot accept it, given that Cambodia is a tributary of Siam, and I fear to commit any offense. . . . It is for Your Excellency to judge whether or not this treaty exceeds the limits, for Your Excellency is the refuge on whom I depend for my well-being."[9] These sentences reveal the degree of Cambodia's enfeoffment to Siam. Siam indeed continued to scheme with the easily influenced Khmer monarch, which probably accounts for his subsequent about-faces, in particular the signing of a Khmer-Siamese treaty on 1 December 1863.

After a great deal of bargaining, Bangkok yielded; it had no choice. In its text the treaty signed by France and Cambodia in August 1863 did not mention the provinces of the Mekong delta (lower Cochin China), certain zones of which were claimed by Ang Duong. Although the Vietnamese had recently installed their administration in part of the contested territories, the Khmers did not accept the amputation, considering these provinces—in which Cambodians were the majority—an integral part of the Khmer monarch's domain. They looked to France for help in regaining the lands. As for the regions that had been lost for two centuries, it seems that the Khmers themselves had partially given them up in recompense for Vietnamese military assistance.[10]

Thus, when the French arrived on the Cambodian scene in 1863, the country was disintegrating, given over to anarchy and rent by individual ambitions, paying tribute to both Vietnam and Siam. France had to throttle insurrections led by the Achar Sva and then by Pou Kombo, who, supported by the Vietnamese, were preoccupied above all else with usurping power by passing themselves off as princes. France also faced the animosity of Sivotha,

Norodom I's rebellious half brother, who fought the French when they began supporting Norodom. The establishment of France caused no spontaneous popular reaction among Cambodians, and Adémar Leclère explained the people's acceptance: "Recognizing that France had reestablished order, assured the kingdom's security, and substituted itself for Annam and Siam, the people were not concerned."[11]

France's intentions were certainly not pure, and few projects of real benefit to the Khmer people were carried out during the entire ninety years. Nevertheless, in the beginning France had no annexationist designs, as the reports and correspondence exchanged by the governing admiral of Cochin China and the minister of the navy and colonies make clear. Cambodian affairs were directed from afar by the governor of Cochin China. In January 1865 the minister of the navy and colonies reported:

> [Siam] must understand that, determined as we are to remain in Cochin China and to be the masters of it, we will not permit Siam to invade Cambodia and thus to install itself on our borders; that if such an action would be harmful for us, it would be just as harmful *and perhaps even more dangerous for Siam*; that it would not be long before conflicts would break out between us; that our civilization, our religion, and our customs would soon clash with theirs; that the best solution is to place between us *an independent and neutral state* . . . ; that we have no plans for the conquest of Cambodia; that, on the contrary, we want it to be strong enough to defend its independence and civilized enough that our commerce will find fruitful exchange there.[12]

The Khmer sovereign did not give in to this idyllic perspective. Faced with Norodom's reluctance to cooperate, the minister considered replacing him and wrote to the admiral on 14 March 1867 to remind him: "But do not lose sight for a single moment of the goal that I have set as the object of your energy and discretion, a goal that must be attained: to extricate ourselves from the *permanent military occupation* of Cambodia." On 15 April he reiterated: "As for King Norodom, it is evident that he will always be a source of difficulties for us and that there will be grounds for discarding him if you can find a successor who is sympathetic to the people and devoted to our cause. I see no other way of escaping the obligation of permanently occupying Cambodia."[13] France was interested only in the Mekong, which it viewed as a useful base for maintaining its control of Cochin China and as a route for communicating with Siam and penetrating China. A peaceful Cambodia was thus essential; were it not for this imperative, the country would probably have held little interest for Paris.

The people continued to be tormented, exploited, and humiliated by mandarins great and small. Chaos reigned. According to Leclère, the administrative reforms envisaged by the royal ordinances of 1877 were to have suppressed these abuses. But the king himself was uncooperative. He refused to implement the administrative decrees that he had nevertheless signed on 15 January 1877. France showed so little interest in Cambodian affairs that for seven years the governor of Cochin China did not know that the king had not carried out the reforms. France then challenged Norodom to sign the convention of 1884. Its consequences were immediate:

> An insurrection instigated by mandarins under orders from the king himself, which lasted eighteen months. It was not particularly bloody, but it destroyed the country. We were the more powerful party, and the king in Phnom Penh was in our grasp; we could have abducted him, placed the *obareach* [heir] on the throne, and finished the war by taking the king to France or to one of our African possessions. But we did not take this course, preferring as we did to bring influence to bear on the country, on the mandarins, and on the king himself so that we could, with their cooperation, undertake the necessary reforms.[14]

The true protectorate of France over Cambodia, with the designation of a resident superior for Cambodia, began in 1884. From that date onward, Paris began to take Cambodian affairs seriously. Despite the early difficulties caused by the scant attention that France paid the country for several decades, in effect the French protectorate saved Cambodia from probable absorption by the kingdoms of Siam and Vietnam.

## RESPECT FOR TRADITIONS AND REVIVAL OF THE ARTISAN CLASS

Individual French politicians and administrators intended to respect the indigenous culture and maintain contacts with the Khmers. This was undoubtedly not the case for everyone, but there were enough of them so that friendly and intellectual relations tinged with respect were established between the two groups.

Respect does not mean interest, however, and very few administrators or even colonists were interested in Khmer habits and customs. They never learned the rudiments of the language, which would have made them better at understanding the people. Cambodia (like Laos) was a country where officials were sent as punishment. Few researchers, aside from historians and archaeologists, studied the country; the remarkable work of the École française d'Extrême-Orient on the temples of Angkor constitutes a major contribution to our knowledge of ancient Cambodia.

While no serious research was undertaken in the first decades of occupation, at least the inhabitants suffered little from the colonizers' presence in their daily activities. There were changes, recognized seventy years later by the general government of Indochina:

> Indeed, since our arrival in Indochina indigenous arts have decayed through contact with the Western models that we inevitably brought with us. . . . We are undoubtedly responsible for the decadence of the Indochinese arts. For a long time, the general organization of our protectorate absorbed all our efforts, and we did not have the leisure to worry about the artistic and artisanal question—despite its great importance in this country—until the damage had been done. . . . We sought to attract customers with cheap goods; artisans were taught to make faulty and defective work, and thousands of miserable products that could not find a buyer were made. We then realized the need for instruction.[15]

Once the French became aware of the impoverishment of the arts, they opened schools, first of all the École des arts cambodgiens de Phnom Penh, created by a royal edict issued on 14 December 1917. The great humanist George Groslier supervised its operation. With the sole exception of himself, all the personnel were Cambodian. Few Khmers still had technical skill and artistry in traditional crafts, and Groslier devoted himself to searching for them. He assembled skilled artisans, who taught students the artistic traditions of their ancestors. Many crafts were thus kept from oblivion and passed on by the Cambodians themselves: drawing, silver work and other casting, hand-loom weaving, sculpture, and lacquer ware. In reassembling this artisan class France simply followed its duty and, in so doing, preserved and revived arts that the previous centuries' wars had certainly not favored. Khmers today are their beneficiaries.

Furthermore, Suzanne Karpelès made a major contribution to the preservation of Khmer culture; she worked for the revival of Buddhism, creating the famous Institut bouddhique de Phnom Penh.

## ADMINISTRATIVE AND FINANCIAL REFORM

For twenty years of the French protectorate the people's living conditions did not improve. After 1884 and well established in Cochin China, France became aware of the political and economic interest that the neighboring country could have for it. The convention of the protectorate gave France prerogatives that the treaty of 1863 had left to the king, in particular administrative, judicial, financial, and commercial powers. France then moved to reorganize the country to permit more efficient use of its resources. The reforms were stretched out over several decades, and the new administration then began to benefit the Cambodians. Early in the twentieth century, local potentates still held sway:

> There is still one result that I do not abandon hope of attaining before long, and that is the suppression of the old feudal regime that predominates here. . . . Already the principle of election of village chiefs has been adopted, and soon, instead of finding in each settlement four patrons, one for each of the four provincial authorities, we will have but a single chief under the [Cambodian] governor and the French resident.[16]

Villagers did not, it seems, really participate in the elections of their mayors. Nevertheless, the presence of the French limited abuses and contributed to social peace; from that time onward, the people saw them as a recourse against mandarinal depredations. In this domain, results were thus positive. This reform also permitted progress toward the beginning of recording civil status and a census.

In judicial matters the people benefited, and, at the end of the nineteenth century the abolition of "slavery"—proclaimed several times but never carried out—spread effectively to the national level with the suppression of slaves bound to the king, the state, and the monasteries.[17] The practice, however, remained in force within families through the use of indentured debtors as domestic servants. The magistrates, for their part, complained that foreign Asians escaped their jurisdiction because they were henceforth under French justice.

The new financial laws exploited the Khmers; an avalanche of taxes and assessments fell on them. The resident's reports stated that peasants were taxed to the limits of endurance.[18] The application of this reform provoked dissatisfaction, especially after the decision to levy the population for public works. These corvées—from which individuals could buy their way out—further burdened peasant households, and the Khmer officials responsible for collecting the redemption fees increased fees at will. The first evidence of serious popular discontent was the Bardez affair. This French resident of Kompong Chhnang province was killed along with his Vietnamese secretary in 1925 during a tax-collection tour.

Cambodian raw materials (including fish, wood and other forest products, and agricultural products) went to Cochin China or France. The country offered manna from which the neighboring colonies and the home country profited. Moreover, the local budget determined by the French had to cover public works that normally fell under the general budget of Indochina. The French hardly favored the Khmers' access to administrative positions, even after the opening of certain offices to those they called

"Indochinese," that is, people from the four protectorates and one colony; for help in administering Cambodia they continued to prefer Vietnamese to Khmers.

The neighboring territories, particularly Cochin China, Annam, and Tonkin, enjoyed different treatment: France considered them the pivot of its occupation in the region and favored them to the detriment of Laos and Cambodia. Continued isolation from all progress was even more noticeable in the domain of education.

## SLIGHT GAINS IN EDUCATION AND HYGIENE

Khmers complain today—and rightly so—that France did not set up the same school system in their country as in Annam, Tonkin, and Cochin China. Until the beginning of the twentieth century, pagoda schools offered education in the vernacular language, morality, and religion only to men; women were practically illiterate. Of course, Phnom Penh had a French private school, Collège Sisowath, which became Lycée Sisowath in 1935, serving French youngsters and Cambodian mandarins' sons.

The accepted view held by the first French administrators that Khmers were naturally "non-perfectible," that they possessed defects "inherent to their race" such as laziness, contributed to the colonial power's lack of interest in educating them.[19] Rather than try to understand their protégés, to show them a little patience as did Jean Moura, Auguste Pavie, Étienne Aymonnier, Adémar Leclère, and other less known residents, the colonists in general adopted this convenient stereotype. Indeed, very few had the means to get an idea of the Khmers' strong and weak points since they could not communicate with them. Sensible people asked that French officials sent to Cambodia be given language training in Khmer so that they would not depend on the grudges and interests of Vietnamese interpreters, whom the Cambodians barely tolerated. But clichés are tenacious, and France, having from the outset preferred the quicker-witted Vietnamese, continued to ignore the Khmers and Laotians in its educational programs. Certain people even advocated the teaching of French in the pagoda schools, arguing that French was "the only language capable of defeating the routine of Buddhist education"; in this country, "so attached to its ancestral customs, to its past traditions [*sic*], to its religion, it is indispensable to allow these simple minds to have the time to evolve and to understand our intentions." Furthermore: "It is nothing new to observe that, in this domain [education], Cambodia has allowed itself to fall behind the other Indochinese countries."[20] This report has no hint of critical thinking, not a trace of humanity to benefit the Khmers, as though they bore the responsibility for their own lack of education! Furthermore, the small number of teachers in Cambodia is revealing.[21]

In 1924 the conversion of pagoda schools into renovated pagoda schools proved a welcome initiative that would lead to the modernization of certain large traditional pagoda schools and the creation of new ones. The education given by Khmers (religious and lay) treated more diversified subjects than did the traditional schools, with the exception of French. Students there could take "native" examinations analogous to those of the French schools. Thanks to the renovated pagoda schools schooling spread throughout the kingdom—at least among men—but occurred very late, which explains the imbalance among the different protectorates and the colony.[22] In 1945 when France began to grant them autonomy, Laos had no lycée but Cambodia, Tonkin, Annam, and Cochin China each had one; Laos had one secondary institution, Tonkin four, Annam two, Cochin China two, and Cambodia none. The only university founded by the French—in Hanoi—consisted of two schools, law and medicine. Each territory had one technical school.

The opening of the pagoda schools in Cochin China deserves mention:

> The four hundred thousand Cambodians living in Cochin China [Khmer *krom*] were forced to attend the Annamese school, even if Cambodians were in the majority. The Institut d'études boud-dhiques requested and obtained from the government of Cochin China scholarships to pay for the education of Cambodian monks. These monks were to attend Cambodian renovated pagoda schools for one year to relearn how to speak and write their own language—which was larded with Annamese words—and to relearn Buddhist doctrine in all its purity. After one year, these monks returned to Cochin China and opened classes in their pagodas, thus permitting young Khmers from Cochin China to receive an education in their own language.[23]

Some Cambodians wanting to pursue their studies went to the lycées of Hanoi or Saigon. Few parents could offer their children this luxury, and in any case no peasants could. As for higher education, it remained the privilege of several princes or mandarins' sons, sent to Hanoi and France. Cambodia remained underdeveloped at this level of education.

The medical situation seems to have been little better. When France arrived in Cambodia in 1863, the public health policy was nonexistent; when France left in 1955 it was rudimentary. Very few medical personnel were trained. In 1909 there were thirteen medical zones including one at Phnom Penh. Elsewhere, a single French doctor practiced in each zone (group of provinces); generally, he traveled throughout his territory. In 1920 epidemics of plague, cholera, and small pox broke out frequently. In 1948 official statistics showed 3,750,000 inhabitants of Cambodia compared to approximately 4,500,000 of South Vietnam (Cochin China and part of Annam). The disproportion of the figures relating to hygiene and health personnel in the two states shows the scant interest Cambodia received. Several figures on personnel will suffice to clarify the picture (the first concerns Cambodia, the second South Vietnam): medical doctors (from France?) 4 and 135, respectively; Indochinese doctors, 10 and 35; dental surgeons, none and 5; state-certified midwives, none and 9; Indochinese midwives, 7 and 104.[24] These figures speak for themselves. Very few local personnel had training—this should have been a priority.

## YOUTH MOVEMENTS

Aside from scouting, imported to Cambodia by a Khmer who had lived in France, other movements came about at the initiative of France. The Jeunes du Cambodge movement, created in 1941 when the Japanese occupied Southeast Asia, had its equivalent in the neighboring countries under French control. All were under the jurisdiction of the Commissariat à la jeunesse et aux sports, founded for this purpose and led—a revealing detail—by a military officer. Members learned how to march; training also included "civic instruction, a study of morality, and the teaching of various skills as in the Scouts," according to a former member.

Shortly afterward, the French created the Mouvement de rassemblement, including youths, teachers, and civil servants, who received training that was essentially military. A provincial governor's report, written in 1944, was specific: "The results achieved among youths are satisfactory. The population shows an amused curiosity, seeing it as a kind of military training."[25] If, as rumor had it, the French were considering using these recruits in the resistance, the opportunity did not present itself; the Allies liberated the region, forcing the Japanese to capitulate. The youth movements sunk into oblivion, leaving only scouting. But henceforth Cambodians knew how to organize. This asset was useful to King Sihanouk, who in 1953 easily remobilized the assemblages under the name of *chivapol* (active forces) to support him in his royal crusade for independence.

## FRANCE'S NEGLIGIBLE ROLE IN MODERNIZATION

If the artisan class benefited from a renewal, other sectors did not. The peasants, lacking fertilizer, reaped poor harvests. No factory existed beyond a few on the rubber plantations in which France invested substantially from 1921 onward.[26] Moreover, the French did not process the raw materials on the spot but exported them. When they needed local intermediaries for commerce, they turned to Chinese and Sino-Khmer compradors, agents and intermediaries in business affairs. Nonetheless, they taught foresters (a corps created in 1940) the principles of land management, strictly applied until 1970 and—come what might—between 1970 and 1975. The competence of the Cambodian foresters makes us regret that the French did not extend training in other technical domains to Khmers capable of contributing to the development of their country.

The French-built road system, regularly repaired after independence (except for abandoned trails in remote regions), linked the capital to the main provincial towns, as did the Phnom Penh–Trapeang Chong (in Battambang) railroad line. Construction of these systems had costs for the people, as the minister of colonies recognized in 1917, upon his return from an inspection tour. Writing about the progress realized in the realm of public works, he stated that "it was obtained at the expense of the population, exploited beyond all limits."[27] Requisitions of people for labor were excessive. Furthermore, France built no ports in Cambodia. One such project, planned for Ream, was not completed until the French Union period (late 1940s) at Kompong Som. France was content to move Cambodian foodstuffs through Saigon.

Voices were raised in protest. Among them was that of the minister quoted above, who added, "It is evident, moreover, that the residents and their representatives do not maintain enough contact with the population. They rarely leave the roads traveled by cars. I know of a representative who states that, during more than five years at the same post, he never went more than thirty kilometers from his home except to travel the road that takes him to work."[28] This, however, was a matter of general policy: if a few administrators protested and several humanists established personal relationships with the indigenous population, everything was decided in high circles. The lack of interest, the contempt of low-level bureaucrats, simply reflected that of the central authorities.

## DECOLONIZATION: TERRITORIAL AMPUTATIONS

As a result of the French occupation, Siam was forced to return to Cambodia the territories that it had occupied, especially the northern and western provinces of Sisophon, Battambang, Siem Reap, Kah Kong, Mlou Prey. The French arbitrarily incorporated to the Bassac (lower Laos) a part of the newly restored Tonle Rpou province; Stung Treng province underwent several successive modifications. Sarin Chhak studies the evolution of this province and neighboring regions and evaluates the juridical value of this dismemberment.[29] Contrary to all geographical and ethnic logic France administratively united Stung Treng province, restored in 1883, to Cochin China and then to lower Laos, and finally returned it to the kingdom of Cambodia on 6 December 1904. In the meantime Darlac province had been separated from Stung Treng (see appendix 2) and attributed to Annam on 22 November 1904. Sarin Chhak emphasizes that these transactions took place without the Khmer king's approval. Nevertheless, the king hardly protested; his subjects were the victims of the economic covetousness of the French and the slackness of their sovereign. On 12 April 1932 the French president ratified the treaty "restoring" to Annamese territory Darlac province, which belonged to the Cambodian crown.

Regarding southern Cambodia, the colonial archives bear out the fact that the Tay-ninh province, inhabited almost exclusively by Cambodians, belonged to the Khmer crown.[30] Further, the territories consisting of the lands between the Vaico rivers were being administered by Cambodians when the French arrived. The new delimitation effected by France in 1870 was primarily based on the presence of Vietnamese hamlets in these sparsely populated regions, without taking the Cambodian villages into consideration. Sarin Chhak remarks, "When we perceive the ease with which the Annamese carried out encroachments and voiced claims against Cambodian territory, we become aware of all the harm that was to come to the Cambodian people from the dispositions of the inspectors, always ready to endorse Vietnamese claims." The author adds: "Unfortunately, Cambodia was represented by incapable people who should have argued with the French delegates. . . . It is thus evident that they played a laughable role in this commission."

Contributing to the situation was the low esteem the French had for the sovereign, captured in the archives Chhak quotes: "The work that my colleagues and I undertook was simply a topographical operation, little of which the mandarins or the king himself could have understood. . . . I cannot fathom what future plans or thoughts could have upset the king, and it seems to me that we will very easily be able to do without his approval."[31] The situation perhaps also reflected the scant interest that Norodom had in important affairs concerning his kingdom. He did protest but after the fact, and he was given back only a minuscule part of his previously usurped territories. The richest lands remained part of Cochin China, as did the regions further north. Moreover, the growing interest in rubber plantations led the protectors to include in Cochin China part of the rich basaltic lands favorable to rubber cultivation.

Thus, between 1870 and 1914 a series of delimitations was effected to the detriment of Cambodia (see appendix 2): France took advantage of its power and the Khmers' inertia in order to take zones that were economically advantageous. The maritime delimitation (the Brévié Line) was not respected since Cochin China was given the administration of Kah Tral island (Phu-Quoc). After decolonization, the Vietnamese considered this French administrative decision as a political acknowledgment, which they put forward when they refused to return the island to Cambodia (see appendix

3). But responsibility for determination of Cambodia's borders rests as much on the Khmers' apathetic sovereigns as on the French.

Sarin Chhak explains the juridical invalidity of these successive border delimitations:

> Here also, based on the exposition of the facts as much as on the juridical discussion, we must conclude that, whatever the authors' intentions might have been, the present border demarcations have never been anything but an administrative redrawing unlikely to contradict the Khmer character of the territories administratively attributed to Cochin China. This situation should have lapsed either upon the cession of Cochin China to Vietnam, or upon the abrogation of the protectorate, or indeed it should have been expressly ratified at the latter date by Cambodia. We know that nothing of the sort occurred—on the contrary. In theory, Cambodia thus retains sovereignty in these lands.[32]

Kampuchea Krom (a part of South Vietnam) is a more uncertain case. Beginning in 1856 with the previously quoted letter, King Ang Duong had explained the problem to Emperor Napoleon III. He listed the Khmer regions[33] in Vietnamese hands: "That of Dong-nay, seized more than two hundred years ago; but much more recently those of Saigon, Long-Hô, Psardec, Mi-tho, Pra-Trépang, Ongmor, Bassac, Moat Chruk, Crémuon-Sà, Tiec-Khmau, Péam, and the islands of Cô-Trol and Trelach." He added: "If, by chance, the Annamese would offer any of these lands to Your Majesty, I beg him not to accept them, for they belong to Cambodia. I beg Your Majesty to have compassion for me and my people so that we may see an end to our losses rather than suffocate in this narrow kingdom."

A personage like King Ang Duong would undoubtedly have hindered the French in their policy of territorial annexations. Yet we should have no illusions as to the guarantees for the future that he might have obtained; at least he would have limited French pretensions.

On 9 March 1949 the Assemblée de l'union française, created after decolonization, wrote the following item on its agenda: "Cambodia. Negotiation of a treaty with the royal government," and discussed the point in Versailles on 4 April.[34] The Cambodian representatives recalled that, at the time of France's arrival in the region, the die had not yet been cast: Cambodia and Vietnam each claimed provinces in the Mekong delta that should logically have been returned to Cambodia. Sok Chhong and Sim Var made powerful speeches in favor of Cambodia's territorial rights in Cochin China, the future of which the assembly was to discuss the following month. Faced with France's decision—to entrust the fate of Cochin China to local representatives by means of a referendum, a proposal the Cambodian representatives denounced as improper—Sok Chhong protested: "What Annam could not obtain from Cambodia, Vietnam is going to obtain from the French republic. What Cambodia confided to France, the government of the French republic is going to give to Vietnam with the guarantee of an international treaty." Sim Var concluded:

> It is a fact that . . . not only do children who behave well go unre-
> warded, but their interests are sacrificed in favor of the very ones
> who do not. . . . We can only record, once again, the sacrifice that
> has been unjustly imposed on our country. But after this sacrifice,
> what is going to be done to compensate Cambodia for its excessive
> good behavior? Certainly nothing that can permit us to envision
> the future with confidence, for we are too accustomed to the meth-
> ods of pressure and coercion employed by the colonialists to allow
> ourselves the luxury of a misplaced optimism.

Their firmness was criticized by Princess Yukanthor, Norodom Sihanouk's aunt: "I would hope that, given my age and experience, I am not obliged to follow Mr. Sok Chhong in everything he does."[35] In an account that was more personal and royal than political, she recalled her lofty ideals, the blood that flowed in her veins, the princes who died for France (but not all the other Cambodians who died during the war of 1939–1945), and the Cambodians' respect for and confidence in the French.

The Cambodians showed themselves divided on a question as important as the restitution of territories. In the Assemblée de l'union française, as in Cambodia, the Phnom Penh court was opposed—yet again—to the government, and France learned of this disagreement through a member of the royal family. M. Juge, a deputy belonging to the Mouvement de rassemblement populaire (MRP), declared: "I observe with regret that the Cambodian representatives are not in agreement among themselves." The Khmers won over only a few socialist representatives. For political and economic reasons, the MRP (then in power) did not accept the return of the Cochin Chinese provinces to Cambodia; nor did the Communists, who were supporting Ho Chi Minh.

In addition, the Cambodian claims arrived late. The Khmer representatives took the floor of the assembly in November 1948—when France had already decided to conserve and then install Bao Dai in an empire that would oppose the Democratic Republic of Vietnam, proclaimed by Ho Chi Minh in 1945. And this empire could be built only with the Cochin Chinese lands and part of Annam. Norodom Sihanouk's first claims letter, dated 20 January 1948 and addressed to the high commissioner of France in Indochina, reminded him very politely that Cambodia had not wanted to intervene earlier because of the war in Vietnam but reaffirmed "the sacred rights of the Khmer kingdom to these Cochin Chinese provinces, in which Khmer minorities have never ceased to reside." This demand followed an oral statement of 25 June 1945; during two and one-half years the crown had said nothing, no doubt trusting the French. The latter disregarded the message of 20 January 1948 and on 5 June 1948 concluded the Along Bay accords that granted Cochin China to Vietnam.

On gaining independence in 1953 Cambodia regained none of its territories, neither the contested Cochin Chinese provinces nor the strips of land sliced off during the redrawing of the borders from 1870 to 1914. The war in Vietnam froze the situation. The former king, who assumed leadership of an anti-Vietnamese coalition government in 1982, declared in 1986:

> I never accepted the Vietnamese fait accompli in Kampuchea Krom from the juridical point of view. . . . In 1975 the Khmer Rouge told me: "We are going to recover Kampuchea Krom." And you can see what attacking the Vietnamese cost us. . . . We must distinguish between the juridical side of the matter and the political side. Now, we cannot claim Ha-tien, Chau-doc, Moat Chruk, and so forth, because it is too dangerous. The proof is that the Vietnamese are in Battambang, Angkor, Svay Rieng, Phnom Penh. . . . We must use the poor means at our disposal to attempt to regain just the present Cambodia and not try to return to the past.[36]

Despite these wise words, the Khmers continue to feel the injustice of their losses. The absence of discussion on the eventual restitution of some Cochin Chinese provinces left bitterness and disappointment. France had brought about the retrocession of northern Cambodia, occupied for more than a century by Siam, and the Khmers thought France would likewise return to Cambodia the Cochin Chinese provinces, claimed in the middle of the nineteenth century and populated in the majority by Cambodians before being placed under French tutelage. The status of these provinces did not seem clearly defined in 1862, at least not in favor of Vietnam, if we judge by the Chinese reactions to French colonization. Peking intervened as the suzerain power when France seized Tonkin and Annam. But China did not budge when Paris signed with King Tu-duc of Hue the first treaty (1862) relating to the Cochin Chinese provinces, administered by the Vietnamese and claimed by the Khmers. Does this mean that the Chinese did not consider these provinces to belong to Vietnam? Likewise, the Khmers hoped that France, having failed to restore the provinces to them, would agree to persuade Vietnamese authorities to extend minority status to the Khmer *krom*. Paris denied their request. The Khmer *krom*, who still inhabit the land of their ancestors (the present South Vietnam), have always been fiercely hostile to this partition of Khmer territory. They opposed South Vietnamese leaders until 1955 and then fought the northerners. In 1975 they formed a resistance movement, which was repressed in 1976. Monks participated and were incarcerated or killed along with the other partisans. The movement reformed and was repressed anew in 1985. Many of its members reached the Khmer-Thailand border in 1986 and, probably, the end of their forty-years' struggle.

# 3 The Birth of Nationalism

The Indochinese Communist party, founded in 1930 at the initiative of Ho Chi Minh, had little success in Cambodia, where its members were mainly Vietnamese plantation workers. Son Ngoc Minh, a Khmer *krom*, participated in and later became the official head of the *issarak* movement (usually translated as "Free Khmers").[1] It was not until 1951 that the local Communist parties (Khmer, Vietnamese, and Laotian) assumed individual identities, and the first congress of Khmer Communists took place in 1960.

The first Khmer to speak out for Cambodian independence in the 1930s was a Khmer *krom*, Son Ngoc Thanh, then in Phnom Penh. An anticolonialist and anti-Communist, he lapsed into extremism, becoming fanatically anti-French and then equally antimonarchist. His stay in Khmer lands was interrupted by periods of exile: to Japan at the beginning of the 1940s, and to France from 1946 to 1951. Fighting first with the *issarak*, he founded the Khmer *serei* in 1956 to distinguish himself from the now-dissolved *issarak* movement, whose members had expressed their ideological adherence by taking refuge in Hanoi after the Geneva Accords. The Khmer *serei*, considered "rightist" because they had the support of the United States, South Vietnam, and Thailand, where they were based, were a real problem for Norodom Sihanouk until 1970. As long as the prince headed the country's politics, Son Ngoc Thanh remained in opposition. He became prime minister (for several months only) in 1972 under the Khmer Republic. Often linked to foreign powers, he remained an incomprehensible figure to many Cambodians. To fight the French he was forced to make the most of all available means, fair or foul, and collaborated with the Japanese, who occupied Cambodia beginning in 1941. After Sihanouk's intervention in 1952, the French ended his exile. Son Ngoc Thanh refused a governmental ministry offered him on his return to Cambodia by the Democrats, then in power.

Without telling them, he took to the forest, and from a clandestine radio station there he broadcast attacks on the king. The latter then accused the Democrats—whose attitude toward Son Ngoc Thanh was ambiguous—of conducting this subversion from behind the scenes. According to Keng Vannsak, a contemporary political actor, Son Ngoc Thanh had been pushed by the left to join the maquis in order to unify the resistance movements before they could all be undermined by the Vietminh.[2] According to another witness, the maquis had already staked out their territories, and Son Ngoc Thanh fell back to the Dangrek Mountains, which were still unclaimed. From there, he abandoned the call for unification and asked the dissidents to rally to him. Whatever happened, the Democrats were duped. A recently published letter from Son Ngoc Thanh to the Burmese prime minister U Nu suggests that Son Ngoc Thanh acted only out of patriotism. Dated 25 February 1956, the letter asks U Nu to intervene with Sihanouk in order to awaken the latter to the dangers of the Vietnamese invasion. In a text composed in the Dangrek Mountains and bearing the same date, he declared: "The most serious danger for the Cambodian people is Annamese expansionism. It is now multiplied by Indochinese communism. It can be fatal for the Khmer people, as it was for the Cham people. At present, we must expect the wave of invasion to come from North Vietnam."[3]

Son Ngoc Thanh's clairvoyance probably derives from the fact that, as a native of Kampuchea Krom (now part of Vietnam) and moreover a militant, he knew Vietnamese of all political stripes. In 1956 he created the Khmer *serei* movement with American support. This aid from "imperialists," coming after the difficult and troubled period when the *issarak* was partially infiltrated by the Vietminh, tarnished his image and, despite the documents quoted above, reduced his credibility among Cambodians.

Moreover, if Son Ngoc Thanh was the first Khmer to demand Cambodian independence, if he played a role in the *révolte des ombrelles* in 1942, he was unable to create a large-scale movement rallying the Cambodian people. Perhaps as a Khmer *krom* he lacked the Cambodian courtesy needed to make an impression among the masses; his broadcasts against the king in 1952 may also have appeared as ingratitude; and perhaps he was believed to be on the payroll of the imperialists. Today he evokes mixed feelings: some see him as the father of nationalism and emphasize his constant passion for Cambodian independence; many accuse him of opportunism while crediting him for earlier patriotic feelings.

In the 1940s the *issarak* movement contained groups such as those of Son Ngoc Thanh, Prince Norodom Chantaraingsey, and others, who fought for Cambodia's independence. It later became well organized, forming into a succession of committees, and was officially unified in 1950 by the Khmer *krom* Son Ngoc Minh, a pseudonym the Vietnamese used to call to mind

Son Ngoc Thanh, who was considered a patriot by the Khmer elite, then in the process of politicization. Nevertheless, if the Vietnamese indirectly exploited Son Ngoc Thanh's renown, they did not consider him the artisan of Khmer independence, no doubt because of his anti-Communist sentiments; the booklet published by the *issarak* movement in 1954 did not list his name among the individuals who had contributed to the departure of the French.[4] This omission suggests that Son Ngoc Thanh had retained his autonomy. Officially, the *issarak* movement rallied Khmers fighting for the liberation of Cambodia (in fact, after 1950 it was under Vietminh control) and had the support of patriots such as Ea Si Chau. Based in the Cardamom Mountains, Ea Si Chau managed to come to terms with the Vietnamese for a while. He and many other Khmers affiliated with the *issarak* movement turned against the Vietminh elements who had largely infiltrated it. The result was a split into *issarak khmer* and *issarak yuon* (Vietnamese). Besides the Vietminh, the latter included Khmers loyal to Hanoi who went there in 1954 after the dismantling of the *issarak* movement. Many of them returned to Cambodia in the 1960s and 1970s to participate in the Khmer Rouge's activities; among these was the future leader of the People's Republic of Kampuchea, Heng Samrin, who took refuge in Vietnam in 1977 after the failure of a group plot against Pol Pot in which he was involved. Others, such as Pen Sovan, returned in 1979 to act in the People's Republic of Kampuchea regime (see chapter 8).

Alongside the movement led by Son Ngoc Minh, some Cambodians joined small groups that also bore the name of *issarak*. They were either linked to the Thais, who hoped to retake northern Cambodian provinces (with the help of opportunists such as Dap Chhuon), or like Puth Chhay's gang they were bent on enriching themselves.

Despite the sincerity of their initial efforts, the *issarak* were infiltrated by foreigners and bandits and cannot be considered a Khmer movement for national liberation. Some of their leaders are responsible for the awakening of nationalist sentiment. But the first purely Khmer mass reactions originated elsewhere.

The 1940s were decisive for Cambodia's future. Not only did France disengage itself but the first generation of Khmers with advanced education and training became aware of the country's social and political problems.

## THE REBELLIONS OF YOUTH AND CLERGY

Lycée Sisowath students were the first to demonstrate. In 1936 the French resident superior decided to make high school students of twenty years of age and older pay the head tax. On 5 May high school students went on strike, as some of them related:

We wrote a letter to the resident superior saying that we did not want to pay the head tax. Each of us made a copy and sent it to him. This strike could not have taken place without a degree of reflection on our condition. There were a certain movement of emancipation in the air, manifested in the *Nagara Vatta* [Angkor Wat] newspaper, and this did not please the French. The result of this incident was a degree of organization inside the lycée. Previously, there had been no national-level consultation. The resident's clumsiness made us conscious of the fact that something was wrong.

On 7 May the governor general of Indochina denied the political character of the strike and blamed the students' laziness. In contrast, the monthly report of Cambodia for May 1936 had a detailed account of the Lycée Sisowath affair.[5]

The reason given . . . was the desire to protest against a recent decision limiting to twenty years the age exemption from the head tax for students. Rather than bringing their grievances to their teachers through the normal channels—a procedure repugnant to their pride and sensitivity—the lycée students, of whom only thirty were directly involved, preferred to confront the superior authority with a demonstration that was intended to make an impression.

The official report continued, "It should be added that a certain discontent was already present among the boarders because of the lycée's administration's efforts to substitute a stricter discipline for the rather relaxed habits inspired by Cambodian customs that prevailed in the establishment." French officials were concerned to clear their names with respect to the affair and also mentioned an analogous incident that had occurred in a private institution, the Royal, following a disciplinary measure taken against a student.

Contradictorily, another paragraph of the report stated that the strike at the Lycée Sisowath, "while retaining a purely scholastic character, nevertheless revealed a certain general political side that should not be ignored. This incident, related to various manifestations that can be found specifically in the anonymous petitions obviously coming from the most advanced Cambodian milieux, denotes, among those commonly called the Cambodian elite, a rather alarming political development."

The lycée students did not perceive these events as an anti-French act. Today former demonstrators declare:

We did not feel that the French were oppressive colonialists. We adored our French teachers, and we did not have much contact with the administrators or police. . . . Prince Monireth, who was very independent but not anti-French, played the role of moderator. It was he who created the scouting movement, and young people listened to him. . . . At the time, Sihanouk did not yet have a political role; he was young and rather a spoiled child. . . . With the creation of the *Nagara Vatta* newspaper, we started to get interested in politics.

The rebellion of 1936 was not the high school students' only action, as one student explains:

The discontent manifested itself again among the Sisowath students in 1941, still on the taxation question. A little later, during the war, there were problems. I was seventeen then. The French made the mistake of assuming Cambodians accepted the Japanese more readily because they were "yellow." Huot Sambath's older brother, accused of pro-Japanese collaboration, was incarcerated in a barracks beyond the Phnom and tortured to death by Commander Gallois. In Battambang they arrested a teacher, who met the same fate.

In 1942 the *révolte des ombrelles* took place, fomented by Son Ngoc Thanh, who was then assigned to the royal Buddhist library. According to Cambodian sources, the revolt had its origin in the announcement that monks over the age of twenty, previously exempted, were to be subject to taxation. According to David P. Chandler—who consulted unpublished Khmer documents—the monk Hem Chieu was imprisoned on the island of Poulo Condore under the official pretext of a vague anti-French plot; the manner of his arrest—which disregarded his status as a monk—caused the nationalists to ask the Japanese to sponsor a demonstration organized on 20 July to protest this arrest.[6] Pach Chhoeun, defender of the monks, was arrested, condemned to death, and deported also to the Poulo Condore jail; he was liberated by the Japanese in 1945. Hem Chieu died in prison. This account of the facts is somewhat different from that of the French secret services, which claimed that a plan to massacre French nationals brought about Hem Chieu's arrest.[7] Both accounts mentioned anti-French sentiment. Another individual imprisoned during the protest, Buon Chan Mul, wrote about the origins of the nationalist movement, the *révolte des ombrelles*, and his own three-year incarceration on Poulo Condore.[8]

These groups were the first to demonstrate Khmer national feeling and to work in an organized way for Cambodia's independence. The formation of the first Khmer political party, the Democratic party, formalized this political awakening.

## THE FORMATION OF THE DEMOCRATIC PARTY

After invading China, the Japanese took advantage of the European war to bring troops into French Indochina. The Japanese worked for several years with the Vichy government and its representatives in the colonies before seizing all French command posts in March 1945. They abandoned them in August of the same year, following the Allied victory. Nonetheless, Cambodia (and Laos and Vietnam too, for that matter) experienced six months of independence, granted by Japan and proclaimed by the king; no one welcomed the return of the French protectors. Sihanouk did not resist the notion of an Indochinese federation within a French union but, acting in accordance with the elite's desires, demanded the independence of his country within this federation.

Several Cambodians were already studying in French universities in Paris, where they followed the train of events in Cambodia: "One day we learned that the French had returned to Cambodia. We thought that the treaty they were going to sign with the Cambodians would be very unequal." Before returning they discussed plans for their country's future. Sisowath Youtevong, a very learned prince with intelligence to match, was the leader of the Parisian group. After earning a doctorate in physics, he left Montpellier for Paris and worked as official representative at the ministry of colonies. He was said to be a member of the Socialist party in France (the Section française de l'Internationale ouvrière, or SFIO). In 1945 he founded Fraternité khmère, an association of Khmer brotherhood (see appendix 4) regulated by the law of 1901, with the collaboration of Chhean Vâm, a philosopher, Thonn Ouk, a historian, and Ngin Kareth, a geographer. The brotherhood's purpose was to help Khmer volunteers and draftees serving alongside the French during the Second World War. They fought at Bir Hakeim against Rommel; they were then sent to the colonial artillery base in Draguignan (in the département of Var). Most of them would remain there as laborers; only a dozen, chosen for their musical talent, were permitted by French military authorities to come to Vincennes, another colonial artillery school near Paris. They formed an orchestra and learned French from a member of the association. They were also trained in tailoring and sewing before returning to Cambodia in 1947. The association was based in Prince Youtevong's home and funded through a subsidy granted by the ministry of colonies. At the time seven Khmers were studying in France: aside from the four members of Fraternité khmère, there were also a prince of the Norodom branch and a mandarin's son, very rich and with little concern for the fate of others. The seventh, Au Chhieng, who later became an expert on Khmer epigraphy, was known for his xenophobia. The four students from various backgrounds—the son of a peasant, the son of a prince, and two sons of high-ranking mandarins—had thus begun to militate in France for humanitarian goals. Their political discussions were animated. Two of them had already had the opportunity to express themselves during the Lycée Sisowath rebellion in 1936.

Chhean Vâm, instructed by Youtevong, was the first to return to Phnom Penh. The others left several months later. In Phnom Penh, other intellectuals also wanted to create a political party and may have been in touch with their compatriots in Paris during the 1940s. The two groups held discussions. Three of them, advised by a French jurist, drew up statutes for the first Cambodian political party, the Democratic party (Pak Pracheatipatey), created in March 1946 by Sim Var (who held a brevet d'études du premier cycle du second degré), Chhean Vâm (who had a licence [B.A.] in philosophy), and Ieu Koeus (who studied at the École supérieure de commerce de Hanoi). Thonn Ouk (with a licence in history) and Youtevong joined when they arrived. The Democratic party did not get off the ground until the latter's return in June 1946. Aside from Youtevong's personal talent, his status as a prince gained him the attention of a vast public. The majority of the Democrats—except for the left wing—defined themselves above all as reformers favoring an evolution toward a parliamentary system. The Liberals, who organized as a party during the same period, were conservatives. From the beginning, two individuals were reluctant to join the Democratic party: Son Sann (who studied at the École des hautes études commerciales) and Penn Nouth (who had a diploma from the *kromokar* or administrative personnel school in Phnom Penh). The latter, then governor of Phnom Penh, made a place available for the group's first meetings. He opportunely joined the party in 1947 when the Democrats offered him the constituent assembly's presidency, which had been vacant since the overthrow of Chhean Vâm. Son Sann declared himself a monarchist and, suspecting the party of republican ulterior motives, initially refused to join but, reassured by Prince Youtevong's presence in the movement, joined several months later. Others enlarged the Democrats' circle: some who had degrees from France such as Huy Kanthoul, Son Voeunsai, Pach Chhoeun, Sam Nhean, Yem Sarong; and scholars who had remained in the country and spoke little French such as Iv Uot, Meng Nakri, and several others. "The executive committee met in a shop on the Quai Picquet; there were about twenty of us. At the beginning we met once or twice a week because we had to get organized. The office was always open to the public."[9] The party's motto was Peace, Independence, Discipline, Courage. Its emblem was an elephant's head, which symbolized courage, and three lotus flowers representing royalty, religion, and the people.

The Democrats came from three sources. The first faction, back from

France with advanced degrees, were the most numerous group and founded a French-language weekly named *Le Démocrate*. The second faction, trained in Cambodia or Hanoi and led by Ieu Koeus and Sim Var, came from *Nagara Vatta*, a newspaper begun in 1936 by Sim Var and Pach Chhoeun and closed in 1942 by the French, who accused its leaders of inciting the *révolte des ombrelles*. Hem Chamroeun and Son Ngoc Thanh were their collaborators; at that time Son Ngoc Thanh apparently sought the country's independence above all. This group's press organ was a Khmer-language weekly, *Pracheatipatey* (the democrat), the content of which, according to witnesses, differed from that of the French-language version (see below). The scholars back from France and those who had remained in Cambodia had convergent political lines: "We wanted to put an end to Sihanouk's whims and make a constitutional king out of him." The third faction, drawn from leftists such as Son Ngoc Thanh and several *issarak*, hardly grew until 1955. At that time, young men with fresh diplomas returned from France, among them Prince Norodom Phurissara, Sin Khem Ko, Svay So, and Keng Vannsak. Thiounn Mumm stayed in Cambodia only a few months before returning to France with the mission of politicizing Khmer students there. Saloth Sar (later known as Pol Pot)[10] and Ieng Sary gravitated around the party without joining. The importance of the left in the Democratic party would only really appear in 1955 and then only for a short time. The others considered the left-wing Democrats disruptive elements.

The Democrats set themselves two goals: obtaining the country's independence through dialogue with Paris, and bringing about a democratic evolution of the regime. "By democracy, we wanted to be the masters of our own house. We had no intention of taking up arms against the French."

## THE FRENCH REPRESSION

The halos of learning worn by the intellectuals returned from France quickly earned them great popularity. "In France, we became aware of certain things. When we came back, we had the prestige of greater learning, so much so that we were considered leaders. Our stay abroad had opened our minds, and we had information that was not available to our compatriots who had remained in the country."

The Democratic party was not a party born with independence, composed of bourgeois with the single goal of monopolizing power. A part of the leadership came from modest strata of the population (Sim Var, Chhean Vâm, Sok Chhong, and Ieu Koeus) and had been involved in the lycée revolt of 1936. The Lycée Sisowath alumni association, founded in 1934, was advised by Son Ngoc Thanh and supported by monks of the Mohanikay sect.[11] Many civil servants joined them because they seemed likely to defend social justice, which was increasingly desired by urbanites. "Aside from the intellectuals who had come from France and those from the *Nagara Vatta* line, there was a general movement among the elite. Consequently, from the time of its founding onward, the Democratic party took on a national dimension. We served as a catalyst to this disparate group."

But France was watching. As far back as the *révolte des ombrelles* in 1942, "the French police came and broke down the walls of our printing house [*Nagara Vatta*] and confiscated our stocks of paper," Sim Var said.[12] Faced with the Democratic party's success, the French applied two measures—related to politics and to police. In order to oppose the Democrats' action, the protectorate's authorities provoked the creation of another party, the Liberal party—conservative—led by a man favorable to them, Prince Norodom Norindeth, who received considerable material aid while the Democratic party received nothing.

> The Liberal party had all possible facilities while we were in a dire period. We lacked paper and had very little gasoline; yet we needed these things to undertake an electoral campaign. We procured paper to produce two newspapers and posters, but it amounted to very little when compared to what the Liberal party received. We immediately created two newspapers, in French and in Khmer. Their topics differed, but some articles had a common basis. We had to reduce the number of pages in order to increase circulation. Finally, the papers were only half a page in length; we called them pocket-sized papers and printed about twelve thousand copies.

The protection provided by France to Prince Norindeth made him suspect in the eyes of many Khmers. The great landowners and provincial monks were faithful to him, but he had little support in the administration.[13]

Nothing had foretold the Democrats' electoral success in 1946. After their triumph the French police intervened, as a former democrat explains:

> The French still had the police, the army, finances, and the economy. What scared us was the security service that they called military security, the headquarters of which was located in front of the monument to the dead. They arrested party leaders, among them Sim Var, Chhim Phonn, and about twenty railroad men. Phonn was tortured; they plunged his head into a bathtub to make him confess. Sim Var was accused of being the leader of a pro-Japanese movement, the Pavillon noir . . . , and Chhean Vâm of heading another movement, the Étoile noire, both of which threatened to exterminate the French.

In the words of Sim Var,

> They arrested innocent people, people who had never been involved
> in politics. Uy Keo, another railroad man, was manhandled. The
> worst case was that of a magistrate named Khin Chhe, a former
> classmate. Hem Chamroeun, a forester, and several others were im-
> prisoned with me in Saigon and held in solitary confinement. We
> had not been tried. The king did nothing to save me, a palace in-
> sider. One year later, since there was no evidence against us, we
> were released but placed under house arrest in Kompong Cham. In
> addition to my alleged membership in the pro-Japanese Pavillon
> noir movement, I was accused of furnishing arms to the *issarak*
> movement, in revolt against the French. The resident's name was
> Pénavaire, and he was the one who had us all locked up. They came
> to arrest me right in the middle of a National Assembly meeting, ig-
> noring parliamentary immunity. I had been in office only three
> months. Even when I was in France in late 1949, I remained under
> surveillance. In fact, the most annoying thing was that I was look-
> ing after the *Nagara Vatta* newspaper. . . . The French withdrew
> and left the way open for the Liberal party, which had recruited
> thugs or bogeymen to scare us. Our lives were threatened.[14]

In 1948 the new resident superior had most of the prisoners released.

The Democrats' next skirmish involved the most redoubtable of Cambodian politicians, Norodom Sihanouk.

## THE DIFFICULTIES OF GOVERNING WITHOUT THE KING

In 1946, when the Democratic party was born, Sihanouk was leading the
traditional life of kings and scarcely concerned himself with politics. France's
return had been consecrated by the Modus vivendi agreement signed on 8
January 1946: Cambodia gained domestic independence, while France continued to handle foreign affairs and as adviser exercised control over the
government of Prince Sisowath Monireth (the king's uncle) that came into
existence the same day that the Japanese proclaimed Cambodia's independence. In October 1945 General Leclerc personally traveled from Saigon
to Phnom Penh to arrest Son Ngoc Thanh, who had become too anti-French.

The Democrats easily won the universal-suffrage elections held for the
Constituent Assembly on 1 September 1946, winning fifty seats out of
sixty-nine. Prince Youtevong was the obvious person to form a government
replacing that of Prince Monireth. Aside from members who had not yet
registered, such as Penn Nouth and three independents, all the ministers
belonged to the Democratic party.[15] The government's main objective was
to prepare the kingdom's future constitution, passed by the Constituent
Assembly on 6 May 1947. As the Democrats had hoped, Cambodia adopted

a parliamentary monarchy with a bicameral system: a National Assembly and a Council of the Kingdom. But the Democrats, lacking experience with power and seeing Sihanouk as a French tool rather than as a potential politician, adopted an ambiguous text that the latter was able to exploit when he saw fit to do so. He had the constitution amended, modified, and supplemented several times over. Moreover, the constitution stated: "We . . . , Norodom Sihanouk Varman . . . , king of Cambodia, an independent and sovereign state, grant to Our people this constitution, the text of which follows." The use of the word *varman* (shield, protection) in his title, a term unused since the era of Angkor, and the emphasis on the fact that the constitution was a gift freely given by the king shows that he was not pleased with the role of constitutional monarch that the Democrats wanted to assign him. He thus reminded everyone that he was still the master. Tensions developed between palace and government. Nevertheless, one of the constitution's authors stated: "We tried to safeguard the king's dignity and supremacy by stating that 'All powers emanate from the king. They are exercised in the manner established by the present constitution'" (article twenty-one). Referring to this article, Sihanouk was to make unpopular decisions between 1949 and 1953. Older politicians said: "Injuries to individuals aren't serious; but he injured the constitution."

Yet the king was not opposed to democracy. He read with interest Youtevong's articles in the weekly *Le Démocrate* and favorably received the reforms proposed by the Democrats. In May 1947, and still in basic agreement with the French—whose wishes he rarely opposed—Sihanouk sided with the Democrats, choosing their draft constitution over the one written by the French, who in this instance did not hesitate to intervene in a specifically Cambodian matter. Despite several minor problems, the working arrangements between the king and the Democrats were fairly comfortable.

Prince Youtevong, who, according to witnesses, "impressed the king with his implacable logic," died of illness on 11 July 1947. The Democratic party could offer no one of his caliber or his moderation. Its experience with power was still too recent to permit the emergence of a leader of Prince Youtevong's stature. Sihanouk's personality, however, was asserting itself.

Sihanouk later gave the following explanation: "Until 31 October 1947, when you take everything into account I was a very malleable sovereign, rather submissive to the suggestions of the French, for whom I felt, moreover, esteem and warmth. My reaction was an important turning point in my conception of my duty as head of state."[16] On that day the king refused to give a speech written by the French and aimed at the Democrats, despite the antipathy he had said he felt for them. This event marked the first sign of the king's political interest and also marked the beginning of a struggle between a rising will for power that still hesitated between authoritarianism and liberalism, on the one hand, and, on the other, the democracy desired by Prince Youtevong and his friends.

The elections of December 1947 confirmed the preeminence of the Democratic party, which won fifty-four seats (the Liberal party obtained twenty-one). The victory was all the more notable in that other parties, including Khmer Renovation, led by military men, had been created in the meantime. None were represented in the National Assembly; they had seats in the other chamber, the Council of the Kingdom. At the age of thirty-two, Chhean Vâm became president of the Council of Ministers.[17] This government was overthrown six months later, and like those that followed it was short-lived. Penn Nouth, once rejected as minister of state because of misappropriation, was promoted to president of the Council of Ministers and thus became a member of the Democratic party. His government fell because of a scandal involving fisheries uncovered by Yem Sambaur, who had close ties to the palace.

Next came the Yem Sambaur incident. Ieu Koeus, president of the National Assembly since 1946, went to the royal palace for consultation and let the king convince him to designate Yem Sambaur, a dissident Democrat, as head of the government on 1 February 1949, with the support of some Democratic votes but to the great displeasure of certain Democrats: "The consequences were very serious. Ieu Koeus wanted to avoid a conflict with the king, but the Democratic party did not have to vote for Yem Sambaur. People were strongly opposed to him because he was considered the king's man. He had the unfortunate idea of running a casino, which was a fiasco on the political level." In fact politicians were not the only ones who expressed their disagreement with the opening of this casino: the high school students protested and the minister of education, Meas Saem, had the Lycée Sisowath closed. "There were students' demonstrations that, in the rhythm of a popular dance, chanted a slogan: Meas Saem, Yem Sambaur, *baeuk casino bet vichilay* [Meas Saem, Yem Sambaur, you open a casino and close the lycée]."

Thus the Democrats, through their own blundering and inexperience (ambiguous constitutional text, dissension within the party), managed to put an end to the first governmental experience, opening the way for the king to intervene through a proxy. From this moment, perhaps, we can date the monarch's desire to lead. Yet the party enjoyed a great popularity and was remarkably well organized.

The Yem Sambaur government fell in September 1949. Probably weary of this ministerial instability, Sihanouk intervened in an energetic manner on 18 September. He dissolved the National Assembly and formed a government without the assembly but with Yem Sambaur still in the presidency. In so doing he took almost unnoticed liberties with the constitution that the king justified by the seriousness of the situation (Khmer dissidents and Vietminh soldiers were causing a reign of insecurity in the country) and by his right to modify certain articles if necessary since it was he who had originally given the constitution to the people. He asked each party to delegate two members whom he would appoint as ministers.[18] This system functioned for two years but brought no more stability, with four presidents following each other at the head of six governments.

The Democratic party lost another of its faithful members: Ieu Koeus, Youtevong's successor in the presidency, was murdered early in 1950 (by the French, some say; by the king's men, others suggest). And the party expelled four former ministers who proved to be favorable to the dissolution of the National Assembly, and it made ready for the new elections to be held in September 1951. Once again, the Democrats triumphed, taking 70 percent of the seats.[19] And on 12 October 1951 Huy Kanthoul presented his government, composed entirely of Democrats.[20] The king intervened a second time; he dismissed the government on 15 June 1952, dissolved the National Assembly on 13 January 1953, and had nine Democratic deputies imprisoned on charges of terrorism. Student strikes and demonstrations followed throughout the country.

This time the sovereign apparently decided to shut out the Democrats, whose credibility had remained intact in the country for seven years. In these conditions, to allow them to govern would keep anyone who was not one of them, even the king, from exercising power. Part of the royal reaction was the dismissal of the Huy Kanthoul government, which was doing its job in arresting officials and private individuals engaged in corruption. Sihanouk began to protect those who remained loyal to him. Of the partisans thus created, many would become courtiers.[21]

And apparently the Democrats sought either the total submission of the king or his aid in winning independence, for none at the time suspected that underneath his youthful timidity Sihanouk was hiding an alert mind combined with an acute sense of politics. They did not succeed in regaining power.

In 1955 the last party congress took place in the Lux cinema. Many prominent individuals were absent: "Chhean Vâm had retired, Prince Youtevong was dead, Ieu Koeus had been murdered, Huy Kanthoul was in business, and Thonn Ouk was in France." The seats of the new executive committee were filled with leftist elements, with the exception of Son Sann—the only veteran—who refused the presidency. Prince Norodom Phurissara accepted it and, with Kheng Vannsak, Sin Khem Ko, Svay So, and several others, took the party in hand. They were apparently sincere, as the following testimony suggests:

The left-wing Democrats were young students who had not compromised themselves. We thought that the young ones would have
more guts in facing Sihanouk and fighting corruption; that conservatives such as Thonn Ouk, Chhean Vâm, Son Sann . . . did not
resist enough. . . . We believed that we would not have to get involved in the fighting between the Americans and the Vietnamese.
We wanted neutrality and an end to corruption; we were naive to
think that it would disappear easily. For people of goodwill, that
took the place of a program.

This naivete no doubt prevented them from realizing that their elders
had designs on the Democratic party: "Saloth Sar came to see us from time
to time at Democratic party headquarters. He said he was in the resistance;
I don't know if that is true or not, for he was teaching at Lycée Chamroeun
Vichea. . . . The Khmer Rouge tried to bend our policy so that it would
correspond to theirs, but they did not attempt to take over the party."

In fact, that was indeed their intention: in 1955 they had at their disposal
no political structure because they belonged to no party, not even the
People's party (Pracheachon). According to a former member of the Democratic party, "Saloth Sar told us: 'Now that we [referring to the left] have
obtained victory [over the Democratic party], we must use the Democratic
party as an instrument of propaganda.'" But the young members on the
spot resisted.

THE DEMOCRATS' ACHIEVEMENTS

The Democrats, like most Cambodians, wanted the independence that
France was late in granting. The Khmer delegates to the Assemblée de
l'union française in 1949 complained with a hint of bitterness about France's
attitude:

We knew from experience that domestic sovereignty would be a
dead letter as long as it was not completed by sovereignty in foreign relations. For example, France integrated us into the Indochinese federation without consulting us, disregarding our sovereignty
over foreign affairs. France signed a treaty with the Chinese government for directing waves of foreign immigrants toward our country
without consulting us and even over our protests.[22]

At Phnom Penh, the French sensed the determination of this young team
right away, and they rejected it in favor of a more malleable man, whom
they launched with fair success into political life—Prince Norindeth. They
thus stripped the Democrats of all possibilities of opening negotiations with
them about the road to independence. Furthermore, the party lost its most

outstanding leaders, who were imprisoned. The only means of expression left to the Democrats were their newspapers and, more officially, the Assemblée de l'union française in Versailles. There they energetically defended their claims, but French policy in Southeast Asia had already been set before they entered the assembly. Moreover, the conflict between the palace and the government, which reverberated inside that tribune, reduced the impact of Cambodian claims. Nonetheless, the Democrats launched the slogan of Cambodia's neutrality for the first time.

They were no more successful in vanquishing the chronic corruption, which sprang back to life after 1946. They themselves were not exempt. Some leaders proved themselves to be intransigent in this domain. The twenty-two months during which they exercised the powers of government (twenty-eight if we count the consultative assembly's six months) were not sufficient to clean up the administration.

In the social domain, the Democrats have the merit of developing education. "There were only 13,000 students in elementary school in all of Cambodia . . . the provinces were asking for teachers. Money collected during certain religious celebrations was reserved for the construction of pagoda schools. But cadres were lacking: teachers were rushing into administration because they were better paid there and received illicit commissions." The Democrats created high schools in Kompong Cham, Battambang, Svay Rieng, Kampot, and perhaps Kompong Thom. Phnom Penh's high schools could not absorb all the students; the (Catholic) École Miche taught a certain number of them. Two individuals invested their own capital in the construction of a private school in 1953. At first an association, Kambu Both became an educational establishment once a hut was built on land belonging to a Democrat's family.[23] Foreigners came to help in its operation, but all the teachers were Khmers, paid from the tuition. There was another measure of democratization: the *sala srok* (district office) was furnished with benches "so that people could sit and not be obliged to grovel when they talked to the *chau vay srok* [district head], for we wanted to attenuate the rituals of protocol." Furthermore, "the king himself made it known that he was favorable to erasing these signs of servility; in practice, however, he reacted differently: he was displeased if one did not prostrate oneself before him."

The death of Youtevong struck a severe blow to the Democratic party. Another handicap was its inclusion of Son Ngoc Thanh, the idol of youth before what many in the party considered his "treason." The party's ambiguity toward Son Ngoc Thanh led to Sihanouk's blaming them for collusion with him; yet only Ea Si Chau, a very Spartan individual, and about fifty lycée students followed him into the maquis. The sovereign purposely accused the party of "leftism" whereas the Communists became a majority only in 1955 when the Democrats no longer controlled policy. Paradoxically, the former monarch accuses them of going astray in the coup d'état of 1970.[24] "Today Prince Sihanouk speaks of republicans and includes the Democrats among them. This is an error. The republic was founded by Sihanouk's men, coming from the Renovation party. Lon Nol, whom the National Assembly had refused to invest with the prime ministership, was raised to this position in 1969 thanks to Sihanouk."

Nevertheless many Democrats were devoted to the idea of a republic.

> With time, the Democrats drew the lessons of the past. We were young and inexperienced. We sinned by lack of communication. The most serious problems were caused by misunderstandings. When we were invited for the evening to Chamcar Mon [Sihanouk's palace], we left early because we had to get up early the next morning to work. We failed to understand that we needed a small group of our people near the king. There was no one around him to convince him that we were not fundamentally antimonarchist.

The party displayed another typically Cambodian characteristic: "The Democrats were a bit like the prewar French radical party, a gathering of people opposed to something"—in this case to the French and to royal absolutism.

They may also have wanted to go too fast. Given their enthusiasm and the skill later shown by the king, we can imagine what Cambodia could have become if, instead of opposing one another so clumsily and inopportunely, the sovereign and the Democrats had marched hand in hand. From exile, former militants remember: "I retain an indelible memory of the Democratic party, for it mobilized people."

# 4    Sihanouk's Politics
## *A Fragile Equilibrium*

In 1953 Cambodia was in ferment, with calls for rapid and total sovereignty from most of its parties except the Liberals, who favored a gradual evolution that would leave France freedom of choice. The government was again in the hands of a single man, Sihanouk, who did not lack courage despite his pro-French attitudes and who sought total independence.

## THE ROYAL CRUSADE FOR INDEPENDENCE

Three years after the Modus vivendi agreement of late 1946, Norodom Sihanouk signed with France in 1949 a treaty granting Cambodia partial independence. No further commitments followed, although the king hoped for the granting of total sovereignty in the short term. Disappointed, he went to France in 1953 but gained nothing; he then went to the United States, where he made a sensational announcement, threatening to fight alongside the Communists if the French government did not prove more generous. Returning to Cambodia, he withdrew into the northern provinces to lead a royal crusade for independence. Since one argument put forward by the French for maintaining troops in Cambodia was that the country, with its ten thousand soldiers, could not defend itself against Communist expansionism, Sihanouk revived the dormant Mouvement de rassemblement under the name of Chivapol (vital forces). This time women, known as *neary klahan* (courageous women), participated; among them was Khieu Ponnary, the wife of Saloth Sar (known later as Pol Pot). The first priority was the independence struggle. The members of Chivapol received no civic instruction; their action was to be military. Lacking sufficient firearms, they trained with wooden rifles. Undertaken on Cambodia's own initiative, the mass mobilization included civil servants, who were obliged to participate, as well as other able-bodied members of the general population. Former members speak with nostalgia and admiration of the goodwill and determination of these men and women.

Prince Sihanouk went to Bangkok, hoping to obtain Thai support in his struggle against the French and the Vietnamese. His trip was in vain: the system of traditional alliances had broken down. The prince would never forget this rebuff.

Few Cambodians believed in a successful outcome, yet success came on 9 November 1953, the date on which the Khmers recovered full sovereignty. Undoubtedly, the members of Chivapol and their wooden firearms alone did not force France to yield; the royal crusade and Sihanouk's courteous obstinacy surprised Paris and helped resolve the problem. However, all these demonstrations took place in favorable regional and international contexts. In Vietnam the French were caught up in fighting that had already caused many deaths on both sides. Besides, the worldwide decolonization process had started in 1947 with India's independence and the concomitant collapse of the British Empire. Even so the Khmer sovereign undoubtedly deserves credit for skillful maneuvers that avoided all or almost all bloodshed. Only mopping-up operations were carried out in northern Cambodia against the *issarak* (Khmer and Vietminh Communists). During the early 1950s the king had personally participated: operation *samakki*, which he began in autumn 1954, sought out the last pockets of *issarak* rebels, who had regrouped near the Thai border. On the whole, the Cambodians did not clash with the French, who were fighting only against Communist elements.

Overnight Sihanouk became a national hero and the "father of independence." He said not a word about the nationalists who had preceded him in the struggle. The peasants considered his success to be a demonstration of the monarchy's magical political power and henceforth showed their young monarch, whom they called *Samdech Ov* (Monsignor papa), an unfailing devotion that endures to the present day, despite all the vicissitudes of recent decades.

## CREATION OF THE POPULAR SOCIALIST COMMUNITY

Sihanouk was thus to rely on the peasantry; he knew that it would remain faithful. Yet his status as king did not allow him to enter the political arena. Therefore, early in 1955 he abdicated the throne in favor of his father and launched himself in pursuit of power. The Sangkum Reastr Niyum (popular socialist community; hereafter Sangkum), which he created in 1955, is described in its statutes as "a community of citizens . . . composed of comrades who have freely responded to the appeal addressed to them. . . . Our community is not a political party. [It is] the symbol of the aspirations of the common people who are the real people of Cambodia . . . for the communion of the people with their two natural protectors—religion and the throne" (articles 1, 2, 4).

Turning his back on traditional political parties, the former king henceforth appealed chiefly to the peasants to legitimize the power he sought. He referred to the fourteenth-century legend of Ta Trâsâk Phâ'em, said to have been created to justify the establishment of a new royal dynasty of popular origin, to legitimize the reign of a usurper.[1] Say Bory explains the interest of this new doctrine and its use by Prince Sihanouk. Since the time of Ta Trâsâk Phâ'em, "a new theory came to be advanced: the royal power is no longer exclusively of divine origin. It can also come from the people. . . . In the modern political struggle, Norodom Sihanouk relied on this tradition, on this new theory, to prove that he also came from the people, and that the new Khmer monarchy is democratic and popular."[2]

At the same time, this dynasty "lost its 'sacred character' and would no longer be spared the palace quarrels, the intrigues, and various critiques" (30). In reality, Cambodians criticized the head of state's policies, sometimes sharply, particularly in the 1960s. But in the rural milieu he remained the divine king. And the king—now a prince—demonstrated his shrewdness by stipulating that, in order to belong to Sangkum, individuals must "belong to no party." Thus, the parties were dissolved, except for the Pracheachon and the Democratic party, part of which joined Sangkum.

In the 1955 elections Sangkum gained 83 percent of the votes. Some virulent left-wing Democrats had been imprisoned before the electoral campaign; the police-state atmosphere reigned, as one of them would later say. The Democratic party kept only 12 percent of the seats. It had suffered from the rallying of some members to Sangkum, from intimidation, and from Communist infiltration. In addition, it could not compete with the prince in rural society. Nevertheless, the Democratic party had the support of those who knew the most about the state's problems—the townspeople. Faced with the vexations that they endured even after the elections, Democrats who did not renounce their party remained in the shadows. The party fell into inactivity; it would come back to life only under Marshal Lon Nol's republic. The Pracheachon obtained 4 percent of the seats; its faithful pursued their activities clandestinely. The party recruited other partisans, future Khmer Rouge among them.

Sangkum's electoral victory marked the end of the multiparty system and democracy in favor of a single party in the hands of a single man; its statutes notwithstanding, Sangkum was merely a political tool that excluded the other parties. Sihanouk would dominate political life for the next fifteen years by organizing and relying on Cambodian youth.

Created on 5 September 1957, the Jeunesse socialiste royale khmère (royal Khmer socialist youth, or JSRK) sought, in the words of journalist Ros Chantrabot, "to indoctrinate intellectuals and watch over them. Civil servants and students comprised its membership. An entire hierarchy came into being."[3] Mao Chhay assumed the organization's leadership, which then passed to Yim Dith. The JSRK served only as a facade: there was no civic and even less political training. "Once a year, we took a training course lasting three days to learn how to march and salute. We were told to love the monarchy and the country but were given no explanation," said a former member. Their main mission, in point of fact, was to serve as honor guards whenever the prince came to inaugurate one of Sangkum's projects: "For me, being in the JSRK meant having a pretty uniform for parading around in front of the girls. In any case, it was hard to refuse; almost all the young people were in it." Some of them helped peasants improve their skills in growing rice, as did the *Samdech Ov* teams described below. Military men used them (to the benefit of officers and mandarins) to develop lands in Battambang province belonging to the peasants who launched the Samlaut rebellion in 1967 (discussed in chapter 5).

Contrary to other reports, this youth movement was completely non-militarist and did not follow basic scouting principles.[4] Solely a tool of Sangkum, its positive action was negligible. Privately, many Khmers ridiculed the JSRK.

## A MARGINALIZED LIBERAL PRINCE

The prince first prepared a revision of the constitution, passed by Sangkum's National Assembly. The revision was supported by the arrival of provincial delegations in Phnom Penh and the receipt of petitions signed by several hundred thousand persons. All these means of propaganda were part of the traditional power of leaders to manipulate the people. Significant changes are evident:

> The king will thus choose and appoint the members of government. ... The king will have the right to interpret the texts of the constitution in the last instance. This provision simply corrects the anomaly that existed in Article 101 of the constitution. As a matter of fact, the constitution is bestowed by the king upon his people. Since the king is considered the father of the constitution, the task of interpretation logically reverts to him alone.[5]

The other decisions served to give a democratic appearance to the amendment: new electoral apportionment, replacement of the National Assembly by a popular assembly (which was ephemeral), and control promised (but not given) to the people, who, according to the text, became "the supreme judge." Peasants simply endorsed—without understanding—all that was offered them because they hoped to keep the peace. The revision resulted from Sihanouk's desire to protect royal power against the Democrats rather than to implement a reform to benefit the people, as the following lines indicate: "In my opinion, the failure of democracy in Cambodia was caused by blunderers to whom the king had confided the writing of our constitution" (662). Unwilling to be supplanted, criticized, or even advised, the prince preferred to take matters in hand from the beginning of his mandate.

Shortly thereafter Sihanouk included in the constitution an institution that he had created in December 1955, the biannual National Congress, where in theory each person could present personal or village claims, criticize delegates, or have unworthy officials removed.

These various measures gave the regime a democratic veneer.[6] At the outset apparently the prince himself sincerely desired liberalization although later things went wrong. In fact, many Cambodians would say that his first reaction was not always negative. Open to new projects, he reversed himself if he lost control of them, lest an ounce of power escape him. The prince nevertheless understood that the elite, whom he could not bypass in governing the country, remained for the most part hostile to absolute power. To conciliate the elite, he tried to include its members in his successive ministries. Thus Chau Seng, a leftist, became his chef de cabinet for many years; Khieu Samphan, now the Khmer Rouge's number one man, rose to minister of commerce; the right, represented by General Lon Nol (founder of the Khmer Renovation party), would govern the country from 1969 onward at Sihanouk's insistence. But the majority of the members of the administration were Sihanouk's faithful followers or even opportunists who took their Sangkum cards despite their lack of conviction. Some acquired the card under constraint: once nominated for a position, they had either to get a card or to turn down the job. A young man reported: "People like my father, a former Democrat, were under psychological pressure to join Sangkum. . . . The security police arrested suspects on the right and left. If one did not agree with the regime, one was forced either to submit or to join the guerrillas." Ros Chantrabot explains that the National Congress, "imposed like an institution of state," took off rapidly and gained the upper hand over the popularly elected National Assembly: "Popular consultation was thus transformed into a systematic approval of the decisions made by the head of state. Following a well-rehearsed scenario, the prince's proposals were supported by several speakers selected beforehand and were adopted by a show of hands by the indifferent audience. Sensitive subjects—corruption, injustice, unemployment—were always dodged."[7] The journalist adds that the National Assembly simply ratified the decisions that Sihanouk had the congress make.

There were thus serious restrictions on democratic liberty. "For Khmers liberty is something given by the sovereign," writes Say Bory, "a liberty granted and not, as in France, won by the people themselves. . . . 'Bestowed liberty' is in fact only a decoy to fool the people. This is what one finds in the practice of Cambodian democracy. Formal democracy existed, but genuine democracy failed to appear and simply gave way to pure demagoguery" (131–132).

Furthermore, excesses increased. A plot, fomented in 1958 by the rebel pirate Dap Chhuon, then minister of security, was discovered; arrests followed. The repression fell also on the supporters of rightist Sam Sary, a partisan of Dap Chhuon. Approximately two thousand suspects were held at the Stung Mean Chey camp at Phnom Penh: "In the middle of the camp was a large straw hut for eminent persons and civil servants; surrounding it were wooden huts for lower-class people. It was a military camp, surrounded by barbed wire. Officially, ten people were shot during the five months I spent there."

The killings caused publicity and shocked the Khmers. "On the news, we saw the executions of Chau Bory and Priep In. It was really bloody. We couldn't take it and waited outside." Some believed that the prince made a grave error. "The brutal manner in which Sihanouk acted against Sam Sary's people made a number of Cambodians move to Lon Nol's side later on," explains a left-wing opponent. Likewise, in the late 1960s photographs of the executions of Khmer *serei* covered the foyers of movie theaters; newsreels showed several scenes.[8]

Sim Var, whose honesty and integrity are above reproach, and who had been excluded by the Democratic party's left wing, became Sangkum's first secretary general. A committed enemy of personal power and favorable to the peasantry, from which he originated, he had an independence of mind that brought him into conflict with the chief of state. Penn Nouth, a man who did not lack wisdom and talent, enjoyed the prince's confidence; he was to dominate governmental life for a dozen years.

Sihanouk decided on three priorities: development, neutrality, and struggle against corruption. The Sangkum era began auspiciously. Sihanouk, who appeared to be one of the uncontested leaders of the third world countries, was to gain a following, particularly in Africa.

## DOMESTIC ACHIEVEMENTS

### PUBLIC SERVICES AND THE FIGHT AGAINST CORRUPTION

After independence the communes acquired a certain autonomy. Yet theory and practice rarely coincide. Frequently the subprefect chose the mayor, who was accepted with confidence if he was a native; if he came from elsewhere, the peasants feared—often rightly—that they would be exploited.[9] Speak-

ing of Sangkum and the republican period—his book dates from the latter—
our Cambodian civil servant Say Bory explains that the decentralization
desired by the leaders was intended merely to "deceive the vigilance of the
rural population in order to attach it to their cause, the cause of the dominant
central power. It was not and is not a decentralization for the genuine
progress of the peasants. The peasants only served as the stakes for power
hungry political parties and as taxable subjects for the administration" (12).

Since 1946, when—by necessity and then by choice—the French left the
Cambodians a degree of internal autonomy, corruption developed anew.
Now without supervision, high authorities and civil servants returned to
the comfortable practices of yesteryear. Tith Huon summarizes the postin-
dependence phenomenon:

> An ancient tradition, a people whose mentality still remains far
> behind the changes of the modern world, the consequences of
> colonialism and decolonization, ridiculously low public salaries,
> the weakness of statutory protection for civil servants—here are
> the many factors that contributed to the birth, development, and
> the maintenance of corruption in Cambodian public offices.[10]

In addition to civil servants, people in business, in the military, and in
Sihanouk's entourage gave themselves over to corruption; the posts of
governor and sometimes ambassador were sold at auction, without the
knowledge of the head of state. Accusations of trafficking in money were
brought even against someone as worthy and honest as the queen mother
Kossomak, often by people who were unable to influence her and by the
American press. In fact, the crown did own compartments for rent.[11] Likewise Sihanouk's wife, Monique Sihanouk, president of the Cambodian Red
Cross, was accused without proof of misappropriating that organization's
funds. We should remember the view of Sim Var, whom Sihanouk now
considers his worst enemy: "Sihanouk's hands alone are clean. He knows
all about the corruption, including that practiced by his in-laws, but he
pretends not to know."[12]

Thus Cambodia's first politician and several men of Sim Var's generation, trained under the protectorate, were honest and wanted to clean up the
administration, as did the students. Consequently, when the first Sangkum
government of October 1955 set up a general anticorruption ministry, hope
was reborn but soon withered. Prince Monireth, a man whose "integrity
and energy were known to all," according to Charles Meyer, was appointed
to head the ministry:

> Monireth immediately announced his intention to strike high and
> hard; the first haul was to include a dozen notoriously corrupt

individuals. Several days later Monireth presented the Council of Ministers with a plan for exceptional tribunals for this purpose. Consternation and then panic followed. Sihanouk demanded his resignation, which he refused to give. One month later a governmental crisis occurred. There was no more talk about cleaning up except during the meetings of the anticorruption committees who punished policemen and unfortunate secretaries by means of reprimands "placed in their personnel files."[13]

No fewer than two years were needed to clarify the "organization of the ministry, which, moreover, remained theoretical," according to Tith Huon (177). The organs that successively replaced the anticorruption ministry were like parades intended to deceive, as the Khmers say; their roles were ridiculous. The sharp check that Sihanouk gave to the anticorruption struggle in October 1955 indicated that the cleaning up would never occur. Monireth, Sihanouk's dynastic adversary and the person everyone expected would receive the throne in 1941, did not spare palace habitués, somewhat motivated perhaps (some suggested) by a desire for revenge. The application of these measures would involve Sihanouk's intimates, even his family members, and a good number of otherwise competent civil servants. Such personal and political considerations allowed corruption to linger and even to spread; as a result of colonization and the American presence, many civil servants—whose numbers grew after the French left—wanted to live in the Western fashion, which their salaries did not allow them to do.

The disastrous consequence was that still honest young degree holders entered the system of corruption and were swept along despite themselves or from a desire to climb the administrative hierarchy in a normal if not rapid fashion. Moreover, Tith Huon points out that Sangkum had instituted the "variable-salary policy" consisting of giving higher pay to civil servants who lacked the opportunity to enrich themselves illegally (employees of the agricultural service and teaching corps, for example). He considers this "an implicit authorization granted by the state to certain categories of civil servants to practice corruption" (42).

Numerous scandals erupted between 1955 and 1970, some implicating the chief of state's in-laws. Overall, the real culprits were never punished.[14] The failure to deal with corruption dates from the beginning of the Sangkum regime.

BORDER DEFENSE AND THE DEMOGRAPHIC BOOM

Conscious of the covetousness that Cambodia's sparsely populated border regions attracted, Sihanouk (who became head of state in 1960 on the death of his father, King Suramarit, as Queen Kossomak became guardian of the kingdom and the throne remained vacant) developed an intelligent regional and national policy to improve the situation in these neglected regions.

To deal with demographic concerns at the national level, the head of state undertook a campaign at the beginning of the 1960s to increase the birth rate. Its success could not overcome Cambodia's earlier population loss; the country had emerged greatly weakened from the wars of succession and foreign invasions from which it had suffered since the sixteenth century. It recovered slowly at first under the protectorate and then more rapidly following independence, attaining about seven million inhabitants in 1970, still a minuscule population compared with the approximately forty million Vietnamese and as many Thais who then threatened Cambodia's security.

In the administrative domain, Sihanouk created new provinces in the late 1950s in order to protect Cambodian territory from covetous neighbors; the military administered these border provinces and carried out surveillance at the same time. Further, Sihanouk envisioned the creation of a highway network to encircle the country. Military officers and civil engineers began its construction. Unfinished in 1970 after Sihanouk's overthrow, it became impassable in parts from lack of upkeep after the arrival of the Khmer Rouge as attention shifted to the construction of other roads.

Finally, some of these new provinces were declared pioneering regions, and programs for population transfer were prepared under military leadership. They proved effective along the coastal regions of the Gulf of Thailand. The mountainous back country of the west did not attract the Khmers, people of the plains. In many cases schemes were developed without considering the venereal diseases and malaria that decimated the montagnards and alienated potential candidates for relocation. The one sensible action to remedy this sector's demographic decline—medical care for the people—did not occur. In the east, near Vietnam, Mondolkiri and Ratanakiri provinces received few new arrivals, except for rubber plantation workers, who were recruited with difficulty and wanted to leave at the first opportunity. Charles Meyer states that volunteers received land, farming tools, a pair of oxen, and one year's salary. Once this period had elapsed, they sold the tools and animals and returned to their native regions. Aside from provinces' remoteness and the danger of malaria, Khmer soldiers stationed there took advantage of them. Moreover, the presence of Vietcong soldiers, already established on the border, generally caused Khmers to flee. Sihanouk's authorization of the Vietcong's military presence in these areas ran counter to the announced measures, and he must have known this. Generally speaking, administrative centers and highways attracted settlers, but the distant regions remained desperately uninhabited.

In theory, the plan included judicious measures for education and health.

Had it been part of a coherent overall policy, over the long term it would have given Cambodia improved means of defense or, in any case, of dissuasion. Weaknesses and gaps in the infrastructure, combined with the Vietnamese threat, contributed to the plan's failure.

## THE DEVELOPMENT OF PUBLIC HEALTH AND EDUCATION

At the beginning of the 1950s the health and sanitation situation improved slightly: seventy-seven physicians (including those of foreign origins) practiced in Cambodia compared to fourteen in 1948. That number was still not enough, and several measures were taken: scholarship students were sent to foreign countries, particularly France, to study medicine; a corps of health officers was created in Cambodia; and dispensaries were built.[15] There were approximately four hundred Khmer physicians in 1975, a figure that represents a major effort by the Cambodian and French governments to promote medical training. Phnom Penh founded a school of pharmacy that produced doctors of pharmacy who replaced the pharmaceutical health officers previously trained by the school of medicine. But Cambodia did much more than this. The other corps (nurses, midwives, rural midwives) increased fivefold; the new sanitation agent, the health officer, received training on a level between that of a physician and a nurse; the first appointments would temporarily compensate for the lack of physicians. Infirmaries were built and inaugurated by the head of state, who cared little about what happened afterward.

With the development of tourism, it became necessary to modernize hotels and restaurants, which often lacked suitable septic tanks, and to train managers who could deal with hygienic problems. In health and sanitation, the greatest success came from the training (in hygienic concepts and anatomical knowledge) given to matrons who became fully competent rural midwives.

What must be emphasized is that medical care in Cambodia was free: patients were not charged for medicine or hospitalization. This aspect of medical care was not without problems—as education progressed, the inhabitants increasingly rejected traditional medicine in favor of modern practices, causing a growing demand for medicines.[16] But the budget did not increase accordingly. The creation of a laboratory to manufacture pharmaceutical products in 1964 helped considerably, producing syrups, solutions, cachets, tablets, and especially injectable vials, for "Cambodians love injections—it's psychological," adds Chhay Han Cheng. Medical personnel undertook vaccination campaigns (against smallpox, typhoid, poliomyelitis, and other diseases) in cooperation with the Institut Pasteur, which, in exchange for a subsidy, furnished all the vaccines.

Faced with a lack of funds, the then-minister conducted propaganda campaigns to convince communes to build infirmaries. The state supplied iron to reinforce concrete; villagers had to supply sand and bricks and do the construction work. This program began in 1964, when the Cambodian economy struggled to deal with the effects of overspending and the rejection of American aid.

In terms of the number of buildings constructed, the program's success appears immense. In the hard-to-reach border zones (northeastern, western, northern, southwestern), state participation was greater. The works were expensive, since some materials were brought in by plane; and, once construction was completed, buildings had to be supplied with furniture and medicines, for which communes did not have a single riel. So they borrowed them from the capital or a neighboring village. A typical scenario for many communes—the infirmaries in Ratanakiri and in Kah Kong, at Russey Chrum, and at Spean Khda–Thmar Bang—might unfold in the following manner: when the inauguration was over, furniture and medications were sent by plane back to the generous lender; the deserted buildings then served to lodge foreign travelers. The head of state did not know about all these difficulties; his temper and sharp tongue sheltered him from all unpleasant revelations. No one dared tell him: "One could not tell the prince that something was unattainable," a majority of the townspeople reported.

Normally the infirmaries would be supplied with basic medicines, in particular those made in Cambodia. The ministry sent the chief physicians of the provincial hospitals a supply to share among the various establishments. Because of negligence and corruption, the most needy received the least; they lived so far from the center that they presented no real danger to dishonest officials.

No real network was set up to handle personnel. Education was not always available, and nothing was done to clear malarial regions because no funds were available. An official thus left his family in the plains. Finding himself in a remote village with unnavigable roads, he would grow homesick and, at the slightest sign of disease, desert his post, often permanently.[17] The promise of rapid granting of tenure for nurses, teachers, and other employees accepting service in these zones did not increase their enthusiasm.

Isolated from reality and unaware of his country's real needs, Sihanouk went as far as to refuse precious aid from China: "In 1965 Chou En-lai proposed building a medical institute [in Cambodia] to train country doctors, the principal goals of which would be to improve medical services for the inhabitants of remote regions, a version of China's 'barefoot doctors.' But Sihanouk refused, saying that medical services in the countryside were sufficient."[18]

If health policy undoubtedly progressed in the plains, the situation remained unchanged elsewhere. In 1970 the population of the communes of Ta Tey Leu and Chumnoap in Kah Kong was in decline from lack of medicine to treat venereal diseases. Spean Khda–Thmar Bang village had only thirteen households left and an average of one child per couple; rates of sterility were rising.

The greatest changes came in education. Sihanouk wanted his country to close the enormous gap that had developed during the colonial period. Khmer elites had to be trained and education extended to the entire population, especially to women. In 1955 the latter gained the right to vote. Concrete schoolhouses were built everywhere, even in the most remote spots, for educating children—boys as well as girls. Illiterate adults were to learn to read and write, as ordained by the law of 31 May 1965. But we must see the law in its proper context. It required adult Khmer citizens, men and women, to know how to read and write by the end of 1965; educated Khmers had to instruct at least three illiterates who wanted to learn. Finally, foreign residents had until the end of 1965 to learn to write in Cambodian characters. In fact, many considered that the law had as its exclusive target Chinese and Vietnamese, who were regularly visited by police, whom they had to bribe in order to live in peace. Among Khmers, the law's results were poor.

The state created nine universities during the 1960s. In the first stage, France aided in the reorganization. More than three hundred French professors taught in secondary and higher education. The Faculté de pédagogie was to respond gradually to demands; greater progress for the future was expected thanks to the École normale that France promised to provide. Finally the Khmerization of education was decided on. In addition to public education, there were poorly developed private schools and above all the pagoda schools, which increased in number until 1960 (when their total was 1,615) and then decreased until 1964 (to a total of 1,365). This diminution resulted from a disagreement between Prince Sihanouk and the head of the Buddhist clergy (Mohanikay order), Chuon Nath. Officially, the number of students did not decline: 79,000 compared to 84,155. But these statistics should be treated with prudence since officials sometimes modified the figures to please the head of state.[19]

*The Creation of Universities*

Cambodia certainly needed institutions of higher education; in 1955 it had no universities. The creation of the Université royale khmère in January 1960 as well as the Buddhist university were in response to real needs. The former brought together the sciences, medicine, humanities, public administration, and pharmacy; the latter trained monks in philosophy and Buddhist doctrine. Logically, technical education should have received the same priorities, given the hydraulic agricultural works to be undertaken and the birth of industry. Virtually nothing was in place at the time except the École des arts et métiers; the Université technique royale khmère did not open until 1965. The Soviet Union contributed mightily to developing education through the construction of the Institut technique supérieur de l'amitié khméro-soviétique, staffed entirely by Soviet professors. Next came the Université royale des beaux-arts; such a course of instruction was appropriate for a country possessing numerous archaeological remains and theatrical and musical forms that were well integrated into daily life, both in the countryside and in the cities. But perhaps an institute would have sufficed. Aside from these first universities, all located in the capital, others were created in the provinces: Kompong Cham (mechanics, tropical agriculture, physical and mathematical sciences), Takeo-Kampot (mechanics, electronics, oceanography), Battambang (food industries, applied geology, technical training). Finally, there were two other establishments in Phnom Penh: the Université royale des sciences agronomiques and the Université populaire (the former École des arts et métiers), where evening courses taught agriculture and mechanical arts to unemployed youth.[20]

## The Khmerization of Education

The twenty-third national congress, held from 10 to 13 July 1967, adopted a policy of progressive Khmerization of education.[21] Since courses in primary schools were all taught in Khmer, these measures affected only secondary and higher institutions. At that time, three subjects were still taught in French in the seventh through twelfth grades: mathematics, natural science, and physics. Khmerization, first applied in seventh-grade lycée classes, would gain one grade level each year; it was to begin in September 1967 with the next academic year. This schedule indicates that administrators and teachers had little time—two or three months—to prepare. They had to translate textbooks from French to Khmer and invent appropriate terminology. Committees organized for this task were told to use international technical terms. Nevertheless, many words still had to be translated. The preeminence of monks on the committees explains why Pali, the language of Buddhism, served as the medium for new terms; the resulting vocabulary was extremely difficult for students to learn.

According to teachers of the late 1960s, this hastily applied measure lowered the quality of education; young people, for whom arrival at secondary institutions was an important change, suffered. Furthermore, it led to the training of students who would have difficulty understanding courses taught by French professors, whose replacement at the university level by

Khmers was not possible for many years. Experience showed that, with few exceptions, only those who had studied in French high schools proved able to handle typical university courses. Cambodians from Khmer high schools found themselves at a disadvantage with their classmates from the French lycée. To deprive the former of a modicum of bilingualism in secondary education further accentuated the privileges of the most well-to-do. Besides, Cambodia needed the vehicle of the French language—English was scarcely known—because in international relations Khmer was not useful.

Moreover, the progress of Khmerization slowed in 1973 because the translation of twelfth-grade textbooks suffered from the dispersion of members of the Khmerization committees. As refugees in France some of them continued to work conscientiously on the project, but coordination with Phnom Penh and the application of this measure suffered during the war. Thus educational reform in Cambodia was characterized by an immense goodwill and a great burst of enthusiasm coupled with ultranationalism and a lack of realism.

Despite efforts to extend education to all, a high level of illiteracy remained among both adults and children in 1970. The remote regions remained as disinherited in the educational realm as they did in the realm of public health and sanitation. The materials needed (e.g., furniture) could be made locally with wood from the forest, but teachers were no more willing to go there than nurses. Most people from isolated northeastern provinces as well as Kampot, Battambang, Kompong Speu, and Kah Kong provinces remained unlearned, and the Khmer Rouge indoctrinated them easily from 1967 to 1975. A number of peasants arriving at the frontier after 1979 could neither read nor write. Their illiteracy confirms the fact that the educational effort was badly implemented in regions far from the sizable market towns—and perhaps poorly conceived.

Many Khmers wondered if Cambodia really needed so many universities. The country needed technicians and engineers, but did this mean that every establishment built had to be a university? Simple institutes, with lighter administrations and fewer personnel, would have sufficed for the technical training of the young. Phung Ton points out that, "aside from the former Université royale khmère and centers for professional training, 3,500 students were divided among seven universities and twenty-four schools."[22] Phung Ton adds that the Université de Takeo-Kampot "was built in the middle of nowhere for 114 students" and, despite the fact that it housed a school of oceanography, was located fifty kilometers away from the sea. On the one hand, intellectuals regarded these projects as indicators of a policy based on prestige (well illustrated by the building of an extremely expensive Olympic stadium in Phnom Penh); in their view, technical education from the 1950s onward would have better responded to the country's urgent needs. Likewise, the opening of the École de commerce did not take place until 1964, and this at a time when the untrained Khmers were unable to compete with the Chinese, who were accused—and rightly so—of taking advantage of the situation: "In the economic situation, we blame Sihanouk for investing in extravagant projects such as the International Festival of Cinema, the stadium, the numerous universities, the production of mediocre films. . . . The historic visit of General de Gaulle in 1965 was as expensive for Cambodia as the construction of the Chruoy Changvar bridge."

On the other hand, the development of secondary education was positive for Cambodia. Indeed, students who were unable to find positions in the administration and accepted working in industry proved to be much better prepared than youths from the pagoda schools. But many young people refused to become workers or subordinate technicians, positions of little esteem, and they formed a mass of unemployed intellectuals who dreamed of becoming officials, the only rewarding profession.

Another serious lack drew their elders' attention: the fact that educational programs did not include civic instruction, an omission that they regretted for a people with such particular relations to its public affairs.

## HYDRAULIC WORKS AND COOPERATIVES

Cambodians are consumers of rice. Each family worked two hectares of wet rice on the average. On the advice of Chinese experts, Sihanouk studied the benefits of developing small-scale projects for irrigating the fields. They allowed him to help poor Cambodian peasants—who remained faithful to him—without giving up grand projects such as Prek Thnot. The first projects suffered from inadequate technical training and the latter ones from their very size.

On the technical level, the Chinese gave him frank advice, but the prince wanted everyone to contribute to agriculture as in China. Thus, he ordered obligatory manual labor for officials, who could be seen wielding picks and shovels. Handling a trowel proved difficult for them, and many technical projects suffered. Above all, peasants were terrified to see officials replanting rice, trampling plants already in place. The practice of paying peasants to carry out these tasks spread rapidly among officials, and the administration closed its eyes. This practice deprived manual labor of its original ethical context, but at least the peasants avoided disaster. However, some did suffer from the hydraulics authorities' incompetence: peasants from Takeo province saw their harvest destroyed because the water from a dam for their neighbors flowed in the wrong direction and flooded their rice plants. In the 1980s refugees from various regions told of similar failures.

In 1970 a mere two thousand motor pumps served two million peasant users. Cambodians wanted more of this kind of small equipment, so useful to rice growers. Many protested against the construction—under the aegis of the United Nations—of the Prek Thnot dam, which they considered a prestige project. The project suffered many successive reductions that diminished its scope. These long-term projects that could not be completed absorbed enormous financial resources at a time when peasants lacked water.

In 1956 Sihanouk created the Office royal de coopération (OROC) to help peasants organize production, market consumer products, and obtain credit. As in other domains, malfeasance flourished, and Chinese ended up in control of all the key posts. A Cambodian study by Hu Nim assesses the cooperative projects: "By assuming too many tasks in the beginning, without defining and planning the necessary steps, the OROC could only play the role of a commercial enterprise whose practical goal was to make profits and distribute them among members."[23] Given the deposits required of members, landless peasants and those holding less than one hectare rarely met the requirements for membership, much less for applying for a loan. Thus, "from 1956 until the present [1965], the peasantry began to think twice about the cooperatives. And the cooperative movement lost much of the enthusiasm that it had generated in the beginning." Moreover, Hu Nim adds: "The products sold by the OROC were often priced higher than in the private stores."

To a certain degree, these different failures explain the peasants' situation in 1970: they worked the land with traditional agricultural implements (swing plow and harrow pulled by oxen or buffalo) and brought water to their seedbeds in scoops; they used no fertilizer to improve the soil. The average yield of rice fields remained low: 800 to 1,000 kilograms per hectare, from a single annual harvest. Aside from a lack of irrigation works that would yield two harvests from a single parcel of land and a general lack of interest in technical innovation on the part of rural people, peasants did not want to work harder because many individuals' indebtedness to Chinese usurers in 1970 was so great that the latter would benefit from any surplus production. They thus contented themselves with assuring the survival of their families.

Yet in Battambang province the state developed the rich soils with fertilizer and machines. Considered Cambodia's rice basket, the Battambang region supplied most of the annual average of approximately two hundred thousand tons of rice for export, the sale of which brought significant amounts of foreign currency. But on the technical level, individual families hardly altered their method of working the land since independence. For want of proper direction and inspection, hydraulic works and cooperatives were usually failures, and rice growers had to face a new phenomenon—indebtedness.[24]

## THE BEGINNINGS OF INDUSTRIALIZATION

The French heritage was a meager one in the industrial field: a distillery and plants for treating latex on the plantations. Nothing had been envisioned for development, not even light industry useful to the people. Sihanouk, who became the responsible political authority after 1955, set himself to the task.

> Chou En-lai supported me in the policy of industrialization of the country; I saw him for the first time at Bandung . . . ; I had no experience with industry. . . . He told me: "Your country is a rich agricultural country. You should take advantage of the richness of your agriculture to have industrial development rationally coordinated with agriculture. Do not attempt to develop heavy industry . . . [but rather] a reasonable industry; no prestige, [but] a practical industry that benefits the masses." That was how Sangkum Reastr Niyum's industry was born.[25]

China supplied complete factories free of charge to Cambodia: textile mills at Kompong Cham and Battambang, situated near the black soils suitable for growing cotton to be developed by the planters; a plywood plant in Dey Eth (in Kandal), located on the Mekong's banks to harvest the Cambodian woods; a paper mill in Chhlong (in Kratié), where the cutting of abundant bamboo growth gave river dwellers income; a cement factory in Chakrating in the calcareous region of Kampot; and a glassworks in Stung Mean Chey (Phnom Penh). Construction was long and difficult; the glue, long used for making Dey Eth's plywood, was inferior and the Chinese were forced to change it; the quality of paper produced at Chhlong remained unsatisfactory.

Other countries granted loans. Yugoslavia built the Kirirom hydroelectric dam. Czechoslovakia supplied material to build other factories: the pneumatics plant at Ta Khmau (in Kandal), for recapping used tires, the sugar refinery at Kompong Trach (in Kompong Speu), the truck- and tractor-assembly plant at Kompong Som, a plant subsequently developed by Renault. Finally, France granted loans for the petroleum refinery and the brewery at Kompong Som. The Elf-Erap Company, which managed the refinery, began petroleum drilling offshore near Khemarak-Phouminville.

Sometimes Khmers financed these enterprises themselves, such as the sugar mill of Kompong Tuol in Battambang, part of Sonasucre's system, built in the midst of a sugarcane plantation, where raw sugar was produced; and the fish cannery of Kah Kong or Sonacop.

Two public water stations and two electric power stations were in operation; all these plants belonged to the state. The Kirirom dam supplied Phnom Penh. Another one to supply Sihanoukville was planned. A mixed economic sector was developing, including the jute plant in Battambang and the phosphates plant in Tuk Meas in Kampot.

Other small factories not far from Phnom Penh—Pepsi Cola; Sokilait, producing powdered milk; cigarette factories; a bran oil plant—were privately owned, as was the oxygen and acetylene company. To this list must be added many workshops that belonged rather in the category of handicrafts: mechanical repairs, brickmaking, nailmaking, and rice mills. The Chinese who owned these rice mills husked the peasants' rice free of charge, keeping only the bran to feed livestock. However, "the machines were adjusted for maximum scraping of the grain, and it came out completely white, which was not healthful," remarked Keat Chhon, then minister of industry.[26]

Under Sangkum this small-scale industry allowed a great number of persons (e.g., factory workers and suppliers of raw materials) to make a living. Khmer factory directors bought peasant products directly. Moreover, by producing manufactured goods, Cambodia imported less and conserved its foreign exchange stock. Accordingly, for the end of the 1960s other factories were planned, some to be linked with the establishment of a free zone in Sihanoukville.

Until 1962 industry grew at an annual rate of 8 percent, according to Rémy Prud'homme. Afterwards, "the advancement of industry in Cambodia apparently ran into several obstacles. In 1964, the last year for which we have figures, a clear decline was noted, because of a significant decline in building activity and public works. The fragmentary data available for succeeding years do not allow us to say if the secondary sector regained its growth rate. They suggest pessimism."[27] Keat Chhon confirms a decline in construction; since Sihanouk rejected American aid, townspeople stopped building villas that they rented to Americans.

Nonetheless, in 1967 the secondary sector had no more than a minor role in the national economy. Early in the 1960s the government nationalized Cambodian and foreign enterprises, leaving little initiative to the private sector. This operation failed for several reasons. First of all, as previously explained, civil servants believed that public property belonged to everyone, especially to them, and therefore helped themselves to public money and supplies. Besides, the business community and even the elite disagreed with the nationalizations if the rationale behind the changes was hard to see and even more so if the changes threatened their own leisure activities. The replacement of floating dance clubs by one state-controlled dance hall located ten kilometers from the capital and solemnly inaugurated in the presence of monks resulted in the semiclandestine opening of bars and clubs (with bribes to police to protect owners from sanctions) where the traditional dance or *roam vong* yielded to modern dances. The prince was apparently reacting to moral concerns: facing Saigon and Bangkok, paragons of vice, he tried to preserve Phnom Penh and counter moral depravity, which was on the whole rather minor, given the Cambodians' prudishness. The October–December 1965 edition of *Études cambodgiennes* echoed his concerns by reporting a decision of the twentieth Sangkum congress: "To close the small dance clubs, which had proven harmful to the moral health of young people, and replace them with a state-controlled dance hall under the jurisdiction of SOKHAR (Khmer society of royal inns)." Privately, people referred to the state-controlled dance hall as "SONAsluts" or "SONAsex."

In the late 1960s the rightist administration undertook denationalization, without thereby managing to attract Khmer capital. Why did the construction of small-scale factories useful to the country not interest the Cambodian bourgeoisie? If, as Sihanouk emphasized, Phnom Penh's inhabitants preferred to seek riskfree financial ventures, such as the construction of villas for rental to foreigners, the reasons for this lack of interest were apparently more profound and are to be sought in Cambodia's domestic and foreign policies.[28] The semisocialist type of economy resulting from nationalization diverted private capital from industry; the Khmers thus chose construction. Further, the regional context was not reassuring for holders of capital; the risk that the conflicts raging in Vietnam and Laos would spill over into Cambodia and the business community's marked disagreement with the head of state's foreign policy constituted powerful brakes to investment. The wealthiest Chinese and Sino-Khmers put their money in Hong Kong. A new investment code in 1968 tried to encourage private individuals to invest more capital in industry.

Aside from the financial aspect, technical and administrative problems arose during the Sangkum period. In the beginning, former officials took over factory management. When the Chinese experts departed, the Khmers, for better or worse, handled administration even though they knew nothing whatsoever about technical questions—some spoke of "disaster." Thus, engineers gradually assumed leading positions in the factories. A national productivity center was created to rationalize industrial management: "Young men who were more open to modern managerial methods than the former provincial or district governors were placed at the head of the enterprises." But these measures were late in arriving.

Besides, one or several planned industrial zones were not set up because—except in the first years of Chinese aid—authorizations to create
factories were granted in accordance with the system of illicit commissions.
According to Khmer sources, they sometimes went to the chief of state's
friends. Thus, Phnom Penh produced beer bottles, while the brewery was
located two hundred kilometers away. This dispersion of plants was very
harmful and led to high management costs.

Khmer labor was a positive factor. High school students who had completed the tenth grade became workers who, according to the former minister, "surprised the Chinese and the English with their technical skill"; even
so, they needed outside motivation to learn new skills. Industrialization
marked the birth of the Khmer working class (plantation workers, an older
group, were mostly Vietnamese). Yet this period was not the blossoming of
an organized proletariat: in 1967 only 4 percent of the country's active
population were workers.[29] Unions remained illegal, and the term—although it was in use—did not appear in the dictionary published by the
Institut bouddique and considered the official dictionary.

The rejection of American aid, announced by Sihanouk in late 1963, was
a difficult turning point for Cambodia. Foreign exchange stock grew increasingly rare, and aid from other countries was insufficient. The Cambodian
economy entered a period of crisis. More than twenty years later, the former
head of state declared: "There is one mistake that I should have avoided: if
I could do things again, I would not break with the Americans. The rupture
with the Americans was fatal for me. . . ."[30] And for the Cambodian economy as well.

The major shortcoming of Sangkum's policy regarding technical and
social projects was its irrationality; instead of planning, it improvised and
adopted ad hoc methods. Sometimes prestigious projects of little use for a
small country such as Cambodia resulted. Exemplifying the lack of management in these national construction projects was the Olympic stadium. If a
section of a wall had a slight aesthetic flaw, it was completely demolished
and rebuilt. The waste of cement and, as always, misappropriation raised
the stadium's cost to three hundred million dollars, half of which had to be
paid in foreign exchange stock. Although the head of state was not directly
guilty, he nevertheless ordered the completion of projects but did not follow
through to check their progress, and thus, on closer inspection, his responsibility is great. Sihanouk was isolated from reality by the lack of interest
that he displayed in projects he conceived (and, in effect, ordered) and wished
to carry out. Competent individuals hardly had a chance to direct projects
to fit technical and financial necessities because the original plan was not to
be modified in any way. Authoritarianism and unrealistic thinking often

went hand in hand during the country's modernization, and the responsibility rests with Norodom Sihanouk.

## THE DEVELOPMENT OF TOURISM:
### FOREIGNERS LACKING CURIOSITY

While the war was brewing in the 1960s Khmers and foreigners lived out—without their knowledge—Cambodia's final moments of peace. Prince Sihanouk yearned to make Phnom Penh the most beautiful city in Southeast Asia; his neighbors, plunged into war, poverty, or corruption, could no longer compete with it.

When the head of state decided to develop tourism in the late 1950s, hotels and transportation were insufficient. The capital's only legacy from the colonial period, the Royal, had been modernized but kept an old-fashioned charm with its ramshackle facilities; it nevertheless remained the most sought-after hotel in Phnom Penh, even after the construction of other establishments such as the world-class Monorom, the Sukhalay, and the Khemara. In the grounds of Angkor, the newly built Auberge des temples, facing Angkor Wat, offered tourists the reddish glow of sunset over the monuments. The neighboring town, Siem Reap, lodged travelers at the Grand Hotel, a vestige of colonialism, at the Villa princière, open to the public, and at the Hôtel de la paix. At Sihanoukville, bungalows were built on the beach and a modern hotel overhanging the sea.

The Siem Reap airport served passengers coming from Phnom Penh on Royal Cambodian Airways. After expansion, it became an international airport in 1970; Boeing 747s made direct flights between Paris and Siem Reap without stops in Phnom Penh. Air France built a luxurious hotel nearby; it never opened because the Vietcong occupied the grounds of Angkor just before the scheduled date in early June 1970. The hotel's furniture was removed by villagers, and the hotel itself was bombed during the war.

There was a genuine increase in tourism. Angkor is a unique ensemble of monuments, and they attracted people from throughout the world. Many Americans came to visit "the ruins," as they called Angkor; a special agreement gave them access to Angkor for two years after the rupture of diplomatic relations between the United States and Cambodia. Scheduled tour buses unloaded their contingents of Yankees who walked along the temple's long causeway under a sometimes overpowering sun. They usually stopped at the foot of the second-story stairway and then returned to the vehicle taking them to the Bayon, where they had just enough time to admire the many four-faced towers and perhaps an eighth of the bas-reliefs showing scenes from daily life, battles, and the Buddhist hell.

No one missed visiting Ta Prohm, left intentionally untended and overgrown by large creepers and roots of silk-cotton trees[31] that gave visitors the impression of being lost in a virgin forest. Few tourists had the opportunity to contemplate the enigmatic smiles of the Bayon's faces by moonlight. Although their visit was short and part of a tour, the Americans went out of their way to see Cambodia's wonders, as did foreigners coming directly from their countries and also those stationed in the region—they came to Cambodia to forget the fighting, the gaudiness, and the waste of dollars. Cambodia was a haven of peace, a paradise. The smiling amiability of the Khmers, their courtesy, the simple and good-natured way that they solved a stranger's problems, and the tranquility that reigned everywhere soothed the visitor.

Western residents, most of them French (fewer than two thousand), showed little curiosity about the country and its customs. In attractive apartments or superb villas they led a semicolonial life, surrounded by servants. After six o'clock they opened their doors to friends for conversation and the evening whisky. The Royal's bungalows, next to the main building, sheltered those who were truly attached to Cambodia or nostalgic for French Indochina. Social events were in full swing in the capital, but stratification was respected. Even the most insignificant of diplomats would not consider conversing with dynamic lycée teachers; university professors kept for the most part to themselves, except those who could claim wealth or relatives powerful enough to open doors for them. Embassies snatched up businessmen and bankers for official receptions. Mixing was permitted only on Bastille Day, although even then each social group recreated itself on the embassy's lawns.

To be sure, Phnom Penh hardly offered cultural diversions, aside from the movies shown in several theaters—a number of spaghetti Westerns, Italian epics, Chinese and Indian films, and old French movies. The French cultural office showed a film each week; sometimes a speaker would discuss art or literature. These generated little enthusiasm. The coolness of the evenings on verdant riverbanks attracted Khmers above all. The French community preferred socializing and, on weekends during the good weather, driving to the white sands of Sihanoukville. Some took the Kirirom road to hunt for tigers. Some fanatics chose to go admire the site of Angkor; they were few.[32] Others, still rarer, went off to explore the countryside. Most of the French people who lived in Cambodia were drawn there by an exoticism from which they hardly benefited, by a life-style almost beyond the wildest of dreams, by hefty salaries that allowed them to buy apartments and/or second residences, and by the indulgence of material advantages (annual trips to France at the homeland's expense, arrival bonuses, moving expenses, and tax exemptions). Beside the pool at the Royal or the Cercle sportif, women maintained their tans from the preceding weekend by the ocean. In the 1970s a good many journalists wrote their articles on the war from the famous poolside at the Royal.

Others passed their time at the Taverne, an unpretentious café across from the post office where they picked up their mail every morning. Old Indochina hands met at the bar; newcomers got together on the patio. In the evening, snobs ate at the slightly overrated Café de Paris; they rubbed shoulders with military officers and local haute bourgeoisie. Some preferred the Venise's home-style cuisine. Foreigners sometimes topped off the evening in one of the floating dance clubs or at Mère Chhum's place, an opium den catering to Westerners.

The country and its inhabitants were of scant interest to the French residents, and their behavior was probably what it would have been in Africa or South America. The majority of them knew little about Cambodia and even less about the Khmers; they avoided even casual contact with popular strata by choosing to hire Vietnamese domestic servants, considered efficient, rather than Cambodians, thought to be honest but lazy. In doing so, they simply upheld a practice common during the protectorate. Foreigners who hired Cambodians did not regret it. Although the complexity of the Khmer mentality escaped them, they learned about popular reactions through this domestic network. Others could not understand domestic political changes and would be astonished when the regime gradually transformed their paradise into a gilded prison.

Making friends with Khmers was certainly not easy, despite the fact that Khmers accepted the French more than other foreigners and forgave them much, including their refusal to consider them for some jobs. A gesture would suffice to strike up a conversation and exchange ideas, even if the interlocutor would not tell all. They could look around, learn about the Cambodians, and give them the pleasure of conversation and of appreciation. Overall, the French and other Westerners established fashionable relationships at Phnom Penh, few acquaintances, and very few real friendships. Cambodians were invited to official receptions by virtue of their official status; others attended intimate dinners because of their social positions—very few were invited for their personal qualities. Nevertheless, most of them felt attached to France in one way or another.

The few dozens of French people who loved Cambodia and its inhabitants remained faithful after the 18 March 1970 coup and continue to show their loyalty at the present time. For others—the great majority—their sojourn in the land of Angkor was only an interlude of which they have, for the most part, happy memories that supply topics for the old Cambodia hands' conversations in Paris.

Despite the good intentions of some Americans stationed in the region, they did not understand much about Southeast Asia. Convinced of their mission that combined politics with salvation, they overwhelmingly reinforced the privileges of the well-to-do at the expense of the poor. Rarely were they able to communicate with Khmers, even when they spoke their language.

Who has not marveled at the physical harmony of Cambodian peasants, admired the shy country girls and played with the children; who has not returned the generous smile of elderly women eager for information about foreigners, or discussed rice harvests with the men and listened to the sounds of night or early morning in the village—such visitors have cut themselves off from the many indelible memories unique to the real Cambodia.

### THE ETHNIC-MINORITIES COMPLEX

From the moment he took up the reins of power, Sihanouk proved himself to be punctilious about Cambodia's image abroad. As anthropologists throughout the world worked to recover and transmit knowledge about the cultures of peoples on the path to assimilation, as linguists recorded dialects spoken by a few dozen individuals—in short, as scientists amassed information for regional histories of civilizations—the prince made a decision. He believed that bare breasts, apron-belts, and ivory cylinders that distorted the earlobes of the northeastern montagnards did not bring honor to a modern state. Instead of considering the cultural enrichment for Cambodia that these ancient customs embodied, he dismissed them. Minorities—particularly men—lost the costumes, headdress, and ornamentation essential to their dignity. The adoption of Western attire, the benefits of which were not evident, marked the beginning of acculturation. Khmers in the west, that is, in the Cardamom Mountains, were also under pressure: certain of their rituals had to be practiced in secret, and their dialect was declared to be old-fashioned. Although they derived benefit from social works such as infirmaries and concrete schoolhouses (to which they contributed), they were forced to adopt the cultural practices of the plains' inhabitants.

These changes were imposed by administrators. Sihanouk was little known in these remote regions, far from the plains. The plains as well were not exempt from the chief of state's decrees. On his return from a visit to the People's Republic of China, he decided that all Khmer schoolgirls had to abandon their magnificent heads of hair in favor of a standard square cut; another time, he ordered officials to perform several hours of manual labor each month. The prince even went as far as to compel foreign diplomats to practice sports. Jakarta served as the model for university development, and North Korea's influence was felt in the JSRK's songs.

In contrast to cultural assimilation, these measures were little more than momentary whims and—except for manual labor—hardly affected the people. Nevertheless, peasants in the plains were also fenced in: instead of graceful clusters of fruit trees sheltering each wooden house, a cement fence was to surround the habitation, a symbol of modernity; it was often too expensive, and many rural inhabitants did not finish it. Under the Sangkum regime, beautiful wooden pagodas were also replaced—abandoned if not destroyed—by less elegant and more costly concrete monasteries. In the cities unsupervised projects arose or developed and harmed the prince's popularity.

A PARALLEL GOVERNMENT:
THE RETURN OF FEUDAL PRACTICES

Despite everything, Cambodia's development continued at least until the mid-1960s. Difficulties in domestic policy came out into the open after 1965. The country's financial situation became a subject of concern, and many Cambodians questioned the prince's policies. Since the king ran the affairs of state, he also determined the rules of the political game. On the one hand were the masses, still attached to the royalty but politically unsophisticated, loyal to their monarch, who thus remained all powerful. On the other were Cambodian elites who could not compete for power on an equal basis. Unable to express their ideological convictions freely under pain of police harassment, they felt excluded. Their frustrations were to weigh heavily on the future. But abuses of another kind gradually turned a majority of young people against the head of state.

Despite the growing number of high-level technicians trained in Cambodia and abroad, Sihanouk did not trust individuals with advanced degrees who expressed their personal scientific opinions. Those who did not flatter him became potential enemies in his eyes. He implemented a system of supervision that permitted him to have eyes everywhere and to have his ideas put into practice. Almost all the ministries had a *Samdech Ov* team, commissioned to execute projects ordered by Sihanouk. Officially, it reinforced the qualified technicians employed by the governmental services. As the prince himself explained the choice and purpose of these teams:

> There are ministers who do not always take their tasks seriously, and we had to appoint men [on the spot] to watch them. . . . Sihanouk cannot be everywhere. I was forced to create special extragovernmental bodies in order to compel my administration and government to work better. . . . I could not trust everyone, and I thus covered them with *Samdech Ov* teams. They [the team members] had their own professions. Some were detached from teach-

ing, others from parliament, and they continued to serve as representatives but also led a *Samdech Ov* team. The youngest ones were teachers and secretaries of the royal palace. I chose some trusted men who then chose their teammates. That is how we proceeded.[33]

These teams were supposed to help peasants. Given their diverse training, some members lacked expertise. Their essential role was political surveillance, and often the groups' lack of technical competence was evident. *Samdech Ov* teams also operated in the ministry of health: a magazine shows two infirmary trucks with posters that read, *Samdech Ov* Medical Team for the common people of distant villages.[34] The head of state did not know that these gifts rarely reached their intended targets. Speaking of these mobile teams, Kao Kan points out that some of them were assigned to help peasants "improve their nonmechanized farming tools," whereas Chinese agricultural experts had recommended the installation of small-scale mechanization.[35] Likewise, Sihanouk's unconditional supporters held important positions: OROC had a royal delegate, as did Kompong Som municipality. When the right assumed governmental power in 1966, it limited the prince's powers; he created a countergovernment (to be discussed in chapter 5).

Finally, the townspeople reacted strongly to what they called the "parallel government." The prince surrounded himself with loyal supporters, through whom passed all requests for private audiences, popular justice, and public affairs. An honest official could not see the prince to explain a technical or human problem unless he was the friend or client of one of these intermediaries. Less scrupulous individuals paid them off.[36] The resurgence of clans and patron-client relationships brought back or strengthened feudal institutions, giving free rein to corruption and extortion. Within the ministries networks appeared, with the single role of intervening—for a fee—with higher-ups in order to advance a client's business; the higher-ups usually received a share of the proceeds. Businessmen and travelers who used public transportation were victimized by racketeering. Speaking of a high-level official, a former politician observed: "Diamonds were growing on his wife's hands." Under the Sangkum regime not only was it necessary to purchase the administration's services but, Tith Huon says, "one had to pay to avoid harassment" (62).

After 1967 the system became even more complex because of the official preeminence of Sihanouk's lowest ranking wife, Monique Izzi, born of an Italian father and a Cambodian mother, Madam Pom, whose legendary cupidity caused several major scandals. Henceforth, Phnom Penh's residents discovered that what they called "Madam Pom's parallel government" or the "Chamcar Mon court" (a reference to the prince's residence) had usurped the wisely used influence of the queen mother Kossomak and of counselor Penn Nouth. Penn Nouth's role was insignificant from that time on. Urban Cambodians overall did not accept the shunting aside of an authentic princess of the blood, Thaveth Norleak, in favor of a commoner. And the people, Ros Chantrabot writes, "attached to the old traditions, customs, and manners, had great difficulty accepting her as a queen. . . . And rumors circulated everywhere that she had Vietnamese blood. Monique Sihanouk and her family contributed much to the head of state's unpopularity."[37]

All these extragovernmental practices of the late 1960s acquired a bad reputation within Phnom Penh's elite; the opening of a casino was equally unpopular. Yet to voice opposition attracted the interest of the police. Even the press suffered: on 11 September 1967 private newspapers were suspended and replaced by four dailies under the ministry of information's supervision. Peasants, however, felt secure on their lands and remained there, except for children who went to the towns to study; there was no rural exodus. But what destroyed the last fragments of the elite's confidence in the head of state was his conduct of foreign affairs.

## SANGKUM'S FOREIGN POLICY

Sihanouk's major concern was to save his country from war and foreign occupation. He directed his entire foreign policy after 1955 toward this goal. The results were mixed but none question the prince's good intentions. He fought courageously against the naive arrogance of some and the greed for conquest of others; and certain journalists slandered him. Despite his keen sense for politics, his immaturity (at least before 1956) caused him to steer his country's policies in questionable directions.

Cambodia initially received aid from many sources: the United States, China, France, the Union of Soviet Socialist Republics (USSR) and other Eastern European countries, Great Britain, and others. In this domain France always ranked among the leaders. Nevertheless, two countries alternatively predominated in giving aid and thus, in a roundabout fashion, in foreign policy.

### AMERICAN AGGRESSIVENESS AND THE WAR IN VIETNAM

When Mao Tse-tung vanquished Chiang Kai-shek in 1949, the prince did not realize how important this event would be for the former Indochinese colonies. Busily negotiating with France for his country's independence, Sihanouk did not see communism taking shape on his borders or foresee the subsequent importance of China as a great regional power. The prestigious and powerful United States seemed to be best suited to help Cambodia defend and modernize itself. Thus, Cambodia accepted much needed assistance from the Americans in 1955, signing agreements for military equipment, cultural cooperation, and economic treaties.

American aid, however, presented two major problems. First, it was conditional: the dollars provided for the economy were not to be used to benefit state-owned enterprises—they had to be invested in private ones. And acceptance of American aid precluded accepting military aid from socialist countries. Second, it flooded the country with dollars, which encouraged the officials' penchant for corruption. The most tangible result was the construction of the Phnom Penh–Kompong Som road, linking the capital with the sole maritime port, just built by France. However, the road gave way in several places the year after it was finished because local entrepreneurs had been stingy with materials, preferring to divert funds for personal profit. The United States was blamed for its "poisoned gift."

Nevertheless, industry on the whole benefited. Besides, in Sihanouk's eyes, the American presence ensured that his borders would be respected. At that time even neighboring countries doubted that the Vietnamese might win. But some of Cambodia's young people opposed the American presence. Aside from the political aspect, Khmers were shocked by the Americans' coarse behavior, beginning with the ambassador, who attended official meetings in shorts. American advisers associated little with Cambodians and treated them as inferiors, sometimes contemptuously so.

The intensification of the fighting in Vietnam in the early 1960s had repercussions for Cambodia: American planes "mistakenly" bombed Khmer villages. The United States would have liked to bring the Khmer head of state into the war, but Sihanouk clung to a neutrality that he had written into the constitution, a fact that he never failed to bring to the attention of foreign visitors and journalists.

The rejection of American aid in 1963, followed by the rupture of diplomatic relations in 1965, was by no means unanimously approved. It provoked economic decline. The pretext for burning bridges with the Americans was a defamatory article on the queen mother that appeared in *Newsweek*, but in reality the affair was more complicated.

## CHINA'S DECISIVE ROLE

In April 1955 Sihanouk met Chinese officials at the Bandung Conference, the founding conference of the nonaligned movement. The meeting was followed by many others. The prince, while agreeing with the principle of "neutrality" advocated by the Chinese, did not thereby comply with all of their suggestions. On the political level, China gained Cambodian support for its admission to the United Nations (and thus for Taiwan's expulsion) and exchanged ambassadors with Cambodia on 17 July 1958. We have already noted the important contribution made by the People's Republic of China in the economic domain. Delegations of all kinds were exchanged until 1962. If, as Kao Kan writes, "in Chinese eyes, neutrality meant the absence of Americans in Cambodia," the Khmer chief of state did not follow their advice in that the Americans established an embassy in Phnom Penh in late 1955.[38] During this period the majority of Cambodians supported the prince's foreign policy, which relied on the Western and Communist blocs at the same time. The country developed in peace, and it was a blissful period during which Cambodia deserved its description as a paradise.

Sihanouk was received at Peking with the same honors given the head of state of a great power. Punctuating his departures were speeches by Mao Tse-tung or Liu Shao-chi; the latter visited him at Phnom Penh. Kao Kan notes that these speeches and visits demonstrated a measured and progressive escalation by the Chinese leaders, who tried to bring Cambodia to China's side in the "struggle against the American imperialists."[39] Border incidents provoked by American aviation irritated the prince and made him fear for his country. And the compliments showered on him by the Chinese probably pleased Sihanouk. Finally, developments in Vietnam made him realize that the Vietnamese Communists would ultimately emerge victorious. The Americans, as potential losers, no longer appeared able to defend Cambodia's borders. These considerations partly explain the Khmer chief of state's about-face, resulting in the rejection of American aid in late 1963, the rupture of diplomatic relations with the United States in 1965, and the military pact with China in the same year.

Henceforth, Sihanouk trusted China alone to protect Cambodia's territorial integrity. The honeymoon lasted three or four years. The people, unaware of the full details of Khmer foreign policy, did not react at first. However, the stationing of Vietnamese Communists on Khmer territory, which was rumored to have been consecrated by a secret Khmer-Vietnamese pact, disturbed the inhabitants. Furthermore, because of the established political links with Peking, Sihanouk allowed the National Liberation Front of South Vietnam (NLF) to set up a permanent mission in Phnom Penh on 22 June 1967 and allowed that of the Democratic Republic of Vietnam (DRV) to become an embassy on 24 June 1967. The Chinese Cultural Revolution of 1966 and its impact on Cambodia led Prince Sihanouk to change his tack again. If Khmer-Chinese relations to that point had provided Cambodia with a positive economic balance sheet, we must note that China had subtly controlled the political game.

The prince thus sought to resume diplomatic ties with the Americans to counterbalance China, whom he now considered too dangerous ideologically for the Cambodian elite. Besides, in 1969 Norodom Sihanouk was convinced that the situation in Vietnam was evolving once again in the United States' favor. He saw the United States as the victor and sincerely hoped for the successful conclusion of negotiations that had been going on for three years. At a press conference in early 1969 the head of state condemned the Vietcong sanctuaries. On 2 July 1969 Phnom Penh announced the reinstatement of diplomatic relations with the United States. Links with China were loosened, but Cambodia had made agreements with China that could not be revoked and that would cost Cambodia dearly.

Once Sihanouk had ceased to trust the Americans to safeguard his borders, he began a game that he initially called a "policy of equilibrium." The goal was to gain new allies—the Chinese—without displeasing the old ones, whose dollars Cambodia needed. Each was to believe itself particularly privileged. He thus harangued the Americans and the Communists in turn, depending on the regional military context that weighed so heavily on Cambodia.

BORDER PROBLEMS

Border problems with Vietnam and Thailand had existed for centuries. In 1954 the Geneva Accords partitioned Vietnam: Ho Chi Minh led the Communist-dominated north, and the authorities in the south were quick to request the assistance of the American army to repulse northern infiltrations. The Thais likewise requested American aid. Cambodia thus had two covetous and conquering neighbors on its borders, neighbors who were made even more arrogant by the United States' military and financial support.

Thailand had never accepted France's removal of the northern provinces of Cambodia from Thai control and their return to the original owner in the early twentieth century. Thailand thus took advantage of World War II to invade the territories again but was obliged to return them in 1947 after the Allies signed the Treaty of Tokyo. This act in no way signified that Thailand had given up, despite a lull brought about by a pacific leader. After the Geneva Accords, Thailand supported and trained the Khmer *serei* movement led by Son Ngoc Thanh (an opponent of Sihanouk). Further, the Thais provoked numerous border incidents and occupied a northern Cambodian temple that they claimed, Preah Vihear, located on the rim of the Dangrek Mountains. The verdict of the International Court of Justice at The Hague stipulated that the temple belonged to Cambodia and thus forced them to evacuate it in 1962; during October 1961 Phnom Penh had broken off diplomatic relations with Bangkok. But these developments did not protect

Preah Vihear, and tensions rose when Thai troops briefly reoccupied the temple in 1966. Elsewhere attacks continued, aimed mainly at Khmer military posts in Dangrek and at villages in the western province of Kah Kong. Bangkok did not permit foreign planes transporting Khmers to land at its airport. Thai fishermen constantly violated Cambodia's territorial waters, which resulted in the temporary arrest of some of them. In 1969 the Khmer army captured military men and civilians belonging to the Thai security services in Battambang. They were working, respectively, for the Bangkok government and for private Thai businesses but on the same project: the large-scale development of Phnom Malay's inhabited forests, located not far from the border. To do so, Thai industrialists had signed contracts with the Khmer *serei*.

Despite Bangkok's transgressions, Sihanouk made several attempts to reestablish relations. Since his proposals required the recognition of Cambodia's borders, Thailand refused. In 1963 the Thai chief of state, Sarit Thanarat, insulted the prince, and in response Cambodians celebrated Sarit's death by wearing pink ribbons—the symbol of festivities—on their clothing.

South Vietnamese leaders first attacked the Khmer minority inhabiting the provinces of the Mekong delta, the Khmer *krom*. These Khmers did not have minority status (which Sihanouk had requested from France in 1953). Furthermore, Saigon transformed the Franco-Khmer school of Soc-trang into a Vietnamese establishment in 1957; Khmer *krom* could learn their language only surreptitiously in the pagoda schools. Vietnamese Catholics treated Khmer traditions and Buddhism with contempt and ridicule. Frightened monks and families fled their lands and took refuge in Cambodia, where they were well treated. As their numbers grew in the 1960s, they began to pose financial problems for a country with such a precarious economy. In 1961 negotiations took place at Siem Reap between the Cambodian and South Vietnamese governments for the repatriation of Khmer *krom* wanting to return to their homes. The negotiations settled nothing, and on 27 August 1963 Phnom Penh severed diplomatic relations with Saigon. For several years, Cambodia's permanent representative at the United Nations informed the member states through the intermediary of the Secretary General about the Khmer *krom* problem. They continued to enter Cambodia until 1970, after which living conditions under the Khmer Republic caused some of them to flee in the opposite direction.

In 1964 Saigon claimed coastal islands belonging to Cambodia. Violations of the land borders and air attacks on peaceful Cambodian villages became frequent. Backing up the South Vietnamese were the Americans, who had not forgiven Phnom Penh for staying out of the Vietnam war. Some bombardments turned into slaughters.

When Cambodia reestablished diplomatic relations with the United States in July 1969, the border situation did not improve. On the contrary, these regions were to suffer B-52 bombings intended to destroy the Vietcong sanctuaries on Khmer territory, which led to the obliteration of the Dak Dam post in Ratanakiri in November 1969. Moreover, the Americans provided military training to Khmer *krom*, who were then sent to Thailand to fight alongside the Khmer *serei*.

Faced with such dangers, Sihanouk attempted to win over his neighbors; he went to Saigon in 1957 in order to come to terms with Ngo Dinh Diem but to no avail.

The Khmer chief of state harbored a legitimate obsession—to guarantee his country's territorial integrity. Unable to come to terms with his counterparts, he requested the support of the International Control Commission (ICC) in 1961. Great Britain vetoed the motion first, expressing the Americans' position. In late 1963 the prince demanded an international conference to guarantee Cambodia's neutrality such as the one he had initiated for Laos in 1961. It did not take place because Great Britain—a cosignatory with the USSR of the 1954 Geneva Accords—delayed the proposal, thus supporting the United States in refusal. Finally Sihanouk proposed a "last-chance conference" to include the United States, South Vietnam, Thailand, and Cambodia. On 9 March 1964 the assembled press learned that, because of the Americans' decision, the conference would not occur. Sihanouk nonetheless discussed the affair in unambiguous terms several times: "I have always—and the Americans should know this—kept my promises. It is completely up to them if we remain peaceful neutrals or become the ally of China and North Vietnam. I hope with all my heart that we receive the basic conditions that we are asking for."

The following day he spoke more specifically: "That which cannot be settled with South Vietnam will finally be settled with North Vietnam." And he delivered another very clear comment: "If we must align ourselves, it would never be anything but an extreme solution and as a means of saving our nation from imminent death."[40] There was thus no ambiguity in the Khmer chief of state's words, and the alliance that he entered into with China the following year was merely the result of the failure of his negotiations with the Westerners. The latter, to be sure, had excuses: they did not always understand what they termed the prince's fickleness and about-faces.

### THE LOSS OF NEUTRALITY

The situation did not improve in the following eighteen months. Sihanouk went into action. On 25 November 1965 General Lon Nol, chief of staff of the Forces armées royales khmères (royal Khmer armed forces, or FARK), went to Peking on Sihanouk's orders and signed with General Lo Jui-ching, his Chinese counterpart, a military treaty.[41] Most notably, it stipulated the following terms: "(1) Cambodia would permit the passage and the refuge of Vietnamese combatants in the border regions, granting them protection if necessary and permitting them to establish command posts; (2) Cambodia would permit the passage of material coming from China and intended for Vietnam."[42]

The contents of this treaty, which were revealed by China four years later in a booklet entitled *Essential Account of the Penetration of Cambodia by the Chinese Communists*, is known thanks to the work of Kao Kan. From that day onward Cambodia lost its neutrality and attached itself to the Communist camp. Thus the secret accords in favor of the Vietnamese Communists, mentioned so often by Cambodians, were indeed signed but first with China and not with Vietnam, which, on the foreign policy plane, had much greater significance in terms of consequences. The economic aid that China extended free of charge to Cambodia was not, it seems, truly unconditional because Peking succeeded in bringing Cambodia to its side politically, even though the Americans unwittingly contributed to the process.

Sihanouk certainly did not sign the treaty because he accepted Communist ideology. The West had not responded to his overtures. Besides, the Americans did not recognize Cambodia's neutrality. Finally, the relation of forces in Vietnam had changed, and the Vietnamese were going to win.[43] In the prince's view, only China could assure that Cambodia's borders would be respected, given the influence that he believed the Chinese leaders had over their Vietnamese comrades. He also hoped that services rendered to the Vietnamese Communists would earn him their gratitude once peace returned, particularly in terms of Cambodia's territorial integrity. And he believed that he had done the right thing when the Democratic Republic of Vietnam (DRV) and the Provisional Revolutionary Government of South Vietnam (PRG) recognized Cambodia's borders in 1967. Paradoxically, it was therefore to protect his country's future interests that the chief of state, who had bet everything on the principle of neutrality, brought his country into the Communist clan.

Even though the prince never revealed the treaty's existence, there were nevertheless leaks from within his administration after its signing. It became an open secret in 1967. The people could not have been ignorant: the border regions' inhabitants noted the stationing—with complete impunity—of the Vietcong on Cambodian soil. And covered trucks passed through villages on their way to the border, where their cargoes of rice and munitions were unloaded. Furthermore, Cambodia itself participated in the supplying of rice to the Vietnamese guerrillas. A veritable trafficking was organized under the army's supervision; traces were left in the ministries, and many Cambodians knew about it.

Nonetheless, in 1968, in a final effort to free himself of the tightening hold that China and North Vietnam had on young Khmer progressives, Sihanouk suggested the creation of a federation among Cambodia, Thailand, and South Vietnam, a proposal that remained a dead letter.

On the political level Cambodia had lost its neutrality. After signing the military pact with Peking, Cambodia was unable to retain the International Control Commission, established in accordance with the Geneva Accords in 1954, on its soil. The commission left at the end of 1969 for reasons officially described as financial. But a statement six months earlier explained Cambodia's position:

> The royal government desires that the ICC no longer concern itself with the question of the establishment and the infiltration of Vietcong-Vietminh forces on Cambodian territory. This is to avoid further complicating the situation. . . . The government believes that this question concerns only Vietnam (the DRV and the NLF of South Vietnam) and Cambodia and should not, in any case, concern third parties. The royal government believes that it is capable of settling this question by itself with the authentic representatives of the Vietnamese people at the appropriate time.[44]

This was equivalent to accusing the ICC of interfering in Cambodia's internal affairs, when in fact it was simply carrying out its mission. According to many Cambodians, moreover, when the ICC was invited to enter regions where its presence might have disturbed the Vietcong, the latter, forewarned, had disappeared.

Was Cambodia in a position to refuse asylum to Vietcong units under pressure? Probably not, and coming to terms with them was certainly more adroit than giving them an ultimatum, as General Lon Nol did in 1970. Nonetheless, after the treaty Cambodia no longer had any recourse. A reinforced ICC would not have been able to make the guerrillas disappear, but at least its presence and inspections would have prevented what inevitably happened after its departure—the spilling over of the Vietnamese Communists into large parts of Khmer territory. Sihanouk, aware of the danger of these concentrations of Vietcong on the border and of his own impotence, began to denounce them to journalists in early 1969, presenting them with a map of the Vietcong sanctuaries. In so doing, he was admitting what he had previously denied, but the Sino-Khmer treaty remained secret, and the ICC's mission had been postponed. In October he tried one last time. Lon Nol, sent as Cambodian representative to the Chinese national day, was assigned to ask the Chinese to pressure the Vietcong to cease their advances into Khmer soil.

Prince Sihanouk's foreign policy was thus more coherent than it would seem at first glance. It sometimes appeared disordered and ill conceived because we did not have all the keys. His foreign policy was a difficult burden for him to bear, all the more so in that the prince could not simultaneously rely on his administration and keep it in the dark when he made important decisions—decisions that he certainly could not reveal abroad, much less to the people, who knew little about politics. Even those in the center of urban society, closer to state affairs, had very little sense of duties and responsibilities. This complex situation shows the degree to which Cambodian society needed to restructure itself and how illusory it is to think that a single person can resolve all problems.

# 5 Harbingers of Change

In 1955 Sihanouk had at hand everything he needed to make a success of his country's development: support from the people, hope from an elite ready to cooperate, movement with loyal followers, and promises of various foreign aid. Twelve years later only the peasantry's enthusiasm survived. In 1967 the head of state no longer mastered the domestic situation, and the elite was concerned. The final years of Sangkum's power were littered with warnings that foretold the troubles to come.

The developments related below are particularly important for Cambodia's future. In fact, it was in Paris that the future Khmer Rouge leaders gained the attention of foreigners and created a structure that rallied the majority of the left-wing Cambodian intellectuals whose support would prove decisive in their victory.

## THE POLITICIZATION OF KHMER YOUTH

Dissent could come only from the city and from intellectuals with rural origins. For reasons that were both historical and sociological, peasants remained passive, loyal to the divine royalty or to the one who represented it, regardless of his behavior.

Nationalist ideas germinated in the heads of studious youth. We recall that the first demonstrations against the French in 1936 came from Lycée Sisowath students and then, early in the 1940s, from lay and religious elements. At the same time that the lay group created the Democratic party, their younger comrades from the lycées of Phnom Penh, Saigon, and Hanoi experienced democracy in France. Most held scholarships from the Khmer government, and they reacted differently to the political environment: some remained outside any form of agitation while others became militants, among them the future Khmer Rouge leaders.

OVERSEAS KHMER STUDENT ASSOCIATIONS
UP TO THE COUP D'ÉTAT

The first associations of Khmer students abroad were founded in France.

*Creation of the Association des Étudiants Khmers*

In 1946 this Khmer students' association, the AEK, was born in Paris during the French Union, to which Cambodia belonged. At its origin the group, regulated by the law of 1901, brought together young men and women from all backgrounds and political tendencies whose essential goal was education. It had then no declared political orientation and contented itself with demanding the independence of their country, "which annoyed the French," according to a former member. At the organization's head were Ea Si Chau, its president, considered to be a pure nationalist, and Yem Sarong, a moderate Democrat. Ea Si Chau remained president until the end of 1950 and returned to Cambodia shortly after that. Its headquarters was the Pavillon de l'Indochine at the Cité universitaire de Paris, but the association would never be represented on the pavilion's executive committee. The AEK published a biannual bulletin, *Khemara Nisset* (Khmer students; its French title was *Bulletin de l'Association des étudiants khmers*),[1] which contained reports on the association's activities and articles on Cambodian economy, history, and art, as well as several news items on foreign issues. There was virtually nothing on politics, at least until the end of 1950. At first the group was not politicized; nationalist spirit predominated.

If no major problem emerged during the first three years, dissensions appeared in 1950, provoked by Communist elements, of whom Ieng Sary, newly arrived in French, assumed leadership. At the general assembly, at the end of the academic year 1949–1950, on 1 November 1950, Ea Si Chau evoked recent difficulties and "encouraged members to remember the unity of the community that they comprised in France and to continue the behavior that they had always practiced in their relations with their comrades: to respond to intolerance with tolerance and misunderstanding with understanding." On the same day, "he asked them to double their efforts so that the coming year, by the brilliant results that it would bring, would testify to our desire to prove worthy of the many sacrifices that our compatriots and government have made and continue to make for us."[2]

Unity did not survive. From 1950 onward the left-wing students created a Marxist cell. Ieng Sary and Saloth Sar then abandoned their studies, in which they were apparently not performing brilliantly, for politics. Hou Yuon and several others continued to study and joined the cell. But not every student arrived in France completely apolitical. Saloth Sar had read Karl Marx's *Communist Manifesto*, and Ieng Sary was already conversant with

Communist doctrine; after several months in France, he had divided the AEK. On 1 November 1950 the association elected its second president, Vann Molyvann. A student at the École des beaux-arts, he became a talented architect whom students from this period described as a "moderate and tolerant" element. He would not retain the presidency for a full year. In August 1951 a large delegation led by Ieng Sary and Saloth Sar went to the youth festival in East Berlin to represent the AEK. "They brought back the first documents on the *issarak,* on Son Ngoc Minh, given them by the Vietnamese, for the *issarak* movement was under Vietnamese influence. This armed struggle stimulated us because we did not believe in the prospect of gaining independence through negotiations." At that point the Communists decided to act.

In autumn of 1951 "the Marxist cell decided to take over the leadership of the AEK. Thus, Hou Yuon was appointed president," Keng Vannsak reported.[3] Immediately the association began to display a political orientation: "Members of the AEK sold *L'Humanité.* . . . Some of them frequented the people's universities of the PCF [Parti communiste français]," said a former student. In the early 1950s AEK members considered King Sihanouk, the honorary president of the organization, a vassal of the French. They seized the pretext of a frivolous minor scandal focusing on him in Paris, to ask him, in a letter signed by its president, to renounce this honorary title. On 23 March 1961 Phnom Penh's daily, *La Dépêche,* launched into a diatribe against the PCF: "The French Communist party has a perfect right to proselytize but exclusively among the French and not among those who are guests of the French. For this enterprise of 'conversion' of our young people in France is to us an indecency, an abuse of confidence that is linked to a certain Western missionary tradition that we find repugnant."

With the arrival and progress made by the Communists, the association split. Among the moderates were Vann Molyvann, Yem Sarong, Hang Tun Hak, and Tan Kim Huon. The right wing included Mau Say, Long Pet, Douc Rasy, Douc Phana, Sam Sary, and Prom Tos. In 1950 they created the Amicale des Cambodgiens de France (Cambodian friendly society of France, or ACF) and later the Communauté khmère d'outremer (Khmer overseas community, or CKOM). Among those on the left were Ieng Sary, Saloth Sar, Thiounn Mumm, Khieu Samphan, Keng Vannsak, Sin Khem Ko, Hou Yuon, and Phung Ton. The last two were considered sympathizers: "They were grudgingly accepted and criticized for their individualist tendencies and their love of diplomas, women, and wealth. They were tolerated, but Ieng Sary, Saloth Sar, and the others reproached them for wanting to obtain their law degrees."[4]

Relations between this left-wing faction and the French Communists seem to have been good, despite a certain distrust on the latter's part for their Khmer comrades. A former student explains one point on which they disagreed: "We wanted to take power and believed that we could do so only with popular support, which necessarily means violence. We opposed the PCF's view that we could come to power through universal suffrage." Says Keng Vannsak, "At the beginning, we were very Stalinist. . . . We turned toward China in the late 1950s because the Russians were playing the Sihanouk card and neglecting us. . . . When everyone began to criticize Stalin, we became Maoists." Even so the association had pro-Soviet members.

The Communists quickly became preponderant because they held the association's key positions. They created another bulletin, unofficial and in manuscript form, entitled *Reasmey* (light). Five years and eighty issues later, it ceased when Ieng Sary returned to Cambodia in 1957. Saloth Sar signed articles with the pseudonym *Khmer daeum* (original Khmer), an expression used to designate the inhabitants of the Cardamom Mountains, who lived from grubbing and gathering.

Hou Yuon's mandate expired on 9 February 1953 when the AEK was disbanded by France, on the demand, according to rumor, of the Khmer king. On the one hand, the AEK criticized members of the ACF, who supported Sihanouk; on the other, Hou Yuon and his friends had established links with the International Union of Students, based in Bucharest. The latter development reportedly caused the king to lose patience.

For three years Khmer Marxist students had no official organ at their disposal to spread their ideas; the cell continued to function, and at the first opportunity the association reconstituted itself.

## Resurrection of the Union des Étudiants Khmers

The union of Khmer students (UEK) was officially founded on 26 November 1953, thanks to a French friend. This time, the political orientation was more uniform because moderate or right-wing elements had created or would create their own groups (the CKOM in particular). The UEK, moreover, disassociated itself from the administration by establishing its headquarters in the home of a member residing in Sceaux. While waiting for the constituent assembly that met on 28 December 1956, a provisional executive committee named Ieng Sary to the presidency and, as his assistants named students with similar convictions, Thiounn Mumm, Khieu Samphan, and In Sokan. One month later the election of a new executive committee took place, an election that looked more like an appointment than a vote. The new president, In Sokan, was to be helped during his mandate by well-known

Communist figures such as Khieu Samphan and Dy Phon. Ieng Sary had a very brief official role, but he installed an executive committee of his followers, which gave him the time to conduct politics on a higher level. With Khieu Thirith (who had a degree in humanities and became his wife) he made a name for himself among Khmers and foreigners. The UEK participated in all the youth congresses, including that of Helsinki, and the student festivals held in Eastern Europe.[5] In France it had especially close contacts with the Union nationale des étudiants de France (national union of students of France, or UNEF).[6] The UEK's bulletins contained no information on the other foreign student communities living at the Cité universitaire or on possible relations with them.

The association thus did not conceal its ideological preferences; to anyone taking the trouble to follow its activities of the period, the situation would have been clear. Nevertheless, it did not play fair in regard to Sihanouk, whom it always supported in public although the rupture had existed since 1953. Official accord was a tactical maneuver, for this small group of Communists could do nothing without powerful supporters, and only the chief of state enjoyed an exploitable popularity inside and outside the country. Furthermore, the UEK took into account the privileged relations that Cambodia maintained with China from the end of the 1950s, despite the American presence, and the facilities accorded to the North Vietnamese and the Vietcong in the 1960s, for the group was determined to use the national leader for its purposes. Each issue of the UEK's bulletins praised "national unity behind the policy of peace, national independence, and neutrality led by *Samdech*, the chief of state."[7]

From 1957 onward Khmer students arriving in France and wishing to become politically active had the choice between a right-wing association (CKOM) and a left-wing one. The UEK enjoyed a certain success among the new arrivals—for several reasons. First, the majority of the young people, at the beginning of independence, supported Sihanouk against the position of several Democrats who did not believe that there would be a genuine liberalization in Cambodia (time would prove the latter correct, and lycée and university students joined the opposition's ranks). This did not mean that they approved of one party more than another, as two of them relate: "On arrival we had a vague idea of social justice; we didn't understand much about politics." The other adds, "The young people coming to France had a desire for justice and social progress. This vague sentiment was the beginning of an awakening that occurred in three-fourths of the students. The other fourth was composed of the group of Sihanouk supporters, children of wealthy families who came to France to have a good time and didn't take their studies seriously. Among the three-fourths who were politically conscious, approximately one-third joined the UEK." Students who were progressive intellectuals did not consider joining the other organization, which officially supported the chief of state and had his recognition. They saw the UEK as a left-wing structure that was already established and wanted nothing better than to receive them. Most of them did not initially realize the association's Communist orientation; some never perceived its extremist cast.

Second, Khieu Samphan's presence in the UEK caused students to join because they considered him to be a pure and honest nationalist. Many admired him: "I joined because there was no other leftist association and because Khieu Samphan was part of it. Further, they were serious-minded and worked harder than the others." This last remark obviously did not apply to Saloth Sar and Ieng Sary, who remained outside the UEK and were known to few of the youths in France because they returned to Cambodia in 1953 and 1957, respectively.

The CKOM and UEK fought over new arrivals. Those few who had declared political ideas chose right away and more or less consciously. For the hesitant ones, in the beginning (before the Cambodian government intervened by eliminating or reducing scholarships, particularly of those affiliated with the UEK), it was the better organized and most cooperative group that won their membership. From this point of view, the CKOM could not compete with its rival, which, with an acute sense of organization and a persistence rare among Khmers, tried to help young people resolve their material problems, often successfully.

Third, the political program that the UEK proclaimed, emphasizing the anti-imperialist struggle, reassured the undecided and the lukewarm ones, flattering their national and personal pride with the idea of their tiny country standing up to a superpower. In 1958 the UEK approved an appeal to candidates for elections in 1958 to maintain unity around the head of state and to avoid, during the campaign, any incident that would permit foreigners to interfere in Cambodia's affairs.[8]

These different factors explain the Communists' success within the Khmer student community. It was not a question of political consensus but rather of agreement on vague ideas of social progress and opposition to those whom a large part of the young people considered to be the worst enemies of Cambodia, the Americans. "I was against the American presence in the region. At the time, the Americans did not have very good press in Cambodia, and Sihanouk himself was anti-imperialist."

The UEK maintained, at least in appearance, good relations with the Vietnamese. One student stated, "Early in the 1960s I participated in the UEK's activities without being a member. The thing that bothered me was the favorable attitude the association had toward Vietnamese comrades. If I criticized the Vietnamese, they didn't like it; if during a meeting I used the word *yuon*, they reprimanded me—we were supposed to say 'Vietnamese comrade' or 'Vietnamese friend.' If it weren't for that, I would have joined."[9]

After the departure of the great figures (Ieng Sary, Hou Yuon, Saloth Sar, Khieu Samphan) for Cambodia, the UEK had various presidents, one of the best known of whom after 1959 and in the 1960s was Toch Kam Doeurn, under Soviet influence like his elders; he was reelected for several legislatures and enjoyed a certain prestige among the students. In the 1970s the Khmer Rouge, who, given his declared sympathies, had no confidence in him, eliminated him. In 1969 Suong Sikoeung, who was pro-Chinese and frequented a Maoist cell in Paris, assumed the presidency until the absorption of the UEK by the Front uni national du Cambodge (FUNC) in 1971; he was not well liked, and rumor had it that he was an opportunist.

In the provinces, Montpellier had the most Khmer students. For the most part, they belonged to Montpellier's branch of the UEK, where Chau Seng was an activist. Khieu Samphan obtained his law degree before coming to Paris to work on a thesis. The branch did not remain inactive since letters were read at the general assembly in Paris from all the members of Montpellier and Switzerland in which they affirmed their solidarity with the general assembly's work and decisions.

Abroad, the USSR and the German Democratic Republic (GDR) received Khmer scholarship students, one hundred for the former, and for the GDR approximately sixty in the 1960s. These two countries sheltered the two most active UEK centers in Eastern Europe, although the two associations that spread their ideas had different names. In East Berlin it took the name of the Union de la jeunesse khmère (union of Khmer youth, or UJK) and functioned as a catchall. Only a dozen persons were politically active. In late 1966 the UJK took on a revolutionary orientation with the arrival of a peasant's son who had been a militant in Phnom Penh in a leftist association, the Association générale des étudiants khmers (general association of Khmer students, or AGEK). Phnom Penh recognized the UJK but was ignorant of almost all its activities. In Moscow the Marxist group was called the Union des étudiants cambodgiens (union of Cambodian students, or UEC). In September 1968 the *Sangkum* journal violently attacked its members and gave a list of the most virulent ones:

> Then we see them putting on plays that attack our political system,
> chanting slogans that celebrate the superiority of the ideology
> whose cause they serve, participate in demonstrations whose activ-
> ist character is clearly visible. . . . They have even released two clan-
> destine bulletins that they have had distributed in the USSR, in

France, and even in Cambodia. . . . Their courage is not great—they are careful not to sign their real names.

In the 1950s and 1960s the UEK reinforced its support of Sihanouk in his anti-imperialist struggle, adding liberal amounts of chauvinism and xenophobia.

> Few Khmers know their history. And we repeatedly tell them that it is regrettable that, until the present, the most important pages of our history have been written by foreigners. Without being chauvinists, we think that it is dangerous for our country to neglect the training of a team of historians worthy of the title. Moreover, the specialists in our history are, in almost all cases, content with describing the Khmer monuments as perfectly as possible and then studying their chronology in conjunction with the chronology of Khmer kings.
>
> The present study consists of three parts: the correct statement of the problem to be solved; the reasons advanced until the present to explain this phenomenon; our hypothesis. [Signed] Thnot[10]

Considering the quality of the French historians whom the UEK author criticized without a trace of embarrassment, as well as the absence of Khmer historians at the time, we feel no surprise at the emptiness of the article that followed and recognize the first touches of the wild arrogance that Khmer Rouge leaders would openly display. Ieng Sary and Saloth Sar, the Khmer Rouge's two most prominent leaders, never impressed other students— among their contemporaries or younger groups—as profound thinkers. They did not take the time to attend the courses in which they had enrolled in Paris. These were the men, who read extensively in Marx and Lenin (especially Ieng Sary) but had little culture or humanism, who took power in 1975.

The UEK organized a vacation camp each year in the Vendée. It enjoyed modest student participation and was a formidable propaganda tool. In 1959 Phnom Penh officially appointed Chau Seng, a well-known leftist, as permanent representative of the Khmer students in Europe.

### The Right-Wing Separatists

Little information is available on the Amicale des Cambodgiens de France (ACF) and on the Association khmère (AK). The ACF was created at the beginning of 1950 by some AEK members who disapproved of the rise in power of the Communist members within the association. More specifically, they objected to these leftist elements' associations with the PCF's cells. The first president, Mau Say, was succeeded by Douc Rasy and Ly Chin Ly. The

ACF had thirty to forty members and received funds from Phnom Penh. According to former members of the AEK-UEK, the ACF barely managed to survive until 1952–1953. In fact, it lasted for a dozen years and must have bothered the UEK because, even today, former UEK members denigrate the ACF's partisans. The latter defined their actions in the following terms: "We hoped for a democratic evolution with Prince Sihanouk. We didn't want to betray him. We were thinking of an English-style monarchy." This bears a strange resemblance to the Democratic party's program. Nonetheless, according to their fellow students, there was nothing democratic in the behavior of the ACF's members. The ACF supported the Sangkum regime; its members detested the members of the UEK, and the feeling was mutual.

The association declared its dissolution in January of 1961 when it decided to merge into the AK in order to form the Communauté khmère d'outremer.

The AK, born in the mid-1960s, is said to have had several dozen members. It supported Prince Sihanouk's policy and, more specifically, was influenced by General Nhiek Tioulong. They first met on 27 February 1955 with Chau Xeng Hua as president of the executive committee; other members included Dy Balen, Roger Kosal, Samair Phalcun, and Srey Pong. The association lasted almost six years.

The distinction between the ACF and the AK is unclear. Perhaps the former had republican ulterior motives, while General Tioulong remained an unconditional supporter of Sihanouk. The prince and his advisers probably found the differences so minimal that they asked the two associations to merge. It is also possible, as a former ACF member asserts, that the chief of state sought to stiffen the character of this not-very-royalist organization by larding it with elements loyal to himself.

### La Communauté Khmère d'Outremer

And the CKOM? "Yes, I heard about it vaguely, but I didn't have any contact with those people," said the prince.[11] Sihanouk remained just as evasive about the Association générale des Cambodgiens de France (general association of Cambodians of France, or AGCAF), another association created, it seems, following his advice and for the purpose of supporting him.

Chea Thay Seng, an archaeologist, remained at the head of the CKOM during its four years of existence. Long Pet, Uy Phatna, Phu Si Uy, Boramy Tioulong, Nouth Narang, and Cambodia's only future psychiatrist, Chamroeum Sam Eun, who has now disappeared, were also members. Three bulletins appeared, the last in April 1964; aside from political news and articles, their content was probably the most cultural of all the previously issued bulletins.

The bylaws stipulated that the association had its headquarters in the Seine department. The second bulletin gave 21 rue Franklin as the editorial address, the premises of the Cambodian Embassy. Membership forms and dues were to be sent to an officer whose name changed, but the address remained the Pavillon du Cambodge at the Cité universitaire de Paris. As we shall see, when the Pavillon opened in 1957 all the associations held their activities there.

The CKOM received funds from the Sangkum regime and supported Prince Sihanouk's policies. When the rapprochement between Phnom Penh and Peking become obvious in the early 1960s, "Khieu Samphan said that he supported the prince's policy. At the CKOM, that did not sit well with us because, at that time, we were proud of being on the prince's side. And then, all of a sudden, the Communists were doing the same thing."

The group met infrequently, and its activities consisted mainly of dividing the money supplied by the government among the needy. An annual vacation camp was held at Lavandou. The CKOM would probably have continued to jog along, but the UEK's activities bothered Sihanouk, who decided to merge the diverse political tendencies into a single organization.

## L'Association Générale des Cambodgiens de France

The AGCAF was created in 1965, after Sihanouk's visit to Paris. In August 1967 a periodical controlled by the prince, *Sangkum*, announced: "The Association générale des Cambodgiens de France, born thanks to the initiative of *Samdech*, chief of state of Cambodia, at the time of a speech delivered at the Pavillon du Cambodge in June 1964, took shape on 8 July 1965 under the acronym AGCAF." The main goal was to merge the UEK and the CKOM into a single movement. For its part, the UEK, in an undated communiqué stated that it "enthusiastically welcomes the proposal made by *Samdech*, the chief of state, at the time of his very brilliant lecture at the Pavillon du Cambodge on 28 June 1964, asking our compatriots to create a single association democratically joining all our compatriots living in France." But, when the time came, the UEK did not merge with the others. Seang Hac, a graduate of the École centrale, assumed the AGCAF's presidency.

This time, the situation was clear: in order to obtain a scholarship, one had to be an AGCAF member. The association used for students requirements like those the Sangkum Reastr Niyum used among the population of Cambodia. Many students joined: "Joining the AGCAF was like joining Sangkum. You did it to avoid problems. It was political pressure: no AGCAF card, no scholarship." Many Khmers expressed this viewpoint. On the other hand, the director of the Pavillon du Cambodge, Sarin Chhak, an honest man who was concerned above all with the well-being and academic success of the young people, favored a broad distribution of financial aid. He and Seang Hac were considered moderates. Students of the same political tendency gathered around them and formed the AGCAF's centrist wing. Long Pet and Chhieng Kim Suor belonged to the right wing. There was no left wing. The progressives, forced to join in order to obtain scholarships, comprised the centrist wing, and the Communists set themselves up within the UEK. But tacit arrangements existed, and future alliances could be glimpsed: "From 1966–1967, the UEK supported the centrist wing of the AGCAF; Seang Hac had the support of the UEK for his work on the executive committee of the Pavillon du Cambodge because the two associations were represented there." And, according to centrists from the AGCAF, relations were "friendly":

> We got along better with the progressives from the UEK than with the AGCAF's right wing; UEK members were nice, they said hello to us, and we played volleyball together. In the beginning, some members of the AGCAF-center even went to the annual vacation camp organized by the UEK. However, our disagreement with the UEK hinged on a fundamental point. Its members said that you couldn't reform society, that you had to destroy it and build up another one. We said that you had to change certain things while remaining within the system.

The right wing soon split, and replacing Long Pet was Chhieng Kim Suor, a less radical individual. Sangkum supporters in the provinces organized mainly at Lyons. The Ouk Thol brothers, of whom one, André, called himself Prince Suryavong in 1979, were active.[12] The group formed the Association des étudiants cambodgiens de Lyon (association of Cambodian students of Lyons) and, copying the other movements, organized a vacation camp in the Haute-Savoie. In 1969 the *Sangkum* review published several letters from the students in Lyons supporting Prince Sihanouk's policies.[13] Branches of the AGCAF existed elsewhere, but their activities remained weak.

In the 1950s diverse groups (right and left) were able to get along within the Pavillon du Cambodge without many problems. After 1960 relations deteriorated, with occasional exchanges of arguments or fighting words. Statements were sometimes made through Khmer newspapers. The 29 January 1962 edition of *La Vérité*, a Phnom Penh daily, reported a protest made by the CKOM, probably directed against the UEK. It denounced the Khmer authors of a "common communiqué [of 17/12/61] on the situation in Cambodia, Laos, and South Vietnam by a group of Cambodian, Laotian, and Vietnamese students and intellectuals in France" that attacked American imperialism and improperly made itself the voice of all of the Khmer community of France; the text showed that Cambodian Communists lived in harmony with their Vietnamese counterparts. These skirmishes were of little importance compared to the outbursts of student violence in 1973 that would result in the closing of the Pavillon du Cambodge at the Cité universitaire (discussed in chapter 6).

## THE YOUTH OF PHNOM PENH AND STATE INTERVENTION

The Lycée Sisowath, which had always been the home of young progressives, was the scene of a new rebellion in 1949 following the signature of the treaty with France and the dissolution of the Democratic government by the king. According to a witness, "Ieng Sary must have been involved in this strike; that is why he and several of his friends were sent to France." Most leftist professors taught at two private lycées except for several in the state lycées: "At the Lycée Sisowath, when I was in my fifth year, a professor of Cambodian analyzed literature in a Marxist fashion. Approximately 10 percent of the students reacted favorably." Those who were favorable spread propaganda in the institutions: "Even in primary school, I already knew who Marx was. Some comrades from the higher classes had talked to me about him." Little information is available about developments in the provinces: "On 10 December 1952 at the lycée at Kompong Cham we went on strike against the French. I was in my first year there, and I was influenced by the boarders who were in their fourth year. . . . All the young people admired Son Ngoc Thanh. We didn't know whether or not he was a Communist; we knew that he wanted Cambodia's independence, and that he considered the monarchy to be a thing of the past."

At Phnom Penh, twenty years would pass before the members of the youthful opposition organized themselves in political groups. Initially, a single youth movement opposed to the regime emerged—a general association of Khmer students.

### L'Association Générale des Étudiants Khmers

Created on 17 January 1965, this group, the AGEK, brought together young people from different universities and private schools: the Université populaire (technical), the Institut de pédagogie, the Kampuchea Both (better known under the abbreviation Kambu Both), and Chamroeun Vichea.

Kambu Both began as a Democratic group. Its name came from the pseudonym Prince Youtevong used when he wrote in the local press. The group set up a private lycée; several individuals taught there who had not been accepted by the state lycées because they lacked diplomas. Among the first to come was Saloth Sar in 1953, joined in 1957 by Ieng Sary and then later by Khieu Samphan, Hou Yuon, Thiounn Thioun, and others who had passed their university examinations. The establishment opened its doors widely to all dissidents, teachers and students alike. Some of the students would learn Marxism through courses taught by the future Khmer Rouge leaders. "Students from Stung Treng, Takeo, and Kah Sotin district in Kompong Cham were of modest origins and too old to enter the public schools. Others from wealthy families had failed their examinations at the state lycées; they rode bikes or motorcycles. The teachers were Communists, almost all of them from well-to-do families; they had been educated at the university."

But the Democrats had not foreseen the political coloration that the high school would assume, and they gradually withdrew from it on that account, and it became a Marxist fief. Many progressive students spent one or two years there, and all appreciated the gentleness and the poetic sensibility of teacher Saloth Sar, who recited Verlaine by heart. The school—which had sheltered the future greats of Democratic Kampuchea (to be discussed in chapter 7)—closed its doors when the latter installed their regime of terror in April 1975.

Little is known about the second private lycée, Chamroeun Vichea, except that the same teachers taught there for a time and propagated the same ideas. In similar fashion the Université populaire (Sala Dek) furnished recruits to the AGEK:

> At the beginning of the academic year 1965–1966, I entered Sala Dek. A friend arranged meetings for discussions between university and lycée students. Since political meetings could not be freely held, he organized excursions that lasted one or two days, and discussions occurred then. It was then that I joined the AGEK. At the beginning I was assigned merely technical problems; gradually I became politicized and had an important role in the association; I was a political commissar. Later, we realized that politicians backed the association, but we didn't know it at the time. In 1967, 1968, and 1969 the AGEK's leaders rejoined the Communist guerrillas.

Some of them perhaps awakened rather late, but most of the leaders were probably not dupes. Tiv Ol, murdered by the Khmer Rouge in the 1970s, was the ministry of education's representative on the AGEK's central committee. Phouk Chhay, who was then deputy general commissar of the Jeunesse socialiste royale khmère (JSRK), was also president of the AGEK during the three short years of the association's life. At the AGEK, "we met once a week. There was a general assembly that included several thousands of people from the universities of Phnom Penh and Takeo-Kampot, and many from Kompong Cham."

Finally, the Institut pédagogique, created in 1958, was the fief of Son Sen, another Khmer Rouge leader, and it supplied recruits to the AGEK. The institute was known for its Marxist teachers who gave students a politically oriented education.

At the beginning, the head of state favored exchanges with Peking, to which Phouk Chhay traveled in August 1965, at a time when all was well between the two peoples. At Phnom Penh, the AGEK organized shows at the Chadomuk auditorium. "We were conducting political activity through art. Some of Hou Yuon's students, too young to be members, came to the cultural evenings." It seems that non-Communist intellectuals attended. Well organized, the association successfully recruited militants, several hundred of them in 1967, according to former members. It maintained close relations with the UEK in Paris. In 1967 the chief of state dissolved the association "because of its subversive activities," reported the 15 November 1967 issue of the review *Kambuja*, which announced its replacement by the Association des étudiants cambodgiens (association of Cambodian students, or AEC), created on 4 November 1967. Another detail was given: "*Samdech* defines the role and the mission of the AEC." This was, therefore, an association controlled by the government.

The same year, the chief of state found himself the target of another group that he had authorized but that had escaped his control. A foreign country was involved—China.

*L'Association d'Amitié Khméro-Chinoise*

The Association d'amitié khméro-chinoise (Khmer-Chinese friendship association, or AAKC) dates from September 1964, when Sino-Cambodian relations were very cordial. It was part of a series of Cambodian–foreign associations (for example, with France, USSR, India, Eastern European countries). The AAKC had a single president, Leng Ngeth, who was reelected at each renewal of the governing body. All political groups were represented on the executive board, including the Khmer left with Hu Nim, who was later assisted by Hou Yuon. Officers, among them Hu Nim, would go to Peking in 1965, but the excesses of the Cultural Revolution in Phnom Penh beginning in 1967 and the openly Maoist position that the Khmer Marxists gave to the AAKC irritated Sihanouk. On 1 September 1967 the prince announced the dissolution of the association and had several persons arrested, among them Phouk Chhay, former president of the dissolved AGEK, who was later released by the leaders of the putsch of 1970. The AAKC was reborn the following day under the name Comité national pour l'amitié khméro-chinoise (national committee for Khmer-Chinese friendship), with Penn Nouth as president and without the Khmer Rouge leaders, who took to the maquis. (That year all the friendship associations with foreign countries were transformed into national committees.)

With the dissolution of these two groups, Communist youth and left-wing youth in general were reduced to silence. Only one means of opposition remained—guerrilla warfare. But not all educated Cambodians rejected Sihanouk's policies. Teachers who were members of the Association des professeurs khmers (association of Khmer teachers) remained loyal, as did law students. Both groups sent him motions expressing their support. Members of the bourgeoisie, bureaucracy, and military, enjoying their privileges, did not utter a word. Peasants remained apart from these movements.

In Paris and elsewhere in the world Khmer students, unhappy about the violence done to democracy and liberty, began to agitate. They were probably angered by the denial of political pluralism. To be a supporter of Sangkum meant nothing. Leftists received ministerial posts because they belonged to Sangkum or because the chief of state wanted to attach them to himself but not for the political orientation they represented. Sihanouk was also hoping that these positions would cause them to become more bourgeois. "My practice was to utilize young Turks as much as possible. Some say that I was Machiavellian, but it was not so. I wanted to coax them by offering them honey and candy in the form of an under secretary's portfolio."[14]

In fact, the chief of state's intervention within the associations constituted a warning to China, and, without Chou En-lai's cleverness, Peking and Phnom Penh would have moved toward a severing of relations.

## THE RIGHT'S RISE TO POWER
## AND PRINCE SIHANOUK'S MISTAKES

While Sihanouk governed Cambodia, he had tried to rally all those whom he could not push aside. In 1966 Communists who were elected representatives were given ministerial posts: Hou Yuon, Khieu Samphan, and Hu Nim. But they did not take the bait and remained honest, especially the first two. They gave up their positions in 1967 and 1968 and took refuge in the maquis when their lives were threatened by the prince's men and rightist elements in the government.

### THE ELECTIONS OF 1966

A turning point in Cambodia's domestic politics came in 1966. Until then, Sangkum's executive committee had chosen candidates for deputation from among Sangkum's members. Following criticism from foreign observers, the chief of state did away with this preliminary classification, which amounted to appointment pure and simple since the number of candidates was no larger than the number of seats. The elections, open to all, took place on 11 September 1966. Most Cambodian politicians had no definite positions, and Sangkum—this enormous catchall government—was certainly convenient for many of them. Only a handful of Democrats who opposed absolute power (and remained outside), the Communists, and several pro-American rightists had declared their positions. Those in the last group are the ones who would benefit from the elections of 1966. After the rejection of American aid in 1963, "they began a systematic action to seize power . . . [and] this faction rapidly succeeded in placing its least well known partisans in important positions in the central and provincial administration. In fact, the ringleaders were few, remarkably discreet, and prudent. Lon Nol himself seems to have been but a confederate like so many others."[15]

Of the 82 representatives elected from among 415 candidates, 27 (from the 42 who presented themselves) had belonged to the previous legislature; a dozen powerful men and officials who were not above commerce represented the business world. This was, witnesses say, an assembly of opportunists. The Lon Nol administration, half of whose members belonged to the pro-American right, was invested on 22 October with a comfortable majority of seventy-three votes (no vote against; four abstentions). Two days later, when the decree appointing this administration appeared, Sihanouk announced the formation of "a Sangkum Reastr Niyum countergovernment entrusted with making known the views of the opposition to the royal government duly invested by the National Assembly."[16] This organ, with the chief of state as its prime mover, published a daily bulletin and gave those it questioned a right of response. This was, in fact, one of varying means that the prince created each time that he wanted to check or influence a group. "There was a government and a countergovernment, always in the Sihanoukist framework; there was a governmental press and an antigovernmental press, always patronized by Sihanouk. . . . It was similar to Communist countries, where you have political commissars next to the heads of each unit."[17]

In reality, things were a bit different, and this organ allowed the prince to continue to express himself on everything and above all to exercise a counterweight to the actions of his adversaries. The government being rightist, the prince brought leftists such as Phouk Chhay, So Nem, Tan Kim Huon, and Chau Sau into the countergovernment.

The Lon Nol government was forced to resign at the end of April 1967, following the Samlaut affair and the opposition of the left, which demonstrated tirelessly for several months. An extraordinary government replaced it, presided over by Sihanouk, who was succeeded by Penn Nouth on January 1968; but this change brought no improvement in the internal situation. It would take the right more than two years to return to power, "two years during the course of which Prince Sihanouk, with an astonishing lack of political understanding, pitilessly destroyed all who could oppose the reactionary right. Yet this repression of leftists had the effect of pushing toward Lon Nol the mass of hesitant individuals who were still waiting for a confirmation of the new orientation."[18] At the time, Sihanouk was attempting a rapprochement with the United States, which had already decided to withdraw militarily from Southeast Asia.

In August 1969 the chief of state, aware of the economic stagnation in which the country was foundering, summoned General Lon Nol to form a salvation government to succeed the last-chance government. Lon Nol refused. The pro-American right returned en masse and offered, most notably, a program of denationalization. From this moment onward political initiative escaped the prince. He asked the four ministers loyal to him to resign in hopes of bringing down the government. The maneuver failed: Prince Sisowath Sirik Matak, then first vice-president of the council, accepted the resignations and did not allow the ministers in question to take back their positions.

The net result of the chief of state's maneuver was to promote the return of a right wing that was hostile to him. Rightist elements found support among the people since the prince had committed errors or allowed practices to emerge that served his adversaries' propaganda purposes.

PEASANT REVOLTS

Samlaut (in Battambang) gave the first important alert. What made the peasants unhappy was the collection of paddy by the national company Sorapa, which was created to collect paddy and forestall traffic in rice with the Vietcong. The explosion came with the confiscation of lands from the peasants of Samlaut. The government had decided to open a road that was to be followed by land development.

> Lon Nol had been governor of Battambang; it was his former fief.
> He opened many plots of land there. Lon Nol, who placed great importance on agricultural matters, wanted rice fields, orange groves,
> pepper trees there. . . . Concessions were thus granted to military
> officers who intended to plant profitable crops such as fruit trees
> and to exploit lumber and precious stones. Nobody cared to find
> out if these fallow lands were available or not. When the peasants
> to whom they belonged demanded their return, their claims were
> dismissed because they did not have titles of ownership. . . . The
> security chief, In Tam, knew about the plan.

This was a case of dupery. Private ownership, which had been established in Cambodia by the French, coexisted with the traditional land system that still ordered a part of the lands. Custom had it that the king was the sole possessor of the soil, with the peasants having usufructuary rights to land on condition of cultivating it; but most of the peasants had never held titles of ownership.

According to what inhabitants of Samlaut said in 1970, the first initiative for the rebellion was the peasants' alone. They in no way challenged Sihanouk; they raised their sticks and machetes against the military officers who had taken their lands. Contrary to the statements of one journalist, the JSRK had no responsibility for the distribution of the lands that it cleared on the orders of military officers.[19] The April–June 1967 issue of *Études cambodgiennes* reported that the FARK were given the responsibility of "containing the rebellion within its geographical limits" and that it had been settled "without bloodshed." Such would probably have been the case if General Lon Nol had not savagely retaliated against the people (probably on his own initiative); the previously mentioned article was quiet on the point. Told to return to their villages, from which they had fled into the forest, where the Khmer Rouge of Phnom Vay Chap had welcomed them, the peasants were attacked and pursued by the military. "All who protested were accused of being Communists, and their homes were burned; the peasants responded by burning the barracks. Rebels taken prisoner were confined by the military at Treng, left exposed to the sun, without food. . . . People burned bridges. Many inhabitants joined the maquis, where they would remain until 1975."

The chief of state appeared much troubled by these events; he certainly did not want to have peasants killed. Nonetheless, in a speech given at Kompong Thom and broadcast live on the radio, he approved of the retaliation (carried out without his agreement), although he criticized it severely the following day.

The Khmer Rouge had nothing to do with the peasant rebellion, even if they subsequently turned the affair to their advantage by dating their action in the maquis from the time of this Samlaut rebellion. At least this was what Pol Pot said after taking power. In Paris, however, the UEK explained:

> The officers of the UEK told us that the Lon Nol group was responsible for these events. They based their analysis on tracts distributed in Cambodia. The people of Samlaut accused the vice-governor, a civilian, and the military governor. The vice-governor had agreed to send the JSRK to clear not virgin lands but cultivated lands belonging to peasants, who rose in rebellion. . . . Members of the government were able to ascertain that there were no Communists involved.

"The Khmer Rouge were not ready to do anything at Samlaut," a militant stated. "They recognized that they were outstripped by the peasant movement and that the rioters had been calmed by them."

In Ratanakiri a similar phenomenon caused the montagnard peoples to rebel. The government requisitioned some of their fallow lands to enlarge the Labansiek rubber plantation, created in 1960. This region was particularly sensitive because the Pathet Lao and the Vietminh had been developing there for several years and exploited the discontent of the montagnards to turn them against the central power. The most serious incidents occurred in 1968 when, armed with their crossbows, the Brou, Tumpuon, and Jarai tribes confronted or ambushed Khmer troops. Here too the military reacted harshly. The stakes were unquestionably greater in this region than in Samlaut: there, it was a purely internal problem among Khmers; here, foreign propaganda was an additional factor. These events, painful for the montagnards of the northeast, would help the Khmer Rouge leaders in the early 1960s.

Besides, these minorities felt closer to their counterparts living on the other side of the borders, in Vietnamese and Laotian territory, than to Cambodians. Some of them who remained outside the conflict even though they had endured the same wrongs nonetheless suffered the consequences—their villages were moved. Outsiders could still visit these new sites in 1969.

Aside from these specific episodes peasants certainly had social demands to make; on the whole they remained passive. Yet these incidents revealed, in the case of Samlaut, discontent and the possibility of spontaneous outbursts of violence, and in the case of Ratanakiri, a movement Communist neighbors already had well in hand. Probably other structured cells existed elsewhere. In Kompong Cham and Battambang, salary demands were presented in 1967. Khmer Rouge were stationed in these two regions. A union, led by Nguon Eng, functioned on a clandestine basis.

As soon as Phnom Penh ascertained the presence of Khmer Rouge guerrilla forces, the witch-hunt was on. "Superior officers had received special funds from the general staff. The governor and his military intelligence officer received a great deal."

As for the inhabitants of the border zones whose regions were invaded by Vietcong soldiers, it seems that their displeasure was not always directed at the Communists. According to the inhabitants, the depredations reported by the Cambodian press were more often committed by nearby South Vietnamese civilians rather than by NLF soldiers. A former official reported: "In my village, on the left bank of the Mekong, in Kompong Cham, the inhabitants sided with the Vietnamese Communists because during the war they gave them many things. . . . The people were sympathetic to the

Vietcong because they lacked everything. The smallest thing given by them, for example, the opportunity to pillage American and South Vietnamese barracks, represented a windfall."

The anti-NLF demonstrations on the borders in March 1970 had been, moreover, organized by the Phnom Penh regime. This understanding between the Khmer villagers of the east bank of the Mekong and the Vietcong explains, in part, the mistrust that the Khmer Rouge felt for this population, most of which was deported and massacred in 1978, at the high point of the war between Democratic Kampuchea and the Socialist Republic of Vietnam. In rural society, contention remained localized in several specific centers. Disapproval of Sihanouk's politics surfaced above all in the cities.

URBAN DISCONTENT

Growing corruption, a collapsing economy, Sihanouk's increasingly frequent and arbitrary meddling with affairs of state, and unemployment among the educated all constituted sufficient motives to push townspeople to action, but no movement took shape. Nonetheless, beginning in 1968, the discontent expressed itself openly on two issues that added to the misfortunes of the Khmer people: the supplying of Cambodian rice to the Vietcong and the opening of a state-run casino.

Until 1968 Cambodia had served as a route for arms, munitions, and foodstuffs coming from China and destined for the NLF's soldiers. Very few Khmer officials knew of the existence or, in any case, the details of transactions that their country had concluded with China. But when Phnom Penh delivered Cambodian rice to the Vietnamese Communists, the existence of accords could no longer be denied. Some officials and military officers took charge of this transportation of rice and munitions. Individuals acquired huge fortunes overnight, and corruption spread. Worse still, approximately one hundred thousand tons of rice, equivalent to half of Cambodia's annual exports, traveled the road to the border. If this sale improved the income of an entire chain of profiteers belonging to the regime, it also caused a deficit in foreign exchange stock important for an economy that was already ailing; this was its coup de grace. The chief of state was not unaware of the transactions. "The clandestine commerce in rice was not the result of uncoordinated activities by Chinese merchants alone. On the contrary, it was an operation that was well organized in advance, with the participation of the FARK. Sihanouk knew about this operation, but he personally gave his approval for its implementation."[20] The operation also had the active participation of General Lon Nol and the endorsement of the governor of the National Bank of Cambodia, Son Sann.

Residents of Phnom Penh who had relatives in the border zones were aware of the Vietnamese Communists' advance into Cambodian territory. Foreigners could see them moving freely about the rubber plantations. From that time onward people talked freely about them in the capital, blaming the prince directly. No longer master of the situation, Sihanouk denounced the Vietcong sanctuaries in a press conference, all the while closing his eyes to the traffic in rice and its consequences for the country's economy. Tempers flared, and the ancient hatred of the *yuon* (Vietnamese) rose again; preparations were underway for the atrocities that General Lon Nol would unleash in 1970.

The opening of the casino in January 1969 proved to be just as problematic for the chief of state. Officially created to help fill the treasury's empty coffers, "the contribution it made to the treasury was but a drop of water in relation to the deficit; and then a great deal of money was diverted by these same corrupt officials or dignitaries of whom we wanted to rid ourselves." Khmers paid less attention to the economic failure and the profits reaped by several individuals than to the suicides. Asians can hardly resist games of chance, which were, moreover, forbidden in Cambodia. Khmers could enjoy them only during the three days of the New Year Festival, in April. To throw open this type of establishment, ordinarily reserved for foreigners, to all citizens was bound to have disastrous consequences. Having lost everything, including his oxen, a peasant dared not return home and preferred to kill himself; an urban husband having wagered his wife did not have the heart to face her. The Monivong bridge was the scene of numerous suicides. At the time, to hear the latest of these developments, residents needed only talk to the pedicab driver transporting them or listen to the community of Khmer servants of the *phsar kap ko* (the neighborhood of the Front du Bassac building), where many teachers and foreign experts lived. The press was not allowed to report the suicides, perhaps to conceal them from foreigners, for all the Khmers knew about them. Discontentment grew, and Prince Sihanouk's common people, not understanding the reasons behind this murderous casino, concluded: "If *Samdech* doesn't stop this, soon there won't be anyone left in Phnom Penh."

During this period, the Cambodians saw their leader transformed into a film director, using up miles of film paid for through the state's budget, at a time when young people who lived in the city could not find employment. In retrospect some Khmers thought that Norodom Sihanouk, having lost control of politics, had found in cinema a diversion and a means of attracting attention. At the same time, the chief of state conducted a campaign of repression against the left-wing opposition that capped the elite's discontentment.

All these events made the prince extremely unpopular, especially in

Phnom Penh, and played a determining role in the support that the Cambodians would give to the right during the Sangkum congress of August 1969. From that time onward all the right-wing forces, closely aligned, left Sihanouk without the slightest initiative. The latter did try to provoke the breakup of the Lon Nol government; this show of strength (his last ace in the hole) was to occur during the congress on 27 December to 29 December 1969, but it failed.

THE LAST SANGKUM CONGRESS

The twenty-eighth Sangkum congress marked the end of Sihanouk's political preponderance. According to participants, all was not lost in advance: "The prince needed only to explain in precise terms the situation as to the Vietcong sanctuaries and ask for the masses' support in resolving the problem; he would have had it because many still wanted to believe in him." The authorization given to the Vietcong without the agreement or even the consultation of the people reduced the prince's margin for maneuver. He thus conceived of a show of strength: "It was his last chance, and he ruined it by giving free rein to his verbal intemperance, which made him announce his intentions beforehand."[21] Thus, his adversaries took the same precautions that he had by surrounding themselves with devoted partisans. The confrontation could have resulted in violence, which the prince refused, preferring not to act.

Furthermore, it must be noted that the Khmer chief of state always preferred to resolve important problems peacefully, notably when foreigners were involved: for example, in obtaining independence, in making Vietminh soldiers leave Khmer territory, and in avoiding war with the Vietcong. In the first two cases he appealed to the population. In 1965 the population would have probably refused to grant sanctuary to the Vietnamese—their hereditary enemies—and Sihanouk, unable to expose himself to the humiliation of a rebuff, thus made the decision by himself and found himself alone in the final ordeal. When deaths occurred, they resulted from the resolution of strictly internal affairs and did not commit the Cambodian nation: for example, in eliminating right-wing (Khmer *serei*) and left-wing (Khmer Rouge) opposition who completely escaped his domination and made no concessions whatsoever. The fifteen years of peace that Cambodia enjoyed were certainly the result of this desire to avoid bloodshed, and all Khmers benefited.

And yet the chief of state never made even the smallest personal sacrifice. He abandoned none of the privileges and deportment of a feudal prince, refusing to bring about social, civic, and political transformations that would have given the country national stability and international standing.

# Part Two

## CAMBODIA IN AGONY

Encore s'il suffisait de quelques hécatombes
Pour qu'enfin tout changeât, qu'enfin tout s'arrangeât
Depuis tant de grands soirs que tant de têtes tombent,
Au Paradis sur terre on y serait déjà.
Or l'âge d'or sans cesse est remis aux calendes
Les dieux ont toujours soif, n'en ont jamais assez.
Et c'est la mort, la mort toujours recommencée.

Georges Brassens, "Mourir pour des idées"

Jamais les crépuscules ne vaincront les aurores
Étonnons-nous des soirs mais vivons les matins
Méprisons l'immuable comme la pierre ou l'or
Sources qui tariront.

Guillaume Apollinaire, *Le guetteur mélancolique*

# 6    Disasters of the Republican Period

A common interpretation of Sihanouk's abrupt departure from Cambodia on 6 January 1970, several days after the Sangkum congress, holds that the prince took flight. More generously, Charles Meyer writes that "more probably he was attempting to gain his second wind."[1] Having in all confidence left power in the hands of Lon Nol, the man whom he had installed as prime minister, Sihanouk left for France. In early 1970 there was nothing in the head of state's behavior to indicate that he had given up. When he learned of his deposal by the National Assembly and the Council of the Kingdom, he was in Moscow, where he had stopped on his return trip to try to convince the Soviet Union and China to restrain Hanoi's settlement of Vietnamese Communists in Cambodian territory.

## THE COUP D'ÉTAT: PREPARATIONS AND IMMEDIATE CONSEQUENCES

According to unconfirmed rumors, Prince Sisowath Sirik Matak was scheming to depose Sihanouk when the latter traveled to Hanoi to attend Ho Chi Minh's funeral in September 1969. The coup d'état occurred early in 1970. While the head of state was in France, administrators in charge of the frontier provinces complained to Lon Nol about problems they could not bring to Sihanouk's attention: the penetration of Vietcong troops into the interior of the country. Lon Nol then closed the port of Sihanoukville to deliveries of arms intended for the Vietcong. In fact, Ros Chantrabot (who served in the military under the republic) states that preparations for the change had been in progress since 1968: Commander Lon Non (the general's younger brother), very likely aided by Sirik Matak, "had started to assemble small cells of intellectuals hostile to Sihanouk's absolutist regime."[2]

Sirik Matak hated this cousin whom the French had placed in power in

121

1941; everyone had expected that the throne would go to his uncle, Sisowath Monireth. Yet it seems that his hatred for Sihanouk had another cause as well. A conscientious statesman, Sirik Matak could not tolerate the constant fluctuations of a head of state who made decisions in the evening only to annul them the next morning, who modified policies on fleeting whims, and who became enraptured with Chinese or Indonesian projects and wanted to implement them immediately in Cambodia. When the retirement age for officials was changed to fifty-five, it forced a reluctant Sirik Matak into retirement. He had refused to cajole the court of Chamcar Mon, though he might thereby have retained his position. And yet he regretted its loss.

We have every reason to suppose that Sihanouk had little confidence in Sirik Matak. Moreover, many Khmers were certain that Sirik Matak's ambition was to seize the throne for himself. All recognized his intelligence, and his fellow students remember him as a young man of slender means from a respectable milieu. "My mother-in-law always told us to associate with Sirik Matak's family because his family was a modest one, more realistic and closer to the poor than the royal palace was." "He was a decent sort, competent administratively; but he was a prince, and like all princes, he was always susceptible to flattery. Nevertheless, he was one of the best of the princes." Further, "He was tough on the job, but as soon as we left the office, we were friends again, we laughed and had a good time." Despite these qualities, it seems that the desire for wealth gained control of him as he rose in the hierarchy. Some said that he liked money too much.

This man was to become the principal architect of Sihanouk's overthrow. Despite Sirik Matak's sympathy for the Americans, their involvement in the plot has never been proven. The coup d'état advanced their interests, and they immediately began to support the new regime; perhaps they even added the finishing touches. But it seems clear that the decision was a Khmer one and that it involved political factors as well as individual ambitions and antagonisms, so tenacious is rancor in Khmer hearts. No witness has accused Lon Nol; those who knew him well declared him incapable of treason. They say that he even hesitated to vote for Sihanouk's deposition.

Few are the Khmers willing to tell the truth about such an important affair, whose full impact is yet to be felt. Here are a few excerpts from a conversation I had in April 1986 with a former politician: "'The coup d'état was neither Lon Nol nor the Americans.' 'Then it must have been Sirik Matak? [Silence] Even if you don't want to name names, you must have presumptions?' 'I have more than presumptions—I have certainty.'"

Curiously, the head of state contributed to his own downfall. While in France for treatment, Sihanouk asked his prime minister to organize popular anti-Vietnamese demonstrations in support of his initiatives with the two

Communist giants. The success of the demonstrations was assured: the Cambodians have detested their Vietnamese neighbors since the beginning of the nineteenth century if not earlier.[3] The demonstrations took place on 8 and 9 March 1970, in the border provinces. Subsequently, an angry crowd in Phnom Penh sacked the diplomatic missions of the Democratic Republic of Vietnam (DRV) and the Provisional Revolutionary Government of South Vietnam (PRG) as well as Vietnamese-owned shops. Sihanouk then released a statement condemning the outbreaks of violence and criticizing his prime minister and the government: "When *Samdech* criticized him, Lon Nol did not understand because he had only followed Sihanouk's orders; but he still hesitated [to overthrow him]." Everyone agrees that if the prince had returned immediately, he would have been able to turn the situation in his favor. The pillaging of Vietnamese civilians continued in the provinces and in Phnom Penh, and there is every reason to believe that the excesses were deliberate. The violence of Khmer *krom* participants (Khmers from South Vietnam), known to be rightists, suggests that Sirik Matak was active behind the scenes. Had he not used Khmer *krom* elements among others during the December 1969 congress to stand up to the chief of state's partisans? Moreover, according to a close friend, Commander Lon Non had contacted Son Ngoc Thanh in order to organize the outbursts; the hypothesis is a plausible one given Lon Non's subsequent role. In any case, General Lon Nol did not control the situation, neither on the spot nor within his own government. As Meyer observes, the ultimatum given to the DRV and the NLF demanding that they withdraw their troops had supposedly been composed "on his own initiative [by] the secretary general of foreign affairs."[4]

On 14 March 1970 Sihanouk, still in Europe, declined to receive two emissaries, one from the queen mother and one from the government, who had come to explain the situation to him. It is rumored that his wife Monique and General Ngo Hou heavily influenced his decision to refuse them. Before leaving for Moscow, the prince announced confidentially to his entourage that he was going to deal ruthlessly with the plotters. The conversation, recorded without his knowledge, made its way to Sirik Matak, who had Lon Nol listen to it, adding that Sihanouk should be deposed. Everyone believed that bloody reprisals would follow. Still Lon Nol dissented. In the meantime, military men knowing the situation sided with Sirik Matak so that Lon Nol had no choice but to follow the movement against his will. Perhaps Sirik Matak seized the opportunity in order to take revenge. In the words of an associate: "He shouldn't have carried out the coup this way; he should've just deposed Sihanouk but left the queen mother on the throne."[5] Apparently Sirik Matak considered this possibility, but Lon Nol's entourage did everything possible to preclude it.

Nothing was left to chance. Owners of businesses in Phnom Penh were to let employees off work so that they could attend demonstrations. "I had to mobilize workers to demonstrate against Sihanouk," one owner said. "I supplied four hundred people, but I didn't allow them to take along any implements." Students also were requisitioned. Everyone had been told to gather spontaneously on March 16 in front of the National Assembly to protest against the presence of the Vietnamese Communists in Cambodia. The president of the asssembly, In Tam, read a message condemning it. "Vietcong out of Cambodia!" the crowd screamed. Following this slogan there was to be another: "Down with Sihanouk!" But someone in the crowd yelled, "Long live *Samdech Ov!*" and a number of other voices took up the cry. As several people reported, "In fact, the youths had been requisitioned without knowing much about what they were expected to do. As usual, some had brought banners favorable to Sihanouk." Abashed, In Tam withdrew; the first attempt had been a failure.

At the second meeting two days later, Sirik Matak took the precaution of having the National Assembly surrounded by tanks; the proceedings were held in camera. Not a single deputy or council member failed to vote for the chief of state's overthrow. Witnesses assert that the general wept after the decisive vote was cast. The manner in which the vote was conducted (each had to sign his ballot) no doubt discouraged heroics if anyone was so inclined. In this sense, the affair may be termed a military coup, for the army was waiting outside.

Cheng Heng became interim head of state, and Lon Nol headed the new government with Sirik Matak as adviser. The government tried to negotiate with DRV and PRG diplomats in Phnom Penh, but the attempts proved futile, and the latter closed their missions. In reply to the Khmer government's ultimatum, Hanoi initiated hostilities on 29 March. The inferno that Sihanouk had kept under control for fifteen years violently exploded in the several days following his deposition.

## A PEOPLE IN DISTRESS

A large part of the Khmer elite who had remained in the country welcomed the overthrow of Sihanouk. For several months, the capital was euphoric. Most of the intellectuals applauded, as did members of the military, with officials still divided. The most politically conscious young people remained hopeful: "For a while we felt something was going to happen; we thought they wanted to get rid of the rot, but the result was completely different. You must realize that at first young people had high hopes." As for the politicians, they proved opportunistic. The peasants, troubled, disturbed, or angry, could only wonder; they were no more able than the prime minister had been, several days earlier, to understand the situation.[6] On 29 March Cambodians from the provinces bordering Vietnam, badly informed or misinformed, went to Phnom Penh "to welcome *Samdech*." Two representatives who tried to explain the situation to them died—at whose hands we do not know. Although the majority of the people supported him, the former chief of state could no longer return to the country after the threats to decapitate the traitors that he had uttered at Paris. The new government, presided over by General Lon Nol, resolved to assassinate him if he returned to Khmer soil.

Phnom Penh rejoiced. The "twenty-four-hour soldiers," as Lon Nol called them, left for the front, that is, for the Vietcong sanctuaries, singing, piled up in old Chinese buses, many without shoes, some without arms. In April 1970 the courage, the patriotism, and the lack of awareness of these young recruits were simultaneously and clearly visible to all. The coming tragedy was suffused with exultation, with the feeling that a grand exploit lay ahead. This attitude confirms a compatriot's assertion: "It seems the Khmer people always go to war through arrogance, as a game, through megalomania." In fact, before the intervention of American bombers on 30 April 1970, there was wholesale slaughter in the republican ranks.[7] For more than a month, Phnom Penh had called for arms for its soldiers. The West responded by sending B-52s: "Lon Nol, faced with a fait accompli, cried when he realized that bombs were falling on the border villages, killing Khmer peasants" and chasing away others, who poured into the cities. As a matter of fact, the United States had not asked him for his opinion; it had been waiting fifteen years for the opportunity to put Cambodia to use in its war against the Vietnamese Communists.[8]

People in the cities, particularly the capital, were advised to raise vegetables, fowl, and pigs. Those who did not have gardens were encouraged to use their balconies. Charming Phnom Penh thus lost its beauty and cleanliness. At least this measure, which was ridiculed by Westerners, who continued to live in the greatest of comfort, would allow many inhabitants to avoid famine. Some of them joined the Khmer Rouge camp, not because of ideology but because of the economic difficulties of the republican regime. Likewise, peasants who were refugees from various provinces had scant financial resources. For the areca nut that they cultivated in their villages to prepare betel-leaf quid peasants found substitutes: they stripped the superb *koki* bordering avenue Norodom. The government fortified strategic locations of the city; and with time, the sacks of cement came apart and gave way under the rains. Maintenance left something to be desired because of a lack of personnel, with the men leaving for combat. The building at the Front du Bassac, where a great many foreigners lived, suffered a water shortage beginning in April 1970. The broken pumps were no longer repaired, and the inhabitants had to share one for every two or three staircases. Huge rats ran about among piles of garbage. The worst off among the civilians were Khmer city dwellers of modest means who could not endure the inflation and accelerated increases in the cost of living, as well as peasants who were victims of the bombing and other survivors from the countryside who took refuge in the city. In the beginning, family and friends lined up to welcome these outcasts. Many of them knew nobody in Phnom Penh, and they had the choice between a hastily erected shantytown on the outskirts of town or camps that the government opened for them. The first camps, in Tuk Thla, Tuol Bakha in the Chak Angré neighborhood, started operating in December 1970. Others followed, at O Baek Khaâm–Stung Mean Chey, Vat Kah in July 1972, and then at Pochentong. The unfinished Hôtel Cambodiana, bordering the Four-Arms, also sheltered a number of the emigrants. During this period an affluent and corrupt minority built sumptuous villas and profited from renting them to Americans. The great problem for the state remained to nourish and care for refugees, who for the most part were fleeing the B-52 bombings. In a cruel paradox, Washington could not aid them without recognizing their status as displaced persons, thus admitting that Khmer civilians were bombing victims, which the Department of State denied. These unfortunates had to wait a year before receiving any American aid. Phnom Penh created a refugee commission. The Cambodian Red Cross did its best. Dedicated individuals as well as charitable and humanitarian organizations came to aid the needy, but their help was insufficient. From the end of 1970 beggars took over Phnom Penh; city residents and refugees, abandoning their dignity, searched for a few riels to survive. Military skirmishes along the national highways, frequently cut, allowed only irregular transportation of rice from the rich province of Battambang to the capital, and the exorbitant prices bore unjustly on the poor. On 13 July 1971 the government created the Mixed Economic Commission and gave it the task of forming convoys to supply the capital and the provincial cities. Despite several brief respites the food situation worsened over the years. The shortage of rice was deeply felt; for Cambodians, "to eat" means "to eat rice." The hope of successful change gave way to regret and hunger. Even the most staunch opponents of Sihanouk recognized that the depredations committed under Sangkum were slight compared to the general misery that had taken over the country.

The misfortunes of these impoverished people contrasted with the ostentatious spending of nouveaux riches who benefited from the war and the American presence. They led the good life. The rich ignored their ravenous compatriots and shifted the blame for everything onto foreigners. In the

October 1971 issue of the *Revue de l'armée* the editor-in-chief wrote: "All Khmers, Chinese, Malays, and Vietnamese of Cambodia must fight together against the aggressors, the Vietcong–North Vietnamese. There must be a true alliance among all citizens of the Khmer Republic." He attributed the rise in prices to insecurity and concluded,

> It must be understood that when one lives in conditions of extreme privation, he is forced to use all means, even illegal or immoral ones, to survive. It is very regrettable, but one cannot do the impossible. . . . This is why we ask merchants, who are for the most part foreigners, to cooperate openly with our authorities in order to put an end to the rise in prices. These "profiteers," whoever they are, should put a brake on their cupidity. It is in their own interest to do so, for, pushed to extremes, people are capable of committing acts whose consequences will be regrettable for everyone.

Here was a thinly veiled threat aimed at Chinese merchants, who certainly profited from the situation; but they were not the only ones responsible for the rising cost of living. This denunciation whitewashed the role of the governmental authorities and gave free rein to the Khmers' xenophobic penchant.

For urban society, cloistered by its insouciance and lack of awareness, everything became the object of a game; during the Khmer New Year celebration of April 1975 people wagered on the number, day, and hour that rockets would be fired on Phnom Penh. During this period rural people, displaced from their habitual sociological context, tried to survive in the camps, no longer knowing which spirits to honor; their entire lives were dislocated. Women and children had fled without husbands or eldest sons, who were dead or involved in the fighting; family units were shattered.

If some foreigners were moved by the spectacle of such misery, most continued to live as before. Disturbed by the first power outages and frightened by the first rockets, they organized themselves, grew accustomed to the changes, and continued to throw parties. People no longer went to the rubber plantations for receptions that had sometimes ended with the guests plunging fully dressed into the pool: the Vietcong circulated freely there; French planters then held their gatherings in Phnom Penh, which was less grandiose but just as fashionable.

LON NOL AND THE AMERICANS

The military has never had good press in Cambodia. It was not a career that attracted the best students. As one of them explained, on leaving high school, these "students went on to higher studies, becoming physicians, magistrates, engineers, and so on. Those who for various reasons were too old to enter the lycée headed for the École normale and learned the profession of teacher, or indeed they signed up at the technical school. The rest joined the army or the police.... In our country, military officers are mediocre people, incapable of studying."

General Lon Nol corresponded perfectly to this portrait. An unassuming individual, he did not seem to be at ease anywhere except in his military career, and even there his talents were questioned. For many years he had remained commander-in-chief of the general staff of the Forces armées royales khmères (royal Khmer armed forces, or FARK, which became national, the FANK, in 1970). His days as an administrator had left an impression of mediocrity. A former minister reports: "When I asked Lon Nol, my subordinate, for a study on a specific question, he would give me six lines, which bears witness to his limited ideas." Anyone who has ever met Lon Nol is hardly surprised by this statement. Uncommunicative, his eyes staring into nothingness, the general left the conversational initiative to his interlocutor, answering briefly or by gestures—sometimes a half-smile—and entering, if his opposite did not react, into a silence that was sometimes taken for meditation. But his friends respected him and considered him honest. While serving Sihanouk, he remained loyal and stuck to his work, except during the Samlaut repression, for which he was not held accountable.

On 18 March 1970 he took up the reins of power, with Sirik Matak as his second. No one doubted that the latter was the real leader, given his intelligence. Disagreements soon emerged, in part stemming from the general's entourage, particularly from his brother, Commander Lon Non, hungry for power and wealth and also more artful than his elder brother; he obtained much from the general. Witnesses reported, moreover, that Sirik Matak did not desire the proclamation of the republic and intended to retain the monarchy. Some maintain that he hoped eventually to take the crown himself; others say that he wished to reserve it for Prince Sihamoni (the son of Sihanouk and his wife Monique); according to them he resented Lon Nol, who, after giving his assent, did not keep his word.

Late in 1969 the general had the misfortune of losing his wife, whom he worshiped, and who was highly respected. "It had been predicted to Lon Nol that, as long as his wife lived, everything would go well for him, but afterward it would be different." His second companion meddled in politics and was unanimously disliked: "She wanted to know about everything. You couldn't have a meeting without microphones being installed in her rooms. If his first wife had lived, Lon Nol would probably have acted differently. She would have prevented him from listening to his brother because she had great influence on Lon Non."

Just after the coup d'état, rumors flew and were reported in the foreign press. According to Kao Kan's text, the most precise one, an emissary from Peking, Kuo An, proposed to Lon Nol that China would "treat the fall of Sihanouk as a domestic affair if the Lon Nol government would agree to continue to grant the same diplomatic and logistical support to Vietnamese combatants. This conversation lasted until 5 May, that is, one month and seventeen days after the change of regime in Phnom Penh."[9]

Lon Nol refused. On the same day Peking announced the breaking off of diplomatic relations with Phnom Penh and the recognition of the Gouvernement royal d'union nationale du Cambodge (royal government of national union of Cambodia, or GRUNC), composed of Khmer exiles. In late January 1971 the Vietcong launched a surprise attack on the capital's airport, Pochentong, destroying most of the planes. Several days later the general was struck by hemiplegia. He saw his disease as a punishment, since all Cambodians believed that anyone who betrayed the palace after swearing allegiance to it would die young. This disease and the military setback constituted signs that reinforced his mysticism. After treatment in Hawaii, he returned diminished but held onto the power that his brother, through intrigues with the Americans, guarded for him, against the wishes of Sirik Matak, who considered him henceforth incapable of governing. His ability to work was then estimated at two or three hours per day, and he remained the supreme leader, conducting battles from his bedroom. Preoccupied with religion, astrology, and agriculture, he spoke at length about the Khmer-Mons.

This last point deserves several lines because it illustrates the ignorance and stupidity of the man who, with the Americans, led the country (and reveals also the opportunism and cowardice of his entourage). Owing to the complex blend of humanity in Southeast Asia, the notion of physical traits does not help in identifying the populations that inhabit the region. The tendency is to classify them according to a linguistic criterion. Within the vast Austroasiatic group, the Khmer language belongs to the Mon-Khmer family, so named for the languages of the two ethnic groups that were best represented at the time of its definition, the Mons of Burma and the Khmers (the Vietnamese have since been included). After long bargaining between France and Cambodia, at the beginning of 1970 Phnom Penh announced the founding of the Institut môn-khmer to promote social science research in Cambodia and initiate collaboration between Khmer and French researchers. With a typically Cambodian chauvinism, Lon Nol inverted the order of words in an expression that had been consecrated for more than fifty years: the institute's modified plaque henceforth carried the inscription, Institut khmer-môn. Because of the war, the organization remained relatively inactive but did, from 1972 onward, publish a bulletin. The same period saw the publication of *La Civilisation khmère-môn*. Then, in a burst of mental confusion the general arrived at the concept of the "Khmer-Mon race." The absurdity reached a pinnacle when he sent a delegation to Burma with the assignment of researching and reporting on the original Khmer-Mon dress. Keng Vannsak, probably the only Cambodian specialist on Khmer civilization, agreed to head the delegation. It was, according to Sim Var, "one of the first missions that Lon Nol sent abroad in 1970."[10]

New magazines appeared: *Revue de l'armée* and *Chadomuk*. During a time when shortages of food were at their most acute, *Chadomuk* included among the measures intended to develop the capital the planning of a park in the style of the Bois de Boulogne and the construction of several subway lines. In this same issue of November 1971 the general, promoted to field marshal in April 1971, wrote: "The Chams are Malayo-Polynesian Khmer-Mons, thus also of our race but of a mixed culture, slightly differentiated."[11] In light of the fact that the magazine was created by the committee assigned to follow the evolution of mind and ideas in the republic (Comité chargé de suivre l'évolution de l'esprit et des idées de la république khmère, or COMESIREK), the intellectual poverty—not of the republicans in general but of their leader, who, in the image of his predecessor, imposed a style that his entourage faithfully reproduced—becomes manifest. Finally, in the preface to an opuscule entitled *Néo-Khmérisme* (a very obscure text) he observed: "It is to be hoped that neo-Khmerism will contribute to prolonging the Buddhist era for five thousand years as foreseen, to bringing peace back to Southeast Asia, and to avoiding world war in the future."[12] In 1971, in the context of the general mobilization, Lon Nol created a whole series of committees, including the Coordinating Committee for Khmer-Mon Friendship Activities and for Malayo-Polynesian Khmer-Mon Culture, as well as the Religious Struggle Activities Coordinating Committee.

The field marshal did not remain inactive in the areas of religion and magic. Invulnerability became the dominant theme characterizing, not the career officers, some of whom had already seen combat, but the inexperienced privates who left for the front with a magic scarf—a square of white cotton decorated with diagrams drawn by mediums and astrologers—around their necks. The army had a garden with magical rhizomatous plants near the Pochentong airport. Wearing a small piece of these rhizomes or swallowing a concoction before battle took the place of real protection. Thus, these young men left for combat with a smile on their faces, at least for the first few months. Moreover, to protect Phnom Penh from attack, Lon Nol had helicopters spread consecrated sand around the city; this measure was intended to approximate the ritual boundaries of pagodas, which delimit the sacred enclosure. At the Festival of the Dead in November 1971 residents of Phnom Penh marched and assembled before the stupa on the train station's square. One of the banners proclaimed: The spirits of the victims demand justice.

After setting himself up in the princely palace of Chamcar Mon, once Cheng Heng was shoved aside in March 1971, Field Marshal Lon Nol began to consider himself a great leader, but he was over his head and gradually revealed his mediocrity. His regime became more and more authoritarian: in 1973 he abolished freedom of expression and censored the press.

We may wonder why the Americans nevertheless maintained in power an individual who combined such incompetence and eccentricity, whereas they would have had, in the person of Sirik Matak, a man who was just as devoted to their cause but was also intelligent and respected. The latter admitted to a Sihanouk loyalist who had remained in Phnom Penh that he could not do much. "Sirik Matak told me that it was the republican military officers who held power." In particular Lon Non, the *petit frère*, had an important role in the removal of this man, who loved his country and was a leader. Perhaps the White House did not wish to deal with someone capable of defying it. The hemiplegic Lon Nol thus remained in power until the regime's collapse. The Americans did search for an alternative but ran into obstacles. John Enders, the American ambassador and an unconditional supporter of President Richard Nixon and Henry Kissinger, gave the field marshal strong support. When John Gunther Dean succeeded him in 1974, the situation was nearly irreversible, and attempts to bring Sihanouk back to power failed.

The field marshal may have had belated regrets. Exiled to Hawaii in 1975, he lived a relatively solitary life, although he received some visitors; he had time for reflection. When he left to move to Los Angeles in 1979, he assembled the Khmer military officers living in the United States and told them, "If there's one man who can help Cambodia, it's *Samdech*; I beg you, help Sihanouk."

## PROCLAMATION OF THE REPUBLIC
## AND THE OPPOSING KHMER FORCES

According to Ros Chantrabot, then a friend of Lon Non's: "The proclamation of Cambodia as a Khmer republic was to occur on the night of 18–19 March 1970. But numerous difficulties and strange mysteries completely blocked this. . . . That is why Professor Keng Vannsak, with the approval of General Lon Nol, head of the 'national salvation government,' had organized a committee of intellectuals in support of the government."[13] The manifesto published by this committee on 18 March 1970 stipulated:

The intellectuals' committee demands the abolition of the monarchical regime, which has proven incapable of defending the Khmer cultural and territorial patrimony. . . . National salvation for a Cambodia that has been enslaved, diminished, and humiliated by millennia of absolutism, despotism, and tyranny can be found only in the radical transformation of the kingdom of Cambodia into a Khmer republic.

For seven months onlookers had been waiting for Cambodia's new status; official paper bore the letterhead: State of Cambodia. On 28 August 1970 Ros Chantrabot participated in two preparatory meetings for the proclamation of the republic, called in urgency by Commander Lon Non "to 'help him' resolve the problem of the proclamation of the Khmer Republic, which 'the other side' was not accepting" (17). In this context, "the other side" clearly designated Sirik Matak. The influence that Lon Non exercised in the government seems undeniable. The republic was instituted on 9 October 1970. Nevertheless, just as the kingdom had functioned for ten years without a king, the Khmer Republic had no president for seventeen months; Lon Nol granted himself the title on 17 March 1972. As for the republican constitution, it was born on 30 April 1972 after a long and difficult gestation. In the same fashion the Sangkum Reastr Niyum, created by Sihanouk in 1955, was not dissolved until 18 February 1971, "at the end of a congress on the recommendation of its central committee."[14]

When they were military officers, Lon Nol and Nhiek Tioulong had created the Renovation party. Following the coup they found themselves divided, with General Tioulong remaining loyal to Sihanouk. Thus, after the government declared the dissolution of Sangkum, the officers in power created a new organ, the Social Republican party, which assembled around the field marshal the majority of officers implicated in the earlier regime. In practice, Lon Non led the group. Sirik Matak soon took discreet exception to the head of the government. When the rupture became public in 1972, his supporters, civilians for the most part, regrouped within a new party, the Republican party. The two parties had very similar political programs.

The Cham minority (Islamic Khmers) made its appearance in the country's political and military affairs. Lon Nol, for unknown reasons, was interested in the Front unifié de lutte des races opprimées (unified front of the struggle of oppressed races), created in central Vietnam in the mid-1960s and presided over by Les Kasem, an Islamic Khmer who fought under the Khmer Republic's banner. Oppressed by the Khmer Rouge, the Muslims would reemerge in 1979.[15]

At the time of the march for concord, on 11 April 1970 at the sports complex, the monarchy was banned, the republic was unofficially proclaimed, and the flag, coat of arms, and national anthem were modified. The JSRK became the Jeunesse de sauvetage (salvation youth). Of no great usefulness, it engaged in acts without political impact such as the initiation of a combatants' day on 6 January 1971, the distribution of gifts to combatants, and so on. The only active youths remained the students who turned against the regime when they saw that corruption, against which they had been fighting for several years, was increasing daily.

In March 1971 a group of intellectuals created an association, the Alliance pour la paix (alliance for peace), with the goal of rallying the various Khmer antagonists—Sihanouk loyalists, partisans of Lon Nol, and Khmer Rouge. The promoters, who were former members of the École royale d'administration, sincerely believed in contributing to the ambitious project of restoring peace. Sirik Matak, who was then interim president of the Council of Ministers (in the absence of Lon Nol, in Hawaii for treatment), ratified the creation of the organization. According to participants, Son Ngoc Thanh attempted for his part to coopt the association for political ends, but it resisted. During a two-year period, young people and administrative officials attended meetings and seminars on Cambodia's problems, meetings that brought no concrete results. The association was dissolved after a financial scandal attributed to one of its members. "Even if our association had continued to function well," one of the founding members recalled, "we could no longer do much, given the situation in the country. It was a mess; we were living materially from day to day." After 1973 the inhabitants were mainly preoccupied with survival: "We needed money to survive, and we sold whatever we had, but there were few buyers. At that time, only the officers could eat in restaurants and build villas. At the ministry, the coolies were starving."

Economically, the failure was total. The government no longer exported rice, rubber, or wood, from which it had gained most of its foreign exchange stock; it became totally dependent on American dollars. In June 1971 Sirik Matak decided to tackle the problem of prices and speculators, at the risk of making himself even more unpopular with the military, whose excesses he could not stop.

Some republicans longed for Sihanouk's return. From Phnom Penh and then from France, Son Sann, the former Sangkum prime minister, corresponded with Penn Nouth, then at Peking, hoping to bring about discussions between the two opposing sides. France served as intermediary in 1970 but without success—Sihanouk refused to negotiate. Attempts continued in 1971. According to one of the Khmer participants, Sirik Matak himself considered negotiations: "Sirik Matak was for a compromise solution, bringing Sihanouk back but imposing on him conditions that would prevent him from resuming his previous policies. It must be said that the partisans of the two men, in their confrontations, obstructed the behind-the-scenes work." Besides, the republican officers were watching. And the Khmer Rouge, for their part, were unwilling to let their standard bearer Sihanouk leave; as we shall see, he had concluded an alliance with them. The Americans hesitated. In 1972, establishing a balance sheet of men capable of assuming leadership of the state, they identified only General Sak Sutsakhan as a man without declared enemies, but he lacked the energy to redress the situation. General In Tam, despised by the army, was unsuitable, as was Son Ngoc Thanh, compromised by association with the Central Intelligence Agency (CIA). As for Sirik Matak, the only competent man of the day, they hardly took him into consideration because students and other youth had demonstrated against him, declaring him to be corrupt and despotic. Yet, as was often the case, the order to demonstrate came from above, in the event from the field marshal (or his brother?); having tasted power, he sought to undermine the popularity of his counselor, who did not share all his views. "If there were demonstrations and strikes, they were the work of some 'apprentice sorcerers,' and the rest of the crowd was nothing but sheep."[16] We may be tempted to see here the *petit frère*'s hand because, according to fellow students, "Lon Nol and Sirik Matak were like two brothers since they had studied together in the Lycée Chasseloup-Laubat in Saigon."

At approximately the same time Son Sann considered forming a third force, probably with the backing of the Americans. In France since the end of 1970, he had discussions with former colleagues who, like him, had taken refuge in Paris; no one doubted that he was contemplating action. He went to Cambodia in 1973–1974. Questioned on this, he stated that, at the request of the president of the Khmer Republic, he went on a mission of conciliation aimed at bringing Sihanouk back to power. It seems more plausible that the Americans had invited him to do so, even if Sirik Matak served as intermediary, for they controlled all of Cambodian politics. Whatever the truth of the matter may be, the Democratic party, in suspended animation since 1955, awakened and brought its support to Son Sann. "I was prevented from reaching the people," Son Sann said.[17] A witness would affirm that he acted without the consent of the government. "He believed that three groups were important: the Buddhist clergy, the parties, and the students. He met first with the young people. But the military suspected something." On 12 January 1974 at the Faculté de commerce, he gave an address on foreign aid and, Ros Chantrabot writes, "took advantage of the occasion to launch his third-force idea" (17). Although Son Sann had to leave the country, he remained in the political arena. The Cambodians had at their disposal three parties—Social Republican, Republican, and Democratic, with so many potential leaders—but this did not mean that they could choose freely among them. They were constrained to endure the malfeasance of field marshal Lon Nol and his allies, the Americans. Members of the Social Republican party alone sat in the two chambers.

The new regime that began on 18 March 1970 had little political stability. It took shape not around a republican doctrine but against Prince Sihanouk, against his authoritarianism and his alliance with the Vietnamese Communists. No one, with the possible exception of Sirik Matak, ever gave any thought to the postcoup period or envisioned any alternative solution. Isolated, the instigator of such a change could not impose his views. Where the Cambodians had destroyed, they proved unable to rebuild; they had hardly been educated to this end. In illustration of the Khmer saying, Garbage floats and gourds sink, worthless people were promoted and competent ones cast aside, which partially explains the republic's failure. Opponents remained numerous: Prince Sihanouk and the Khmer Rouge but also the elite.

## PRINCE SIHANOUK'S CHARISMA IN THE SERVICE OF THE KHMER ROUGE

At Peking the deposed leader was discreetly received, even though he was still regarded as a chief of state. Prime Minister Chou En-lai asked him if he wanted to join battle, leaving him time to think it over. On 23 March 1970 Sihanouk announced the imminent formation of a Front uni national du Cambodge (FUNC).[18] Its composition and its program (which placed the words liberty, equality, fraternity, and democracy side by side) were not made public until 5 May, at the time of the proclamation of the Gouvernement royal d'union nationale, placed under the FUNC's aegis.[19] The same individuals held posts in both bodies, with leftists (five Communists and two progressives) outnumbering those loyal to Sihanouk (five). Three former Communist ministers, Khieu Samphan, Hou Yuon, and Hu Nim, supposedly murdered by Sangkum's police, were members. The alliance with the Khmer Rouge was thus sealed. In the first speech that he gave at Peking, Sihanouk called on "all Khmer patriots to trample and chase the American imperialists out of the country. . . . Our soldiers [those of FUNC] have received the order to cease defending the borders and the national territory, to turn against their own compatriots, to pitilessly bring to heel all those who dare 'raise a finger.'"[20]

Two observations are in order here. First, Sihanouk was calling on the Khmers to turn against the Americans but also against other Khmers; the charge that he had called for civil war, which the prince denied, is thus valid. Second, "the order to cease defending the borders" means permission for

Vietnamese Communists to penetrate Cambodian territory with impunity. "In politics," a Cambodian exile commented, "it is the national interest that should take precedence and not personal opinion. Sihanouk should have stayed in France after March 1970; he would certainly have been asked to return to the country before the situation had become irreversible."

In Sihanouk's text, written in Peking, we find a very personal style alongside Communist jargon—a clear indication that Sihanouk was not entirely free in writing his speech. From that day forward, he depended on the Khmer Rouge, who exploited his popularity among the peasantry for propaganda purposes, as they did with the townspeople, who listened to him regularly on Radio Peking. The stand that he took on 23 March would prove decisive help in bringing about the final victory of the Khmer Rouge. Backed by China, the Khmer Communists knew how to take full advantage of their standard bearer Sihanouk, whom they did not permit to return to Cambodia during the republican war except for a month-long visit in 1973. This brief sojourn confirmed their fears—the prince's popularity remained intact in the countryside. In Siem Reap province enraptured peasants cheered him wildly.

By 19 March Hanoi reacted. Prime Minister Pham Van Dong gave his support to the prince. On 24–25 April the alliance among the Vietnamese and Laotian Communists on the one hand and the Khmer Rouge and the Sihanoukists on the other was made public by the meeting of the PRG, DRV, Pathet Lao, and FUNC in a summit conference of the Indochinese peoples, held in southern China. The final communiqué emphasized the unity among the four parties.[21]

What did the FUNC represent on the ground? In the beginning, it was only a handful of Sihanouk's partisans who linked up with two or three thousand Khmer Rouge in the maquis. Poorly armed and unaccustomed to fighting, the partisans had little military weight compared to their Communist comrades. Yet they had the peasantry's attention because they represented royalty. Besides, the Khmer Rouge soldiers (*yothea*) and the Vietcong who supported them in the struggle brandished the portrait of the former chief of state. The peasants naively believed that this war corresponded to Sihanouk's wishes and that the *yothea* and their Vietnamese comrades served him. The appeal launched from Peking was widely approved. Afterwards, notably after 1973, when villages, communes, and districts passed into the sole control of Khmer Rouge soldiers and cadres, the people would begin to question their sincerity. But then it was too late: solidly organized, they exacted total obedience from the people who already suffered under their abuses. Some daring souls would succeed in fleeing and thus would escape the beginnings of collectivization and the depredations.

Why, in 1970, did the prince become the ally of the Khmer Rouge whom he had fought for three years? Sihanouk himself gives a partial answer in his *Souvenirs doux et amers* (200):

> To be completely honest, my hostility toward the United States and the Free World during the 1950s and 1960s, my association with the Khmer Rouge in the early 1970s in opposition to "American imperialism," are in large measure a reaction to the numerous attacks, many of which appeared to me to be unjust or malicious, directed at me by Western newspapers. I can say, with the perspective of hindsight, that these attacks contributed mightily to turning me against the West and throwing me, during a rather long period, into the arms of the Communist world, the hypocrisy of which I have never ignored, but which, by calculation, refrained from criticizing me and sometimes showered me with compliments that struck a responsive chord.

Sihanouk did not accept his deposition, which he considered illegal based on the fact that he had been "implicitly" named chief of state for life; he intended to retake power. After six months of the republic, many in Phnom Penh would have approved of the prince's return—without his wife, Monique, and above all, without his mother-in-law. The republicans conducted a campaign to denounce the former chief of state's abuses, not without a hearty dose of calumny, which the former monarch could not allow. Just as the republic took shape in opposition to the prince and his intrigues, the prince's reaction to certain individuals determined his response to his deposition. In the midst of these campaigns, no one thought of the Khmer people and nation, of the means to save them and to oppose the lack of solidarity and national fervor. It was Cambodian society, trapped by its anachronistic values and its inability to act, that allowed political authorities to govern in accordance with their personal inclinations. It was the state, keeping the peasants in total political ignorance and with an unintended but very high rate of illiteracy, that left them no choice but naive belief in their future executioners, the Khmer Rouge. Sihanouk, without illusions about his Marxist comrades, nevertheless remained in Peking, thereby sanctioning their activities inside Cambodia. Despite his efforts to obtain the recognition of the GRUNC, the United Nations kept the republican regime of Phnom Penh within its ranks. From that time onward the head of the GRUNC remained in exile in China, as did the ministers who supported Sihanouk. Khmer Rouge leaders went back to the interior, with the exception of Ieng Sary, who returned to China in 1971 to watch over the former king. According to witnesses, Penn Nouth agreed to participate in the GRUNC against his will; moreover, he abandoned the prince's ranks after his departure from Phnom Penh in 1979 and sided with Son Sann. Several hundred Cambodians lived in Peking in late 1974—Sihanouk loyalists, Khmer Rouge, and progressives. Unity did not reign: "Sihanouk had his partisans, Penn Nouth had his, and the Khmer Rouge personnel serving at the embassy distrusted the progressive intellectuals who came to join up with the GRUNC headquarters."

Thus during the lifetime of the FUNC the Khmer Rouge, supported by China, dominated resistance against Phnom Penh and the Americans. Ieng Sary, who was already jockeying for the post of foreign minister, focused on the incumbent, the progressive Sarin Chhak, a hatred that caused him to dissociate himself from this comrade in 1979. He undertook no international action to free Sarin Chhak and his wife, whom he knew to be in the hands of the Vietnamese by 7 January 1979.

## THE WAR

When war began in April 1970, the Khmer military acted in a way that is impossible to explain or justify: they massacred Vietnamese civilians living in Cambodia, declaring that the *yuon* were Cambodia's enemies just as the Vietcong were. To be sure, many Vietnamese did help them, either from conviction or to avoid harassment. The military's first victims were in the provinces; the *yuon* residents of the Chruoy Changvar peninsula, opposite the capital, were next: bodies could be seen floating in the Mekong. For several days violence was unleashed and was not condemned by the Khmers; for most of them this bloody episode was consistent with their logic. Soldiers executed several hundred *yuon*. If foreigners had not intervened, the victims would have been even more numerous: four hundred fifty thousand Vietnamese lived on Khmer soil. American journalists (Henry Kamm among them) stopped a massacre in progress at the Université de Takeo-Kampot by threatening Commander Lon Non, the instigator of the action, telling him that they would report the story if he did not calm his unchained men. They might have disappeared along with the other victims, but the journalists were heeded. The massacres—of which reports nevertheless made their way to the West—ceased. On the grounds of a Catholic school in Phnom Penh the government opened a camp where Vietnamese from the town and from the Catholic village (seven kilometers north of Phnom Penh) took refuge while waiting until a solution could be found; the wealthiest of them purchased their tranquility. A South Vietnamese delegation came to discuss matters with the Cambodian authorities, and after a month of negotiations many Vietnamese civilians returned to Vietnam. Others took Khmer names and, thanks to their generosity toward Cambodian soldiers and police, continued their lives in Cambodia.

During the entire month of April 1970, while the war raged on the border, carnage ruled: the Vietcong made short work of these smiling and inexperienced young men, some of them armed with nothing but a stick, who left the border and plunged into the interior of the country. If the intervention by American air power stopped the massacre of Cambodian soldiers, it killed a great many civilians. It also facilitated the advance of the Vietnamese Communists and gave them an excuse vis-à-vis the West, for they had not waited for the bombs before pushing deep into Cambodia. Khmer forces were not inactive, but Prince Sihanouk's rejection of American aid in 1963 had caused him to reduce the budget of the armed forces and thus their numbers. Furthermore, the thirty thousand men enrolled had hardly had appropriate training. They had mainly built roads, except for the most competent, who had patrolled near Vietnam and Thailand. From Sihanouk's point of view, an "operetta army," as it was often called, was sufficient for a Cambodia that he wished to see neutralized. Some Khmers did not approve of the army's weakness and believed that, to avoid being attacked, a dissuasive force was necessary. Was this a sensible policy for a country flanked by two more populated, more aggressive, and better-armed countries? Sensible or not, such had been Sihanouk's reasoning, a view that led him to help those with the best chance to emerge victorious.

For the United States in the 1970s, the important thing was not to find a way to eliminate the Vietcong but to have the South Vietnamese pursue them into Khmer territory and give the illusion that the Vietnamization of the war, that is to say, the replacement of American forces by South Vietnamese soldiers, was really making progress and would thus let the GIs come home. Nor did this point of view lead the Americans to protect the lives of the Khmer peasants whose villages were cratered by the B-52's bombs. Gross mistakes added to the losses, in particular that of Neak Luong, a strategic village on the Lower Mekong, completely destroyed in 1972. The American raids on the border stopped officially on 1 July 1970, but the United States continued to supply arms, munitions, and advisers. The marshal was compelled to call on South Vietnamese soldiers for help. He did not have to ask twice. The South Vietnamese bombarded rubber plantations and pillaged the villages. Their slender, elegantly dressed silhouettes paraded arrogantly through Phnom Penh. By 1971 they were the masters of Neak Luong, and Marshal Lon Nol had to ask the Americans to make them leave. In August 1971 the Khmers and the South Vietnamese met in Saigon to determine "the schedule for the withdrawal of South Vietnamese troops stationed in Neak Luong in Prey Veng province and their replacement by Khmer troops."[22]

The Khmer people unwillingly submitted to the presence of the hereditary enemy, who simply added to their troubles; the president of the republic thus lost his scant popularity. The inhabitants endured the abuses of the Americans, the South Vietnamese, and, increasingly, the Communists, whom the certainty of victory made less cautious.

Bangkok remained more discreet. In 1970 people in Phnom Penh spoke of the probable intervention of Thai soldiers in Cambodia; it did not occur. The Thais contented themselves with training Khmer soldiers on Thai soil and sending several military advisers, notably to Siem Reap. The officers made fruitful arrangements with their Cambodian counterparts: wood and precious stones from Pailin crossed the border, bringing enormous profits to the partners. The Khmer state did not receive a single riel. Other young recruits received military training in South Vietnam.

Phnom Penh declared general mobilization on 25 June 1970. Khmer *krom*, trained by the Americans, came to help their Khmer brothers. They formed the republican army's elite troops; others joined the NLF. The absence of competent leaders meant that young republican volunteers were left to their own devices for the first months. They went off to the front the day after joining, without a single order. Later they trained in Phnom Penh, where the inhabitants watched with amusement as recruits learned to march. The civic instruction manuals for army soldiers distributed in 1970 by the FANK's training center could hardly have helped the recruits. It was a patchwork of banalities intended to motivate the army to wage a "people's war against the *thmil* (atheistic, barbaric) North Vietnamese, Vietcong, and Pathet Lao invaders," reminding them that "misguided Khmers are in effect the *thmil*'s auxiliary forces while waiting to become *thmil* themselves." It advised soldiers and noncommissioned officers to "know the postoffice box number for writing to your family" and taught them that, among other advances in world science, "beefsteak could be fabricated from stones and wood." Subsequently, the troops were victimized by dishonest officers who stole their salaries. The numbers were inflated by inclusion of "phantom soldiers," unreported combat deaths and recruits who never joined. Those who did join pillaged in order to eat, and their officers did not interfere. From December 1970 onward the *Revue de l'armée* reported malnutrition among the troops. In 1971 troop inspections were planned, particularly to cross dead soldiers' names off the lists and to ensure that aid went directly to victim's families without going through unit commanders. In January 1972 FANK's general staff announced sanctions against officers who did not pay salaries on time. These make-believe measures remained dead letters, the army being corrupt at all command levels.

Faced with such inequalities, depredations, and incompetence, some townspeople joined the guerrillas, followed by a group of intellectuals after the attack on the Pochentong airport in January 1971. Greater and greater numbers of people who were without work made their ways to the forest and became so many artisans of FUNC's victory. On two occasions angry students, stirred up by high-level authorities, went on strike. In 1972 the minister of education and one of his colleagues were taken hostage and shot. After the bombardment of the Chamcar Mon palace in 1974, new demonstrations broke out and were suppressed by Prime Minister Son Ngoc Thanh. Banners condemning corruption and demanding the departure of Vietnamese Communists decorated the streets of the capital. The atmosphere was highly charged. Conversely, villagers continued to pour into Phnom Penh. Several teachers, Ith Sarin among them, returned to Phnom Penh after a few months with the Khmer Rouge; they expressed their disagreement with the severity of the regime that the Communists were preparing; Ith Sarin's booklet published in 1973 attracted little attention.[23] The massacre of the Oudong high school students in December 1972 and that of the inhabitants of Sasar Sdam in Siem Reap in 1974 failed to alarm the elite and the military and governmental authorities. The highest ranking individuals were certain that the Americans would whisk them away in helicopters if things did not work out. Others quietly made arrangements to go abroad. This time the Khmers did not succeed in uniting against the Khmer Rouge nor even in coming to an agreement to help them present a strong and united front for the initiation of negotiations.

Opinion united on a single point, the neutralization of Angkor; the conservator Bernard Philippe Groslier, the government, the students, the women's association, and Sihanouk—all called for it. But in vain: the Khmer Rouge refused this proposal. And they turned down the marshal's request for the return of the International Control Commission, to be composed of representatives of countries more neutral than those that had served during the 1960s. After the signature of the Paris Accords between the Americans and the Vietnamese Communists in January 1973, the Khmers counted on the withdrawal of foreign troops from their soil, as stipulated in the accords. When it came to nothing, the president of the republic launched an appeal for "the strict application of the Geneva Accords of 1954." In the midst of this disorder, the government nonetheless passed democratic measures: the creation of unions; the abolition of certain rituals pertaining to etiquette; the abolition of *Samdech* status for civilians, a title thereafter reserved for monks; and the reopening of the École nationale d'administration, closed under Sangkum for political reasons. But the government also examined proposals whose urgency and practicality appear questionable: the creation of a free zone in Sihanoukville; the building of a Phnom Penh–Saigon railroad; and the construction of an Asian highway.

During the five years of fighting, Phnom Penh announced practically nothing but successes, speaking of republican revolution and denying the existence of civil war. Officially, the only fighting in Cambodia involved foreign aggression against the Khmers. On the Communist side, this view was nearly true in the early period, and the Vietcong dominated the conflict militarily until 1972. The Khmer Rouge could not have won without their help. On the republican side, however, the official view ignored the presence of American advisers and air raids, which began again for six months in 1973. After that the Khmers—governmental forces and guerrillas—were face to face.

After the settlement of the Vietnamese problem in 1973, the Khmer Rouge refused to negotiate with the Americans and quarreled with their Vietnamese comrades-in-arms, who temporarily stopped deliveries of arms to the Khmer guerrillas over the Ho Chi Minh trail. The Khmer Rouge, wanting to win the victory by themselves, forced the Vietcong to leave Khmer soil, which they did more or less willingly. The Vietcong and Prince Sihanouk certainly contributed to the Khmer Rouge's victory; likewise, the Khmer Rouge found moral support among the starving people and the intellectuals disillusioned with the republic. Yet every issue of the *Revue de l'armée* mentioned the imminent collapse of the enemy, its great losses, and its extremely low morale. Although the Khmer Republic's army was suffering striking defeats—Chenla I, Chenla II, Pochentong airport, and many others—every battle was presented as a victory. The Khmers nevertheless fought courageously as long as they had faith. Officers made names for themselves, and soldiers acted like real patriots. But the system was undermined, and the army fell apart. The authorities learned of this state of affairs and began to make peace proposals.

In October 1972 Phnom Penh informed the United Nations of a first peace proposal. Hanoi refused it, declaring that the conflict was a civil war among the Khmers. In January 1973 the marshal unilaterally ordered a cease-fire, but the republicans alone observed it. In March 1973 the government announced possible elections in which the Khmer Rouge would be able to participate. The latter, of course, did not reply. The Khmer Rouge hoped to win the war on the ground thanks to the republicans' failures and to the support given by the people to Sihanouk, whom the Khmer Rouge claimed as their patron, but they had little chance of winning power through elections. In July 1973 the government renewed its call for negotiations; FUNC refused. "Beginning in 1973, the Khmer Rouge army was sacrificed," Khmer observers would say. "The more bombings there were, the more the soldiers advanced. The Khmer Rouge wanted to break the opposite camp psychologically, and the number of deaths mattered little." The outcome had not yet been decided. Students gathered in the Boeung Trabek reeducation camp reported that, in 1976 in the course of a seminar, Khieu Samphan confessed to them that "until 1972 victory was not foreseeable and that they had found themselves faced with the following dilemma: to accept either Vietnamese domination or the American presence. But the adroit and clairvoyant party finally resolved the problem by expelling both enemies."

Finally, in July 1974, acting on the advice of the American ambassador, John Gunther Dean, the president of the republic announced that he would negotiate unconditionally with the other side—in vain. For his part, Prince Sihanouk requested a meeting with Henry Kissinger in 1973 but was rebuffed. Against the Khmer Rouge's wishes, the Chinese tried to help him negotiate with the United States. The Khmer Rouge, as obstinate as Washington, blocked any limited possibilities of accord. When Washington finally realized that the sole solution was to have Sihanouk brought back to Phnom Penh, it was 11 April 1975. On 12 April American embassy personnel left Cambodia. The Khmer Rouge were at the gates of Phnom Penh and had no intention of negotiating.

With the Americans gone, the republican forces, having no other alternative except to fall into the hands of the Khmer Rouge, whose cruelty they knew too well, desperately fought on for another week. But Phnom Penh fell on 17 April 1975, happily at first, although its joy would later turn to horror. The republican war had cost between six hundred thousand and seven hundred thousand lives.

GOVERNMENTAL REACTIONS

The Khmer Republic had had its partisans. Regional alliances were thus modified: Saigon and Bangkok renewed the diplomatic relations with Phnom Penh that had been broken off under the Sangkum regime. The other countries then in the Association of Southeast Asian Nations (ASEAN), Thailand, Malaysia, Singapore, Indonesia, and the Philippines, maintained neighborly relations.

China and the Republic of North Vietnam on the one hand, and the United States on the other, who supported opposite sides, exercised their influence, as we have seen. From 1973 onward China, however, was convinced that only the return of Sihanouk to Phnom Penh could save Cambodia from disaster. Moscow prudently replaced its ambassador to the Khmer Republic with a chargé d'affaires, at the same time supporting the FUNC. This "treason" caused the Khmer Rouge to move Soviet diplomats along with the other foreigners to the French embassy, where it assembled non-Khmers.

France was among the states concerned about Cambodia. In view of the misfortunes of the Khmer people after the coup d'état, France had suggested a kind of international conference on Cambodia. Washington turned a deaf ear, and Sihanouk showed little enthusiasm.[24] The French ambassador in Peking regularly met with Sihanouk and transmitted news supplied by the latter about the GRUNC and FUNC to Paris. On the one hand, the prince's opinions had little political weight because the Khmer Rouge decided everything without asking his advice—in 1970 they had not even allowed him to attend the funeral of General de Gaulle, whom he much admired. On the other hand, these same Khmer Rouge leaders screened the information supplied to the prince about the Cambodian guerrillas. For his part, the chargé d'affaires on mission in Cambodia seemed to be ignorant of what was happening among the Khmer maquis, unaware of the divisions into clans, which were quite real among the soldiers of FUNC and the members of GRUNC, and were spoken about by everyone. In early January 1975, while the capital lived out its last few months as a republic, under rocket fire and increasingly threatened, a misplaced optimism reigned in the embassy: the massacres reported by refugees were credited to accidents or exaggerations. French diplomats uttered the same reassuring words that could be heard in Phnom Penh: once the Khmers found themselves alone with one another, reconciliation would follow. Paris lacked any sort of information. It did not change its orientation until one week before the Khmer Rouge's victory, when it finally recognized GRUNC.

## THE KHMERS' RATIONALIZATION OF THE COUP D'ÉTAT AND THE WAR

Once the initial anger and uncertainty had passed, everyone tried to explain the changes that had occurred. Even the most reticent recognized that there had been signs: "When I was little, I often heard predictions by the *cak kompi*.[25] I remember one of them: black crows would take off from the forest—harbingers of troubles, famine, and massacres. Several years later, they would return to the forest. These black crows obviously designated the Khmer Rouge."

Numerous predictions circulated in Cambodian circles, many of them of unknown origin: a Khmer king, called the *sdach piel* (wicked king), would mount a white horse and fly off in the direction of China. For some, he was Pol Pot; for others, Sihanouk. With subsequent events to support their claims, the Cambodians reported the following: "Houses will be empty; there will be rice, but people will have nothing to eat." "When the blood reaches the level of an elephant's stomach, Saigon will fall, Phnom Penh will be destroyed, confusion will reign in Bangkok, and happiness will return to Angkor Wat." After the fact, Khmers saw in these bloody words the prediction, either of the massacre of Vietnamese civilians in 1970, or the Khmer Rouge regime with evacuation, famine, and executions. They were attributed to Put, a sort of Khmer Nostradamus whose prophecies were recorded in a collection—*Put Tumneay*. The printed text does not conform completely to what is passed on by word of mouth, and it concerns the period when the Buddhist era comes to an end in 2500, that is, in 1956 of the Christian era. Some prefer to see 1956 as an error in dating but remain attentive to what they consider as ineluctable for their country in the short term:

> Then, King Naong Snao will lead his troops to the Four-Arms [Phnom Penh]—exactly in the middle of the Buddhist era. They will go on killing one another for seven years until the blood reaches the level of an elephant's stomach, that is, from Boeung Srang [about thirty kilometers from Phnom Penh] and in the direction of Kompong Tuol [near Pochentong]. The troubles will reach Phnom Penh and its vicinity. Then the wicked atheists will go until Lovea Em [Kandal province], and then they will rejoin the river of blood, that is, Chadomuk [Phnom Penh].[26]

Today some intellectuals still fear that the foretold blood is an indication of new conflicts between Khmers but also between Cambodia, Vietnam, and Thailand.

For one week in 1969 a comet lit up the night over Phnom Penh: "The Mekong will run with blood," Khmers said. In February 1970 a man climbed up to the royal pole planted along the river in front of the floating house where the royal family and its guests stand during public ceremonies. He went into a trance, claiming to be possessed by the spirit of Sivotha, Prince Norodom's half brother. He asked to speak to the queen mother, saying that the throne was at risk and that war was imminent for Cambodia.

This last sign is perhaps the most easily explained: the individual came from Roleak Kang Cheung in Kompong Speu, where there was a Khmer Rouge base. He may have simulated the trance to reinforce the Cambodians' beliefs in destiny and fatalism, which makes them accept adversity. Whether the other signs were providential or invented, Khmers—still very much attached to the ancient beliefs—remained easily influenced, particularly peasants. Even townspeople believed in these predictions.[27]

This belief partially explains the absence of spontaneous demonstrations under the Khmer Republic. Rural people who took refuge on the border in the late 1970s said, moreover, that people living under the Khmer Rouge were waiting for the end of their reign, as foretold. As a Khmer proverb had it, When there is no longer a king, anything is possible. Because of the population transfers, the absence of personal houses and rice fields, and the cadres' prohibitions, "new people" (to be discussed in chapter 7) ceased to honor the spirits protecting the habitation or the harvest, or those responsible for illness. Thus they endured the Khmer Republic and then Democratic Kampuchea, convinced that the prince would return and they would live normally once again.

Today, it is up to Cambodians to judge the coup d'état: only those who have lived within a system can evaluate its benefits, its impact, and its dangers. Nevertheless, if the coup was necessary, it occurred at a most unfortunate juncture, when the Vietnamese Communists were in the process of negotiating with the Americans who were looking for a way to disengage; they found it by bringing Cambodia into the war. The new regime benefited not only those who promoted it but also their foreign allies.

## THE CAMBODIANS OF PARIS

Khmers studying abroad reacted to the coup d'état in various ways. In France there was excitement, especially among the left-wing militants. In Cambodia most people could not express themselves or even acquire a solid political training. They enthusiastically accepted the ideological structure offered them by the Khmer Communists and were convinced that the Communists were doing something useful for their country.

### THE STUDENT ASSOCIATIONS

Early in 1970 there were only two organizations in Paris: one was a group of Communist and progressive elements (Union des étudiants khmers, or UEK); the other favored the government (Association générale des Cambodgiens de France, or AGCAF), an assembly of Sangkum's partisans as well as Sihanouk's opponents, progressives, and people who were politically indifferent, compelled to belong in order to keep their scholarships. Owing to the changes that had occurred in Cambodia, the political tendencies of each side would assert themselves.

Aside from the minority of right-wing students, the others for the most part reacted negatively. The UEK declared against the American presence; Sihanouk loyalists protested; the progressives, who had been concerned for several months, expressed new fears: "Emotionally, I was against the coup d'état. Despite its tensions, Cambodia was an oasis of peace. I did not suspect that we would soon be at war," a progressive belonging to the Union nationale des étudiants khmers (national union of Khmer students, or UNEK) recalls. The AGCAF centrists regretted the eviction of the prince:

"Sihanouk no longer had a hold on power; the disappearance of the left wing in parliament weakened him. So he looked for diversion by directing films. . . . I was shocked when he was deposed; I said to myself that it was the end of an era, that life would be thrown into confusion, that we could not go back again. Now, one supported the right or the left."

Partisans of social progress stated: "We had always been against Sihanouk's policies. When the coup d'état occurred, we said that it was going to be worse with Lon Nol. . . . We did not think that Sihanouk, in allying with the Khmer Rouge, would change, for the simple reason that one does not get wine from a cow."

To the students, Sihanouk seemed locked into behavior and practices from which he could not escape. The AGCAF was the first to experience a crisis. On the very day of Sihanouk's overthrow, 18 March 1970, elements of the extreme right (including Long Pet and the virulent anti-Communists) left the group in order to create the Association des patriotes cambodgiens à l'étranger (association of Cambodian patriots abroad, or APCE). From the beginning they declared for the proclamation and the construction of a Khmer republic. Openly anti-FUNC, they published several editions of a bulletin of which no trace remains, and no more was heard of them. The movement disintegrated after the several-months' visit of one of its members to Cambodia. He could not help observing the new regime's failure: "We were disappointed; it was a lost cause. The republicans were cretins, incompetents; only Sirik Matak proved worthy and meritorious."

Progressive though non-Communist elements—who made up the centralist wing—were next to leave the AGCAF, on 19 March 1970, to form the Association des Khmers de France (association of Khmers in France, or AKF), which desired the modernization of the country and social justice. With the coup d'état, legality had been destroyed by Lon Nol, some said; one could not remain in the AGCAF because, after mid-1969, the AGCAF's right wing no longer supported Sihanouk but rather Lon Nol. Approximately thirty persons joined the AKF, which criticized the general's policies. "On the ideological level, we were close to the Union nationale des étudiants khmers. We advocated armed struggle in Cambodia." As with the APCE, there seems to have been no breakup.

The APCE and AKF both refused to fight alongside the Vietnamese and to consider them as allies. The most neutral members of the AGCAF continued to militate under the same label. They prepared a statement, dated 30 March 1970, which appeared in the newspaper *Le Monde*, denouncing the politics of the blocs, imperialism in all its forms—particularly Vietnamese annexationism—condemning the Khmer politicians responsible for the war, and placing themselves on the side of the Khmer people in demanding

Cambodia for Cambodians. After the setbacks suffered by the APCE, the AGCAF, infiltrated by right-wing elements, lost the principal neutralists, who resigned on 22 March 1973. Without its active members the group slowly fell apart.

Despite apparent unity, the UEK did not escape dissension: "The UEK supported armed struggle, but we questioned their advocacy of a common fight alongside the Vietnamese. This led to the split." Initially, the young people of the UEK and nonaffiliated individuals solicited by the former to join envisioned giving the association a less radical turn. On 1 May 1970, the general assembly of the UEK was to elect a new executive committee:

> We proposed young candidates in order to counter the older ones. We fell several votes short of winning. We decided that things could not continue like that because the seniors remaining on the executive committee were ruling on the candidatures and rejecting the young ones. Seeing that we would never be in the majority, in May 1970 we, about thirty members of the UEK, left the association. We found Ok Sakun, Thiounn Mumm, Toch Kam Doeurn, and others too sectarian; that is why we formed the UNEK, under Chinese influence. It was in fact a split between the senior members of the UEK, who were then pro-Soviet and pro-Vietnamese, and the junior members, who were rather favorable to China.

At Lyons the Ouk Thol brothers attempted to create a Sihanoukist national front several months after the coup. It is not known what came of this except that they did not belong to the FUNC. In East Germany the UJK divided into two branches, one pro–Lon Nol, the other pro–Khmer Rouge: "From that moment onward, the other parties were considered rivals. We didn't talk to one another anymore, and former friends became enemies." One final change would determine the positions of the politicized students' groups for a long time to come.

### THE CREATION OF A FUNC BRANCH IN PARIS

In order to assemble those who supported the anti-imperialist struggle, left-wing students created, immediately after the coup d'état, the Comité des patriotes khmers à l'étranger (committee of Khmer patriots abroad), which addressed a message of support to the FUNC. The UEK, UNEK, AKF, and the centralist wing of the AGCAF were all represented.

> In 1971 Ieng Sary asked each left-wing student association to delegate three or four representatives to go to Peking to participate in a conference on Marxism. There were two students from Yugoslavia,

one from Czechoslovakia, two from the German Democratic Republic, three from Paris, two from Moscow, and three or four from North Korea. The seminars lasted eight days. The principal themes dealt with general politics, the peasants' class struggle, and the Front's program. In particular, we discussed the meaning of the terms democracy, revolutionary youth, revolutionary intellectual, centralism, and so on. I had the impression of learning something, of having a line for carrying out our action. . . . Ieng Sary told us that the multiplicity of parties was playing into the hands of the right, that dissension among the groups was the result of French imperialist policy. . . . At the end of our meeting in Peking, the Fédération de la Jeunesse khmère d'Europe was suppressed, and henceforth GRUNC's minister of education, Chan Yuran, made the decisions concerning young people. . . . At that time, all of us tried to do our self-criticism in front of Ieng Sary, whom we perceived to be powerful. Thus, there was agreement on creating a FUNC committee in Paris. Senior members In Sokan and Ok Sakun were sent there to create unity.

The former represented the FUNC and the latter GRUNC. On their return to Paris, the associations' leaders convinced their members that the multiplicity of associations harmed the Cambodian cause.

The FUNC committee was born late in 1971. The UEK and the UNEK merged into the committee; only five to six members of the AKF did the same. The survivors of the AGCAF did not rally, with the exception of one member, an admirer of Sihanouk. Disagreements occurred: some students strongly opposed to Sihanouk did not want to rally to the FUNC, while other hard-core anti-Communists expressed fears about the Khmer Rouge's intentions. Moderates (Khieu Samphan, Hou Yuon, and Hu Nim) were placed in the forefront, and they finally reached agreement.

In this period politicized Khmers living in France defined themselves in relation to American imperialism—for or against. Those who wanted to remain neutral or desired simply the independence of Cambodia in the context of neutrality were submerged by one or the other; they allowed themselves to be manipulated or indeed stopped all political activity.

The young militants, most of them sincere in their convictions, lived through this period in a mood of exaltation. They had above all social demands to formulate and lined up against the Sangkum regime. Some, of peasant origins, had personally suffered from inequalities in Cambodia. A student of modest means from the countryside reported: "Since I was poor, my parents could not buy me the *yuvan* [junior member of JSRK] uniform. At school, they therefore decided not to give me a scholarship for the lycée." Rice growers depended on the goodwill of the Chinese usurer who purchased their harvest at a low price in order to reimburse himself for loans. Likewise, farmers along the Mekong's banks depended on Khmer or Sino-Khmer owners: "In the village, everyone knew that the rich exploited us, but if someone raised his voice to express disagreement on the buying price for our products, he would not receive land to plant the tobacco from which we lived. . . . The poor who were exploited by the rich cried, but they did not experience the situation as a class struggle; they did not know Marxism."

The majority of the students came from well-to-do families. Some, such as Hou Yuon and Hu Nim, were truly concerned about popular well-being, according to progressives. At the time, many saw in Khieu Samphan the incarnation of pure patriotism: his father a magistrate, himself a minister for several years, he had not hesitated to abandon the privileges of the city for the discomfort of the maquis. A number of young people would say: "The Khmer Rouge leaders lured us by giving Khieu Samphan, Hou Yuon, Hu Nim as examples." And then another would say: "We must remember that, at the time, the French Communists and Socialists had elaborated a common program. For us they constituted the French left; within the Khmer left, our position was somewhat comparable to that of the French Socialists vis-à-vis the French left."

Furthermore, young Khmers had no experience with politics. Only a few former Democrats and the handful of Communists who manipulated the young people had a concept of political power. Given their traditional education, students found it normal to follow the advice of their elders who seemed sincere and invariably had an advanced degree, be it a thesis on political economy or a diploma from the polytechnical school, as in Thiounn Mumm's case. The latter impressed only a fraction of the youths because, married to a French woman, he lived in the suburbs of Paris. Overall, the young people preferred Khieu Samphan and his friends who worked on the spot. Among Khmer Communists, however, Thiounn Mumm seems to have best understood Marxism; he coldly analyzed Cambodian society and wanted to raise the educational level of the people. The support that young Khmer progressives living in Paris gave to the Khmer Rouge movement (that is, the FUNC's left wing) logically derived from the system of education given them at home and their lack of political training. It also represented the first time that they could manifest a personal political viewpoint. They thus may have been intoxicated by the opportunity to act and displayed an enthusiasm as great as the previous forced inertia. Moreover, few of them had the political understanding necessary to create an independent left-wing movement. They tried to do so with the UNEK, but the Khmer Rouge, better organized, won out when they created the FUNC committee. They thus offered a readymade structure that the progressives joined, unaware of the ideological danger or seeing no other way to defend their country. The future leaders of the Khmer Rouge were no longer in Paris; their younger comrades, blander though dogmatic, did not seem as dangerous as they would later prove to be.

The second component of the FUNC grouped partisans of Prince Sihanouk. The appointment of the former leader of Cambodia to the head of the GRUNC led some of them to join the Parisian FUNC. Likewise, the appointment of Sarin Chhak, whom the youth say was an honest, moderate individual concerned with social progress, to the head of GRUNC's foreign ministry brought an additional guarantee. Others followed the activities of the movement without joining it. The republicans, it goes without saying, remained apart from this outburst of enthusiasm, without succeeding in counterbalancing the FUNC. To be sure, the behavior of the Phnom Penh government did not help them gain the confidence of the youth. Only the AGCAF attempted to subsist but could not withstand internal dissensions.

At the FUNC, union or at least unity reigned. Two or three hundred members—supporters of Sihanouk, progressives, and Communists—met every Saturday at the place de Barcelone and then at Arcueil, the headquarters of the Comité des patriotes khmers à l'étranger. The Communists, especially In Sokan, led the debates. The students discussed the misdeeds of the Lon Nol "clique" and the Americans, the victories gained inside Cambodia by the guerrillas, the high political consciousness of the people, and their duty, as intellectuals, to act. After 1972 the FUNC eliminated the scholarships that it had been distributing to students since 1970, thanks to Chinese aid. The GRUNC mission, located at the place de Barcelone, created all sorts of paid positions. The majority of the militant students left their studies and instead composed and distributed tracts and spent their evenings listening to interminable speeches. The more motivated were given responsibilities: "I was in charge of a geographical sector, and I went from door to door to see the Khmers arriving in France. I had doors slammed in my face." In the German Democratic Republic,

> since we could not conduct political activities inside the UJK, we created a new association, the Association des Khmers nationalistes, to support the FUNC. We were one dozen members in contact with Paris, the center of Khmer youth in Europe. Then, after the seminar in Peking, the associations of Europe (except Paris) joined us and decided to create a European movement to support the FUNC.

> [In 1972, other students said,] Ieng Sary came to lead a seminar in Albania. There were two Khmer students from Romania, two from the GDR, and about thirty from France. It was the Communist lead-

ers, In Sokan and Ok Sakun, who selected the students. . . . Ieng
Sary's idea was to inform and politicize the young people. He gave
us a report on the situation in Cambodia, on the exploits of the combatants, on GRUNC's foreign policy; he used the sixties as the starting point for Cambodian history and evoked Samlaut. He condemned
the misery of the peasants, in Ratanakiri I think, under Sangkum.
He did not openly attack the prince, but one felt that he did not
agree with him. . . . In theory, there was to be a debate after each
theme, but people remained rather passive. Ieng Sary did not dare
use the term Communist; he spoke of the struggle for liberation,
and it was under that banner that one marched. One sensed, however, that the orientation was Communist. Monique's two sons,
Sihamoni and Narindrapong, did not know Cambodian letters
very well, and Ieng Sary told them that it might be time to learn to
write. He seemed to be more or less jealous of Sihanouk's fame and
desirous of pointing out the importance of the militants of the interior, such as himself and later Khieu Samphan. Sihanouk was in Albania, but he did not attend the seminar. He met the president of
Albania.

Similarly, Ieng Sary, Ieng Thirith, and Khieu Samphan came to speak at
Bucharest in 1973. Khieu Samphan's presence reassured the moderate
intellectuals. However, "one sensed Ieng Sary's brutality and ambition. He
told us, 'The combatants are forced to live in holes to avoid American bombs.
You understand that, after such sufferings, Cambodia can never be the same
again.' Instead of holding the Americans responsible, it was us, the participants, whom he was blaming. Listening to him, we sensed that he wanted
to take revenge on us; he frightened me."

Aside from the Khmer Rouge cadres and several opportunists, the students sincerely wanted to build an independent Cambodia, cleansed of all
corruption, in which social justice would reign. The negative evolution of
the republican regime only reinforced their ideals. Politically speaking,
"Sihanouk, of course, represented the center. But he had held power for
sixteen years after independence and had not succeeded. I thought that the
center might not work in a country so torn between the Americans and the
nearby Vietcong."

Following tradition, the prince's supporters relied on him. The progressives considered France, where they lived, to be the model of social success,
not realizing that an underdeveloped country such as Cambodia could not
set up an analogous system of social welfare overnight. Nor did they
understand that their Communist elders were more avid for power than for

reforms. Most of them imagined that a moderate regime promoting social justice would spring from the alliance of the Khmer Rouge with Prince Sihanouk.

For the adherents of FUNC (Communists, progressives, Sihanouk loyalists), there was no ambiguity regarding the nature of the war. "We were sure that the resistance would neither submit to Lon Nol—because the people were for Sihanouk—nor to the Vietnamese, because we trusted the intellectuals who led the guerrillas (Khieu Samphan and his friends). In our minds, it was a struggle among Cambodians. . . . We relied on the indigenous forces, on the resistance."

Immediately after the coup d'état, the Khmers positioned themselves alongside or against the Americans, who were accused of involvement in the conspiracy. Shortly later many declared themselves anti-imperialists, the enemy being above all the republican regime. Whatever their ideological identification, the Cambodians fought to eliminate the rival Khmer faction: Prince Sihanouk and his partisans wanted to crush the republicans and found a new system in which all people of goodwill would have a place. The progressives worked in the same spirit, differing only in that they were wary of the prince's feudal behavior and did not believe that he could change. In their view, the presence of the Khmer Rouge would help prevent a return to the practices of the Sangkum regime. The Khmer Rouge sought to exclude the moderates (Sihanouk loyalists and progressives) and above all Lon Nol's supporters from the Marxist regime that they were preparing to establish. The republicans' main objective was to repel the Vietnamese, but they also openly opposed the Communists and therefore opposed the Khmer Rouge as well. The Americans simply catalyzed ideological hatreds and rancor.

In Paris the Communists controlled the FUNC. Aside from their structure, they brandished the names of several partisans who had not waited for March 1970 to take to the maquis. "Sihanouk was the champion of anti-imperialism at a certain time. After the coup d'état, that was no longer sufficient. One had to have an overall conception of Cambodian organization for the future, and Sihanouk had no specific plan." These youths demanded a social program promised them by the UEK's leaders:

> We supported Sihanouk because of the coup d'état, and he was at the head of the FUNC, supported by Khieu Samphan. We supported him on the tactical level because he was rallying the resistance forces, but he was disliked by the majority of the students. And above all there were the combatants. . . . They represented an opposition. We placed our confidence in them. . . . In 1970–1971 the Khmer Rouge told us in the meetings in Paris that people were

taking to the forest to fight at Sihanouk's side to defend Cambodia, but they lacked a program and were quickly taken in by the Khmer Rouge system.

The Khmer Rouge took care not to reveal that they were murdering as many of the Sihanoukist guerrillas as possible. Thus, deprived of all contact with the rebels and relying on a handful of intellectuals whom they considered honest, the progressives—who formed the majority of the Parisian FUNC—helped their Communist elders. Further, "the experience of China, an essentially agricultural country that seemed to have made a success of its revolution, was inspirational."

Many former members of the UEK had affinities with the USSR. After the creation of the FUNC committee, they made a shift:

> from Soviet revisionism to a pro-Chinese attitude by means of self-criticism sessions, intended to destroy the Khmers' inferiority complex vis-à-vis the Vietnamese. . . . From the moment when Ieng Sary, representing the resistance inside Cambodia, stressed the value of the Cambodian people, he stimulated nationalistic and patriotic feelings. And we asked ourselves, why not? . . . The Lon Nol group claimed that the resistance was entirely in the hands of the Vietnamese, that few Cambodians were involved. Ieng Sary wanted to convince us to the contrary, and we strongly agreed because we sought an independent Cambodia, without any foreign presence, even a friendly one.

Witnesses nevertheless confirmed that Vietcong participated in the battles:

> In 1971 some youths came to France after completing their military service. Some of them had been to the front, where they had seen many Vietnamese. But even if we had doubts, we had to say that the resistance was Cambodian. After all, we could not say the same thing Lon Nol's people did, for, once with the FUNC, we had to follow the common, official line. We asserted that the Cambodian resistance existed, even though we had no proof.

Meanwhile, the right-wing opposition, albeit in an unorganized fashion, was developing in Paris, and antagonism emerged several times at the Pavillon du Cambodge (Cité universitaire), which brought together all political factions.

### THE PAVILLON DU CAMBODGE AFFAIR

Inaugurated in 1957, the Cambodian pavilion of the Cité universitaire had more than two hundred rooms, in which organizations held their political activities. New developments in the Vietnam war made the climate of the

Pavillon du Cambodge uncomfortable and difficult, particularly after 1965. Sarin Chhak, appointed director in that year, told the students, in essence: "I am here to deal with the problems of the students but not with politicking. I want no fights. I respect your ideas; respect mine." He lasted only one year. According to the students, Sihanouk was jealous of the confidence that the elite had in him. Sihanouk appointed Sarin Chhak ambassador in Cairo, and Prince Sisowath Essaro succeeded him in 1966 (until January 1973). At the same time in Phnom Penh the right took power, which fanned the quarrels among the associations in Paris, each of which had representatives on the pavilion's committee.

Management of the Pavillon du Cambodge proved delicate. The Cambodians did not respect all the Cité universitaire's rules. In particular, they did not pay for their rooms regularly, even though the Maison internationale had agreed not to increase the rental rates. They settled in with wives and children and stayed far longer than the authorized three years of residence (as did clandestine residents, of course). Problems arose between the pavilion's administrators and residents. Nevertheless, while courtesy did not always prevail, a relative calm lasted until March 1970. "After the coup d'état, the Pavillon du Cambodge's committee met. We could not issue a communiqué because Long Pet [of the AGCAF's right wing] did not want to condemn the coup d'état, whereas the UEK denounced Lon Nol and the Americans. They then quarreled."

For the moment, it was of no consequence. The first brawl broke out in September 1973 between UEK members and some republicans, resulting in several trivial injuries. Then an incident set off the powder keg. Prince Sisowath Methavi, a military attaché, returned to Peking. The right and left fought over his apartment; each wanted to occupy the premises, which were Cambodian property. Aided by an officer who supported Sihanouk and had rallied to the FUNC, the left was victorious. The GRUNC mission, drawn only from Communists and progressives, then moved in. The second scuffle occurred on 18 March 1971, when the administrator of the pavilion celebrated the anniversary of the coup d'état in the presence of foreign dignitaries (French, American, and South Vietnamese). Several shots were fired and a few fleshwounds resulted, but the person responsible could not be determined. In 1971 and 1972 the atmosphere grew more tense; insults were common. The Khmer Rouge and the republicans continually harassed one another. During the night of 7– 8 January 1973 a fight broke out. The French police arrested twenty-seven students belonging to the FUNC; released several hours later, they returned to the Cambodian pavilion. Once again shots rang out, causing one death. According to witnesses, the republicans were armed with rifles, and the leftists carried swords and shards of glass.

The Pavillon du Cambodge closed its doors. A trial sentenced a nonresident to one year in prison. Rumors were heard about perjured witnesses; it was said that the true perpetrator left by plane the day after his crime. No official clarification followed.[28]

From this date forward, the building has remained unoccupied. France cannot agree to receive Khmer students again because it recognizes neither Heng Samrin's government in Phnom Penh nor the anti-Vietnamese coalition (the GCKD; to be discussed in chapter 9); it thus has no official interlocutor with which to conclude the necessary accords.[29]

# 7    The Khmer Rouge Genocide

For five years, from March 1970 to April 1975, the Khmer Rouge—who numbered approximately two to three thousand armed men in 1970—conducted an intense propaganda campaign among the peasants by exploiting Sihanouk's popularity. Some of his partisans left the cities and joined the guerrillas. Refugees reported that until 1972 members of the Vietcong also displayed pictures of the former chief of state in the villages.[1] Before the peasants' eyes the FUNC therefore set out two guarantees: the presence of a leader of royal essence, Prince Sihanouk (thus legitimizing the movement), and the activity of Sihanouk's soldiers, the Khmer *rumdâh*. Nevertheless the Khmer Communists, once powerful, eliminated as many of the Khmer *rumdâh* as possible, for the latter were well received by the population.

The Vietminh Khmers, the roughly one thousand former Khmer *issarak* who were exiled to North Vietnam in 1954 after the Geneva Accords, began to return after 1967 to help the Khmer Rouge. Some of them, suspected of working for Vietnam, were murdered in the maquis. Others fled to Vietnam in 1977 and 1978 in order to avoid the same fate.

The role of the Vietcong had been decisive in the victory, as Norodom Sihanouk explains: "The Khmer Rouge and I had the Vietminh with us, and that is why we vanquished Lon Nol."[2] In fact, the Vietcong started and developed the conflict from 1970 until 1972, as border residents attest. In the meantime, the Khmer Rouge had no trouble recruiting in the name of Sihanouk and of opposition to the republicans. The 1975 victory was above all a Khmer victory; the final offensive was unleashed earlier than expected, precisely in order to prevent the Vietnamese, busy taking Saigon, from entering Phnom Penh alongside the Khmers.

When the Khmer Rouge invested Phnom Penh on 17 April 1975, there were still Khmer *rumdâh* and Khmer-Vietminh with them. The Khmer Rouge leaders, that is, the Cambodian Communists who had remained in the forest since the 1960s, were themselves divided. Rivalries and conflicts would rapidly arise, from which Pol Pot's clan emerged victorious.

## THE TRUE LEADERS

### ANGKAR

This was the first word the revolutionaries learned. It means "the organization." Omnipresent, Angkar long embodied an effective and invisible power to which everyone owed total obedience. In September 1977 Pol Pot revealed its true nature: it was purely and simply the political bureau of the central committee of the Communist party.

### THE MODERATES

Hou Yuon and Hu Nim, respected by many progressive intellectuals, did not survive the regime. Hou Yuon, a native of Kompong Cham, married a young girl whose parents owned a pharmaceutical storehouse. "Hou Yuon's father had arranged the union; because of this marriage, he was at odds with the party he belonged to." Having a doctoral degree in law on the Cambodian peasantry and great interest in the problem of cooperatives, he sincerely desired to improve the lot of the Cambodian peasants.[3] He was well regarded in his village, where he went every year to attend a Buddhist celebration: "he was sensitive to life." He taught French in the Lycée Kambu Both and was recognized as having a powerful personality. "Hou Yuon had read extensively.  He said we mustn't confuse suppressing the bourgeois class with eliminating the bourgeois." During the war, he went to Peking several times: "When Hou Yuon came to the political seminars, in 1973–1974, he said: 'If Phnom Penh falls, we'll go there to work; we'll build a new structure.' I believe he wasn't informed about the evacuation until the last minute." After the victory, he went to his native village in Kompong Cham. When he returned to Phnom Penh in June, he noted that each clan had its own sector and reportedly made a fateful remark: "It's Berlin!" Indeed, at least until the end of 1975 the city remained divided into as many pieces as there were zones that the Khmer Rouge had created in the country (southeast, southwest, northwest, north, northeast, and—later—center and west; see appendix 5). For several months, each regional authority administered a part of Phnom Penh that it received in the country's division. Moreover, Hou Yuon is reported to have said: "This evacuation is a pillage." According to a close relative, these words by Hou Yuon expressed an indictment of the state and not an accusation against the leaders. Nevertheless, the latter— who allowed no questioning of their power nor even of their decisions—

decided to eliminate him immediately. The murder was never made public, no doubt because of Hou Yuon's popularity among the peasants as well as among Khmer intellectuals who remained abroad and whom the Khmer Rouge wanted to induce to return.

Hu Nim, like his fellow student and friend Hou Yuon, married a girl who belonged to the wealthy sector of the population. Also the holder of a doctoral degree in law, he shared Hou Yuon's social ideas.[4] He taught history and geography at the Lycée Kambu Both and believed that the development of the country was to be achieved through technology. For professing such ideas, he was eliminated by the Pol Pot–Ieng Sary clan early in 1977, when he was minister of information, along with officials in charge of river transport and, shortly after the suppression of Khoy Thuon, the former head of the northern region, accused of having relations with the CIA.

THE GANG OF FIVE

The gang of five included Pol Pot, Ieng Sary, their respective wives—the sisters Khieu Ponnary and Khieu Thirith—and Khieu Samphan, who was no relation to them.

Born in 1928 (?) to a bourgeois family in Kompong Thom province, Saloth Sar, later known as Pol Pot, received a traditional education; like most Cambodians, he spent six years of retreat in a pagoda. In the opinion of those who knew him well, he was "a reflective man, very sober, very gentle, deliberate. . . . Charming, smiling, he spoke little. He had style; he had a charismatic personality. . . . When he lived in Paris, I believe he was sincerely nationalistic, perhaps still tainted by feudalism. I remember hearing him speak when I was young; I don't have the impression he was lying." As an adolescent he read Marx's *Manifesto*.

Having failed to obtain his *brevet élémentaire*, Saloth Sar came to France in 1949–1950 and enrolled in the École Violet, a technical school in the fifteenth arrondissement where he had no more success. During his three-year stay he was a militant with Ieng Sary, Khieu Thirith, Khieu Ponnary, and several others, and he founded a Marxist circle with them. Saloth Sar lived in the fifteenth arrondissement and then on the rue Lacépède. Known to Cambodians of his age group who shared his Marxist ideas, he remained unknown to others. He was never on the executive committee of the AEK and did not stay long in Paris.

Back home in Cambodia in 1953, he undertook to contact the Khmer *issarak*, then under the control of Son Ngoc Minh and thus of the Vietminh, who had little use for Khmers. Employed in petty tasks such as transporting pots and pans, Saloth Sar would never forget this humiliation. His stay in the maquis ended, at the latest, with the Geneva Accords. He had time to confirm the existence of arms caches left by the *issarak*. He moved to Phnom Penh and taught French, history, geography, and ethics in Chamroeun Vichea, one of two private lycées that were the left's fiefs. Small nuclei of Communists were still stationed in the forest; Saloth Sar visited them periodically and seems to have been their chief from this period onward. Thus the first truly Khmer Communist guerrilla force came into being. In 1955, the future Pol Pot tried to utilize the structure of the Democratic party for the purposes of his politics; this was a failure. In 1963 he settled in Kratié province.

One memory haunted Saloth Sar: a cousin of his, whom he considered a sister, had been among the favorites of King Monivong. He would never forgive the sovereign for not making her his sole wife. From that time onward he bore the monarchy and its representatives a personal hatred that the needs of his cause transformed into a class hatred; he accused it of exploiting the people and condemned the practice of royal harems. Everyone agrees that Saloth Sar knew how to motivate and lead and thus proved an excellent military commander; but his political analyses lacked consistency.

Emphasizing their ties to the people, the revolutionaries decided to assume peasant-sounding names. Khmers traditionally had only given names, which were long and of Sanskrit or Pali origin in the cities or short and Cambodian in the countryside. The protectorate forced them to use surnames. Before 1970 Saloth Sar called himself *bâng* Pol (*bâng* is a kinship term signifying elder). As he gained wider recognition in the West as a leader, he felt obliged to complete the name. He added Pot, a doublet of Pol (doublets are common in Cambodian), to become Pol Pot.

Khieu Ponnary and her sister Khieu Thirith were born of bourgeois parents. "The family lived on Samdech Pann Street, near the royal palace, in a perimeter of lands previously distributed by the king. This means that the parents or grandparents have been palace insiders because all who lived around the palace were former courtiers." Their father was a magistrate (a profession said to be among the most corrupt) who took up a life of dissipation in Battambang, leaving their mother alone to raise five children in Phnom Penh. This past marked the children, particularly the girls, for whom "official" became synonymous with "embezzler." Khieu Ponnary, the eldest, had to look after the other children. Becoming a teacher, she was intelligent and well liked by her pupils and by the peasants as well. Her renown grew; she was one of the first Cambodian women to work. She did not, as her younger sister Thirith did, abandon the traditional education. Having come to Paris to earn an undergraduate degree (the *licence*), she met her future husband there and was an activist with him before their marriage. Once they returned to Phnom Penh, she taught French at the Lycée

Sisowath. "She wrote articles with a double meaning for a newspaper; she was making, as it were, propaganda for Saloth Sar's ideas." "When she militated [as a sympathizer] for the Democratic party, she showed herself virulent against Sihanouk. She was among the first politicized women of Cambodia." In the maquis, before the formation of FUNC, she carried messages inside the hem of her skirt. Khieu Ponnary played a not unimportant role because in her capacity as president of Democratic Kampuchea's women, she controlled the entire feminine element of the country.

> Here was Pol Pot's gray eminence; she helped him as a theoretician. For example, I believe we owe to her the revolutionary vocabulary because she was very good at the Khmer language. In any case, she had an important role as far as we could tell: in November 1978 Angkar invited the intellectuals from the Boeung Trabek camp to the Olympic stadium to see the Chinese circus. Khieu Ponnary presided over the evening, and her mother and Khieu Thirith occupied the seats of honor, near the Chinese general who was the group's guide. When she entered, she was supported by two young girls because she was sick; everyone stood up and applauded.

Ieng Sary, whose real name is Kim Trang, was originally from Kampuchea Krom (South Vietnam). He moved into an uncle's residence in Phnom Penh to study Khmer. His change of identity dates from this time. "Coming late to his studies, he made himself younger; he was born in the year of the pig" (thus in 1993 he was seventy-one years old). He took the first part of the *baccalauréat* at the Lycée Sisowath and arrived in France in 1949 for the second part, which he completed at the Lycée Condorcet. He then enrolled in economics courses but without great devotion. He lived in a studio on rue St-André-des-Arts, in a building where other Khmer Communists also lived; discussions began early in the morning and lasted until late at night.

In contrast to Saloth Sar, he remained eight years in France, until 1957. With his wife, Khieu Thirith, he passed most of his time visiting French or foreign luminaries temporarily in France. He became known to many French people and to Khmer students as well, for which reason he would retain his name. After returning to Phnom Penh, he taught at the Lycée Kambu Both before taking to the maquis in 1963.

Like Pol Pot and other Khmer students, he had taken courses at the PCF's people's university.[5] As an adolescent, Ieng Sary declared that he had embraced nationalist ideas since his childhood in Kampuchea Krom.

> He suffered from his father's position as a landowner, which placed him among the privileged, and from the vexations imposed by the

Vietnamese. . . . He said he hated the bourgeoisie. I do not know if
he was sincere at the beginning, and I have always seen him as arrogant; I also think he's a liar. He is a very intelligent man, with com-
plexes since he is a Khmer *krom*. He has a visceral hatred of the
Vietnamese and, like all Khmers, is prone to delusions of grandeur.[6]

He was said to be an autocrat and was extremely vindictive, another
characteristic of the Khmers. Perhaps his complex as a Khmer *krom* prevented him from being brilliant, despite his immense political culture.
Everyone agrees that he is well read, knows Marxism very well and has
analyzed it, and he has proven to be a skillful politician. Since 1970, he has
continually intrigued to win the position of head of foreign affairs since he
was unable to be the number one of Cambodia. "He reeked of calculation."
Keng Vannsak remembered Ieng Sary's explanation that on his arrival in
France, "the first thing he wanted to do was to meet me to see if I had
remained as politicized as I was in Cambodia and was still a Communist. He
wanted to test me in a way. . . . Ieng Sary was (with Rath Samoeurn) one
of the first Communists of Cambodia; he was already one when he arrived
in France."[7]

Unsubstantiated rumors insist that Ieng Sary "became Marxist" in Paris,
that Pol Pot "first heard of Marxism and imperialism in the Latin Quarter,"
that both were "initiated to Marxist ideas there" or "acquired their Marxism
through contact with the PCF during the 1950s and 1960s."[8] In fact, as stated
above, Pol Pot had already read the *Manifesto*, a meager accomplishment
compared to Ieng Sary's learning. Why did the ambitious Ieng Sary, who
outclassed Pol Pot intellectually, remain in only the second position within
the hierarchy? When he returned from France in 1957, he found Pol Pot, if
not really engaged on a daily basis, at least listened to in the still rudimentary guerrilla forces, of which he soon came to be considered the leader. Ieng
Sary entered an existing structure and could not take from his comrade the
position of guerrilla chieftain; in such struggles, supreme power always
belongs to whoever controls the combatants. Ieng Sary perforce settled for
second place. In compensation, after 1975 he had the upper hand in foreign
affairs, not only because of his capacity as minister but also because "he had
placed a nephew, named Hong, in the position of secretary general of foreign
affairs." "Ieng Sary was hungry for power," a youth reports. "He had settled
his family in important positions, including foreign affairs. He already had
a well-organized structure. Who knows whether, subsequently, he would
not have tried to eliminate Pol Pot."

Khieu Thirith, who had a degree in English (the *licence*), appeared to be
a capable woman. She met her future husband in Phnom Penh and joined

him in Paris, where she married him and committed herself to politicking with him. She kept little of the Khmer tradition, becoming a cool-headed ideologue. She played a direct political role in Democratic Kampuchea: minister of social action, she more or less looked after the people's material life. In any case, she was able to reserve favors for the revolutionaries and ignore the "new people"—townspeople and peasants who lived in areas of the country beyond the control of the Khmer Rouge until April 1975 and who were also called the people of 17 April—and even see to it that their lot did not improve. In fact, she controlled the social as well as the economic and cultural spheres, not without entering into conflicts with Yun Yat, minister of education. Today her intelligence, determination, and toughness remain impressive.

Pol Pot, Ieng Sary, Khieu Thirith, and Khieu Ponnary were probably the toughest individuals in the Khmer Rouge regime. They hated the monarchy and the bourgeoisie so much that they never spoke of them without vilifying them and expressing a desire to see them "smashed to bits." The lust for revenge alone guided them. For propaganda purposes they skillfully presented this personal feeling as a class struggle and, more specifically, as a city-country antagonism.

Khieu Samphan was born in Kompong Cham. His father was an official who had been imprisoned for corruption under the protectorate. As a student at Montpellier, Khieu Samphan obtained a degree in law (the *licence*); he was at that time a militant with the local branch of the Union des étudiants khmers (UEK). Then he went to Paris to work on a thesis.[9] On his return to Phnom Penh, he taught history and geography at the Lycée Kambu Both. "His courses were purely political," one of his students remembers. "He vilified the Khmer monarchy and recommended not following the example of the Khmer kings, who were traitor-kings, including Suramarit, still alive at the time. He even attacked Sihanouk. He was the most virulent of the professors at Lycée Kambu Both." In 1962 he became a representative and then under secretary of state for commerce. He disappeared in 1967 with Hou Yuon. His friends accused Sihanouk of having him killed, but he had taken to the maquis. The scenario repeated itself in 1968 for Hu Nim.

Considered to be an idealist and a true patriot by left-wing youth, Khieu Samphan—who lacked the stuff of a leader—may have had a reputation higher than he deserved. Undoubtedly his opportunism helped him avoid elimination at the hands of his superiors. He was known for his submissiveness and pliability. In 1975 the Americans doubted his political abilities because he had "rather effeminate manners."[10] We also know that in the UEK's dance company this individual, the Khmer Rouge's present number one, played female roles, which the Khmers consider a sign of a weak personality. His schoolfellows asserted that Khieu Samphan was homosexual. Others said that he was forced to marry a peasant woman in the maquis. The support that he continues to give the Khmer Rouge in 1993 shows that his love for the Khmer people did not equal that of his executed friends, Hou Yuon and Hu Nim. Perhaps he was doctrinaire; and perhaps as often happens he became intoxicated by the power (albeit imaginary) that his official title as number one among the Khmer Rouge brought him. In reality, he was well to the bottom of the list of luminaries. Because of his reputation, he will probably never be given real power and instead occupies subordinate roles in the present Khmer Rouge leadership.

One fact confirms the slight confidence in which he was held. Near the village where the leaders lived at the end of the republican war was the Stung Trâng camp for intellectuals (in Kompong Cham province):

> This village had been abandoned, and the cadres ordered us to rebuild it. Some of us participated in the work, and the others saw the results in the Chinese-made film that was shown to us. Ieng Sary's and Pol Pot's houses were side by side at the center of the village; Khieu Samphan's was on the periphery. The location of houses was a clear reflection of rank: the farther from the center, the less important its occupant.

In the same way, students with advanced degrees who returned from abroad remember seeing him seated in the back of the room at a reception; Pol Pot, Ieng Sary, and several others were prominently placed, but no seat had been reserved for Khieu Samphan. Yet Khieu Samphan was a magnet for young progressives. Whereas in Cambodia Ieng Sary looked after the believers, Khieu Samphan had the task of rallying the hesitant. Many joined the guerrillas because of what he symbolized: "Along with many other young people, I liked Khieu Samphan, Hou Yuon, Hu Nim. . . . For me, all the left was the same; I didn't imagine there would be clans." Likewise, his renown attracted to the UEK and then to the FUNC in Paris many students who would otherwise have stood to one side. "When I was arrested by the Vietnamese early in 1979, I still had a photograph of Khieu Samphan with me. I quickly went to throw it in the toilet." His role in the Khmer Rouge's victory was thus not an unimportant one. In November 1974 he stated in *Le Monde diplomatique*: "With the exception of this handful of traitors, each citizen of Kampuchea, regardless of his past, belongs in the national community. Kampuchea needs all its nationals of goodwill for its peaceful reconstruction and development in the context of national unity."

Even if he did not write the text, it told lies that the people longed to believe. An intellectual of Khmer *krom* origins, more realistic than his schoolmates, would say: "Khieu Samphan bears a great deal of responsibility. He was extremely popular, and it is partly thanks to him that the revolution was successful."

## TA MOK, SON SEN, AND THE OTHERS

The presidents of the zones all played important roles in the victory of April 1975, particularly So Phim, Vorn Veth, and Khoy Thuon. Because they opposed the central power, they did not survive the Democratic Kampuchea regime. Only Ta Mok, a rising star in 1975–1978 without a glorious past, escaped.

In 1981 under the name of Chhit Chhoeun, Ta Mok became a member of the new Khmer Rouge government. He was born in Takeo (or Kampot) and took the monk's habit during adolescence. Uncertainty regarding his true identity remains: some said Eang Eng, others Nguon Kang. He was an *issarak*. Some sources state that he withdrew to North Vietnam in 1954; others claim that he did not leave Cambodia. He joined the Khmer guerrillas in 1967 at about the time Khieu Samphan arrived. In the Khmer Rouge's military victory Ta Mok distinguished himself. He is said to have led the evacuation of Phnom Penh. Intellectuals who returned from abroad between 1975–1978 and were assembled in the Boeung Trabek camp saw him in a film they were shown: "Ta Mok was in it from beginning to end, and the film sang his praises." He was the only regional chief faithful to Pol Pot; the others were plotters. He forged an army of highly motivated youths, feared by the people, the soldiers from *nirdey* (the southwest), who set themselves up in all the command posts from 1977 onward, when it became clear that the regime was in danger. Under Ta Mok's direction, they conducted monstrous purges from mid-1978 onward that ended in the massacre of the population of the east, accused of collaborating with the Vietnamese enemy. Ta Mok can be considered a faithful and attentive executor of Pol Pot's orders. He was responsible for a great many deaths. Even after one leg was amputated in the early 1980s, he still exercised a reign of terror in the north and in the west of Cambodia, and the Vietnamese army was unable to dislodge him.

Son Sen, who came to Paris to study law, stopped attending his courses after six months. He wanted to make revolution and accordingly agitated among the Khmer students in France. He lived there during 1953–1956, when no associations existed. Since he obtained no university diplomas, his scholarship was canceled after two years. He thus returned to Cambodia. In the 1960s he was the principal of the Institut pédagogique, where he carved out a fief; in the evenings he taught French free of charge. Joining the guerrillas, Son Sen became chief of staff of the Khmer Rouge forces in 1972. Later, in Democratic Kampuchea, he was minister of defense. He was said to be more moderate than Ta Mok. In 1985 he took the place of Pol Pot as official head of the army. His brother Nikon, who is today the chief military authority in the Battambang region, worked between 1975–1978 at Phnom Penh's foreign ministry.

Nuon Chea spent part of his youth in Thailand. Long a convert to communism and officially introduced as the number-two man of the Kampuchean Communist party, he actually held the third position, after Pol Pot and Ieng Sary, in Democratic Kampuchea's hierarchy. He acted as president of the assembly of people's representatives and above all as minister of the interior. Despite the small amount of information available on his activities, he has been an influential figure in the Khmer Rouge system since 1975.

Very early on, Kompong Speu province was in the hands of the Khmer Rouge. The leaders set themselves up there in a zone called *phumphiek piseh* (special region). Many soldiers (*yothea*) were stationed there until April 1975. In 1974, however, the leaders and their families were transferred to Kompong Cham, in the Stung Trâng district, which was made an autonomous sector. The other regions each had an army; these diverse armed groups and those of the special region would link up in Phnom Penh on 17 April 1975.

THE *KAMAPHIBAL* AND THE *YOTHEA*

These are, respectively, the Khmer Rouge cadres and soldiers. The cadres include holders of advanced degrees at the higher echelons, while other comrades usually have no conception of technical matters. They are taught that an elevated political consciousness allows an individual to solve any problem. They thus cannot understand how people can fail in their work. When they do, the offending comrades are required to perform a self-criticism and improve; if not, a cadre turns them over to the *yothea* or simply kills them in the nearby forest. The *kamaphibal*, needless to say, are the terror of the "new people."

The recruitment of cadres and soldiers during the republican war was significant in regions in which high rates of illiteracy facilitated indoctrination: the montagnards of the northeast (ethnic groups in which only the males speak and understand Cambodian); villagers ensconced at the foot of Phnom Aural; inhabitants of the hinterlands of Kampot and Kompong Chhnang or of the mountainous confines of the Pailin region. Each family in the occupied villages was to supply, voluntarily or otherwise, at least one boy or girl for the army. Recruited from the age of twelve years, these ignorant young soldiers quickly became fanatics, driven by hatred and vengeance and learning a gun's power.

One of them spoke with me in 1980, when he was stationed at the Kamput II camp, which mainly sheltered the "old people"—the base population, also called the people of 18 March, those under the Khmer Rouge's control during the republican war; the camp had been established for *kamaphibal* and *yothea* who came there to rest between battles inside Cambodia. Probably because my informant was an illiterate young rice grower who was not accustomed to speaking, and because the interview took place under difficult conditions, I obtained not a narrative but rather answers to my questions. For clarity, I make small changes in the significant responses but keep their meaning consistent with refugees' accounts.

> My name is Soeung Thoeung, twenty-one years old. I was born in Prey Kri, in Kompong Chhnang. I am unmarried. Until the arrival of the Khmer Rouge in our village in September 1973, I lived with my parents. Some *kamaphibal* were spreading propaganda in order to enroll people. At thirteen, I volunteered to become a member of the militia; there were twelve of us for the commune. I joined because I suffered under the rich people and the capitalists who exploited the poor. This anger led me to become a *yothea* to fight Lon Nol's army. The work consisted of guarding and protecting the base population. At night I stood guard, I kept watch and told the chief about people who spoke ill of us; he tried to correct their errors; there were about twenty of these people, men, women, and their families. In 1973–1974, the population was divided into mutual-aid groups, and in 1975 cooperatives were created.
>
> In the beginning of 1974 I became a *yothea* and fought against Lon Nol's soldiers. After [April] 1975 I worked in the rice fields, and, at the same time, Angkar entrusted me with rooting out Lon Nol's agents among the "new people" who had come to us. In the case of former soldiers, Angkar physically liquidated them. Approximately ten of Lon Nol's soldiers were killed in this way where I was. Two nights a week I mounted guard until dawn; I protected the grounds and watched for Cambodian enemy agents. They were bad men. We killed those who tried to escape; I captured three of them. Those we surprised at night in the act of saying bad things were educated, which means that they worked harder than the others. If they repeated the offense, they were killed with a cudgel or pickax. Then they were buried, and that was that. I heard them scream because I was nearby. During the interrogations, electric shocks were used. Children were also killed if they made a lot of mistakes, if they were traitors. I personally didn't kill anybody; during interrogations, I beat several young boys of fifteen or twenty years old who had stolen.
>
> I agreed with the executions. If I hadn't, they'd have accused me of complicity and arrested me. And those who made mistakes had

to take responsibility for their errors. Angkar judged them on a case-by-case basis. In my heart, I accepted all of this.

Sections met every ten days, and every month there was a general meeting. They talked about our surplus rice production. They told us it was exported in exchange for other merchandise, for example, trucks.

We had four meals a day: before going to work in the morning, potatoes and sugarcane; at eleven o'clock, a meal of rice and various dishes, and we took a rest; at two o'clock in the afternoon, we went back to work after eating *num* [glutinous rice cakes]; the last meal was at five; then we went to sleep.

About one hundred Chinese from People's China came to build the Kompong Chhnang air base.

I think we [the Khmer Rouge] are going to win against the Vietnamese.

I've never been to Phnom Penh or to Pursat, and I don't know about anything outside Kompong Chhnang province. . . .

This account, in which we find peasant language right next to doublespeak, reveals the indoctrination and the blind obedience of a young illiterate (he did not know how to read); he is the image of the majority of Khmer Rouge cadres and soldiers. The widespread spontaneous uprising of the peasantry is a myth. Rural people were not politicized, and when they revolted (in Samlaut and Ratanakiri), it was for strictly material reasons and against the military officers who had taken their lands; it was not for ideological reasons and in opposition to the chief of state. Within this base population, under Khmer Rouge control during the republican war and their source of cadres and soldiers, people had enough to eat and were usually not mistreated, except in 1978 in the sensitive regions of the east, bordering on Vietnam. They did not seek to flee from the regime. The other inhabitants, townspeople and country people who had lived in a governmental region until 1975, were all objects of the Khmer Rouge's violence; some of them did succeed in fleeing.

The fact that the Khmer Rouge generalized peasant practices—the use of the cotton *krâma* (scarf); the use of the term *hop* (to eat), a polite form employed by peasants in isolated regions to the exclusion of any other form—is not evidence of peasants' political engagement in the Khmer Rouge's favor.[11] Claiming to have the support of the peasantry, the authorities—who said that they sought to establish equality among the masses and whose rallying cry was the city-country opposition—could not fail to favor the customs of indoctrinated peasants. Here was no spontaneous and general peasant uprising but only a Marxist movement led in a commonplace manner by members of the bourgeoisie who took advantage of the ignorance of part of the people in order to propagate ideas about the overthrow of powers that be for their own advantage. In the following pages we witness the monstrous evolution of this movement.

## THE LIFE OF THE PEOPLE

> I'm thirty-eight years old and was born in Kratié province; I'm a farmer. . . . I was in the town of Kratié when the Vietcong, accompanied by several Khmer Rouge, entered in 1970 after the overthrow of *Samdech*. The Khmer Rouge immediately closed the school, and everyone had to grow rice. In 1971 and 1972 they set up mutual aid teams of twenty to thirty families, but we still ate individually and had enough food. . . . In 1973 commerce was stopped in town, the circulation of money was abolished, merchants were sent to the rice fields, and cooperatives were created. The inhabitants grew rice and raised animals. We lived in a closed economy. People didn't want cooperatives because it meant meals in common, and so certain places kept mutual aid groups alongside cooperatives. After 1974 we no longer had enough to eat, and the work demanded of us got harder. . . .
>
> The pagodas remained open as usual until 1972. From 1973 onward the problems began: they defrocked the monks in 1974 and used the pagodas as storehouses for fertilizer, rice granaries, or prisons. They destroyed statues of the Buddha. My brother was killed. In particular, they looked for military men, who were all accused of being intelligence agents. There weren't many massacres of civilians until 1975, perhaps because in this province Pol Pot's cadres were former teachers. . . . When the *yothea* entered Phnom Penh, we weren't evacuated because we were considered "old people"; but people from Phnom Penh came here. They were gradually eliminated beginning in 1976 as the cadres discovered their former professions.

In the beginning of 1975 the republicans hardly controlled anything anymore except the towns. On 12 April 1975, after an effort by the Americans—in vain because it came too late—to bring Sihanouk back to Phnom Penh, the last American diplomats closed their embassy and left Cambodia by helicopter, taking 156 Khmers with them. The Khmer Rouge were stationed at the gates of Phnom Penh and put the Pochentong airport out of commission. Five days later, on 17 April, after years of hardship, the people of Phnom Penh welcomed the Khmer Rouge liberators with a sense of relief. For them, it was the end of the war and misery, it was national reconciliation and, possibly, the return of Sihanouk, who, they thought, was not so bad as all that. Very few city dwellers had listened to or believed the accounts of rural escapees who had come from the Khmer Rouge–administered zones during 1970–1974 and told of life "over there."

Phnom Penh's more farsighted and well-off residents—for a visa cost a great deal under the Khmer Republic, and seats on the last planes out of the capital cost a king's ransom—left for abroad eight days before the final assault. Some Chinese and Sino-Khmers gradually moved nearer the Thai border and crossed over when the time came. Most people of modest means had no choice but to live under the new regime, even if they had once experienced but fled from it. The majority of the intellectuals, officials, and businessmen, held in place by traditional inertia and obsolete values, refused to undertake the analyses that could have saved the country; they turned to the gods and the like; they waited for a miracle. It was not unusual, from the end of 1970 onward, to hear Cambodians wishing for the return of the French—so much is recourse to foreigners a constant in Khmer history. Profiteers, who had left with the Americans, had not seen fit to work with these various groups at righting the country's affairs.

On 17 April 1975 the combatants drew their grids and advanced methodically and unhesitatingly through the town, evidently obeying general orders. In response for admiring applause, the residents of Phnom Penh got nothing from these men in black (the Khmer Rouge soldiers) but icy silence and the order to leave the city for three days' time. Some believed what they were told and left their homes intact; others were distrustful and carried away more than was necessary.

A PREMEDITATED EXODUS; INVALIDS ON THE HIGHWAY

> When the Khmer Rouge entered Phnom Penh on 17 April 1975, they used loudspeakers to urge the entire population to leave for three days. My husband, my three children, and I followed National Highway 1. We could only advance several kilometers each day because the crowd was immense; the Monivong bridge was completely blocked. . . . Children screamed, adults cried, the elderly followed miserably, and women gave birth on the sidewalk. The most suspicious had brought large parcels of clothing and food along on handcarts, on bicycles, or on their shoulders. Some had piled everything on their carts, which they pushed, but the Khmer Rouge made them abandon their vehicles. There was indescribable misery, and it was horribly hot. . . . I could take only a very little extra milk for my baby and had no money to buy any; at the time you could still buy and sell among evacuees. My baby had been sick, and he was throwing up. I sold clothing, which let me buy milk and white sugar. But he died during the exodus, at the end of

May or the beginning of June, I don't know what day; he was six months old. . . .

There were stations where the Khmer Rouge required soldiers and officials to declare themselves. We avoided the first classifications because my husband was a career military man. One day, near four o'clock in the morning, two *yothea* came, wearing caps, *krâma*, and B-40s. They told us: "You all love Angkar, but Angkar wants you to be reeducated because you come from the former regime." They took eleven men, including my husband. There were two of us wives there, and they told us: "Wait here. We're going to a meeting; we'll be back in twenty minutes." Three days later a messenger came to ask for my husband's clothes. I included a watch because you have to know what time it is when you're taking courses. I wanted to wait for him before going on. I'd only crossed the Mekong because he'd left on a boat. . . . Some villagers from the "old people" came to tell me: "Neang, don't wait for your husband. They killed all of them [the eleven] twenty kilometers from here. Get out of here, and don't say you're the wife of a military man— they'll kill you."

I took the road to my native village in Kompong Thom. I didn't move quickly; I had nobody to help me carry everything. I spent the night in a stable. Urine from children sleeping on a plank above came down on me. I couldn't stay because the peasants didn't believe I was a merchant. They were afraid to keep me in their houses. I left. I gave a ring to the Khmer Rouge soldiers so they'd let us go to Skuon. There, an epidemic of cholera was going on; cadavers all around, and flies. I tried to draw water from a well. It was black because the Khmer Rouge had thrown in the corpses of people they'd just killed. I fled two kilometers. I exchanged a Montagut[12] jersey and a Cambodian skirt for a bunch of bananas, some white sugar, and some beef. Someone who knew my husband hid us for one month at Baray, and then I went to my village, Banteay, where there were many "new people." We started by building our house.

Anguish quickly took hold of the people from Phnom Penh; this was no ordinary walk. Even the wounded and ill were taken from the hospitals and put out onto the road, on foot, holding bottles of serum, supported by the most able or even left in beds on wheels. Some died in the course of the exodus:

The *yothea* came into the Khmer-Soviet hospital on 17 April at nine o'clock. They told patients who could walk to go home, adding that the hospital and everything inside it now belonged to everyone, that anybody, patients and inhabitants of nearby villages,

could help themselves in the storerooms. It was chaos. . . . Some of
the medical personnel there fled in fear. There were fifteen of us
left. The hospital director, Dr. Samair Phalcun, was taken away in a
jeep. We don't know what became of him. . . . Six seriously ill patients had taken out their intravenous needles in order to flee. They
didn't get far. The Khmer Rouge had us dig a pit to bury them in.
Shortly later an ambulance came to take the remaining patients,
and we never heard anything else about them. . . . We were still
forty doctors and nurses; on 26 April a truck transported us as far
as Ta Khmau. Phnom Penh was empty, but after Ta Khmau traffic
was snarled, and we were abandoned in the crowd of evacuees.

The military hospital on Monivong Boulevard contained several hundred
wounded soldiers. "They forced the wounded to get out and, before leaving
the premises, threw grenades at those who had been unable to move." The
Hôpital Calmette operated normally until 19 April, the date on which the
French personnel had to join the other foreigners in the city at the French
embassy. Khmer medical personnel remained on the spot more than two
more weeks:

On 6 May the *yothea* came to tell us the hospital had to be evacuated tomorrow for three days in order to escape American bombing.
. . . Some patients, accompanied by nurses, preferred to go to their
homes, thinking they'd find their families there. About fifty of
them wanted to follow us; five of them who had recently undergone operations were put on stretchers. They died at Prek Khdam
[thirty kilometers north of Phnom Penh]. Among them was a little
girl of fifteen who had been wounded in the bombing and a man
who had been operated on for a cranial trauma; he screamed endlessly. . . . At the following stop, at Speu, a young boy of fifteen
died. . . . In this way we went on into Kratié province. We had left
Phnom Penh on 6 May, and we arrived at our destination on the
twelfth. Six other patients died in the months that followed, including three women who left the Khmer Rouge hospital where they
were in order to commit suicide. A total of sixteen patients died.

The Khmer Rouge calmly shot down stragglers and the elderly who were,
in their view, going too slowly. All the cities were evacuated, and not just
for three days. The Khmer Rouge feared that they would not be able to
contain their opponents, and they thought that the best way to dismantle
their networks was to empty all cities. The account of a colonel who
remained in Phnom Penh until 27 April shows that the second reason
invoked for the evacuation, the lack of food, is not valid: "The bombings and

the lack of food, *despite stockpiles,* had the effect of making the inhabitants long for peace at any price."[13] The capital thus would have been able to feed its inhabitants, once the refugees from the countryside returned to their homes. The same is true of Battambang, Cambodia's second largest city, which had at its disposal a great deal of rice as well as pigs for slaughter. Furthermore, from the beginning, the Khmer Rouge refused the humanitarian aid offered them by the international community; concern to protect the population did not guide their decisions. This exodus apparently took place against the advice of China, which presumably expressed reservations because it included several hundred thousand Chinese. The evacuation also struck rural inhabitants. Villages that had been administered by the republic until the final offensive beginning in January 1975 were generally abandoned and their inhabitants transplanted to regions that had been held by the Khmer Rouge for several years.

Furthermore, throughout the country, the Khmer Rouge emptied settlements that were far from the axes of communication and thus difficult to control, those too close to the border, from which people might try to escape, and those areas whose soil was too poor to permit the installation of large productive units.

The following measures had been announced to villagers "liberated" between 1970 and 1974: "Peasants must go to the towns, and city dwellers must work in the fields. People should go to the provinces. Those from Ba Phnom have to go to Ratanakiri." The evacuation had thus been planned on a countrywide scale.

### PEOPLE IN THE FIELDS: DISEASE AND FAMINE

Townspeople, born in the city or, for the most part, refugees, were to be punished for the years of republican debauchery that they had experienced. The Khmer Rouge did not take individual modes of behavior lightly: morality and purity were the order of the day. Necessary virtues were humility, but without the dignity that is the greatness of the Khmer peasant; poverty, but without the moments of joy or holidays that normally punctuate peasant life; show of satisfaction despite discomfort, fatigue, and hunger. Further, everyone had to be a producer; all were to cultivate the soil. Accordingly, most of the people worked in the rice fields. Townspeople were plunged into this labor without any preparation whatsoever, the goal being to humiliate them.[14] Whereas before 1975 the "old people" experienced progressive collectivization with, in an initial period, the formation of mutual-aid teams, the "new people" endured without transition the radical measures that were henceforth in place throughout the country.

In agriculture, industry, fishing, transportation, and other activities, at the head of each organization (cooperative, factory, mobile team) was a triumvirate: a president and two vice-presidents. Members were divided into military units: team, group, section, company, battalion, regiment, brigade.

Guarded by *yothea*, the youths of the mobile brigades (fifteen years of age and above) endured an exhausting schedule of work: fifteen to eighteen hours every day, including travel, for rice fields or hydraulic yards might be located several hours away from the base camp. They could be asked to do any kind of work: growing rice, building canals, dikes, and reservoirs; the earth is so dry that it must first be broken up with pickaxes. In the evenings an electrical generating set illuminated the hydraulic yards or rice fields. The youngsters of the mobile units (twelve to fourteen years of age) did almost the same jobs, but their schedules were less onerous and their range of travel more limited. The adult leader of the unit picked subalterns from among the children. These youths formed the country's primary productive force. Children from five or six to eleven years of age were assembled in fixed locations for the rice crops; along with the most robust adults sent from the cooperatives for day work in the fields and rice paddies, they made up the secondary productive force. The elderly and young children (from three to five or six years of age) of the cooperatives, employed on the spot in odd jobs, represented the tertiary productive force. Aside from watching over infants, the elderly worked for six to eight hours each day at secondary tasks under the *kamaphibal*'s direction.

The average diet did not fill people's nutritional needs in view of the enormous effort demanded from them.[15] In normal times, Cambodian peasants ate approximately 700 grams of white rice per day.

> Since 1975 there were restrictions on rice. In that year the harvest had been poor, and there was little grain in the countryside; for ten persons, we received two *kampong* per day [=50 grams per person] as well as a *kampong* of salt per week. In the beginning, each family cooked for itself and did its best to find something to serve along with the rice. Late in 1975 the Khmer Rouge created the mobile brigades. I was twelve years old, and I was assigned to a children's brigade; we moved about in the commune but received more food. In 1976 the cadres granted us a half-*kampong* of rice [=125 grams] per day per member of the brigade, with a bit of *sâmlâ* (soup) or *prâhok* (fish paste). After the first few months we had no rice at all, only manioc root, or some *prâhok* or manioc-based *sâmlâ*. Early in 1977 after the harvest we received one *kampong* of rice for three persons [=85 grams per person per day] with a *sâmlâ* made from

salted vegetables or a bit of *prâhok*. The ration diminished further to increase again in the last months of the year because we were to participate in the digging of the 17 April canal. There we were each given one *kampong* [=125 grams of rice] per day with as much fish *sâmlâ* as we wanted and meat from time to time; sometimes we even had two dishes and a cake every ten days. This lasted until the end of the work in February 1978; then once again it was one *kampong* for three and then for five persons [=85 grams for each, then 50 grams] and a bit of *sâmlâ*. After an early harvest in September there was a new increase: one *kampong* [=250 grams] per person and some *sâmlâ*.

This menu constituted the daily fare for the mobile work teams and more than what was available for the cooperatives' sedentary workers. During nearly three years most of the inhabitants consumed practically no fats and very little protein—although Cambodia is one of the world's richest countries in fish—and an insufficient quantity of glucosides. Further, they had few vitamins since fruits and raw vegetables were rare: "When we celebrated the anniversary of 17 April and then, beginning in 1977, that of the founding of the party, we ate well and had the right to laugh; it was a windfall." From time to time, someone caught a lizard that he shared with his family in secret. "I remember one day I caught two snails, a frog, and a centipede, and for us it was like having a meal at the Élysée." The Khmer Rouge prohibited searching for tubers and gathering leaves for personal use. Some starving people even attempted to eat cadavers:

> I remember a Charlie Chaplin film where he was so hungry, he ate his shoe; we all laughed when we saw it. If you'd been with us at that time [under the Khmer Rouge], you wouldn't have laughed at all—it was reality. We ate grass; there were even people who ate cadavers; they tried to dig down and just get a bit of the flesh. In one case, the Khmer Rouge took them by surprise and killed them.

The alimentary deficiencies caused cases of edema, diarrhea, and generalized weakness. "The elderly and babies couldn't take it as well as we did. My sister lost her two children. Before dying, her little girl cried for rice, and I went to exchange a ring for three spoonfuls. When I came back, she was already dead. . . . Once my sister was alone, she had to join a mobile brigade." In some regions, such as Pursat and Kompong Chhnang, the suffering was more cruel.

> In Pursat province, in *srok* 22, in Khum Thla Ampil, Phum Po, we were about five thousand persons, mostly townspeople. Sometimes we had no rice, only banana stalks and leaves. Late in 1978, of the

four thousand inhabitants belonging to the "new people," only two hundred were left, the others having died of hunger, except for about one hundred who had been killed by the cadres. At the neighboring cooperative in *srok* 23, five thousand persons died of hunger, and one thousand were massacred, leaving mostly women, seven hundred or eight hundred of them, and the "old people."[16]

In view of their physiological distress at a time when the leaders were feasting with foreign visitors, it is understandable that the people snatched at less than inviting plunder:

> When the Vietnamese arrived, people went looking for gold in these famous ossuaries dating from the Khmer Rouge period; they were in fact pits. I saw them with my own eyes. Each pit measured sixteen to twenty meters in depth and four to five meters in diameter. They contained the corpses of inhabitants of the southeast whom the Khmer Rouge were in the process of killing when the Vietnamese arrived. There were some bodies whose decomposing flesh was still reddish. The cadavers of children were right next to those of the adults. Those who opened the holes sometimes found jewels that they tore from the corpses. In each pit, they took forty to fifty *dâmloeung* [1,500 to 1,875 grams of gold]; some of them gathered dollars. The children's delicate flesh had been shredded by blows from cudgels, hatchets, or pickaxes. By contrast, some adults' bodies were quasi-intact. I went to these ossuaries because I had the idea of looking for booty among this tangle of human butchery. But the sight of still fresh cadavers took away my courage. I had nothing at all, and even so my hands could not search the bodies for gold. This happened near Svay Teap, in Kompong Cham, on a plantation that had belonged to the French.

If the cadres and soldiers had district hospitals supplied with doctors and modern medicines furnished by China, among the general population pathological cases existed. People who were casualties or invalids, now nonproductive, saw their already meager ration cut in half. And, to justify their absence, they were obliged to go to the dispensary belonging to the cooperative or the brigade, where the "nurse," a child of twelve or thirteen years of age, trained by the regime, that is, totally incompetent, handed out a traditional preparation in the form of pills, which everyone called *ac tonsay* (rabbit pellets). Patients were lucky if they walked away from this bedless lean-to where they often lay on beaten soil.

> I had chronic diarrhea and went to the infirmary. The nurses, little girls of eleven or thirteen years old, gave me some *ac tonsay* and two injections of vitamin C preserved in BGI bottles [from the Brasseries et Glacières de l'Indochine]. Each time I had abscesses. The

third time I refused the injection, saying I was cured, and returned to the cooperative where I treated my abscesses with medicines supplied by friends.

For these young revolutionary nurses, "the consultation consisted above all of asking questions." They had no idea how to cure infantile diseases: "In our cooperative at Dambok Khpuos in Kampot, there was a measles epidemic; it was late in 1977. About one hundred children died, among them my daughter. . . . I also lost my wife, who had a fever and beriberi. My father had left us early in 1977; I stayed on there by myself with the Khmer Rouge." Individuals with chronic ailments generally did not survive these years of privations: "My father died at Prey Nop; he had cardiac and hepatic problems. In normal times he was taking special remedies every day."

Obviously, Peking did not appreciate the identical treatment given to Cambodia's Chinese minority:

> Some Chinese experts came on mission in 1977; two Chinese working in a hydraulic yard served as interpreters. The Chinese officials and the interpreters spent a good while together, to the great displeasure of the delegation's Khmer Rouge authorities. The Chinese officials looked sad; they must have understood that their compatriots in Cambodia were mistreated, and they gave the interpreters everything that they had to eat.

Wherever they were too numerous, the *yothea* helped with the rice crops. They alone were authorized to use any mechanized tools. The rest of the people used hand tools and the little baskets so common in Southeast Asia. Were more draft animals needed? Human bodies were harnessed in their place. Since the Khmer Rouge were unable to arrest the annual epizootic diseases, the livestock diminished.

On the technical level, the Khmer Rouge did not adequately take into account the local peasants' empirical knowledge when they laid out rice paddies. Those in charge of townspeople clearing lands came from areas of the country where the terrain and soil conditions were different. Furthermore, they followed orders "from above." And yet the Khmer Rouge had model zones laid out with fields of one hectare (100 meters on each side) in order to show visitors the glorious achievements of Democratic Kampuchea; everything had to be aligned and measured off to the last centimeter. In both cases, the cadres scorned the topographical conditions that the former owners had respected. In laying out identical squares, they broke the equilibrium between natural conditions and the peasants' ingenuity. Moreover, they introduced the Chinese method of replanting at the expense of Khmer methods, which were more appropriate for local varieties, and yields fell. Chinese varieties that were more productive and adapted to the new way of replanting—but flavorless—replaced Khmer seeds. The diminution of the varieties used led to an impoverishment of the genetic patrimony of rice in Cambodia as well as to a standardization of taste. Nor did the Khmer Rouge know how to combat diseases of the paddy. The peasants had formerly fought them with traditional remedies prepared at home. After 1975 insecticides imported from China displaced the old remedies. Likewise, Chinese swatters replaced homemade traps for killing rats. Preference thus honored unknown Chinese methods rather than Khmer peasants' proven experience.

The people brought virgin lands under cultivation; yet, according to witnesses, the surface planted with paddy did not increase compared to 1970 because poor soils were no longer cultivated. Despite double-cropping and generalized use of fertilizer, production remained about the same, the construction of many hydraulic works notwithstanding.

In this domain all worked feverishly. The leaders wanted to build a new Cambodia that would equal the period of Angkor. Yet they could not engage in temple building: aside from the fact that they lacked the technical knowledge, a Marxist regime must avoid religion. It thus had to focus on the economy. So they displayed an irrigation network exceeding the grandeur of those Angkor's monarchs carried out; satellite photos offer evidence of the projects they undertook. Given their great number and inaccessibility, we cannot make a fair analysis of the Khmer Rouge's successes and failures. Sometimes they allowed competent men from the "new people" to lead the operations; when they had finished the work, these technicians were sometimes executed by the Khmer Rouge, notably in the east. Most of the time work proceeded hastily and carelessly, for Angkar's deadlines had to be met. Before the 1977 purges, a few qualified people were among the *kamaphibal* in charge of such technical work and labor. In many cases a dike or dam survived more or less intact, but breaches appeared after heavy rains and had to be filled in each year. Some functioned in this way until January 1979. When Chinese advice was sought, notably for concrete dams, the result was consistent with the degree to which the advice was followed. Others, erected through reliance on elevated political consciousness, collapsed in the first rainstorm and caused floods; poorly slanted canals irrigated lands that did not need it, leaving the driest lands to their natural sterility.

These far-reaching projects are indicative of the Khmer Rouge's megalomania, which manifested itself in this domain: they apparently found piling up earth or digging into it easier than making steel, for example. In any case, the development of agriculture was not aimed at enhancing the people's well-being; it was at the service of a few who held power and sought to isolate the country from the outside world.

## THE RETURN TO IGNORANCE

In the midst of all this agitation, children were not neglected, for they were occupied with productive tasks. Yet their education suffered. Boys and girls who were from the "old people" had to learn the rudiments of Khmer. Here is one account of the positive and negative aspects of this education for schools in Phnom Penh:

> The Khmer Rouge leaders are the first who tried to make children of this generation among the most studious, hardworking, and dedicated in all that they do. . . . In terms of political education, there are no more familial values, critical thinking, or initiative. Too arrogant, for the children are aware of the future role that they will have in the country's reconstruction, intolerant of everything that represents weakness (physical and political), pretentious, like their masters, the children are hungry for power. Since the power of money no longer exists, the only substitute is that of a position, which led to well-known excesses. . . . We may ask ourselves how many children really believed in this system as compared to those who only pretended to. Indeed, most of them returned to their former behavior as soon as the regime fell. The Khmer Rouge temporarily deprived them of the freedom to express themselves but not of the freedom to think.[17]

In the countryside the *kamaphibal* and the *yothea*, most of whom were illiterate, could not educate the children, and the Khmer Rouge did not trust teachers from the old regime. With few exceptions, children from the countryside remained ignorant, just as did those of the "new people." In the case of the latter, this cultural vacuum was no accident—it was planned. A people's education presents a risk when its total submission is necessary, especially at the outset in a new era. And it is not inappropriate to suggest that the highest leaders, intoxicated by an experience that they consider unique, really believed in the virtues of an untutored society.

Instead of studying Khmer, arithmetic, or history, children learned revolutionary songs, the only form of education given them. The Khmer Rouge exploited their tendency to obey and recruited *chhlop* (spies) among youngsters of the "old people"; they watched over the words of adults, whoever they were. Some children received a technical education. In any case the people did not have the right to think. "If the Khmer Rouge say rain falls from the earth to the sky, you have to say it too; otherwise, it means you think and thus you're an intellectual."

## A TRADITIONAL SOCIETY IN DISINTEGRATION

The "old people" hardly changed their way of life, at least if they were adults, for children worked in the mobile brigades. Adults remained in their native villages and grew rice according to schedules that were fixed and longer than previous ones, despite the authorized rest periods. But they had enough to eat, lived in the same houses, and continued to plant surrounding areas with fruit trees and vegetables, which they were allowed to eat. Spouses generally remained together, and intervillage communication existed. The spirits and magical practices still retained their importance. By contrast the "new people," the evacuees, completely fell apart.

### The Abolition of the Family

Once the evacuation was finished, townspeople and rice growers had been uprooted from their native neighborhoods or villages. They arrived either in hamlets belonging to the "old people" or in deserted zones where they needed to build everything, houses as well as paddy fields. But that was not enough for the Khmer Rouge, who sought to rub out all links between individuals, thus making them as vulnerable as possible.

Living quarters became collective. Two or three families—and sometimes more, or what was left of them—shared a hastily constructed abode, its walls and roof palm branches or grass. Intimacy no longer existed, and individuals could no longer chose friends or mates. Angkar determined the groupings of individuals, including marriage ceremonies, which were conducted hastily and in mass.

Children, separated from their parents from the age of seven, lived in children's units. They stayed several kilometers away from parents and were authorized to see them only once or twice a year. Sometimes they visited surreptitiously:

> I remember the period beginning in 1975; before, I was too young. I was seven years old, and they separated me from my parents and put me in a children's team. We were about thirty, living one kilometer from Phum Chrap [in Stung Treng province], where my parents lived. This village was divided into two: the adults were downstream, and the children were upstream, near the road. . . . We ate and slept there. We worked in the fields from six o'clock until noon and then from one until six o'clock. We didn't have the right to go to our parents' village; we went secretly. I went there two or three times. My brother, who is now seven, was used in cutting *Eupatorium* stalks to make fertilizer; this began in 1977, when he was three years old.

This organization extended throughout the country:

> Once we got to Pursat, the Khmer Rouge placed us—my brother and me—in a children's unit. I was building small causeways for

the paddy fields. We had to break up earth, put it in small baskets, carry it to the flail, and pile it up; instead of doing that, I threw it quickly without paying attention so I'd be done sooner, for we had a specific quantity of work to complete. . . . Mother was in a cooperative several kilometers from us. I secretly went to see her; that's why I hurried to finish my work. Then I'd run toward her cooperative, I didn't stay long, and then I came back, always running because I had to be back before the meal so nobody would notice.

The impact on other children was different: "At the beginning, I missed my parents. With the self-criticism sessions, I ended up feeling ashamed before Angkar and the other kids; after a while, I no longer thought about going to see them; I had practically forgotten them. And anyway, we were better off in our building because we had more to eat than they did." The adolescents made up mobile brigades of girls or of boys augmented by widowed adults and vigorous unmarried individuals. These adolescents rarely saw their families. Visits depended on the rotation of the mobile team to which they belonged: some traveled about within a commune, others within a district, province, or region. Some young people met their parents again only in 1979 or learned that they had been killed after perhaps three years without contact. Moreover, parent-child relations were practically nonexistent. Everyone avoided conversations, even with infants, because spies prowled about under the houses on piles: "At home in the evening, if my son wanted to talk to me, I whispered in his ear to keep quiet and go to sleep."

In the camps for intellectuals who had returned from abroad, parents and children were similarly separated. A young adolescent who was only five years old in 1976, Yim Nollary, gave her account at Lycée de Laon. Along with two comrades of her own age, she had looked after infants:

> In the afternoons we worked in the paddy fields. Depending on the periods, we cleared land or harvested wood, big logs to build houses. We were separated from our parents. The Khmer Rouge told us we must not go to see them—the party was more important. At the beginning we missed them, but at the end of a year we had no desire at all to see them. They weren't our parents anymore but rather individuals just like anyone else, and rather harmful. I no longer called them mother and father—we didn't have the right. I called them 'sir' and 'madam.'[18]

Parents and elderly people, attached to cooperatives for work such as gardening and handicrafts, cared for the small children, themselves occupied from the age of three years and above with preparing manure for the crops.

Husbands might be absent for several months: put into a fishing team that went off to the great lake or the sea, or sent to cut bamboo in distant and unhealthy mountains. Families were rarely complete.

Furthermore, a politicized child, that is, one who had become a *kamaphibal* or *yothea*, was obliged to consider his parents as strangers and to inflict on them, if they had committed errors, the same punishments as on others. Children considered them to be simple "comrades" in the political sense of the term. Daughters and sons owed obedience to Angkar, which gave its orders through the cadres. "The children were pitiless. I have heard them browbeat their parents. The cadres had taught them a certain number of slogans, such as I'm not killing my mother—I'm killing an enemy." This was the end of the family unit and of familial values.

*Ov* (papa), the diminutive of *opuk* (father), was too reminiscent of Prince Sihanouk, whom the people were in the habit of calling *Samdech Ov* (Monsignor papa). Beginning in 1975, father became *puk*. If the leaders' wives took a political role just as in preceding regimes, Khmer Rouge power nonetheless belonged to the men in the first instance, as the new vocabulary showed. Thus, for designating parents, a child no longer used traditional expression *maê-ov* (mama and papa) but rather *puk-maê* (papa and mama). Any meeting, including those on the border camps controlled by the Khmer Rouge in the 1980s, began with the formula: "Honorable *puk-maê*, elder and younger siblings, comrades . . ." In the villages controlled by the Khmer Rouge inside Cambodia, *puk-maê* was still in use in 1986.[19] More generally, among the "old people," the word comrade replaced terms indicating kinship. Among the "new people," various kinship terms—elder or younger sibling and aunt or uncle, nephew or niece—were common. Among the Khmer Rouge leaders, the terms older and younger sibling prevailed.

## Faith in the Service of Angkar

For propaganda purposes, between 1970 and 1975 the Khmer Rouge dispensed an education of their design but allowed monks in the regions they controlled to carry out their sacerdotal duties:

> In 1970 the Vietcong and the Khmer Rouge came into the village [in Prey Veng]. The Khmer Rouge closed the schools. The only instruction for all, children and adults, was a course in politics. It took place every day from seven to ten o'clock in the morning. For five years, they repeated to us the same thing: you must contribute to the village's development, that is, you must dig canals, build dikes, install a pumping station. . . . They taught us also communism and the doctrine of the mass line, a doctrine that tramples men under-

foot. . . . In my village, there had been a pagoda with many monks, I don't know how many. They remained until 1975, when the Khmer Rouge took away the position of monk. In other villages, the pagodas had been closed well before this, but not in ours.

Indeed, in well-organized hamlets inhabitants did not move about freely and had begun to live according to the rules that were imposed all over the country beginning in 1975. The monks were defrocked and put to work growing rice. If they protested, they were killed, as was any lay person who complained. But there was no systematic killing of monks; the Khmer Rouge simply wanted to transform them into producers and to eradicate Buddhism.

The new constitution, introduced on 5 January 1976, differed from the FUNC's program. It did not mention Buddhism. Whereas previously the monastery had exercised a force of attraction in the rural milieu, individuals could no longer take the initiative to decide their future: there were no more pagodas, no more offerings to the monks, no more merits to assure oneself a fortuitous reincarnation. People were confused and puzzled but in their hearts continued to venerate the Buddha.

The wood from the demolished pagodas was used in the construction of storehouses and workshops. Concrete monasteries often served as prisons. Indeed, the Khmer Rouge did not always kill with a cudgel's blow on the back of the head: they also tortured, allowing victims to die slowly. The peaceful pagodas, usually open for the well-being and repose of the soul as well as the body—a building was reserved for travelers—thus became places of suffering. In the mosques previously frequented by Islamic Khmers (Chams), pigs were raised; what is more, Muslims were forced to eat them. These actions reveal the leaders' desire to humiliate the people by degrading their holy places.

The prohibition also applied to popular religion, made up of beliefs in the many spirits who inhabit the Cambodians' universe. With the changes in location, it would have been necessary for the people to conciliate other deities, render worship to new spirits of the land, to those of cultivated areas, to the goddess of rice. The "new people," initially bothered by this absence of religiosity, soon encountered a problem that would take precedence over all the rest—physical survival.

In any case, people had no choice, for a single god was to be honored: Angkar, the Communist party. An infraction could bring death. However, three and one-half years were not enough to turn the Cambodians into atheists. Buddhism reemerged vigorously after the Khmer Rouge's defeat (to new persecution under the following regime).

## The Destruction of Other Village Values

The pagoda no longer played its traditional religious role. Dispensing knowledge, the monks there taught not only Buddhism but empirical medical craft as well. Each village had its *kru* (master) in the art of healing. In remote regions to which teachers refused to go, the monastery had the role of primary school for boys who wanted to learn to read and write.

Knowledge—of whatever sort—had the force of law in the village. The inhabitants respected traditional healers; the same was true of the *méphum*, the village chief, who was generally a native of the village and chosen by the inhabitants. In the 1960s the Cambodian administration, still new, had not eradicated all of the traditional values. For serious conflicts (adultery, land problems, etc.), the peasants often preferred to turn to the community's elders: *méphum*, in office or retired, traditional healers, masters of rituals, men who had retired to the pagodas for a few years, all those whose knowledge or age earned them a halo of wisdom. They formed a kind of assembly of notables, although it was not officially recognized; the administration could not prevent peasants from solving their daily problems by consulting a community's elders as long as they did not exceed reasonable limits.

In 1975 the former sexual division of labor within the household and within larger social groups—including the entire hamlet during periods of mutual aid (agricultural work)—no longer existed. Replacing it was a distribution of tasks according to age-based categories. The individual rice paddy disappeared, and collectivization spread to the entire country. Gone were the beautiful wooden houses of the charming hamlets, located near springs and surrounded by greenery. In many places, they were demolished and replaced by straw huts, rudimentary shelters, and sheds erected with no vegetation around them. Or indeed people had to construct new settlements in the midst of the unhealthy forest.

Thus, the values were reversed: gone was the beauty of sites dear to the rural people; gone was individual liberty within the context of respect for others, leaving only the masses in Angkar's service. Power passed into the hands of young know-nothings who invoked Angkar's name and despised private expertise. Peasants no longer knew which spirits to call on: "If so many deaths from malaria happened when people went into the forest to cut wood, it's because the spirits were angry that nobody made offerings to them," a peasant would say. Many waited passively for the end of this bloody era foretold by the predictions. Educated Cambodians thought differently: "From the beginning, it was not a question of respect for authority. Pol Pot's was a regime of terror, of arms. You said nothing because you wanted to stay alive; it was a kind of contract."

In 1978, faced with growing border problems and convinced that the Vietnamese would invade Cambodia, the Khmer Rouge tried to rally the people by announcing the imminent abolition of the "new people" status and improvements in the diet. These measures never went into effect. The only new effort involved technical education, as shown by the opening of a school in Phnom Penh.

THE SILENCE OF THE INTERNATIONAL COMMUNITY

The French press—with a few exceptions, among them right-wing papers accused of counterpropaganda—reported few refugees' accounts, or did so with a great deal of reservations and without giving them the coverage they deserved. Nonetheless, early in 1977 Father François Ponchaud (a well-informed source, as we have learned) devoted a book to the question and gave the outside world some idea of the general features of the Khmer Rouge regime.[20] But not until late 1977, after the rupture of diplomatic relations between Cambodia and Vietnam and, as a corollary, the attacks on the Khmer Rouge regime by Hanoi and Moscow, did opinion begin to veer.

There was little alarm abroad about the fate of the Cambodian people. After the expulsion of foreign diplomats by the Khmer Rouge in 1975, the West—including France—on the whole remained silent. At the instigation of Great Britain, the United Nation's Commission on Human Rights condemned the Khmer Rouge. Americans Stephen Solarz and Richard Holbrook convinced Washington to do likewise. But when Senator George McGovern raised the question of Democratic Kampuchea to his government and suggested an international military intervention to stop the massacres, nobody listened. Nothing was done until the overthrow of the regime in 1979, when the press made up for its silence by a frenzy that has rarely been equaled.

POLITICAL PRIORITIES

After completing the transfers of population that were to save the regime from plots, the Khmer Rouge applied its official political line, based on several principles: monopolization of power by a few, physical elimination of the bourgeoisie, generalization of peasant status, development of industry for agriculture, self-sufficiency, and territorial defense.

THE END OF GRUNC AND THE
RESIGNATION OF PRINCE SIHANOUK

In January 1976 Cambodia became the state of Democratic Kampuchea and promulgated its constitution. The government continued to be called the Gouvernement royal d'union nationale until April. Elections were mentioned in March. "This was a decoy; only several containers for ballots were placed in Phnom Penh to deceive Prince Sihanouk, one of the few citizens who voted." In the provinces none of the evacuees voted. After these sham elections, GRUNC was dissolved in April 1976. The leaders installed an assembly of people's representatives presided over by Nuon Chea, a presidium of state of which Khieu Samphan was the number one, and a government led by Pol Pot. All the big names were included: Ieng Sary, vice-president, who received at the same time the much coveted post of foreign minister; Ieng Thirith, social affairs; Son Sen, defense; his wife, Yun Yat, education. The moderate Khieu Samphan served as window dressing, a role that the former chief of state declined.

Sihanouk carried out a mission at the United Nations in autumn of 1975, after which the Khmer Rouge allowed him to return to Phnom Penh. He had not imagined the harshness of the regime. When he had visited the Angkor region in 1973, the people—"old people," approximately ten thousand civilians organized by one to two thousand *yothea*—had cheered him. He thus had the impression that the peasants were not living too badly.

When Khieu Samphan took him to the provinces to visit cooperatives, factories, and hydraulic works early in 1976, reality appeared different. He decided to retire rather than sanction the regime. Khieu Samphan replaced him as chief of state. The Khmer Rouge did not forgive Sihanouk this desertion and sent his family to the cooperatives; five of his children and fourteen grandchildren are missing.

Why did Sihanouk return after eight months of a bloody regime, of which he had certainly heard in the West? The prince gives an answer in his book *Prisonnier des Khmers rouges*: "Out of love for my people, an almost physical passion, to be there with them, [a desire] all the more intense because they were martyrs. I am a Buddhist. Was the Buddha not the Compassionate One?" (17). Cambodians themselves remain skeptical. Did this behavior manifest one of the Khmer character traits, one that takes into account only particular time or circumstance? Let us simply assert that the former head of state responded to the irresistible call of the Khmer soil.

NATIONAL DEFENSE AND AGRICULTURE

Among the regime's priorities was the principle of self-sufficiency and territorial defense.[21] The principle of self-sufficiency—reminiscent of the Maoist slogan of "relying on one's own forces," abundantly used by the Khmer Rouge—had been decided on in the maquis. The guerrillas had tried without success to put it into practice as far as possible. Despite the creation of cooperatives and the abolition of money in order to prevent all commerce with the Vietcong, they did not achieve complete autonomy in food and even less so in the military domain. In the agricultural realm, however, they made interesting experiments that the central power implemented after 1975. In the short term, the country was to produce sufficient foodstuffs, technical devices, and munitions to allow it some independence from the friendly socialist countries on which it depended for commerce. The foreign policy of Democratic Kampuchea had no other perspective except xenophobia. The leaders wanted to transform the Khmer people into a society unique in the world, which meant isolationism, removing all "contamination" from outside. Hence the necessity to do everything alone, without recourse to other countries. Inside the country, each region and even each cooperative was to be self-sufficient in foodstuffs. The strict application of this principle led to absurd situations: the inhabitants of one cooperative died of hunger while a neighboring group in another cooperative had an abundance of manioc. But rice? Here was the point at which other concerns interfered.

In practice, territorial defense was the pivot of all Khmer Rouge action. The leaders were obsessed by a possible Vietnamese invasion, but they did not envision the peaceful resolution of border problems. Between 1970 and 1975 the Vietcong and the North Vietnamese had helped them: with soldiers until 1972; and with transit facilities for Chinese arms for the *yothea* until the end of the republican war. Nonetheless, during meetings in Europe and later in the maquis, the Khmer Rouge knew that the Vietnamese threat persisted. Succeeding fairly well in settling differences with Thailand, they then concentrated on the southern and eastern borders. For a small country such as Cambodia, this represented a considerable military effort. The Chinese were ready to continue the free delivery of arms and munitions to their Khmer allies so that the latter could defend themselves against an enemy that had also become China's own—Vietnam. But the arrogant Khmer Rouge could not accept this offer. They intended to pay for everything that China gave them, and the means of exchange was rice.

The production of rice remained comparable to that of the 1960s when the kingdom exported an average of two hundred to three hundred tons per year. From 1975 onward Angkar decided to pay for its munitions, despite the fact that it had little rice to exchange: the harvest of 1974–1975 had been poor because the countryside was not secure. Angkar had already decided that the "new people" would receive less rice. They were to endure the privations suffered by the revolutionaries during the war, working hard, eating less than before, experiencing hardship. More rice would thus remain for export. All this was planned, aside from the generalized famine that the leaders allowed to take over the country. They needed more and more rice to pay China. MIG aircraft could already be found in the colossal airport at Kompong Chhnang, unfinished in late 1978; a cartridge factory supplied by

Czechoslovakia was in operation, with a second to be delivered by the Chinese. All of this was extremely expensive. Consequently, inhabitants of cooperatives—young members of the mobile brigades who were performing hard labor and receiving a less Spartan though still inadequate regimen— saw more and more truckloads of rice leave the fields. Some people tasted very little rice for three years: after the harvest their rice soup was relatively thick but was clear the rest of the time; sometimes, corn replaced rice.

In order to compensate for the lack of rice available to the inhabitants, the leaders adapted a practice used in the maquis: the growing of strategic plants, by which they meant any species not requiring special care and yielding an easily transportable nutrient that could substitute for basic alimentary substances. After paddy, manioc constituted the strategic starch par excellence. Water bindweed was at the head of the green vegetables. People planted it wherever it did not grow naturally. They also raised sugarcane, beans, bananas, and coconut trees, but these products were soon diverted for export. Water bindweed had to be consumed the day it was harvested, but manioc, bananas, and beans could endure several days' transportation; they could be exchanged for spare parts, cartridges, and so forth. Glucosides became a rarity in the Cambodian diet. The incredibly low rations people received (declining as low as twenty-five grams of rice per day per person, in place of the seven hundred grams rice growers usually consumed) caused numerous deaths. We must emphasize that this process was not the doing of enemies of the regime infiltrated among the cadres who then sabotaged Angkar's orders. The decision to give priority to national defense was made by the leaders, perfectly well informed about the famine that was raging everywhere among the "new people," even if it was not premeditated. The regime, moreover, did not conceal its goals. Propaganda bulletins read as follows: "After rice, we are increasing strategic plants to the maximum degree . . . for internal consumption and for export." The same was true for dried or smoked fish, sent in large quantities to China and also to Thailand, where it was exchanged for gasoline. "We are also preparing excess fish for export. We also have a program for ocean fishing in order to augment production. We envision the export of twenty to thirty tons of salted fish."[22] These revelations date from August 1975, that is, from the beginning of the regime.

Once the country had become well equipped militarily, the inhabitants could have had a less severe diet. Yet on the one hand domestic plots—the first dates from 1976—did not motivate the small group of leaders toward greater clemency; and on the other, open war with Vietnam beginning in 1977 absorbed part of the reserves of munitions and these had to be replaced. Moreover, fearing generalized Vietnamese aggression, in 1978 the Khmer

Rouge diverted rice to build up caches in the hilly parts of Kompong Chhnang, Pursat, Battambang, Kah Kong, Kampot, and Kompong Speu. Hence the Cambodian people fell into the greatest material and bodily destitution, on behalf of a revolution they had not wanted and whose necessity they did not understand—to ensure the defense of a country that would finally undergo invasion by its longstanding enemy, Vietnam.

## PHNOM PENH—INDUSTRIAL CENTER

The elegant city of Phnom Penh, after five years of misery and overpopulation (one and one-half million to two million inhabitants) became nearly deserted and frankly sinister.[23] It sheltered no more than fifty thousand to seventy thousand persons: these were the regime's luminaries and officials, soldiers transformed into workers in time of peace, and cleaning teams. For, although the Khmer Rouge neglected the buildings and houses, they maintained the downtown thoroughfares, particularly in 1978, because they intended to bring tourists there. This downtown region, parts of which were laid out in vegetable gardens, manioc patches, and mini–coconut plantations, was devoted primarily to industry.[24]

In this domain, the Khmer Rouge could not do without technology. The factories were operating until the fall of the republic and then remained silent for two weeks. From 17 April onward, aware of the difficulties that the ignorant young revolutionaries would have in starting them up again, the authorities asked the technicians of the preceding regime to remain. This appeal having been only partially heard—many technicians, Chinese or Sino-Khmer of Chinese culture, remained suspicious—the request would be repeated in the towns that the evacuees had reached by April–May. Several thousand technicians responded to the call; the cadres distributed them throughout the country, especially in Phnom Penh. Among them were Khmers who would remain only several months. In December 1975, following a meeting of industrial cadres, the heads of the southwestern zone, administered by Ta Mok, emerged victorious. It was decided to send Khmer technicians to the rice fields so that they would not influence the workers, to whom, however, they were not allowed to speak. Chinese and Sino-Khmers who stuttered and stumbled in poor Khmer and maintained their distance were not considered dangerous by the regime; they lived in the city with their families. These were the only people kept for their skills who would survive the regime. The Khmer Rouge planned to eliminate them as soon as Angkar had trained its own cadres. The Chinese fully understood this and did everything they could to make themselves indispensable, teaching the workers the minimum necessary to carry out their daily tasks and taking care not to teach them the machines' secrets.

Nevertheless, almost all factories were functioning from 1975 onward. The transfer of Khmer technicians coincided with the first arrivals of Cambodian intellectuals from abroad. In July 1976 the *kamaphibal* selected approximately fifty of them for training in different plants in the capital; later on, they would replace the Chinese technicians. In France, they had participated actively in the revolution through propaganda campaigns and by supporting the FUNC. They were considered "recoverable" or in any case more trustworthy than the technicians—Khmer or Chinese—of the defunct republic. Three months later, the first great plot directed against the central power broke out, and the leaders sent the Khmer intellectuals to the Boeung Trabek camp that the state opened for them.

Foreign experts included North Koreans and above all Chinese from the People's Republic. The former equipped a tractor-assembly plant and built a hydroelectric plant at Kirirom. The latter, who came with their own advanced technicians, repaired the telephone system, railroads, and Kompong Som's oil refinery. They undertook the construction of a gigantic military airport in the hills of Kompong Chhnang. The Romanians attended to deep-sea fishing and the construction of canneries. China remained the most faithful friend; nevertheless, Chinese experts were never allowed to become plant directors.

Dependence on foreign aid in technology did not suit the xenophobic Khmer Rouge's principle of self-sufficiency. They had to become self-sufficient as soon as possible. The regime had opened two technical schools in Phnom Penh, Tuk Thla and Sala Dek, with about four hundred fifty students training to become specialized workers and mid-level technicians, but this did not solve the immediate problem of the factories. Early in 1978 Angkar decided to give a minimum of instruction to the workers; it assigned the Chinese experts to teach theoretical courses and explain the workings of the machines that they had supplied with concise instructions written in Chinese. The young and illiterate worker-soldiers had first to learn Khmer so that they could write down the explanations provided by the Chinese. The leaders thus implicitly admitted the failure of the "Pol Pot theory," according to which an elevated revolutionary consciousness could replace all technical knowledge.

In October 1978, when the regime was living its last months, the leaders decided to open a technical school in the capital to train high-level technicians in seven years and engineers in ten; the instructors, selected from the Khmer returnees, had just enough time to teach their pupils to read, write, and count before Phnom Penh fell.

Aside from the former plants restored to working order, some other sectors were developed, such as weaving and the fabrication of traditional

medicines, which now became industrial; others—such as metallurgy—
were newly created. Industry had two priorities: to satisfy the country's
needs; and to serve agriculture and especially rice growing, the development
of which was Angkar's primary economic objective. Thus, a great number
of small rotating hand beaters, shares for plows, and shovels and picks for
breaking the soil were produced. But machines and tools often broke down,
and Khmers went to Peking to learn the skills and methods of foundry. After
three months of training, they did not achieve better results. Other products
left much to be desired: a blackish and ineffective soap; rubber that cracked
easily. The most obvious industrial progress came in the shipyards. Since
waterways were utilized to move exportable goods toward Kompong Som,
many boats were needed. The workshop at Prek Phneou, modest in 1975,
rapidly became a veritable shipyard. Its means of production did not equal
those of a modern country, but the scale of this industry and the number of
craft produced were impressive. Despite a highly perfected woodworking
craft, problems arose. In order to deliver the boats promised to Angkar on
time, work had to be done quickly, and the wood, without time to dry,
warped. Generally speaking, the quality of finished products remained
mediocre in all domains. Phnom Penh did not master industrial production.
Late in 1978 Angkar became aware of the country's technological insufficiency, when the threat of a Vietnamese invasion was taking shape.

What emerged, unquestioned, was the goodwill of the workers and their
zeal on the job. Even the youngest of them—factories employed children
from the age of eleven years and above (orphans, children separated from
their parents, cadres' sons)—did their best. Some of them achieved feats of
prowess that required great investment of time and effort; yet a minimum
of technical knowledge would have saved both. The daily meetings and the
slogans broadcast on the radio gave them the impression of playing an
important role, and, in fact, they were necessary to the regime's survival.
They thus responded favorably to the daily exhortations launched over the
airwaves:

> Holding firmly to the revolutionary organization of Kampuchea's
> line of sovereignty and independence, the revolutionary workers,
> boiling with patriotism and revolutionary pride, launch offensives
> for the reinforcement and development of workshops and plants by
> utilizing the national resources for giving an impulsion to national
> defense and construction by prodigious bounds, together with the
> peasants of the cooperatives.

The combative spirit was to be applied in the service of war as in production.
Workers labored from nine to ten hours per day, not counting the hours

of "socialist labor" devoted to gardening, maintenance, and shifts of guard duty at night. They ate decently and lived in collective buildings. Job safety was nonexistent. Accidents occurred because of the ignorance of rural people who allowed a hand to rest on an engine or a *krâma* to hang over a gearbox; some were electrocuted. Needless to say, nothing was done to prevent such accidents; it was experience that made the worker, and their enthusiasm should not be dampened. Nevertheless, the common worker-soldiers escaped purges because they remained loyal to Angkar that trained them when they were young; only the cadres would participate in the plots.

The revolutionaries, ready to take up any kind of work, were not specialized. Soldiers helped the mobile brigades in agricultural work. Since the rice crop and its associated tasks were primordial, the worker-combatants from the factories had to participate as well. They had to know how to handle a sickle; they could not put on the airs of a privileged group. Thus, their rare days off were spent replanting and harvesting rice and putting up embankments on the lands owned by the industrial committee in the suburbs of Phnom Penh.

Despite the leaders' wishes, Democratic Kampuchea was unable to produce all that it needed. It resorted to barter, for money no longer existed. China, North Korea, and the Eastern European countries were privileged partners. Thailand caught up with the times and concluded economic accords in 1976, and Madagascar purchased rice, payable in currency, which allowed the opening of a commercial emporium in Hong Kong in 1976 and another in Singapore in 1978 that might engage in commerce with the West and particularly Europe without seeming to do so. Since the leaders failed to elaborate intelligent planning or provide appropriate technical education that might guide the country toward the greatest possible autonomy, they left Cambodia dependent on the West and brought it to the brink of catastrophe, which occurred at the end of 1978 with the Vietnamese offensive. If the leaders were surprised by the rapidity of the attack, they nevertheless expected it. It had been announced from June 1978 onward in the factories; from this time, workers had been learning martial arts and, for those without experience with small arms, the handling of a gun.

THE PURGES AND PROGRESSIVE ELIMINATIONS

These bloody campaigns affected above all the "new people" and the Khmer Rouge cadres. On their arrival in April 1975, the Khmer Rouge first dealt with the two "supertraitors" still in Phnom Penh: Prime Minister Long Boreth, who just missed his place in an American helicopter; Sirik Matak, who took refuge at the French embassy and left it with great dignity when the *yothea* demanded him.[25]

During the evacuation of the city dwellers in 1975, in many places (such as Kandal, Prey Veng, Kompong Cham, Kah Kong, Siem Reap) the people passed through clearing centers: "The Khmer Rouge called on military men and officials loyal to Angkar to present themselves in order to go to Phnom Penh and participate in the reconstruction of Cambodia. Many revealed their identities, and they were taken away that very evening. On the way, I had seen numerous acts of violence. So I kept my mouth shut." Elsewhere the *yothea* held out the return of Prince Sihanouk in order to bring the hesitant around:

> In Battambang, the *yothea* asked if there were among the evacuees any former military men or officials to welcome *Samdech Ov*. A dozen people, including a doctor, came forward. They were immediately taken away and shot on the Pailin road; it was 20 April 1975, at seven o'clock in the morning. Some peasants came to tell one of the wives what had happened. She was able to go to see the cadavers that same night. Three days later, the Khmer Rouge transferred her; they knew that her husband was one of the victims.

Many of the ossuaries found from 1979 onward dated from this time, when the Khmer Rouge rid themselves of the most hated and most dangerous elements, those capable of leading the masses—military officers and officials. These premeditated massacres went on in the same manner throughout the country. The revolutionaries, who announced the physical elimination of only seven people, killed at this time dozens and even hundreds of thousands. Some wives, having understood what was happening and fearing to see their time come, bought off the young soldiers and passed the barriers without difficulty: "I offered the *yothea* my diamonds and watch to let me pass. He didn't know what diamonds were, but he took my watch, and I was able to continue."

When they learned of the end of the republic, almost two hundred Khmer military men in Bangkok for study courses returned to the country. In transit at the Thai airbase of Utapao their fellow citizens, along with Thais and Americans, tried in vain to change their minds. One group returning from the United States found itself in Phnom Penh in mid-1976. There are no known survivors.

Throughout 1975 the search for military men was in full swing. Several hundred were assembled, along with officials, in a camp at Takeo. The *yothea* eliminated them in small groups. The purges also struck the youths of the mobile brigades:

> In our brigade in Kompong Thom they liquidated all the former soldiers and state employees. . . . Several young girls killed themselves

by taking poison; some were saved. Every day several of our companions were "called." They never came back, which means that the Khmer Rouge had massacred them. Shortly before the arrival of the Vietnamese, we had to dig pits. We learned later that they were meant for us because our names were on the death list. For them, we were all traitors because we had been officials. Aside from peasants and workers, all others deserved death.

In certain places, the Khmer Rouge eliminated minority groups because they were not Khmers in the sense understood by Ieng Sary: "In 1977–1978 at Kompong Preah (Battambang), the cadres killed almost all the Islamic Khmers in the commune. There were nearly four hundred of them; they 'took away' twenty to thirty per day. By late 1978 there were only about twenty left. The others had been massacred for the most part; some had died of hunger." Elsewhere they escaped: Malaysia received several thousand of them early in the 1980s, the United States took approximately one thousand, France three hundred, and Denmark slightly more.[26] The Chinese did not receive any better treatment: "In 1979 when we came back to Damdek [Siem Reap], many of the Chinese were missing; they had been massacred in 1977. The cadre in charge of the Damdek commune, Mit Chheng, had more than one hundred of them killed." Nevertheless, entire Chinese families made it to the border in 1979. They had escaped the famine thanks to their capacity to engage in commerce with the "old people"; they had indeed engaged in barter on their own account and for that of the Khmers who were, like them, considered "new people," and took a percentage on rice exchanged.

For three years—in addition to these systematic killings—Cambodians died of hunger or untreated illnesses, or fell as victims one by one to elimination at a local cadre's discretion or Angkar's determination that there were still too many people capable of taking the initiative in these times of want. A small number succeeded in reaching the Vietnamese and Thai borders. Some unfortunates, after an attempt at revolt that forced them to flee, reached the forest, where they often joined groups of republican soldiers who had taken to the maquis after April 1975. The Khmer Rouge called them Khmer *sar* (white Khmers) or In Tam Khmers (after the general who organized the first guerrilla force in 1975 in Phnom Malay, close to the Thai border). State employees and students were the first to be targeted by these more or less discreet eliminations, followed by lycée students.

Everywhere, workers were present at executions or saw the cadavers. To be declared a traitor to the revolution, it was sufficient to have eaten a grasshopper on the sly, to have broken a tool, or simply to have relaxed the pace of work. Offenders were sometimes executed during the evening self-criticism sessions by a single blow with a rattan cane on the nape of the neck; the Khmer Rouge economized on munitions and sometimes killed publicly to set an example.

> We didn't see the executions, but we saw the cadavers. They were superficially buried, and dogs pulled on them by the legs. When we went to work, we also came across cadavers right on the ground; we recognized some by the particulars of their clothing. There were many of them. Beginning in August 1978 the Khmer Rouge made us open the tombs [pits]. Within the brigade, there were teams of men who specialized in this work. They had to dig up the cadavers. These were sometimes in a state of decomposition, but in general they waited two or three months so that the flesh was separated from the bones. The Khmer Rouge had the cadavers piled up to a level of about one and one-half meters and set them afire, saying that the ashes were for fertilizer. Beginning in June 1977 patients who died at the hospital were soaked in basins measuring five by three meters in order to detach the flesh. The water in which they steeped was redistributed by pumps into a smaller basin in which rice seedlings to be replanted were placed during the night; this was to make them grow better and faster. It smelled terrible, but the men assigned this work could not refuse without risking being killed. There was no soap to wash your hands.

Khmer Rouge cadres and soldiers themselves experienced disasters. In Kah Kong, at Thmar Sar, there were massacres from 1974 onward; rival Communist groups confronted each other; Ta Mok's clan (thus that of Pol Pot–Ieng Sary) emerged victorious. Likewise, at Prey Nop in Kampot on 2 November 1975 the civil group, section, and company chiefs who did not belong to the leading clan perished. Beginning in 1976 and above all in 1977, the Khmer Rouge killed the regime's cadres and soldiers en masse, following plots against the Pol Pot–Ieng Sary group. According to the testimony from Cambodians among the "old people," from youths in the mobile brigades, and from cadres and soldiers, plots were numerous. They first broke out in the northern zone, on a greater or lesser scale according to place: in Kompong Cham two soldiers guarding a cooperative turned against a cadre whom they killed; they were captured and executed as they fled. In Siem Reap workers in a hydraulic construction yard left the premises in the midst of great unrest: Angkar arrested the rebellious authorities—who had in their possession rifles and side arms—and dispersed the workers involved in these incidents. In the provincial capital, a serious altercation took place between elements loyal to the regime and rebellious soldiers who set a munitions depot aflame (blame for the incident fell on the Americans). In 1976 the purge of members responsible for transportation of water in the northern zone dealt with one of a series of attempts against the regime. Khoy Thuon, unable to assure security in the zone that he led, was transferred to Phnom Penh. Then, "when Pol Pot learned that Khoy Thuon was implicated in a conspiracy against the party, he had him killed along with three hundred persons who were in league with him; among them was Tiv Ol and an army chief named Chakrey. Afterward Nuon Chea gave a report to all the public services denouncing the 'acts of sabotage' committed by Khoy Thuon and his team."

The purges reached the cadres of the northwest sometime around the middle of 1977. According to cadres and youths from the mobile brigades, Ros Nhim and his entourage were indeed preparing a coup d'état. In the east, zone chief So Phim and his companions, exposed, perished for attempting to overthrow Pol Pot and his entourage. Ministers Vorn Veth and Cheng On, accused of connivance, were eliminated shortly afterward. Soldiers in So Phim's army who had joined him in rebellion confirmed that he was plotting against the regime and established contacts for this purpose with the Vietnamese, whose support he needed.

The purges within the regime were aimed at individuals—Hou Yuon, Hu Nim, Vorn Veth, Cheng On, and the zone chiefs—who represented a threat for the central power because they questioned some of its actions or because they moved from collaboration to discreet opposition before attempting to overthrow the regime. To impute these purges to economic failures alone (as Élisabeth Becker does)[27] follows from a line of reasoning inconsistent with the facts that cadres and witnesses to these massacres experienced. It is not surprising that the use of torture gave the Khmer Rouge leaders the confessions they wanted to hear (acts of economic sabotage committed by infiltrated pro-Vietnamese agents), or that their later declarations corroborated the testimony. The high authorities could not accept seeing their regime and their power contested. Before the eyes of soldiers, cadres, and supporting population, an emphasis on foreign enemies was essential; the regime and the authority of the chiefs thus remained intact. What was termed the "eclipse of Pol Pot" between September 1976 and September 1977 was, according to a witness, a voluntary retreat from political leadership in order to unmask and unravel plots whose scope and danger plots in the north had revealed. Three attempts against Pol Pot—one of them fomented by his adoptive son, Pang—confirmed that the opposition to the main leaders was violent. The end of the regime coincided with numerous massacres—this time of the population at large.

The prisons and reeducation camps housed individuals who were declared guilty of something or other. No one was ever released from the prisons, as two survivors attest.

In June 1978 I was locked up because I complained we were working too hard and not eating enough. There were about a thousand
of us, adults and children, working in the rice fields by day and
chained up at night. The prison was twenty to thirty kilometers
from the town of Kratié, in the middle of the forest. Every day
three, four, five people died of malaria; they "took away" others.
We ate a gruel of water bindweed and banana stalks with a few
grains of rice floating in it. My body was all swollen. I got out
when the Vietnamese came because the Khmer Rouge fled, leaving
us in the prison.

I am a rice grower. . . . One month after our transfer, I was arrested
and put in the Kaun Kreng camp in Siem Reap. They tortured me,
hitting me on the head. . . . I stayed there nine months and thirteen
days. They accused me of wanting to escape to Thailand. Today,
when I talk too much, I have a terrible pain in my head. . . . After
the arrival of the Vietnamese, I didn't dare remain in Cambodia for
very long for fear of another revolution like that of the Polpotists.

Very young children were not thrown into prison, but they endured cruel
punishments that did not stop short of death. Here are two accounts, equally
terrifying, the first by a child:

I saw orphans of seven to eight years old, a girl and a boy who'd
stolen rice, salt, and vegetables because they were hungry. A cadre
caught them by surprise, and he had them beaten until they bled.
Another time, they stole salt to eat with tamarind; the chief tied
their hands and feet and put them for two hours in a place infested
with tiny ants, until blood was pouring out. Then they were beaten
with a cane and then put back with the ants. . . . I saw it with my
own eyes because I'd gone to get some vegetables, and that was
where they were punished. A third time, they were so hungry—
they were nothing but skin and bones—they stole vegetables from
the kitchen. The Khmer Rouge cadre picked eight children to beat
them and then bury them alive up to the neck. I wasn't there, but
the eight children in question said they both died.

At the cooperative, a boy of five or six years old had stolen some
rice. The Khmer Rouge forced his companions to bind his hands
and feet and to cut open on him a nest of big, red ants. He called for
help to his father, who was carrying bananas with me. The father
brought him some vegetables, and the very same day the man was
"taken away." The child never stole again.

THE RECALL OF DIPLOMATS AND STUDENTS

GRUNC had diplomatic missions in Cuba, in several countries in Europe, the Near East, and Africa. In December 1975 Phnom Penh recalled its ambassadors "for two-week reeducation courses." In April 1976 the Khmer Rouge announced the dissolution of GRUNC, and the diplomats did not set out again; with several individuals on mission when Phnom Penh fell, they made up the first contingent of the voluntarily repatriated. Many would survive by accepting the subordinate posts offered them by the Khmer Rouge or by enduring without complaint the life of a reeducation camp; several died under torture. The approximately thirty embassy employees who came with them all disappeared; several of their names were on the list of victims of Tuol Sleng, the Khmer Rouge extermination camp established in a former lycée in the capital.

During a seminar in Albania in 1972 some students had asked to be returned to the country to participate in its liberation. The Khmer Rouge responded that they were performing greater service on the outside and that the resistance did not lack combatants. After victory, their presence inside the country was desired. The Khmer students' return from abroad was to be spread out over three years. The returns were organized by the FUNC representative in Paris and then, after his departure, by the official in charge of the Comité des patriotes du Kampuchea démocratique (which had changed its name from the Comité des patriotes khmers à l'étranger). Approximately one thousand young people living in America, in Eastern Europe, and above all in France responded. The first to return perhaps lacked information about their country, although the evacuation of Phnom Penh had been reported by the international press, and refugees had already reached Paris. In 1976 refugees arrived in great numbers. Some Khmers in France refused to listen to the atrocities that they reported because they could not question the system. "And besides, what they said was so horrible you couldn't believe it." A few argued with members of their families who had lived several months in Democratic Kampuchea. Concerning the revolutionaries, "we told ourselves: since they won the war in five years and one month, they must be intelligent and well organized. We couldn't question them, given their abilities and their results. And besides, the intellectuals who joined the maquis were regarded as being something other than the Khmer Rouge, than those people."

In other respects, the Khmer Rouge brought multiple pressures to bear. The Comité des patriotes showed "an interview with Ieng Sary declaring that the evacuated residents of Phnom Penh had returned to their homes. We didn't know it was false. The entire policy of Pol Pot–Ieng Sary was nothing but deception and lies." In August 1975 "Ieng Sary, during a short stay in Paris, gave a report to the intellectuals on the overall situation in

Cambodia. He showed a film illustrating the development of the war between 1970 and 1975. He added that intellectuals who returned would be able to serve the country's cause in their areas of specialization." The authorities tempted students by telling them that their parents were waiting for them. One important detail should have alerted them: not a single letter came out of Democratic Kampuchea. Some hesitated, undecided:

> On the one hand, I was a bit disturbed because I had never lived under a Communist regime. I thought that if I delayed I would never return . . . , that if I weighed the pros and cons, given my old habits, I would no longer dare. On the other hand, I said to myself that I had to be logical with myself, that having contributed to the change of regime, I should go all the way. That is why I left with the first ones.

"It was a kind of faith," another would say. Two individuals returned to their country in December 1978, two weeks before the final Vietnamese offensive. Up until the last moment Phnom Penh continued to insist; in 1978 Ieng Sary issued a final written appeal. The Khmer Rouge's xenophobia saved those who had married French women, for Phnom Penh did not accept foreigners, and very few Khmers consented to separation from their wives. However, two French women were allowed to follow their husbands: one of them had given sufficient proofs of her sincerity toward Khmer communism; it is not known why the Khmer Rouge authorized the other's return.[28]

None of the young Khmers had any idea what was waiting for them. Their enthusiasm and naiveté were such that they hastily sold their Parisian apartments and, in some cases, donated the money to FUNC. All believed that they would have a role in the postwar reconstruction. The most consistent ones, who had been living in Peking since the beginning of the 1970s, returned in 1975 on the Ho Chi Minh trail or by plane. The cadres welcomed them at the former Khmer-Soviet Friendship Technical Institute and then distributed them in the villages. When the Boeung Trabek camp was opened in September 1976, all the diplomats and students who had returned from abroad, including those from Peking, stayed there. At the end of 1976 another camp, established at Stung Trâng in Kompong Cham, received two hundred and fifty intellectuals.

Some of them began to wonder when they arrived at the airport with no one waiting for them: "If I'd had wings, I'd have turned right around. I can say that, from the very first day, I had it in my mind to leave." Their concern grew when they saw their schoolfellows, who had arrived only two months before them, pale and emaciated. Some committed suicide: an engineer threw himself out of the window of the fourth floor of the Khmer-Soviet Technical Institute. Another hanged himself two days after his arrival; his wife killed herself once she was transferred to the camp in Kompong Cham. Here are accounts from two inmates.

> Boeung Trabek was a sort of reeducation camp, placed under the tutelage of Khieu Samphan. But it was Phum, our political authority, and especially Pang, head of the camp's organization, who had authority, for, judging from what we learned afterward, whenever a question about the camp arose, Khieu Samphan referred it to Pang, a member of the central committee of the Communist party and the adoptive son of Pol Pot.

> Pang was in authority over Angkar Committee 870, or the executive committee for Pol Pot's orders. This committee established the food rations for the entire country. . . . Pang was in charge of the foreign affairs department of committee 870. All denunciation reports went through him before reaching Pol Pot. He tried to assassinate Pol Pot, but he was exposed.

Thus the foreign ministry, that is, Ieng Sary, looked after intellectuals returned from abroad. Angkar took care to place the name of Khieu Samphan, appreciated by the intellectuals, in the forefront. Ieng Sary placed the men he trusted at Boeung Trabek, especially a Khmer *leu* (from the hill tribes of Ratanakiri and Mondolkiri provinces) named Savonn, who succeeded Phum. In the early period, Khieu Samphan conducted a seminar in the camp:

> "You have done the right thing in coming back to Cambodia . . . , you are good patriots, and you have a bright future. [But] intellectuals can help in the reconstruction of the country only if they have acquired a proletarian viewpoint, if they have eliminated all private property, material and sentimental. That is, we have to consider our wives, parents, and children no different from other people, with no special bonds between us. . . ." We didn't agree but didn't dare say so; it's difficult to say why, but we were afraid of the regime. . . .
> He spoke to us about agrarian reform, about the creation of cooperatives between 1970 and 1975.

Most gave all their property to Angkar: money, jewelry, cameras. Before leaving Paris, one intellectual spent his entire savings to buy science books; he found them later in the toilets. During the seminars that followed Khieu Samphan's, one of the cadres was explicit from the very first day: "Gentlemen, coming back to Cambodia was a positive action; you have demonstrated your nationalism. But what are you looking for? A good position? Let us say clearly that we do not need you; we need people who know how to work the land, and that is all." And every day the same leitmotif was repeated:

> One who is politicized, who has understood the regime, can do anything; the skills will come afterward . . . ; one does not need engineers to cultivate rice, grow corn, raise pigs.

> In order to find out if people are friends or enemies, we need only put them in a difficult situation; those who protest are refractory, and those who obey and say nothing are the regime's faithful followers.

Intellectuals learned to keep quiet and to control their behavior: "If, for example, one broke a glass, he was accused of having served the cause of the enemy." For twenty days, participants were required to split into small groups and perform self-criticisms: "Khieu Samphan urged us to tell everything in order to purify ourselves. Each of us talked for four or five hours. . . . It was brainwashing."

In this manner individuals who could have used their technical abilities to contribute to the renovation of Cambodia, found themselves profoundly despised and even humiliated by the cadres: members of the fertilizer team, for example, were required to collect human excrement with their bare hands. Others broke up dry earth and planted cabbages or water bindweed, the latter being picked early each morning to supply the capital; children did the weeding. Despite dietary privations, they did not experience famine, which was general among the "new people." And yet to see these individuals as accomplices of the regime or even as a privileged class is implausible because, out of the approximately one thousand returnees, only about two hundred and fifty are still alive. Between 1976 and 1979 the Khmer Rouge killed the others since they were unable to return to the ranks of ordinary workers.

In late 1978 the government paid some attention to persons with advanced degrees: it brought back to Phnom Penh those who had been sent to Kompong Cham. Ieng Sary became officially what he had always been secretly—the authority in charge of the intellectuals. He went to Boeung Trabek to see the survivors; he said he was unaware of the whereabouts of the missing and blamed their disappearance on a fifth column. After the Vietnamese entered Phnom Penh in 1979, Khmers employed at the foreign ministry found biographies written by these intellectuals in Khmer Rouge archives. Ieng Sary had written notes on them, emphasizing the failings of their authors and the possible danger that they represented for the regime. Here are my remarks and suggestions, he concluded in substance, but naturally the decision is up to *bâng ti muoy* (elder brother number one; that is, Pol Pot), signed *bâng ti pi* (elder brother number two; that is, Ieng Sary). The authors of the biographies that were considered questionable appear on the list of victims of the Tuol Sleng extermination center.

In August and September, Ieng Sary gave the youths from Boeung
Trabek courses in a former elementary school not far away: "He spoke of
the organization of the camp, of the evolution of each person's ideas, and
of what had been learned since our return. He also dealt with the question
of the war with Vietnam, saying that the Khmer Rouge had eliminated
almost all the Vietnamese agents who had infiltrated the country and that
victory was certain." Next,

> Pol Pot invited about thirty of us at the Université bouddhique for
> a seminar. He was accompanied by Ieng Sary and Khieu Samphan,
> as well as minister of economy Vorn Veth, and minister of industry
> Cheng On. He was the only one to speak during two days. He
> wanted the country to be first in all domains and to become the
> model for all nonaligned countries; he wanted agricultural yields to
> be higher than Japan's. He told us that Cambodia was an underde-
> veloped country, that it had to wake up quickly, make progress, a
> great leap. At first, we were a bit surprised, but then these fine
> words encouraged us. And twice he added: "Gentlemen, don't
> worry about your family members. We're looking out for them; if
> they're alive, you'll probably have the chance to see them again." . . .
> For Khieu Samphan had acknowledged in 1976 that there had been
> deaths during the evacuation of Phnom Penh. But Ieng Sary stated
> precisely: "No more than those who die on France's highways dur-
> ing a weekend." Next, Pol Pot spoke about Vietnam's jealousy to-
> ward Cambodia, which had made such progress and where justice
> and equality reigned; about the economic covetousness of the Viet-
> namese, who wanted to have as much fish and fertile land as we
> had. And he uttered a sentence that Ieng Sary had already told us:
> "If it comes to an armed struggle, we're not afraid."

In fact, in the words of a participant, "Khieu Samphan was there for show;
there wasn't even a seat reserved for him. Ieng Sary didn't make a major
speech, but you got the impression he was supervising what Pol Pot said.
By the way he intervened, you sensed he was the one who led the debates."
The meeting focused on the education of young people:

> Pol Pot told us that he wanted to open a technical school; that we
> had to educate our children while maintaining our national charac-
> ter, that is, without copying from abroad; that in foreign countries
> they needed twenty years to train an engineer starting from zero
> but that Democratic Kampuchea would set aside only ten years by
> emphasizing the practical aspect; in France, for example, they put
> too much emphasis on theory. By the end of the seminar, about fif-
> teen persons had been picked to teach in the technical school that
> was to open under Thiounn Mumm's direction. Overall, we were
> proud to be the model for the entire world.

The Khmer-Soviet Friendship Technical Institute opened its doors on 10 October 1978 to three hundred pupils from the ages of twelve to sixteen years, as well as to their professors. The latter's children were not admitted to the courses; they were placed in nurseries outside the lycée. Some parents never saw their children again; they were moved separately on 7 January 1979, on the arrival of the Vietnamese. Courses ended on that date; students were evacuated across the mountainous west in extremely arduous conditions.[29] The nonteaching intellectuals took another itinerary: most of them were able to flee to the Thai border and, from there, reached the West through the embassies' refugee missions.

These progressive or Marxist Khmers with advanced degrees were not, of course, the only indoctrinated people who lost all critical facilities; but their education had trained them particularly well to avoid analysis, to believe elders who expressed wishes for social justice similar to their own. The officers who returned from the United States proved just as gullible. The Comité des patriotes du Kampuchea démocratique in France used them to protest against the anti–Khmer Rouge regime "defamation campaigns" in the West and to urge all their compatriots still abroad to return to the country. The extremist declaration that they made in Paris on 23 May 1976 through the intermediary of this organization (see appendix 6) shows the degree to which they were manipulated.

In France, however, the neutral students remained coolheaded; they were probably the only individuals with advanced degrees who reflected calmly. In June 1977 they circulated in the Cambodian milieu a text that, despite some blunders, constitutes a historical reflection. Entitled *Pour une société khmère meilleure*, this manifesto for a better society condemned the Khmer Rouge authority

> that imposes on the whole of the population a totalitarian dictatorship based on terror, fanaticism, sectarianism, hatred, and malice rather than the true social revolution that was so anticipated. . . . Economic and social progress should be sought in a combination of the positive elements of the Khmer culture and civilization with the elements of technical, scientific, and social progress from the modern world.

The last sentence shows that this thinking minority was aware of the fact that Khmer culture held positive but also negative elements. The signers of this manifesto were the only ones who did something useful for Cambodia in the 1980s: despite enormous difficulties, slender means, and the jealousy of their refugee compatriots, they maintained and disseminated Khmer culture.[30] They were the instigators of another motion, written on 4 January

1978 and published in *Le Monde* when the Vietnamese-Khmer conflict came out into the open: they denounced imperialism and neoimperialism, condemned the suicidal and totalitarian policy of the Khmer Rouge, demanded an end to Vietnamese expansionism, urged Khmer refugees to unify, and called for international aid for guaranteeing peace in Southeast Asia (see appendix 7). These sensible and realistic words drew no response at the time.

### KHMER ROUGE FOREIGN POLICY

Above all a xenophobic state, Democratic Kampuchea practiced a closed door policy. The Khmer Rouge had embassies only in Peking, Pyongyang, and—until late 1977—Hanoi. It allowed none other than socialist countries who recognized the regime to cooperate on the technical level and to open diplomatic missions at Phnom Penh. Even China, the ally par excellence, had almost no political role in the Khmer Rouge's Cambodia. The regime rarely consulted this privileged ideological partner before making its political decisions and called on China essentially for commercial exchanges and technical problems.

The single aspect of foreign policy that interested the leaders had to do with the recognition from the United Nations for their regime, which they obtained and retained until their fall and even beyond. For the rest, the Khmer Rouge wished above all to keep to themselves. Only economic constraints forced them to undertake a commercial opening to the West, their goal being to achieve a complete if temporary autarchy, to construct a society "purified" of all external germs.

### THE REGIME'S CONTRADICTIONS

#### THE DE-KHMERIZATION OF SOCIETY AND INDIVIDUAL PRIVILEGES

The balance sheet for the Khmer Rouge period indicts its leaders. In addition to the sheer record of deaths—one out of every five or six inhabitants—the period inspires disgust in many other ways, all of which converge in contradictions, excesses, and irrationality.[31]

During their time in the maquis Pol Pot, Ieng Sary, Khieu Samphan, Khieu Ponnary, and Khieu Thirith were perfectly organized. They had foreseen everything—except the fact that the pace of events would accelerate, advancing victory by several years. This fact does not, it must be emphasized again, explain the hasty evacuation.

As Lon Nol did, the Khmer Rouge spoke and continue to speak of race without knowing much about the concept's significance. Questioned on the meaning given to the expression "Khmer race," Khieu Samphan preferred not to answer (see appendix 7).[32] This expression shows the degree to which this tiny group strove to present a people different from all others: pure, strong, unique, and above all in no way related to the Vietnamese. A recognition of the positive particularisms of Cambodia was to replace centuries of humiliation and incomprehension. Yet in abolishing social classes, Buddhism, popular religion, and in denying the individual—in short, in adopting communism—the regime effected a cultural leveling at least equal to that of its neighbors, particularly Vietnam. The consequence of the adoption of Marxism was the "de-Khmerization" of the inhabitants, who were indoctrinated in order to transform them into Communist yes-men.

In their arrogance, the chiefs wanted to copy Angkor in order to show that today's tiny Cambodia could create great works. All Khmers justly take pride in this unique ensemble of monuments, but the model was inappropriate. To build a hydraulic system greater than the ancient one, in our time, rapidly but without modern tools, would require mass mobilization and a draconian work schedule very like a nightmarish reworking of the Middle Ages. It would have to do without the moral support of the outside world.

Further, in denying themselves the technical skills accumulated by Cambodians during several decades, the Khmer Rouge prevented the realization of their dream because much of the work did not hold up. In the face of such stupidity and failures, the world was not even willing to recognize the successes described by refugees. Moreover, the refusal to use Khmer technicians made Cambodia dependent on Communist countries such as China and also on the despised capitalist countries, with which commercial dealings were necessary to obtain products that Democratic Kampuchea could not produce but in opposition to the regime's primary goal of closing the country to foreign influences. Young revolutionaries were ignorant of these details, which might have called into question their faith in the all-powerful Angkar.

Finally, the abolition of privileges, even among revolutionaries, was not real. If the "old people" benefited from almost uniform treatment, the "new people" encountered abuse; furthermore, among the Khmer Rouge authorities differences existed: the number of dishes per meal increased along with one's position in the hierarchy (subordinate cadre, middle cadre, higher cadre, military man, etc.). As for the leaders, they had veritable feasts, especially when they received foreign guests; orders were given to throw away the leftovers. Likewise, according to rank, commanding officers and soldiers possessed several cars, including a luxurious Mercedes, or indeed a single jeep, a motorbike, or a bicycle; the rest of the people got around on foot. In 1978 Pol Pot was caught up in the game of power. During an interview with Yugoslavian filmmakers in spring 1978 he takes on mannerisms rather like Sihanouk's. Furthermore, the Khmer Rouge's number one had busts of his person made; they were completed at the end of 1978. Just as under the preceding regimes, there was a cult of personality.

Another factor hindered national reconstruction—the number of deaths and the resulting decrease in laborers. The available population was in such a state of malnutrition and illness that it could not give what was demanded of it. The leaders belatedly took cognizance of this demographic decline; in 1977 they announced that the country was to reach fifteen to twenty million inhabitants in 1990. Aside from the enormity of this figure, the means for improving the birthrate were not brought into play. An adequate diet would have allowed women to regain a normal physiological state; many of them no longer menstruated. Angkar merely sent such girls to the hospital; once recovered, they went back to the mobile brigades and cooperatives and again suffered from malnutrition. In the Khmer mentality, only spectacular results count; since it excluded follow-up, it forced the cadres to handle the problem incorrectly. Instead of coping with the real cause—malnutrition—they resorted to treatments (injections) that, combined with better food during hospitalization, gave temporarily satisfactory results. The health-care personnel had done their jobs, and what happened afterward mattered little to them. Such a compartmentalization of tasks applied throughout in Democratic Kampuchea. Brief reflection would have shown the leaders that the problem was nutrition. But, at a time when the fighting with Vietnam was growing serious, did Angkar really want to divert toward civilians foodstuffs that were so precious for obtaining armaments? In any case, the health-care personnel (ignorant peasants) had received no medical training. "If someone suffers from malaria," Pol Pot said, "he needs only take up a pick and break earth in the sun; he will be cured because of his high political consciousness." Ieng Sary, for his part, took pride in his seventeen-year-old daughter who had never studied medicine but managed a hospital in Phnom Penh! But "young peasant women from *nirdey*, transformed into nurses, did not understand the chemical formulas the Chinese experts came to teach them."

Thus simple logic shows that the decisions made by the Khmer Rouge were counterproductive. Everything was practiced to excess, even obvious acts of stupidity. Only the comfort of a small minority counted; the welfare of the people was not an objective. Sure of themselves and of the *yothea*, the Khmer Rouge leaders believed that they would win the revolution as easily as they had won the war. "What they fear most of all is losing power. . . . [I] think that they are limited by the doctrine." In fact, they failed in both domestic and foreign policy.

## CLAN RIVALRIES

Inside Cambodia, the massacres and famine roused the powerless inhabitants against the regime. Small groups took to the maquis. Those who were armed stayed in the forest. The Khmer Rouge, refusing to recognize their status as an opposition, calls them *cau prey* (bandits, outlaws). Those without weapons joined the republican rebels. The latter, short of means, found themselves dependent on Thailand. "Once, the *yothea* discovered a camp used by these *cau prey*, who had just left. They left behind burning logs and cans of food that obviously came from Thailand, which proved that they had connections with the Khmer guerrillas based in Thailand."

But Thailand certainly did not want war. Thailand's soldiers feared the *yothea*, and the Thais did everything possible to "stay friends." Dating from late April 1975, they opened an annex of the foreign ministry at Aranhaprathet, a border town, to facilitate communications with the Khmer Rouge. They concluded political and economic accords with Democratic Kampuchea. A joint communiqué, dated 31 October 1975, was published, stipulating "the principles of mutual respect, independence, sovereignty, territorial integrity within the present borders, nonintervention in internal affairs, nonaggression, equality, mutual advantage, and neighborly relations."[33] However, the *yothea* launched attacks on villages in Prachinburi, Surin, and Buriram provinces, inhabited by Khmers. Thus, Bangkok maintained several groups of Khmer *sar* precisely on the borders of these provinces, in the Dangrek plateau, to serve as a buffer to the Khmer Rouge. These guerrillas—who carried out periodic raids into Cambodia—could not be much help to the Khmer people. The "old people" enjoyed the necessities of life and did not seek to flee. The "new people" despised the regime but lacked the means to oppose it. Almost everywhere, armed cadres and soldiers rebelled: "There was an uprising on almost all the major anniversaries—17 April, 30 September." Angkar was vigilant and had trusted men everywhere who uncovered suspects, breaking up the plots. Major revolts were planned in all the regions, with the exception of the southwest, but none materialized.

From the beginning, ideologically based coteries existed. Some Khmer Vietminh (several hundred remained after the purges in the maquis) may have fomented revolts on behalf of Vietnam; the leaders of the western region probably contacted bands of guerrillas based in Trat and supported by the Thais. Beginning in late 1977, when the struggle with the Vietnamese came out into the open, some malcontents seem to have found support from them. This does not mean that all the revolts were carried out on behalf of foreigners. The Pol Pot–Ieng Sary coterie sought to monopolize power, and while in the maquis, they themselves massacred Sihanouk's partisans who could invoke neither the Americans nor the Soviets. They believed that other revolutionaries would follow them. But moderates protested against the harshness of the regime and called for a revolution that was less bloody and stupid. They became the first Communists to be killed after the 17 April victory. Whereas ambition may have motivated some plotters, several risings were carried out on the initiative of Khmers and directed above all against the regime's excesses and those who allowed them to occur. And perhaps the plotters rose against the centralization of decision making, which excluded and frustrated many who had worked for the revolution's victory. The pyramidal repression that followed deprived the country of battle-hardened combatants and competent cadres.

The Pol Pot–Ieng Sary clan emerged victorious because it had at its disposal Ta Mok and his army of young and disciplined killers. As soon as a rebellion broke out, the soldiers of the southwest came to purge the *kamaphibal* and *yothea* on the spot and replace them in the positions of authority. Gradually they came to control the entire country. Not all the cadres and soldiers still alive in other regions approved of these radical purges; the Vietnamese found them valuable help when they entered Phnom Penh. Indeed, some of the Khmer troops in the capital may have turned against the regime on 7 January 1979. Likewise, in the first months, civilians would march alongside the Vietnamese against the Khmer Rouge.

There is every reason to believe that the Vietnamese had hoped that the regime would be overthrown from within, with or without their help. The Vietnamese were hoping to gain benefits from their aid to the rebels, or at least to be able to negotiate with the new masters of Cambodia, who would be independent but less brutal than their predecessors. The Khmer Rouge's bellicose attitude gave Hanoi a pretext to intervene and thus, among the other reasons for this invasion, the Khmer Rouge bear great responsibility.

## THE MOTIVATIONS OF THE POL POT–IENG SARY CLAN

Until 1970 the Khmer Communists were generally under Soviet influence. Although distrustful of the Vietnamese, they followed their instructions and advice. Ieng Sary would tell the intellectuals of Boeung Trabek that he had received supplementary training in Hanoi in 1963. When Sihanouk established relations with China in the 1960s, the Khmer Communists took advantage of this in order to enter officially into relations with their Chinese comrades by means of the youth organizations. In 1966 the Cultural Revolution began, and we have seen how it overflowed into Cambodia in 1967. China was not on good terms with the Soviet Union, which had Vietnam in its orbit; to draw closer to China could have the additional asset of restraining the Vietnamese. Moreover, Prince Sihanouk's exile in Peking in 1970 pleased the future leaders, who were newly devoted to Maoism and the Cultural Revolution. The left-wing students who joined the FUNC in Peking would take sides with Ieng Sary, whom they judged all powerful.

Several factors explain the Khmer Rouge's behavior: the masses, the Chinese Cultural Revolution, and Cambodia's montagnard ethnic groups.

## The Khmer Leu

Pol Pot's first guerrilla group was formed in the northeast, in Kratié. He spoke of it in the interview granted to Yugoslavian journalists in March 1978. "My base of support was situated in the northeastern plateau, inhabited by the national minority peoples. I know these national minorities perfectly."[34] Here "northeastern" refers to Kratié and Stung Treng provinces, as well as the mountainous Ratanakiri and Mondolkiri provinces, where the Khmer *leu* hill tribes live. The latter had already been visited by the Vietcong, and certain villages cooperated with them in the 1960s. The Khmer Rouge chose to establish themselves in hamlets that were still free of contact with modern ideology. The Khmer *leu* were distrustful, but the Khmer Rouge were patient; never complaining or raising their voices, the Marxists helped the inhabitants in their daily tasks, living as they did. Little by little, they won their confidence. Then they began their propaganda work, explaining to the hill tribes that they were living in destitution—a notion that had never occurred to them—that Phnom Penh was exploiting them, and that they should struggle together to change things. The Brou, Tumpuon, Stieng, and Bunor are honorable peoples and did not imagine that their interlocutors were intriguing and interested in power above all else: they accepted these new ideas. They spoke Cambodian more or less well but could not write it. In the beginning the trusted agents of the Khmer Rouge were, on the whole, Khmers whose primary interest was protecting themselves in a difficult situation. But the Khmer *leu* showed unshakable loyalty as guards or messengers (*niesa*); some died to save their masters, whom they blindly trusted. Pol Pot and Ieng Sary understood the benefits of the Khmer *leu*'s loyalty; they would make good soldiers and devoted cadres who would execute orders without discussion. The leaders gave them important positions, such as that of political leader of the Boeung Trabek intellectuals' camp. The residents of Phnom Penh who were evacuated to the east remember the high number of Khmer *leu* cadres and their cruelty.

The leaders were very much taken with these hill tribes. Once in Mondolkiri the Khmer *leu* rebelled against the French occupier and even assassinated Commander Le Rolland—acts that do not mean the Khmer *leu* had never been colonized, as the Khmer Rouge believed. They considered the hill tribes to be pure elements and, fascinated by their social organization, decided to apply the tribal social model to all Cambodia. They sought to develop among Cambodians the spirit of mutual aid, to abolish the instinct for capitalistic private property, to bring them to accept Spartan conditions and semi-nomadism, to teach them to live from day to day, to scorn all forms of education, and to swear an unconditional loyalty to leaders. Everyone was to experience what Ieng Sary believed to be the first stage of social life. To apply this system to a society of seven million inhabitants was an insane, utopian project: how could it be possible to bring a people—proud of its brilliant past and conservative yet turned toward the modern world—to transform itself overnight into a giant tribe? Terror would get the upper hand over those who refused to cooperate. But the fact that the leaders did not follow this tribal life themselves—except when they were in the maquis—shows that they had not overcome their feudal mentality.

The hill tribes' role in the revolution explains in part why the term *Khmer* was banished from Democratic Kampuchea's vocabulary. On the one hand, Khmer was too reminiscent of the republican epoch when Lon Nol liked to say, "I am a Khmer." The term referred as well to the kingdom of Prince Sihanouk, who was also proud of his Khmer nationality. On the other hand, it excluded the hill tribes, who were generally despised by the people of Phnom Penh. The Khmer Rouge preferred *Kampuchea* for designating the country as well as its inhabitants. "Kampuchea is a kind of ark in which can be found all those who have spilled blood for the country, Khmers and minorities." Since *Cambodge* and *Cambodia* evoked foreigners, the indigenous term Kampuchea replaced them in French and English translations. The language became more complex with the adoption of many Sanskrit or Pali words that were previously little known except to scholars. They decreed a scholarly language and a militaristic parlance: the peasants "launched an offensive" of growing rice, "raised high the banner of revolution" in building a dam, and "struggled together" to bring in two harvests of rice every year.[35]

### The Chinese Cultural Revolution

The Cultural Revolution would inspire the Khmer Rouge leaders. In 1975 it served as a model for the imposition of their dictatorship. Mao emerged victorious, which meant that the system was a good one, even if it had cost numerous lives. Yet the Red Guards included both ignorant youths and educated people. Furthermore, the cadres had the situation in hand; they allowed excesses but generally maintained control of their troops. This retaking of power by the great helmsman, Mao Tse-tung, had been carefully thought out. The Khmer Rouge revolution, on the contrary, was marked by a lack of realism; Democratic Kampuchea had to surpass China and serve as a model for the Third World. Pol Pot and Ieng Sary displayed more radicalism than the Chinese leaders, with neither their intelligence nor their cultural background.

## The Masses Unchained

In this megalomaniacal context, the masses (soldiers, cadres, and the "old people"), whose patriotism and political consciousness the leaders exhorted each day on the radio, lived in a state of perpetual excitation. The leaders needed their support to maintain the regime—but a people's sacrifices also needed compensation. During the war, the leaders promised to grant advantages to combatants after victory. To be sure, *yothea* had the privilege of living in the towns and working normally in the factories while the city dwellers were spending endless days in the fields, exposed to the full fury of the sun or monsoons; cadres also benefited from special regulations. Both groups ate decently. Nevertheless, they hoped to share in the running of the country. Angkar could not take the time to consider these concessions, for victory came sooner than expected; the regime nonetheless had to give them some leeway. It gave general directives, leaving the local cadres to apply them with more or less rigor. The "old people" could mistreat the "new people" without fear of punishment. Military and civilian authorities could interpret or exaggerate directives; as long as this did not harm the revolution, Angkar would look the other way. The regime's elite were thus able to keep their promises at small cost because the lives of the "new people" mattered little to them. This also explains the local variations that have been noticed in the execution of an order.

> Pol Pot said that the intellectuals had no definite political line, that they oscillated between the right and the left and were interested only in technology. The peasants misinterpreted these words because of their ignorance. They thus sought to suppress all danger of treason because they thought that the intellectuals were going to take advantage of a moment of confusion to leave. Hence they began to kill them.

Revolutionaries who harbored a hatred for city dwellers, learned in the maquis, now took their revenge. "Peasant cooperatives cover the entire country, and the enemy finds it impossible to conduct any activity whatsoever, neither robbery nor espionage. The traitors, those eager lackeys of the American imperialists, do not escape the vigilance of the revolutionaries, who, boiling with class hatred, systematically eliminate them."[36] Everyone had a score to settle. Tension grew to the point that, from time to time, it emerged in violent outbursts; no new animus was needed, and the system of abuses reproduced itself automatically. Informed of these abuses, the leaders still did not forbid them, and a runaway radical system of running the country led only to excesses. Soldiers in the center and the east received complete freedom to eliminate the traitors of the north in 1976, and soldiers in the southwest received equal license in 1977 to purge the inhabitants in the northwest and the north, and, in 1978, to punish the people in the east, bordering Vietnam. But in this activity the ignorant and indoctrinated masses did no more than uphold a regime established by a few.

### THE KHMER ROUGE CAUGHT IN THEIR OWN TRAP

This concentration of power in the hands of a few produced only malcontents. Since a margin for maneuver was left open locally, the zonal chiefs took advantage of it to plot. Their attempts failed, but each cost the regime many lives. The purges (rumors of which crossed the border) and the living conditions for the people constituted Vietnam's trump cards, allowing Vietnam to invade Cambodia while posing as a liberator. It possessed another card as well.

The fact that Ieng Sary was a native of Kampuchea Krom certainly influenced his conduct of foreign policy, above all toward Vietnam. If the Khmers organized their first guerrilla units in accordance with the advice and aid of the Vietnamese, Ieng Sary remained distrustful and waited for the hour of vengeance to come: the Vietnamese of the north and south had to pay for the suffering they had imposed on the Khmer *krom* over the last twenty years. The ease with which the Americans abandoned the game politically, the failure of the Khmer republicans, and the submission of the inhabitants at the entrance of the *yothea* into Phnom Penh caused the leaders to lose what little sense of proportion they had. Ieng Sary was able to give free rein to his desire for vengeance and to convince the victorious Pol Pot without difficulty that the reconquest of Kampuchea Krom was within striking distance. The Vietnamese—unable to come to an understanding with the Khmer Rouge as they had hoped to do, facing ingratitude for their previous aid—remained on the alert. Refugees from the border regions reported that they had been hearing firearms as early as 1975; those who had been in contact with the "old people" learned that the quarrels between the Khmer Rouge and Vietnamese Communists had not ceased since 1975. From mid-1977 onward the engagements became a daily occurrence, and, at year's end, Hanoi severed diplomatic relations with Phnom Penh. On 6 January 1978 the *yothea* repelled the Vietnamese and penetrated several dozen kilometers into Vietnam's Tay-ninh province. During this bloody incursion, some of the "new people" took advantage of the confusion and fled Cambodia. The *yothea* withdrew, and Phnom Penh noisily celebrated its victory. Fighting continued throughout 1978.

The massacre of the inhabitants of the east—whom the Khmer Rouge, in their paranoiac delirium, accused of complicity with the Vietnamese—began in mid-1978. The cadres from *nirdey*—loyal, it must be recalled, to

Pol Pot and Ieng Sary—took over for those of the east, whom they had assassinated the preceding year. In 1978 they began to eliminate entire villages of "new people" but also villages of "old people." The victims first had to dig pits or trenches that would serve as their graves; on their knees near the holes, their hands tied behind their backs, they were clubbed in the neck with a cane or rifle butt and their bodies were simply covered with earth. Beginning in October, survivors were sent to the cooperatives established at the extremes of Battambang and Pursat provinces. Before they left the east, Angkar gave them each a new *krâma*. Since each province had its own distinctive fashion of sewing the hems of scarves, they were easily recognized as evacuees:

> At the cooperative of Thnam and its vicinity, there were about forty thousand people who had come from Svay Rieng and Prey Veng; I don't know how many there were in neighboring cooperatives. . . . They were called on to dig canals; this was from January to April of 1979.[37] Each time they'd take off in three carts, each carrying about ten people. . . . I drove one of these carts for more than a week. . . . Once when we were in the forest, three kilometers from the cooperative, a commando stopped us and accused those who were in the carts of crossing the line of demarcation without authorization, ordering them to get off. While holding them at gunpoint, the *yothea* accused them of being in connivance with the Vietnamese and took them deep into the forest. We heard horrible cries. . . .

Another driver witnessed horrible scenes:

> I had to participate in the digging of the pits. They decapitated people with a machete or hatchet; some they hung from trees by their feet. Old people were tied together in twos with *krâma*. . . . They killed some babies with knives and smashed others against trees. They covered the bodies lightly by throwing a little earth on them. . . . Approximately twelve thousand people were killed; the others were saved by the arrival of the Vietnamese.

By spring 1978 the Khmer Rouge leaders who, in seminars, had spoken of the reconquest of Kampuchea Krom and Surin and Buriram provinces (Thailand)—where there were several engagements—understood that the soldiers from Hanoi, the *bo doi*, had the upper hand militarily. For the first time, they invited journalists from Eastern Europe to film what they wished to show them of Democratic Kampuchea. The leaders warned international opinion and denounced Vietnamese provocations in writing.[38] In December they concluded an agreement with Thailand to allow the visits of tourists; three Bangkok–Siem Reap trips took place. These attempts at opening to foreign countries in order to dissuade Hanoi from carrying out its invasion plans were thus real. In the meantime, Hanoi invited Western journalists to verify the crimes of the Khmer Rouge in the border regions. On 25 December 1978 Vietnamese troops launched the decisive assault. If there was provocation on the part of the Vietnamese—a hypothesis that has yet to be proven—the Khmer Rouge fell into the trap; in any case, they gave arguments to their adversaries, who would occupy Cambodia for ten years.

# 8 The Vietnamese Occupation and the Resistance

From 1979 to 1989 Vietnam imposed on Cambodia a painful and complete protectorate, against the will of the entire population. On 7 January 1979, after fifteen days of combat, Hanoi's soldiers invested Phnom Penh, along with Khmer soldiers assembled during the previous month into the Front uni national de salut du Kampuchea (Kampuchean united front for national salvation). They gradually moved out into the countryside. Even though they systematically pillaged the cities, they did not mistreat the people, who welcomed them as liberators. Almost every Khmer Rouge cooperative turned up plans for mass executions to take place in January 1979; the massacres had already begun in the east on a large scale. The arrival of the *bo doi* brought solace, and the grateful Khmers helped the Vietnamese soldiers uncover arms caches and arrest *kamaphibal*. Slowly withdrawing to the regions bordering Thailand, the Khmer Rouge soldiers established sanctuaries there.

For several months there were incessant comings and goings on Cambodia's roads. Refugees and evacuees returned to their native villages, the implicit place of rendezvous for every family. The balance sheet of the missing was onerous: Angkar had spared no region. Now, Khmers thought, Hanoi was going to restore order militarily and perhaps help in the return of a less brutal regime. Those who had suffered under communism, that is, the majority, had hated it. Growing wary, some hurriedly left the country.

## FORCED RETURNS ALONG THE KHMER-THAI BORDER

Beginning in February 1979 Thailand's eastern border was the scene of a continuous wave of Khmer refugees: former students and officials, peasants dreading the arrival of the Vietnamese and prompted into flight by Khmer Rouge propaganda, which depicted them as executioners. By choice or necessity some of them hid in the mountainous back country, particularly in Kampot; others gambled on Thailand, where they hoped to receive a warm welcome. The Khmer problem overwhelmed Thailand, economically and politically; yet the country took in Khmer Rouge soldiers and cadres who crossed the vast plateau that connects it to Cambodia near Mayrut. Beginning in May 1979 the Khao Larn camp in Trat province sheltered them and the "old people" who accompanied them. This center—the first to accept Cambodians after the overthrow of the Pol Pot–Ieng Sary regime—would never be open to non–Khmer Rouge. Massive numbers of "new people" came to the vicinity of Aranhaprathet. In April the Thai army began to take small groups of them back to Cambodia, into the Cardamom Mountains at Phnom Khieu, an assembly point for *yothea* under pressure from the pursuing *bo doi*, and at nearby Sokh Sann, where supporters of former prime minister Son Sann were organizing. The repatriated Khmers suffered terribly from malaria and lack of rice.[1]

In June Thailand moved forty-four thousand persons back to the Dangrek plateau. Westerners present at the departure of the refugees could save only a small number of those whose requests for asylum reached them. The others, piled up in trucks, arrived at various points on the plateau and had to enter Khmer territory; approximately eight hundred of them died when they set off exploding mines. These deaths (which journalists estimated at between thirty-five and forty thousand), combined with the alarming accounts concerning the lack of food inside Cambodia, roused an outpouring of international generosity. Nevertheless, the impediments that Thailand erected to the provision of sanitary and alimentary assistance to Cambodian refugees cost numerous deaths among the *yothea, kamaphibal,* and the "old people" who were in a state of exhaustion, particularly at Ta Prick, south of Aranhaprathet, and still worse off at Lêm, of which little has been said. The "new people" who arrived to the north of Aranhaprathet were also helpless; as stated above, they had been partially repatriated. Returning to the same spot several months later, they had to wait many months before receiving rice. Unscrupulous leaders, who were supposed to protect them, diverted to their own purposes the little rice that reached the refugees.[2] Afterward regular aid began, and some of the runaways reassembled in reception centers established on Thai territory. While the border was intensely agitated, Phnom Penh was organizing.

## THE PEOPLE'S REPUBLIC OF KAMPUCHEA

In Phnom Penh the Vietnamese installed Heng Samrin and several others who, as Khmer Rouge cadres, had fled in 1977 and returned with the *bo doi* in January 1979. The country took the name République populaire du

Kampuchea (people's republic of Kampuchea, or RPK), and the inhabitants believed that peace and liberty had returned. However, after scarcely a year of Vietnamese presence, the Khmers realized their error—liberation had become occupation. They were to endure Vietnamese domination and a new form of communism at the same time and found both equally detestable. As months and years passed, distress reappeared on faces that had begun to smile. Those who were starving asked for rice; those less hungry demanded freedom of movement; and the most educated denounced the attempts at the de-Khmerization in progress.

EXPERTS AT ALL LEVELS

All officials had a Vietnamese superior in the hierarchy who supervised a single person or an entire department. At the head of each ministry were a Cambodian minister and a "Vietnamese minister," as the Khmers called them. In 1986, for example, in the ministry of health a Vietnamese expert backed up the Cambodian minister as well as the three vice-ministers, while another backed up the chef de cabinet; each of the four subdivisions (pharmacy, accounting, supply, and security) housed one. A dozen experts busied themselves in the ministry of finance, with still more—between twenty-five and thirty—at the ministry of the interior.

Cambodians who held high positions recognized the omnipotence of these advisers and unanimously stated that each text written by a Khmer had to be approved by the Vietnamese authority in the department before circulation. All administrative, political, and economic decisions had to have at least the endorsement of the adviser and were usually dictated by him. The Vietnamese advisers worked under the authority of special bureaus established in Phnom Penh, A-50 and A-68, depending on whether they supervised civilian or military departments. Insufficient data force us to estimate their total number. Only the total number of the *bo doi* has been known since 1979—one hundred eighty thousand soldiers. It seems not to have varied until September 1989, with soldiers finishing their tour of duty being regularly replaced through an annual rotation.[3] Thirty thousand Khmer soldiers fought alongside them.

This foreign domination of the country caused Khmers of all professions to flee: administrators, physicians, teachers, technicians. Hardships also forced peasants to flee this land to which they remained so attached.

THE KHMER ROUGE PROTECTED

In examining the composition of the RPK regime, we note the conspicuously high number of Khmer Rouge cadres. Among them are those who took refuge in Vietnam in 1977–78 and returned in 1979 as potential allies of the

Vietnamese. Alongside them were *kamaphibal* who had not left Cambodia; after the arrival of the Vietnamese, they offered their services. Curiously, not only were they not arrested, but the doors of the ministries were even opened to them.

In 1979 almost everywhere in the country the inhabitants exposed Khmer Rouge cadres who had been in hiding. Here and there, the *bo doi* turned them over to popular justice that led to cruel scenes. Most often, however, these Khmer Rouge emerged with slight harm or none at all; many were arrested as a formality and released several days later or interned in not too severe reeducation camps. At the main prison in Phnom Penh, T-3, some served as jailers. In contrast, imprisoned nationalist guerrillas were harshly treated.

This particularly clement behavior by the Vietnamese toward Khmer Rouge cadres, and the high number of the latter who received key positions, deserve some comment. First of all, did the Khmer Rouge enemy boil down to a few persons, essentially Pol Pot and Ieng Sary? Many RPK officials think that the Vietnamese believed they could win over Marxists, even those under Chinese influence, more easily than anti-Communist nationalists. Furthermore, this course did not go against the ideology on which the Vietnamese rely; it allowed them, in the more or less long term, to plan reconciliation, which would exclude the avowedly anti-Vietnamese leaders (mainly Ieng Sary) whose hostile behavior—Vietnamese authorities constantly emphasized—justified the *bo doi*'s invasion and continued presence. In the second place, were not the Khmer Rouge cadres deliberately left behind by Democratic Kampuchea's leaders with the mission of setting up cells in the RPK regime and preparing for the return of the Khmer Rouge?

THEY'RE TAKING OUR RICE

Since rice was in short supply, the international community responded from the end of summer 1979 onward. After the difficulties that William Shawcross relates, the Khmers who remained in Cambodia benefited from a significant amount of aid.[4] In Phnom Penh the generous donors struggled to obtain authorization to supervise distribution, and aid did not reach the inhabitants, who for two months received from 500 grams to 5 kilograms of rice or corn or—more often—nothing at all.

Late in 1979 the scandal could have been revealed to the press, but the informant, Hea Mean Nuont, the president of the committee to distribute aid in Phnom Penh, had left family in Cambodia and did not want to compromise them. He mentioned the composition of the aid to me and a French journalist, Roland-Pierre Paringaux, and enumerated the location of rice warehouses (there were four for the capital).

Only 4 to 5 percent of the aid goes to the provinces. . . . Fifty percent is not listed on any distribution document. Heng Samrin's soldiers, stationed along the border and having the right to inspect everything that goes to Vietnam, unanimously report that convoys of twenty to thirty Vietnamese trucks come from Phnom Penh two or three times each week and move toward Saigon, loaded with sacks of rice and other foodstuffs bearing the insignias of the UNICEF [United Nations Children's Fund] or the ICRC [International Committee of the Red Cross]. They also contain vegetable oil from Bangkok. Each truck transports five to seven tons of merchandise. . . . The Vietnamese imply that they lack specialized technicians for distribution, but they do not allow the competent Khmers to act. They also claim to be short of trucks. Statistics drawn up in the provinces by Khmer officials and their Vietnamese counterparts reveal that 95 percent of the population has very little to eat. These figures are at the ministry of commerce's bureau of statistics and planning. Furthermore, provincial officials declare that people are dying of hunger. . . . Most of the aid comes from the Western countries, with a lesser part coming from the Eastern European countries. . . . Although there were shortages nearby, I was unable to distribute the foreign-aid foodstuffs. The French deputies who came on 21–22–23 November attended a distribution at Kompong Speu specially organized for them. It was in no way part of a regular cycle; it was an exception. . . . At a meeting, I brought up the problem of distribution to the people. The Vietnamese became angry. I said that if there really was friendship between the Khmer and Vietnamese peoples, we should be allowed to act in accordance with our competencies, that we were a certain number of intellectuals, that there was a foreign specialist in medicine, that, statistics in hand, we could be effective. . . . I said: This aid is intended for the Khmers and, as a Khmer, I am not being given the right to give it to the people, who are suffering from hunger and illness. That very night, I was secretly warned that the Vietnamese were going to arrest me, and I fled. . . . I asked for the protection of the ICRC in the camp [Khao I Dang] because the Vietnamese, who were after me, were looking for me.

Hea Mean Nuont added that the foodstuffs that remained in Cambodia were "partially rotten, especially the rice at kilometer six because it took on water on the boats and during unloading. And medication had been ruined in the Kampuchea Krom street warehouse." Shawcross notes that "ICRC and UNICEF did what they could to keep his story completely secret"[5] but seems to insinuate that this secrecy was ill-intentioned. In fact, Paringaux and I, who recorded Hea Mean Nuont's words, agreed not to release them in order to safeguard his family in Phnom Penh. We were dismayed, but in light of the humanitarian reasons that he advanced, we kept quiet.

The situation did not improve. In the 1980s deserters from the RPK reported having accompanied convoys of rice, cloth, or medications bound for Vietnam. Even if the press in 1979 exaggerated the extent of alimentary deficiencies, the lack of rice was genuine.

To help the peoples of North Cambodia, UNICEF created a land bridge on the border, to which desperate peasants from far-flung regions or the vicinity of Phnom Penh came as well. On 8 May 1980 an emaciated old man murmured: "We came from Kompong Chhnang. There were nine people. Three died of hunger on the way. Our three buffalo died on the road, and we pulled the cart ourselves. . . . During the trip, we had only leaf soup to eat. Tell them to give us lots of rice; we're so hungry."

These Khmers and many others possessed practically nothing and were not lying—they were hungry. In response to their cries of alarm but at Phnom Penh's insistence, UNICEF eliminated the land bridge on 17 January 1981. Whatever the interests may have been—political interests on the part of the West and commercial ones on the part of Thailand, which presided over the passage through Nong Chan of rice and seed grains purchased in Bangkok—this land bridge (to be sure, black marketeers benefited as well as guerrillas) had nonetheless helped nourish many needy people.[6]

In 1980 refugees reported that certain Khmers had access to Phnom Penh's warehouses of rice and medicines. "First, the guard, armed with a firearm, can take all he wants; so could the officials he lets enter the premises at night. Then they sell the stolen medicines, which show up again later in the markets."

Thereafter no one took much interest in the diversion of the aid furnished to Cambodia nor in the real alimentary situation of the Cambodians.

Gradually, peasants who were organized into "solidarity groups" placed their production tools (carts, beasts of burden) in common ownership, with each free to cultivate his plot individually. Elsewhere, collectivization included land, and the state redistributed the harvest. In the beginning, there were incidents, the people not wanting a return to collectivism. In Siem Reap peasants who came to the land bridge to obtain rice stated, "We were unable to harvest because the *bo doi* had confiscated our sickles; they're taking our rice away from us." Faced with the peasants' reluctance, officials sent into the countryside were assigned the mission of educating rice growers and making them accept the production groups. Others, instructed in Marxism beforehand, became in their turn teachers of politics.

In 1979 I was an instructor of politics. . . . I discussed with the officials who took my courses various political documents supplied by
the Vietnamese. . . . We had not yet come to the point of pressuring
people; we were trying to persuade peasants to sell their rice to the
government, which would, in exchange, obtain soap and other commodities. The goal was to prevent traitors [the guerrillas] from coming to buy rice. . . . I believed in what I was teaching because I was
educated—until the day when the Vietnamese put me in prison, accusing me of being in contact with the Khmer Rouge.

The missions of officials of all kinds in the rural areas were also a "return
to the masses" and remained in force until 1991. Despite this organization
of work, peasants did not receive enough rice. The harvest was reduced by
a portion that sometimes exceeded 50 percent, taken by the state without
any compensation at all or purchased at a low price. In all cases, in order to
compensate for this deficiency, peasants purchased supplementary rice in
the free markets at a price that was prohibitive for them. "In the meetings,
the Vietnamese say that selling paddy to the government is a proof of
nationalism. But they transport it to Vietnam in barges and boats; I saw it
with my own eyes in Neak Luong [in Prey Veng province]." Sometimes,
"Vietnamese soldiers help themselves in the peasants' fields, and if we say
anything, they reply: This land doesn't belong to you; it's the land we
liberated." The meager belongings of the inhabitants (poultry, clothing)
might catch their fancy; acts of vandalism also occurred: "The Vietnamese
entered all the houses of the village in September–October 1985 . . . and
pulled out the fencing [around mulberry trees for raising silkworms]. How
could a person live? We didn't have anything left; that's why we came here.
I don't know what the villagers are doing now. I'm desperate."

In the towns, despite Spartan fare, officials remained the least needy
because they could buy rice, water, and electricity at official prices that were
unavailable to most others. These others sold commodities in the markets
that brought them little: soup, beans, fruits, dried fish. Vietnamese settlers
trafficked in clothing, plates and dishes, bicycles, and radios; they paid
insignificant taxes while Khmers paid ten times more. To live in the city
called for sharp wits for those who did not work for the government. "You
can live clandestinely in Phnom Penh but on the sole condition of finding
an accommodating group leader who'd agree to look the other way in return
for substantial gifts."[7]

According to Khmers, the pairing of Cambodian and Vietnamese provinces resulted in the exchange of Cambodian products (rice, breeding ani-

mals, fish, etc.) and natural resources (wood) for manufactured goods from Vietnam such as plastic basins, low-quality cement, toys, kitchen utensils, and corrugated sheet metal.

Faced with these economic difficulties, the Khmer people displayed ingenuity in scavenging: they ate tubers, in the absence of rice, or sold watery bindweed soup for a bit of money to purchase rice on the free markets, where everything was more expensive than in the state-owned stores reserved for officials.

The food and health of the people, officials aside, remained precarious, the aid delivered being insufficient. Despite the efforts of the French Red Cross to check tuberculosis, despite the medicines from international aid, the Khmer people were not in a position to care for themselves. So Sarin, the physician second in charge of the monk's hospital before fleeing, explains: "It was even necessary to purchase the ambulance from the Vietnamese; yet it had been furnished by international aid. Experts from East Germany clashed with the Vietnamese experts about the medicines supplied by their country that the Vietnamese were taking out of the hospital." Esméralda Luciolli, a physician who worked for six months for the French Red Cross, abandoned her obligation of discretion to call attention to the scandal of medical aid that benefited only the regime's privileged few. "Peasants came to the dispensary in tatters. I sometimes exchanged a few words with them, and they complained of the lack of medicines and rice. Beginning in 1985, they spoke particularly of 'clearing operations.'"[8] As many refugees did, she noted a new phenomenon—the extension of malaria.

## WORK FOR NATIONAL DEFENSE

Beginning in 1982 the government levied peasants for "socialist labor" in the collective interest—constructing or repairing public buildings (schools, hospitals). Non-peasants participated in the rice harvest within a production team, and individuals levied could pay others to labor in their place. The projects took place not far from the village and lasted about two weeks, during what the Cambodians called the "gentle phase" of Vietnamization.

In 1983 the second, brutal phase began.[9] The frequency and the difficulty of the levies increased. The work involved cutting swaths in the forest and erecting strategic barriers around villages. The first clearings seem to have taken place in the park of Angkor in late 1982. They then occurred almost everywhere in the country for the purpose of destroying the guerrillas' sanctuaries, situated in the dense forests of the mountains and plains. The result was twofold because the fine logs harvested were sent to Vietnam. The strategic barriers were a response to the same military imperatives:

preventing the people from contacting the guerrillas and aiding them either by selling them food (when people had any) or by supplying them with information useful in the guerrillas' operations.

During the two first years peasants complied with the state's levies and endured the consequences without flinching. They were sent into unhealthy and mine-infested forests where they had to construct strategic roads: the north-east-south-west transversal through the Cardamom Mountains; networks in the border regions of the west and north that made possible the seizure of the guerrillas' sanctuaries early in 1985. A peasant from the Bakan (Pursat) region stated, "During the new year [April] 1985, my husband was called for clearing land. He was gone for a month and a half in the Srok Phnom Kravanh [Cardamom Mountains]. He came back with malaria. He said there were explosions from mines. Si, a young girl of thirteen who was clearing land with my husband, died along with six other persons from neighboring villages. . . . Her body was taken back to the village."

A Battambang official reported that clearing had been in effect since 1983 for the province's peasants:

> I was working in the Transport Service. No one in our service went for clearing or was drafted into the army. We were responsible for transporting those going for clearing duties at Samlaut, Nam Sap, Pailin, Ampil Pram Daeum, and in Oddar Mean Chey, at Ta Nin Ta Kriem. There were about one hundred persons per truck. . . . In 1983, 1984, 1985, for three consecutive months each year I transported people who were going to clear land and coming back. At the beginning, people cleared for three months, then six months, and now it lasts nine months. There were mine explosions; I saw two of them. The first was in March 1984; there were five dead and one wounded. The second time, fifteen days later, there were six people seriously wounded and some slightly wounded. The bodies were buried on the spot. In 1984 I also witnessed a battle on a place being cleared on [the hill] Phnom 130, in Battambang. Vietnamese and Khmer Rouge were fighting. Seven persons who were clearing land were killed.

These mine explosions should not be surprising because people who took part in levies cleared mines without any instruments at all, using only their own ingenuity, after locating the trip wires. The most fortunate survivors of explosions came back missing a leg: "The fate of these millions of amputees is tragic. Every foreigner stationed in Phnom Penh since 1985 is struck by the sight of more and more invalids begging on the streets and in the markets of the capital every day. The victims are destitute of resources."[10]

Finally in 1984 socialist labor was made obligatory for officials, who had previously been exempted. This decision was part of the project for accelerated construction of frontier barrier to isolate Cambodia from its neighbors, Thailand and Laos. The entire able-bodied population had to participate. During these "works for national defense," the official term to which inhabitants preferred the more realistic "cutting down the forest, clearing" (*kap prey*), there were deaths from mine explosions and above all from malaria. On 19 June 1985 *Le Figaro* wrote: "The Vietnamese sent Cambodian officials near Thailand, in the jungle, to construct their defensive networks. The result: twenty-five thousand Khmers seriously ill with malaria in Phnom Penh." Doctor So Sarin explained: "I worked for two months in Pursat's medical service. In Pursat, they had been clearing land since 1982. Of two hundred beds, more than half were occupied by people with malaria after coming back from clearing. And 35 to 40 percent of them were serious cases. During these two months, ten people died of malaria at the Pursat hospital."

Esméralda Luciolli, who was in the capital, wrote:

> The "volunteers," transported overnight into heavily malaria-
> infested regions, are highly susceptible to the disease. Almost all of
> them were soon infected, and the development of serious forms was
> favored by malnutrition and exhaustion. . . . The mortality rate
> from malaria was around 5 percent, and there would thus have
> been fifty thousand deaths [between September 1984 and the end
> of 1986]. . . . Over the long term, the constant movements of people
> for the clearing works risks spreading the disease into non-infested
> regions. In 1986 we already saw occasional cases of malaria among
> children who had never been to the border.[11]

There were even deaths during the fighting between Khmer governmental forces, allied with the Vietnamese, and guerrillas.

> The people of Chumnom, in the Mongkolborei district, were sum-
> moned to go clearing at Nam Sap [Khmer-Thai border region]. I
> went there for three months. . . . I was wounded in the left leg
> during an encounter between the Vietnamese and the Khmer
> Rouge . . . ; the festival of the dead [September] 1985 took place
> while I was in the Ampil Pram Daeum hospital. [I was wounded]
> by fragments from a mine that exploded during the fighting. Two
> people from Chumnom were killed: Pan, married, two children;
> and Sav, thirty-two years old, married, two children. Three others
> died of malaria: Mao, single; Mrin, over fifty years old, four chil-
> dren; Sam, forty-two or forty-three years old, five children. They
> were all from Chumnom.

After this first cycle of hazardous work peasants took fright and fled toward Thailand in order to avoid a second summons.[12]

The closing of Cambodia, even if the term was not uttered, was implied in the statement made in December 1984 by General Le Duc Anh, a member of the Communist party central committee and vice-minister of defense: "Since they [the Khmer guerrillas] are opposed to the revolution and undermine it by force of arms, we must destroy them by military attacks, razing their bases, constructing and consolidating our lines of defense, constructing and consolidating the domination, by our friends [the Heng Samrin government], of the border regions."[13] The Phnom Penh government itself, through the voice of Hun Sen, told *L'Humanité*'s correspondent on 10 June 1986: "We are going to hermetically seal the 700 kilometers of border with Thailand."

In the economic domain the consequences were disastrous for the people. Only members of production groups received part of the harvest. Their departure for clearing work took away from children, the elderly, and spouses—when they were not themselves summoned—the share of rice necessary for survival. They had then to rely on their own resources, a task that only grew more and more difficult in the RPK: "One of my children died of hunger in 1983, and the other died on the road to the border in 1985 because I had gone clearing; my wife didn't have anything to eat, and the baby was sick." Esméralda Luciolli confirms such statements: "Particularly during the time just before the harvest, certain regions experienced famine once again. At Takeo in September 1985 we saw women and children all along the road wandering in search of food."[14]

Despite a political regime that was less severe than the preceding one, daily life—already difficult—involved a real risk of death during socialist labor. Young people, for their part, fled from other forms of requisition.

## SOLDIERS CAME TO SCHOOL TO CONSCRIPT US

Conscription, compulsory for men from eighteen to thirty-five years of age, was extended to those younger than this, who were directly drafted in the lycées and schools without notice:

> A group of about twenty of Heng Samrin's soldiers and five Vietnamese came looking for us at school. Out of one thousand students, they took twenty. They already had a list of names. They told us we were changing schools, without specifying which one. We weren't allowed to go home to say goodbye to our families. . . . In Kandal province, they conscripted eight hundred fifty students. They took all of us to Srok Kien Svay for training. . . . Then we were taken to Nam Sap, near the [Thai] border.

Nam Sap was a dangerous place for these youths, exposed on the front line, often without arms, to Khmer Rouge soldiers (levies of students—which also reduced the time young people spent in school—did not occur in Phnom Penh, probably because the authorities wished to conceal them from Westerners there who, in order to remain at their posts, obligingly ignored the levies' deadly consequences).

Since the militia attracted few volunteers, sweeps of young boys and girls were carried out in the villages. Two girls of thirteen and fourteen years of age, who were levied in 1985 and escaped, described the process of these operations in Oddar Mean Chey: "The Vietnamese came on motorcycle during the day to hunt for young people—boys and girls—for the militia. Trucks were waiting [outside the village] to take us away. They took several tens of people, mostly girls because the boys had run away."

### THAT TORTURE MAY CEASE

> Late in 1979 in Kompong Cham, people were afraid because the Vietnamese brought their handcuffs even into the villages. Fears rose to such a point that the authorities had to issue a denial during meetings attended by Vietnamese "comrades."

The country was crisscrossed with political prisons (see appendix 9), the largest of which, T-3, was in Phnom Penh.[15] *T*, the initial letter of the Vietnamese word for prison, *tu*, also served to designate the principal prison in Vientiane, T-1, and that of Ho Chi Minh City, T-2, all of which people considered "Indochinese" prisons. Tens of thousands of political prisoners, held without trial, inhabited Cambodia's prisons during the RPK regime:

> In September 1980 I was confined in political prison T-3; since I didn't want to work for the government, I was accused of being anti-Vietnamese. I was released in February 1983. . . . I had irons on my ankles day and night. For meals, 230 kernels of corn. . . . I remember one month in which there were ten deaths; they died after mistreatment [during interrogation]. . . . Some prisoners died of illness. . . . I spent one year in a dark cell. They starved us to make us talk; I said anything at all that came to mind. . . . We had showers every ten or fifteen days. We had no right to communicate. Some had broken jaws from being hit; I still carry marks from it. It was the Vietnamese who beat me. The Khmers began it; they struck really hard, but then, when the Vietnamese got mad, they took over and hit even harder.

Early in 1986 Khmer *krom* who had fled Vietnam reported similar occurrences in their native provinces: "I am asking you to do something for the Khmer *krom*, that torture may cease." But the West was reluctant to condemn it; Amnesty International remained silent until 1987. Only the American Lawyers Committee did not hesitate to gather and publish witnesses' accounts.[16]

The better to control its opponents, the regime chose its subordinate jailers from former Khmer Rouge guards, who were not likely to be moved by pity. Very young girls received brutal treatment, and rape was apparently common in the regions where there was an extensive barracking of *bo doi* (Battambang, Siem Reap, Phnom Penh). A deserter stated:

> In December 1984 I arrived in the village of Ta Kong at Nimit (Battambang). Some *bo doi* had just killed three young girls after raping them. The people informed some *sereika* (nationalist guerrillas) and Khmer Rouge, who set out in pursuit of the perpetrators. There were the three bodies. . . . In June 1985 in Phum Damrey Krom, Khum Popel, Srok Damdek (Siem Reap), I saw *bo doi* ask peasants for chickens; when the peasants refused, the *bo doi* shot at the chickens and at the inhabitants. Two people died. . . . In this same village, we saw *bo doi* seize young girls to rape them; we were four [of Heng Samrin's] soldiers, and we opened fire; the Vietnamese fled.

As if all this were not enough, people were also endangered by the chemical weapons the *bo doi* used against the guerrillas, which sometimes polluted the rivers passing through population centers. Several high officials who fled from Phnom Penh have attended meetings dealing with chemical weapons and confirmed, documents in hand, the peasants' accounts.[17]

Problems of physical survival took precedence over all others. And the massive arrival of Vietnamese settlers added to the daily concerns of the Khmers.

## THE LEGALIZED SETTLEMENT OF VIETNAMESE CIVILIANS

In the name of pairing of provinces, Vietnam sent teams of specialists, particularly in construction. But it was the legalized settlement of Vietnamese civilians that most alarmed Cambodians. In May and autumn 1982 Phnom Penh issued memoranda on the reception of Vietnamese settlers and the facilities to be accorded them. Some of these texts crossed the border (see appendix 10); they undercut one journalist's denial of the plan.[18] There would have been no reason for these measures if the plan had consisted of bringing a number of Vietnamese equal to that of the 1960s—four hundred fifty thousand. Newspapers recorded this demographic colonization.[19] In certain neighborhoods of Phnom Penh such as Phsar Toch, Chbar Ampov, and Chak Angré, which were called Vietnamese neighborhoods, Vietnamese settlers predominated. The authorities spoke of making the capital into a Vietnamese city: "In the meetings of the sub-neighborhoods that took place in Phnom Penh on the twenty-fifth of each month, the cadres said that the inhabitants who did not work for the government should go to the rice fields. There have been memoranda about this since 1980, but now they want to apply them."

An escaped high official confirmed the plan and explained that non-official residents of Phnom Penh selected for clearing operations were to move permanently to the location of the works. Moreover, the plan followed the RPK's constitution, which stipulated: "The freedom of movement and settlement of citizens are established by law" (article 36, page 18). So Sarin, a physician who fled in May 1985, reported that during a monthly meeting of the minister of health, a vice-minister, the chef de cabinet, and the hospital directors, the minister read a report from the presidency of the council stipulating that it was necessary to train cadres for the border regions: "In the first stage, it was anticipated that high-level officials from the ministry and hospital directors would go to work on the sites of clearing operations. Nuth Savoeun, [then] vice-minister of health, was requisitioned in spring 1985. The goal was to study the establishment of a minimal medical infrastructure for the Khmer people who were to inhabit these regions."

But no Vietnamese settlers would settle in unsafe places, that is, in regions where the guerrillas were fighting. Faced with quiet disapproval from the people and high officials in Phnom Penh, convoys would arrive surreptitiously at night. The Vietnamese settled in parts of the cities as well as on the banks of the Mekong and other major rivers.

The problem of the massive implantation of Vietnamese civilians in Cambodia was raised by Thailand at the meeting of the General Assembly of the United Nations on 26 October 1983. For his part, the Austrian Willibald Pahr, president of the international conference on Kampuchea, expressed his concern on 7 September 1984, during a stay in Southeast Asia.[20]

The refugees' protests, beginning in 1984, raised personal, cultural, and national issues. On the one hand, Khmers had to give up sections of their houses or—slightly better—gardens and help build houses for the Vietnamese civilians. On the other hand, Cambodian society was still reeling from the shocks of the Khmer Rouge period and could not adequately reconstitute its structures under these conditions. Khmer peasants and lower-class city dwellers no longer felt at home; village or neighborhood life became impossible when it included enemy colonists who, to make matters worse, had a culture very different from Khmer culture. Cultural conflicts aggravated by political interests broke out between the two communities. Refugees expressed their anguish at Cambodia's loss of national identity; Vietnamese civilians acquired Khmer nationality with the privileges it conferred, particularly the right to vote. Hanoi's plan called for several million settlers, approximately one million of whom seem to have been in place by the close of the 1980s. (The Khmers found this settlement policy reminiscent of the one applied several years earlier in South Vietnam [Kampuchea Krom], where Hanoi's leaders had sent Tonkinese civilians to share with Khmers from southern provinces in developing the land.)

Mixed marriages (between Khmer women and Vietnamese soldiers) added to the inhabitants' concerns, even though they occurred only where Vietnamese troops were massed. In rural society, mixed marriages and their offspring were looked down on. Once demobilized, the soldier-fathers returned to Vietnam and to their Vietnamese wives and children. In Phnom Penh, most of the high Khmer officials had Vietnamese wives, freely taken in the case of first marriages or imposed when officials already had Khmer wives.

Taken together, these strains and constraints explain why the inhabitants of the RPK feared for their country's survival, all the more so because their borders were redrawn.

BAMBOO BARRIERS, THE NEW BOUNDARY MARKERS

> I was in the province of Prey Veng when the Vietnamese arrived in December 1978. . . . As soon as the fighting stopped, we could move around. . . . I saw some *bo doi* planting bamboos on a dike as some others finished building it. They'd moved the boundary markers toward the interior of Cambodia. . . . I don't know how many kilometers; what I do know is this: some villages that today are on the other side of the dike [in Vietnamese territory] were in Khmer territory before the *bo doi* moved the boundary markers.

Reports of boundary markers came from many refugees in Prey Veng and from others in Takeo, Kompong Cham, and Svay Rieng provinces. Changes in the country's borders were discussed, moreover, during meetings: "During political courses, the Vietnamese experts ask us to be understanding regarding the Khmer-Vietnamese border. They tell us not to think about the old borders but to think only of the present borders, those of the 'new Cambodia' that Vietnam came to watch over."

These usurpations were confirmed by the signing of treaties. The first, dated 12 November 1982, dealt with maritime borders; in the annexed region to which the Khmers no longer had access the Vietnamese then drilled for oil. The second in importance, eight pages long, concerned terrestrial borders and was signed on 27 December 1985 "in order officially to demarcate the national border between the SRV and the RPK with the goal of constructing a common border of lasting peace and friendship." The border that the same Vietnamese leaders had recognized in 1967 in the name of the DRV and South Vietnam's NLF, Hanoi now acknowledged, was in its eyes no longer valid. In the words of a refugee, "If this continues, instead of our national tree, the sugar palm, we would no longer see anything except the bamboo along the borders."

While the Khmers suffered demographic Vietnamization, the loss of territory, and the takeover of political and economic life by the experts, they also became aware of another danger—the destruction of their cultural heritage.

A CULTURE AT RISK

For ten years, the Vietnamese tried to apply to Cambodia a policy of *ethnocide*—the destruction of a culture within those who carry it—insidiously carried out, particularly in the beginning, in the educational domain.[21] The main features of this policy are summarized below.

*Even Schools' Names Come from Vietnamese*

Nonexistent in Democratic Kampuchea for the "new people," education had to be completely reorganized in 1979. Young people thirsted for knowledge. Teachers were lacking: many had been killed under the preceding regime, and others lived abroad as refugees. Not all abandoned buildings could be reopened. Administrative structures had to be created. Everyone participated: former teachers, students from high school and other levels; adults who knew how to read and write put themselves at the disposal of the ministry of education or its affiliated institutions in the countryside. Despite their poverty, the inhabitants helped build straw huts to shelter the first provincial students since the Khmer Rouge had razed entire villages, considering them too affluent. Everything had to be rebuilt.

In poor and distant villages, former students in the sixth and seventh grade gave a single literacy course to children, who often sat on floors of beaten earth. In the administrative centers of the communes and districts, and in the towns, the curriculum was based on that of Vietnam: the length of academic cycles (four years for primary school, three for the first cycle of secondary school, and three for the second cycle), the numbering of years (from first to tenth instead of twelfth to terminal). "Even schools' names come from Vietnamese," the border people would say. The two military academies established in Phnom Penh did not have Khmer but Vietnamese names, accepted only Vietnamese and Russian professors, and forbade entry to Khmers who were not enrolled as students.

Normally, children had four hours of courses each day, six days a week; the rest of their time was devoted to socialist labor—cleaning the school and gardening. All had to attend classes through the seventh grade (the end of the first cycle of secondary school). This minimum of instruction was beyond the reach of some children, even in the larger towns: "My son, who's thirteen years old, went to look after the production group's buffalo. He doesn't know how to read." Yet on 19 June 1980 Phnom Penh created a national committee to fight illiteracy and celebrated the anniversary each year.

Children received an abridged education, officially because of the shortage of instructors. Those who were recruited taught only several hours a day. They nevertheless worked a normal schedule, for they carried out extrascholastic tasks that took them away from teaching: socialist labor with the students, study of the Vietnamese language, political classes, propaganda campaigns in the rural areas, and clearing operations. Aside from the hours of socialist labor (cleaning the school and gardening), the other tasks did not benefit students. The Vietnamese experts—who regulated the schedules of students and teachers—were thus partly responsible for the poor level of instruction given in the RPK.

## Paying for Education

In theory education was free. In the cities, however, children whose parents did not work for the government paid for it because, normally, they were not supposed to remain there; and they paid more for their books than did officials' children. The country people paid fees that were more modest but still onerous. "The parents are asked to contribute for the upkeep of the school and for their children's care as well," a female instructor stated.

> Often the children were in rags, and the instructors were responsible for washing the children and their clothing. The school committee had us ask the parents for the money to buy soap. Most of the time, they could not pay, and we ended up paying the riel that was asked of them. . . . There was always a reason for asking them for money, a riel here, a riel there; they did not have the means to give it.

The first editions of books were printed in Ho Chi Minh City at Cambodia's expense, even though Phnom Penh had three printing houses in working condition; by offset they printed subsequent editions, greeting cards, publicity tracts, and newspapers. Yet a clandestine classical education was available; for those who were not officials, it was no more expensive than the government's education and had the advantage of giving young people a traditional image of Cambodia. To finance such studies, people who had buried gold before the arrival of the Khmer Rouge used it; those who had none took part in a more-or-less sanctioned commerce with Thailand. Others preferred to send their children to the border settlements to receive courses up to the tenth grade, free of charge in the camp schools.[22]

Aside from the academic examination, access to eighth grade included another stage, a kind of political test (its winners were almost all the sons of officials) that students called "winning your desk." Children of modest origins who had the good fortune to be accepted before the selection became draconian in 1985 were not able to go beyond tenth grade (the terminal year). Like the students who failed to advance to eighth grade classes, they were given the choice between the army and clearing operations.

Phnom Penh had two university schools: the School of Medicine, Stomatology, and Pharmacy, and the Faculty of Agriculture, opened in 1985. At the Khmer-Soviet Friendship Technical Institute students had training in scientific disciplines; a Vietnamese translated the courses given in Russian. They studied humanities at the Institute of Languages, from Vietnamese, Russian, German, and Cuban instructors. At the Institute of Commerce, they learned socialist economics from Vietnamese teachers. At the School of Fine Arts, young people learned dances and songs.

On the whole, education was far from being free and generalized. Its primary beneficiaries were the apparatchiks' families.

### A Sacrifice of Flesh and Blood

When students had learned to read and write, they took courses in arithmetic, reading, history, geography, and "political ethics." Instructors used Vietnamese manuals translated into Khmer or books written by Khmers under the supervision of Vietnamese experts. The official in charge of the editions also handled the press and theatrical performances. By the end of primary school, children of ten years of age had learned, in the reading manual, what was called "political ethics." Here is what they would have learned:

> The Khmers should not forget the flesh and blood shed by their Vietnamese brothers, who sacrificed their lives to liberate us from the Pol Pot–Ieng Sary–Khieu Samphan regime. Each day, in accordance with the instructions given by Uncle Ho, we should remember this. We should be full of gratitude for them and bear in mind that no other country except Vietnam contributed to our national salvation and rescued us from this tragedy. And we use this gratitude as a basis for nourishing an unquenchable hatred for the Pol Pot–Ieng Sary–Khieu Samphan regime and for other gangs of reactionaries who search, by all possible means, to destroy our revolution and Khmer-Vietnamese solidarity.

Arithmetic dealt with the division of collective goods. The history of Cambodia began in 1930 with the founding of the Indochinese Communist party. Courses emphasized the struggle against the American imperialists, attempting to demonstrate the existence of historical bonds among the three countries of the former French Indochina: "The Khmer, Laotian, and Vietnamese peoples are fraternal peoples who have a common history." Prime Minister Hun Sen emphasized: "History has clearly taught us that we have an exceptional weapon for safeguarding the independence, sovereignty, and rights to existence that our people hold by virtue of their status as human beings. . . . This exceptional weapon is the 'fighting solidarity among the three countries of Indochina, particularly the Kampuchean-Vietnamese fighting solidarity.'"[23]

As evidence of the fraternal bonds uniting the three countries, the cover of a history book showed a map of unified "Indochina"—entirely red. This theme of solidarity was also manifested by a three-riel stamp issued on the occasion of the fourth anniversary of 7 January 1979; three women, one Khmer, one Laotian, and one Vietnamese, recognizable by the national flags drawn on their upper bodies, stand hand in hand. Marx, Lenin, and Ho Chi Minh had a place of honor in the classrooms, as shown in the film *Cambodia's Third Liberation*, made in 1984 by Christian Schleimpflug for German television.

## Thailand Excluded from the Indochinese Peninsula

The teaching of geography focused on the Communist countries in the Indochinese peninsula and, as Hanoi clarified elsewhere, excluded Thailand: "After the Second World War, the toponym Indochina was employed in the strict sense to designate only Vietnam, Laos, and Cambodia. And in the new linguistic context, the term Indochinese peninsula no longer includes anything but the territory of these three countries."[24] This assertion has no geographical basis. Indochina refers to all the countries located between India and China. It took on a restricted definition only in a particular political context—colonization. Under the protectorate Cambodia, Laos, and Vietnam comprised French Indochina; under Vietnamese occupation the expression lost its initial term and became Indochina, which itself became equivalent to the Indochinese peninsula, without arousing the slightest protest from neighboring countries.

## Dependent of the Soviet Bloc

Parents reluctantly permitted their children to take the required courses in the Vietnamese language. The teaching of the languages of the Soviet bloc only, and the prohibition against the learning of languages such as English and French, decisions that were logical given the system's perspectives, might in the long run have harmed Cambodia and rendered it totally dependent on the USSR and its satellites. The changes that occurred in 1989 would eliminate this risk. Until 1988 this educational orientation was counterbalanced by the reminders of tradition and history that families hostile to the regime repeated to their children. But not all young people had a chance to live with a relative; orphans sent to Vietnam received an education that had little in common with Khmer practices.

## The Orphans

"From late in 1979 in the province of Takeo, we saw trucks of children enter Vietnam. We were told these were orphans going to study in Hanoi." The Khmer Rouge's massacres produced numerous orphans. Those who were not in the care of private individuals were assembled by the new regime in orphanages—several in the capital and about one for each province. The government considered orphans to be its property and educated them in the desired political sense. The most gifted had their schooling in Vietnam, others in the countries of Eastern Europe. In Hanoi, they were specially trained to take over leadership positions in the RPK.

Soon after their return to Cambodia several of them made it to the Thai border:

> I was in an orphanage in Phnom Penh. In 1981 some Vietnamese came to see us to impress us into the army. We did not go by consent. I first did three months of military training in Cambodia in the Banteay Sleuk barracks, in the neighborhood of Stung Mean Chey [in Phnom Penh]. Then in 1982 I was sent to a military training center on the periphery of Hanoi; there were fourteen of us from an orphanage. . . . I had not chosen to go. I saw nothing of Vietnam; everything was very secret.

This education contained little of Khmer cultural values, and some of these children, like those trained by the Khmer Rouge, would find themselves disoriented and bitter on the day when—assuming a possible return of independence—their powers diminished. They would not feel at ease if Khmer music, dance, and theater regained their place.

## The Arts, Publishing, and Propaganda

The School of Fine Arts, under the tutelage of the ministry of information and culture, trained young people in dance, music, and theater. Moreover, in the ministry's organizational scheme theater was on the same level as publishing, sports, cinema, the society for the preservation of Angkor, political schools, and miscellaneous propaganda. The Vietnamese expert, Bac, handled theater and the printing of newspapers, books, and propaganda documents.

The traditional music that accompanied ballet remained, aside from small changes to emphasize new lyrics; one addition was a section of modern music of Russian inspiration. To the nonspecialist, classical dance seemed little changed, except for its name. Until 1970 the dancers of the royal ballet, known throughout the world, perpetuated this art that, like the rest of Khmer culture, gave the appearance of centuries-old permanence; all the dancers' steps were codified, corresponding to precise words or situations. After 1975 a group reconstituted itself in Paris and kept up a tradition quite different from the one television viewers saw in January 1982 in Jerome Kanapa's film, *Les Enfants d'Angkor* (children of Angkor), and in the May 1982 issue of the *National Geographic Magazine*. The latter depicts the young girls rehearsing in Vietnamese pants instead of the customary *sâmpot câng khben*, while in the film, revolutionary verses replaced the poetic words of the *apsara* dance. A loud gong was introduced to the orchestra to give the new lyrics emphasis. Adaptation of the steps to new text seemed to point toward a gradual loosening of the ensemble; the young girls had no reference to the past and considered theirs to be political dances. This, then, was a means of desacralizing the dances, of removing all symbolic value from them. Moreover, only a small number of the royal dances remained.[25]

The folkloric section, created in the 1960s, was enriched by dances of Cambodian-Laotian-Vietnamese martial solidarity, military parades, and the hammer and sickle dance performed to a background of traditional music. The classical theater (Bassac and *yiké*) depicted revolutionary scenes. Songs and choruses sang the praises of the party and Khmer-Vietnamese friendship. The regime's privileged few had professional singers at their disposal who came to their homes for private ceremonies such as marriages.

Khmer officials in charge of the arts could decide nothing without the approval of the Vietnamese expert, on pain of loss of their positions. Thus, Keo Chanda, who was openly opposed to the wearing of Vietnamese pants by dancers and to the modification of certain movements, lost both his position at the School of Fine Arts and the presidency of Phnom Penh's revolutionary committee. Peou You Leng, in charge of classical ballet, did not accept the wearing of shoes and other changes. His fate was worse: the government canceled the tour that he was to lead to Vietnam. He went there alone and in perfect health; he returned in a coffin.

Television and movie houses showed news and political films. The only books permitted were those dealing favorably with communism and Vietnam. Pin Yathay's account of Khmer Rouge atrocities was proscribed; the author had concluded by stating the will of the Khmer people not to allow themselves to be colonized by the Vietnamese.

Angkor was a special case. Khmer Rouge and Vietcong forces established a stronghold there as early as June 1970. At the time, the site had suffered only a few hits from poorly aimed republican artillery shells. Afterward the Khmer Rouge dynamited statues from Angkor Wat's gallery of a thousand Buddhas that they had piled up in the courtyard and showed no further interest in Angkor. Several heads were exchanged for gasoline in Thailand. Since 1979 the region's inhabitants have once more observed the tradition of picnicking at Angkor Wat on the Khmer New Year. For several years visiting journalists had difficulty obtaining authorization to travel there. But beginning in summer 1987 tours of Angkor organized from Australia and Switzerland were required to pass first through Ho Chi Minh City, where a travel agency held a monopoly on the Cambodian tour. Surrounded by soldiers, visitors contemplated the temple of Angkor Wat and sometimes the Bayon for an hour or two. Since 1989 the Cambodian tourism office organizes these trips itself, with no interference whatsoever from the Vietnamese.

Technically, what the temples have suffered is "practically nothing compared to the sufferings of the Khmer people. The most important thing is to save the people. For the time being, the monuments can wait." So stated Bernard Philippe Groslier, the last conservator of Angkor, to Peter White of the *National Geographic Magazine*.[26] That the monuments are now untended does not constitute a serious threat to their survival. But the premature loss of Bernard Philippe Groslier leaves a void. There is no one with his qualifications and experience to take up the work of conserving and restoring the monuments.

The most notable loss has been the flight of sculptures abroad through Thailand or Vietnam. It is certain that unscrupulous Khmers such as the man who called himself Prince Suryavong stole several statues during the confusion of January 1979. The regime or the occupier is probably to blame for what has occurred since then. In 1979–1980, Ho Chi Minh City had the reputation of being a market for Khmer art, as did Bangkok. Part of the Khmer cultural heritage was carried off as war booty.

In addition, the presence of Vietnamese troops in the park of Angkor constituted another danger: to dislodge them would be to risk damage to the monuments. "Within the park of Angkor, there are two barracks, one at Angkor Thom, and the other at Srah Srang, Vietnamese barracks 479. . . . " Another account offers more detail: "In 1979 the *bo doi* were training in Angkor Wat's second enclosure. At the time one could go there without much difficulty; there was a checkpoint with a barracks on Angkor Thom road. The Angkor Wat pagoda was occupied by *bo doi*. There was also a barracks at Srah Srang." These statements were confirmed in the study published in *Indochina Report*.[27] Khmer Rouge commandos operating in the surrounding areas added to the complexity of the problem.

In the RPK, access to the national museum remained the privilege of a few. After the cultural sterility of the Khmer Rouge years, inhabitants would have taken comfort from admiring the superb pieces in the national museum and gazing at the splendor of the temples. Instead, they were allowed into the Tuol Sleng museum, to recall the horrors of Democratic Kampuchea—which they did not need; nor did they need the Day of Hatred established by the regime.

### Religious Persecution

After the complete religious void of 1975–1978, the reappearance of saffron-robed monks reassured people, who contributed to the reconstruction of some of the monasteries destroyed or damaged by the Khmer Rouge. But significant restrictions took away full freedom of religion from Cambodians: the government authorized one pagoda for each commune, and only unproductive elderly men in limited numbers (one or two for each monastery) were allowed to take the monk's habit; their movements were supervised. Peasants and other workers could not honor the weekly holy day as in former times, for they were not authorized to leave their production teams to visit the monks. The latter did not receive all the offerings: half went to the commune's revolutionary committee. All religious celebrations had to have the approval of the authorities, and processions were required to follow a predetermined route and to proceed in silence, without the accompaniment of a band. All these vexations constituted a disincentive. The government, moreover, hardened its position, and the initial toleration changed to prohibition: "During meetings, the Khmer administrative authorities, accompanied by the Vietnamese expert, told us: 'Religion is a poison, like opium; it is better to give money to help the soldiers fight.'" Khmer New Year celebrations were subject to dissuasion reinforced by sanctions.

Traditional marriages were authorized but became so expensive that Khmers could not observe their original duration (three days). If, on such an occasion, "one wanted to dance the *roam vong* [circular dance] according to custom, one had to ask permission from the responsible official in the revolutionary committee, and it was looked down on." Marriages, celebrated rapidly, lost their religious and socioeconomic significance.

Supervision of religion was, moreover, exercised on the highest level. The superior of the monks in the RPK was, according to the Khmers, a Vietnamese of Cambodian origins, who came from Hanoi. "Maybe he is of Cambodian origins, but he is above all a Communist and has always been devoted to the Vietminh." The title of "false monk," given by the people to the venerable Tep Vong, a native of Siem Reap, is derived from two factors: on the one hand, he combined the role of superior of the Buddhist clergy with those of vice-president of the National Assembly and vice-president of the Front Committee; on the other hand, he served the Vietnamese with such zeal that the people considered him as one of them. The cadres learned that "religion and communism do not mix." Thus, all kept to themselves the attachment they felt for spirits and other occult powers.

## The Standardization of Clothing and the Regulation of Travel

Khmers no longer had the liberty to dress as they wished, especially those who worked for the government. Men were required to limit themselves to plain and sober attire, and the women were obliged to wear dark *sâmpot* (skirts): black (a color traditionally reserved for the elderly), brown (not worn in Cambodia), or navy blue. No bright prints or Western pants were permitted. Women wore a sleeved bodice, preferably loose-fitting, to conceal their busts. The Cambodians, normally highly mobile, were required to have an authorization bearing several signatures if they wanted to visit a relative. This put an end to familial visiting and plant-gathering expeditions. The construction of strategic barriers around the villages in the countryside restricted the movement of the people even though the primary goal was to prevent contacts between villagers and guerrillas.

All these vexations led many Khmers to flee: peasants who were in dire straits economically and harassed by the *bo doi*; physicians and pharmacists who refused to serve a minority of privileged figures; humiliated, threatened, or discouraged officials; progovernmental soldiers protesting against the mistreatment of the inhabitants by the *bo doi* with whom Khmer soldiers sometimes clashed.

Daily life in its entirety as well as cultural practices were challenged. Aside from the fact that Cambodians no longer enjoyed freedom of action, they could no longer lead a normal family life—fathers in the army, sons engaged in clearing operations, daughters in the militia, and mothers in the village production team. The conjugal cell was disorganized even though its elements met from time to time. Relatives and friends, who had visited one another on the slightest pretext, no longer played their social role since travel was regulated; marriages, formerly the occasion of many get-togethers, were celebrated hastily. Traditional village life, with the pagoda as its religious, social, and economic axis, no longer existed. After the terrible years of the Khmer Rouge reign, peasants who had hoped to recover their ancestral customs found that foreigners stood in the way. The model was not simply political but cultural as well: it included a process of de-Khmerization, a dilution of Khmer characteristics into a Vietnamese mold. Hanoi's influence in Cambodia rekindled the Khmers' anti-Vietnamese feelings and provoked the emergence of opposition to Phnom Penh.

## THE RESISTANCE

The resistance was organized inside and outside of the country under various forms.

### REACTIONS OF THE INHABITANTS

After January 1979 the situation progressively changed for the protagonists, all hardening their positions.

### A People Opposed to the Foreign Occupier

For a while, Cambodian peasants believed in the sincerity of the Vietnamese and sought only to rediscover a normal life in a context of peace and humanity, despite the difficulties of reconstruction. Peasants proved willing to exert themselves and make sacrifices to repair the tragic consequences of the Khmer Rouge regime and to conceal the nightmares of this period behind a smile. Rural inhabitants showed their gratitude for the *bo doi* who had saved them from death. This is not to say that they were ready to accept a long and cruel occupation. Deeply attached to *khméritude*—their intrinsic Khmer nature—and to freedom, they began to reject the permanent presence of the *yuon* by complaining; then, in order to minimize the risk of punishment, they kept quiet and responded to orders with inertia. Finally, once Sihanouk returned to the fray, they showed an exemplary unity in coming together to support the anti-Vietnamese resistance. Indeed, their of recent experiences, the difficulties of physical survival, and the impossibility for them to escape depredations by all sides led them to interpret political events in accordance with the following equation "Norodom Sihanouk equals peace." It is for this reason, refugees massed along the Khmer-Thai border said, that they supported the anti-Vietnamese resistance, of which Sihanouk is the president.

In this period of crisis, the masses have been fully conscious of the role that they had to play and indeed played. The resistance, even if it overcame the traditional city-country rupture, did not give enough thought to the peasantry's future. The diaspora, for its part, had forgotten the peasants, and the important exiled leaders only paid them lip service.

### The RPK's Khmer Officials

Some Khmer officials, allied with the Vietnamese for some thirty years, perhaps still believed in a successful collaboration. Others, important figures from the defunct Khmer Rouge regime—and they are numerous in the Phnom Penh government since 1979—were enjoying the advantages derived from a position in the RPK while waiting for the possible total retreat of the *bo doi* before serving their former masters again. Those in a third group were above all concerned with ensuring a bare minimum for their family cell and denounced their neighbors if that could win them a promotion. The encouragement given by the government to informing seems to have borne fruit. Indeed, this practice fits well with the absence of responsibility and lucidity that characterizes the Khmer city dweller; the line of least resistance consists of following orders, taking advantage of personal benefits, and closing one's eyes to the rest. Individuals from a fourth category made their way to the border because they could not endure foreign guardianship or because, after an imprudent word or action, they found their lives endangered. Finally, the most mindful strove to do their work while collaborating as little as possible and trying to remain useful to the people; this group responded as peasants did. Overall, there was no cohesion in public offices; the traditional "every man for himself" remained, even in these periods of extreme danger.

## The Military Men

The Vietnamese, the true masters of the military situation, tried to build up a small Khmer army, first for appearances' sake but then for combat support. The Khmer Rouge threat, constantly brandished to motivate civilians as well as the troops, was effective during the early years. Then the Khmer soldiers, seeing that the *bo doi* abused the people and even killed them, confronted the Vietnamese and helped the peasants. Beginning in 1985 some mutinous soldiers came to the border and joined with the nationalist guerrillas or *sereika*.

The Khmer-Vietnamese anti–Khmer Rouge unity was thus broken and the situation reversed. Even though the people continued to see the Khmer Rouge as deadly enemies—despite the fact that they now helped them—the main adversary of the moment was Vietnam, which could not finish off the resistance. Nevertheless, during the dry season of 1984–85, the *bo doi* took all the border strongholds belonging to the guerrillas, nationalist and Khmer Rouge. Correlatively the *sereika*, often set up near their families who lived in the border camps, were compelled to penetrate further into Cambodia. The *bo doi* had increasing clashes with the Khmer Rouge and the two nationalist forces, according to refugees guided along the road to the border by *sereika*. Insecurity increased inside the country, and apparently largely because of the Khmer Rouge.

### THE KHMER POLITICAL FORCES OPPOSED TO THE RPK

## The Khmer Rouge

In October 1979 the majority of the Khmer Rouge armed forces, routed and having lost three-fourths of their total strength, arrived at the Khmer-Thai border, accompanied by civilians (cadres and some of the "old people") who followed them willingly or under duress; all together, there were slightly more than forty thousand persons. They entered the first shelter, Sakeo, opened by the Thais.[28] Refugees who came from the "new people," mixed with them during the exodus, remained there against their will. The *yothea* left to fight in Cambodia two months later, once they had rested and treated their sick and wounded. In June 1980 the cadres and part of the people returned to Cambodia, to Phnom Malay, which became the seat of the Khmer Rouge government. Although the United Nations High Commission for Refugees (UNHCR) supervised the operation in order to prevent the *kamaphibal* from pressuring the refugees, not all the returnees acted voluntarily. Only the intervention of Westerners could have prevented some of these tragic returns to the Khmer Rouge zones. Refugees not wanting to follow the Khmer Rouge made the following declaration on 8 May 1980:

> We ask the international organizations to help us stay alive. The Khmer Rouge have already killed many people; if we return with them, we know that there will be other deaths. We hope to remain with the international organizations. If they ask us to return to the border, we assert as conditions that they must stay with us and that the place chosen must be to the north of Aranhaprathet, not in the Khmer Rouge area. . . . If not, they will cut our throats. . . . We do not want to return to the country as long as the Vietnamese are there; we are afraid of them and even more so of the Khmer Rouge. . . . We no longer sleep at night; we are afraid they will come looking for us. We have children, babies, and we want them to live; we reject communism.

After the Sakeo repatriations, the people supporting the Khmer Rouge at Phnom Malay stabilized at approximately forty-five thousand persons, nourished and cared for by the United Nations and the International Committee of the Red Cross.

In August 1979 the Khmer Rouge presented a new political program based on individual liberty. None believed it, any more than they believed in the abolition of Pol Pot's Communist party, proclaimed in December 1981. This tinkering, as well as placing Khieu Samphan in the limelight, had as its motive giving the movement more credibility.

Nothing significant had changed in the policy of the Khmer Rouge; similarly, the *yothea*, reorganized into the Armée nationale du Kampuchea démocratique (national army of democratic Kampuchea, or ANKD), fought with their habitual ferocity, and, for three and one-half years, they resisted the *bo doi* by themselves. The violence of their anti-Vietnamese feeling maintained their ardor and morale.

*The Efforts of Son Sann and the Creation*
*of the Khmer People's National Liberation Front*

After April 1975 some republican soldiers refused to rally to the Khmer Rouge and took to the maquis. The first of this group, led by General In Tam, was based in Phnom Malay. Other groups would form further south, or in the north, in the Dangrek Mountains. Most of these forces declared themselves favorable to former prime minister Son Sann, who, in France, attempted to rally the civilians.

In 1976 his followers created in Paris the Association générale des Khmers à l'étranger (general association of overseas Khmers), which assembled Democrats, bourgeois residents of Phnom Penh, other townspeople, and individuals with advanced degrees. Son Sann's efforts to overthrow the Khmer Rouge were thus supported by civilians as well as by soldiers fighting along the Khmer-Thai border. However, the republican guerrillas were too few and lacked supplies. Although Bangkok allowed them to use bases in Thailand, the total was prudently moderated so as not to offend Democratic Kampuchea, with which Thailand wanted to maintain good relations. The republicans were in no position to undertake any large-scale military action between 1975 and 1978.

When power passed into the hands of the Vietnamese and their Khmer allies in January 1979, Son Sann called for armed resistance. In April 1979 he succeeded in unifying some of the republican guerrilla groups into the Force armée nationale de libération du peuple khmer (Khmer people's national armed liberation force), as a preliminary to the creation of a political movement, the civilian platform of which was the overseas Khmers' association. On 9 October 1979 the Front national de libération du peuple khmer (Khmer people's national liberation front, or FNLPK) was born in Sokh Sann, a refugee center created for the occasion in a mountainous region of Battambang, facing the Thai province of Chanthaburi.

Since 1972 Son Sann has sought to constitute an alternative force to the republic and then to the Khmer Rouge, but initially he apparently thought not only of having his own movement but also of rallying the opposition. Thus, beginning in January 1979 and repeatedly that year as the FNLPK took shape, he offered Sihanouk its presidency. Khmer refugees in France were deeply disappointed when the prince refused. The rupture between the prince on the one hand and Son Sann and his followers on the other dates from this period. Why could a unified nationalist movement led by the former chief of state not be formed?

*Prince Sihanouk and the Attempts at Rallying Supporters*

*The Confederation of Nationalist Khmers*    In January 1979 Sihanouk, evacuated in extremis from Phnom Penh by the Chinese, denounced the

Khmer Rouge "butchers" from Peking and, the following day, defended their regime at the United Nations against the Vietnamese invasion. He then turned to the West. After having asked for asylum in France, he decided not to go, since he would not be able to carry on his political activities there; however, recent precedents, such as Khomeini's residence at Neauphle-le-Château, might have been able to make the French restrictions acceptable to him. He also declined to go into exile in the United States. The Chinese, knowing that only Sihanouk, by entering into a new alliance with the Khmer Rouge, could still help to counter Soviet influence exercised through Vietnam in Cambodia, promised him aid for the future.[29] Thus he took up residence in Peking. How was it that the former Khmer leader once again allowed himself to be duped by the Chinese, whose intelligence had always gotten the better of his vacillation?

In June 1979 the prince—apparently abandoned by China, which nevertheless followed his idea of rapprochement with the Khmer Rouge—telegraphed his young supporters who were refugees in France, instructing them to plan for a congress, the result of which was to be the proclamation of the Fédération des Khmers nationalistes de France (federation of Khmer nationalists of France), which, along with those of other countries, was to unite in a *confédération*. Sihanouk's supporters worked actively for almost two months in preparation for the congress, which was to take place in Brussels and was to establish a solid structure capable of receiving all nationalists before uniting with the Khmer Rouge in order to form an anti-Vietnamese coalition. The former head of state thus desired a movement promoted by himself and not offered to him on a platter by a former Democrat. Much to Sihanouk's displeasure, the imminent formation of the FNLPK would rally the majority of the elite, who, unhappy with the princely refusal to cooperate, would not join the Confédération des Khmers nationalistes. Thus Sihanouk, without much support in Europe, preferred to hold the congress not in Brussels but in North Korea, at Pyongyang, in September 1979; some republicans, such as In Tam, Cheng Heng, and several others, came from the United States. Sihanouk was named president of the Confédération but abandoned it on his own account at the conclusion of a second meeting on 2 December 1979 at Nogent-sur-Marne. He announced there his desire to return to Phnom Penh as an ordinary citizen, a proposal that was opposed by some members, among them the president of the Fédération de France.[30] The movement, which was not supported by any foreign power, died of inactivity.

Sihanouk's efforts may be understood as reflecting his desire not to leave the initiative for an anti-Vietnamese coalition to foreigners alone. If the nationalists could have presented a powerful, united front, they would have had more respect and consideration from the Khmer Rouge and their

Chinese friends. This was also Son Sann's thinking in offering the FNLPK's presidency to the prince. Thereafter the two men would each go it alone. Son Sann brought international recognition to his movement, and the former head of state remained in the background.

Meanwhile, the Association of Southeast Asian Nations (ASEAN), which assembles regional non-Communist states (Thailand, Malaysia, Singapore, Indonesia, and the Philippines), pressed on to unify opponents of the Phnom Penh regime. The General Assembly of the United Nations, refusing to accept the Vietnamese fait accompli in Cambodia, continued to recognize Democratic Kampuchea and not the RPK. However, faced with the stagnation of the situation, some members wavered. The seat at the United Nations risked moving in the short run toward the RPK, and ASEAN did not want the international community to recognize a Khmer government favorable to Hanoi. In case of Communist expansion, Thailand would be the first country affected, followed by Malaysia, and so forth. One domino was nevertheless missing: Prince Sihanouk had no political movement.

*The FUNCINPEC*    Pressed by foreign powers and seeing no other solution at the time, Sihanouk created, in March 1981, the Front uni national pour un Cambodge indépendant, neutre, pacifique, et coopératif (national united front for an independent, neutral, peaceful, and cooperative Cambodia, or FUNCINPEC). Former members of the Confédération joined FUNCINPEC. The prince recognized groups of guerrillas who had been fighting since 1979 in his name. The Armée nationaliste sihanoukienne (Sihanoukist nationalist army, or ANS) was born on 4 September 1982 and became the Armée nationale sihanoukienne (Sihanoukist national army) in 1987. But its best leader, Commander Kong Sileah, killed in August 1980, would never see this recognition that he had repeatedly requested. Henceforth, the pieces were all there; it was only a matter of assembling them.

*The Coalition Government of Democratic Kampuchea*

*Formation*    On 4 September 1981, after many delays, a joint communiqué was drawn up in Singapore by the Khmer Rouge (who modestly called themselves the Partie du Kampuchea démocratique [representatives of democratic Kampuchea]), FNLPK, and FUNCINPEC, expressing "the desire to form a coalition government of Democratic Kampuchea, with the goal of continuing the struggle for the liberation of Cambodia from the Vietnamese aggressors by all means." This communiqué allowed the Khmer Rouge to retain the Cambodian seat at the United Nations. In fact, no one—neither the Khmer Rouge nor Sihanouk nor Son Sann—wanted an alliance. The former intended to remain the sole authorities and agreed to share power only because international recognition of their government was seriously questioned. Malaysia, speaking through its under secretary of state for Southeast Asian political affairs, voiced its relief after the Singapore declaration, for "many countries still did not know if they were going to continue to support the Khmer Rouge's Democratic Kampuchea, widely accused of atrocities during their four-year reign from 1975–1979." The two nationalist leaders, for their part, were reluctant to sit at the same table with the Khmer Rouge.

This unease explains why the new tripartite ad hoc committee in charge of studying ways to form a coalition government for Democratic Kampuchea quickly reached a deadlock, the Son Sann and Khmer Rouge camps refusing all concessions. Each party was forced to compromise in order for the negotiations, interrupted since 1 November 1981, to reopen in February 1982. The protagonists ended by agreeing on a formula and nine months later announced, on 22 June 1982 in Kuala Lumpur, the formation of the Gouvernement de coalition du Kampuchea démocratique (GCKD), within which each political movement retained its individuality and functional autonomy. All were represented in each ministry (health, education, defense, finance), which meant that each had three ministers, except for foreign affairs, which the Khmer Rouge monopolized. ASEAN's efforts succeeded in avoiding a reversal, the prospect of which was raised by the Philippines foreign minister who conceded that, without the formation of the GCKD, "we were anticipating a crisis in the United Nations on the question of the delegation of authority for Cambodia."

*Its Usefulness*     Since the promise of alliance made in September 1981 and then the Kuala Lumpur treaty of June 1982, the coalition government—which retained Cambodia's seat until autumn 1990—improved its score in the United Nations. Indeed, resolutions for the withdrawal of foreign forces from Cambodia gained votes each year: 79 in 1980 and 124 in 1989, which, for the RPK's opponents, constituted a diplomatic success. But it must be emphasized that only the presence of Sihanouk at the head of the coalition made this result possible.

Militarily, despite the formation of a GCKD national defense coordinating committee, mutual cooperation on the ground did not come about: few combats united the three factions, and there was only one case of strategic support. Even between the two nationalist forces, theoretically united within a joint military command known as Permico, cooperation remained limited. The *yothea* were still the most effective, although ANS soldiers gained credibility. Son Sann's troops ran into internal rivalries that caused them to lose their combativeness.

Finally, on the political level nothing had changed: the three factions continued to despise one another. Although the two nationalist clans contented themselves with verbal jousting—regrettable as it was—Khmer Rouge went further: Ta Mok's troops regularly assaulted the *sereika*, the FNLPK armed forces, and above all the ANS, which were then the most formidable militarily and especially psychologically in the minds of the peasants since they fought in Sihanouk's name. Soldiers but also villagers were coldly murdered by Ta Mok's killers. Faced with these repeated attacks, the prince threatened to resign several times. Aside from his retirement in May 1987 (for other reasons), these warnings represented the only weapon that the GCKD's president had against the brutality of the Khmer Rouge and China. His Communist partners, well aware of the diplomatic abandonment that would follow his departure, made a minor concession—quickly annulled. The scenario was to be repeated many times.

The GCKD—which proposed an eight-point resolution of the Cambodian problem (see appendix 11)—can be considered a sham alliance that allowed foreign powers to keep their consciences clean while they refused to accept the Vietnamese occupation of Cambodia. But there was no unity among the three factions, and, given the mutual intolerance, particularly between the Khmer Rouge and the FNLPK, it is hard to see how things could have been different.

*Internal Problems*

In practice, each movement reproduces traditional Cambodian society in microcosm: each faction is inspired by the feudal scheme of things. Family clans are in the commanding positions.

It is said that the Khmer Rouge quartet lost one member, Khieu Ponnary, out of action because of her advanced age, perhaps even deceased. Pol Pot, said to be seriously ill, probably had nothing but a face-saving diplomatic illness: with international pressures increasing, his friends were forced to "retire" him in 1988, officially because of his age (sixty); rumors concerning his failing health lend further credence to this measure at a time when he continues to work in the field. The Ieng Sary–Khieu Thirith couple does not seem ready to give up an ounce of their authority to anyone. The docile Khieu Samphan remains the standard-bearer for this infernal trio. These leaders are not above clan rivalries, for Son Sen, Pol Pot's official replacement as head of the national army of Democratic Kampuchea, does not approve of the violence of his colleague, Ta Mok. The Khmer Rouge observe great discretion concerning their internal problems, which do not affect the morale of their combatants. The nationalists, for their part, exposed their differences openly. Only the princes who obeyed FUNCINPEC's leader unconditionally hold power; the others are pitilessly cast aside by the leader and those loyal to him (who are looking to the future or settling accounts). The Parisian bureau thus lost its most politically competent element in 1987.[31] Among the military commanders, the situation is no better; it was nonetheless normalized with the establishment in Bangkok of Prince Ranariddh, Sihanouk's son. The ANS proved its mettle in March 1985 during the battle of Tatum; the valor of the Sihanoukist soldiers raised FUNCINPEC's prestige.[32] Nevertheless, the clans remain. Former courtiers continue to limit access to the former chief of state—the abuses of the Sangkum era persist.

For several years the FNLPK maintained a unity and an organization that could have served as an example. But internal rivalries, unresolved in private, exploded with such violence that the organization splintered, leaving in disarray soldiers, of whom some, without a leader and left to themselves, committed acts of piracy on the Khmer-Thai border and even in the refugee camps. Some youths in Paris had already been disgraced for advocating toleration. In 1985 the quarrels reached the highest echelon of the hierarchy. The FNLPK's committee of wise men stated the principal points of disagreement several times, most notably in a letter addressed to Son Sann in 1985: rejection of the absolute power exercised by Son Sann and the monopoly of positions of authority by his family. In light of the scant attention accorded to its views, the committee resigned. In the border camps and inside Cambodia, FNLPK civil and military authorities seceded. Son Sann excluded them, but, supported by Thai authorities, they retained their posts. Since the commanding general of the FNLPK's army was one of them, the military officers obtained a monopoly over defense-related decisions, but contention remained on other points. The movement lost all credibility on the international plane.

Within the three movements constructive criticism was thus not permitted; nepotism and an absence of realism prevailed. The structure remained feudal, with little hope for change. "This irresponsible characteristic is very pronounced in the Khmer political system. In contemporary Khmer history, no government and none of its members has ever agreed to admit errors and mistakes publicly, even in the most tragic moments."[33]

Sterility and stagnation characterized the GCKD until it was dissolved. Could this situation have been avoided? It would be pointless to rewrite Cambodia's history of the last three decades. Among the politicized Cambodians, many do not understand why Sihanouk concluded a second alliance with the Khmer Rouge; they would have preferred to see him establish himself in a free-world country. Despite their mixed feelings for Sihanouk, they say that they would have rallied around him to counter the Vietnamese threat; they also believe that he would have had a larger international audience. The preference—with many reservations—that considerable numbers of Khmers with advanced degrees have for the violently anti–Khmer Rouge FNLPK represents a reaction to what they consider lack of firmness on Sihanouk's part toward this disgraced group. The young people also see, not without alarm, China appearing once again behind those who killed so many of their compatriots. Thus, the majority of them remain on the sidelines.

Once again, political problems could not be solved by Khmers, who, regardless of what side they were on, appealed to foreigners. The leaders sought in China, among the ASEAN countries, and in the United States the support and aid that they needed internationally, all the more so because they did not find them completely in the Khmer intelligentsia.

## THE ATTITUDE OF THE INTERNATIONAL COMMUNITY

### The GCKD's Sponsors

The Association of Southeast Asian Nations was extremely active, sparing no efforts to bring about the birth of an anti-Vietnamese coalition. The member countries did not all have the same interest in Cambodia, yet all declared themselves favorable to a political solution of the Cambodian problem. Bangkok and Singapore emphasized anti-Vietnamese propaganda; Kuala Lumpur and Jakarta were above all distrustful of China. The distant Manila merely approved the decisions made by the others. Brunei, which joined ASEAN in 1984, seemed little interested in the Cambodian problem.

Thailand (the former Siam), which borders Cambodia, was the first nation drawn into the conflict. A sovereign country, it had escaped all colonization and occupations. Bangkok always had a sole political line: to protect the country's interests at any price, which explains its history of frequent changes of direction. As long as the wars were regional, Thailand was able to escape without loss. Now, with the internationalization of conflicts, small- and medium-sized countries need a powerful ally, and during the Vietnam war the Thais chose the Americans. After the latter's defeat, they preferred China to the Soviet Union, a decision that explains their support of the defeated Khmer Rouge in 1979. In return, China ceased arming pro-Chinese Thai guerrillas. Although it deployed a large-scale diplomatic effort in the Cambodian affair, Bangkok did not exchange ambassadors with the GCKD. Likewise, while Bangkok had carried on commercial and political relations with Democratic Kampuchea, whose *yothea* it feared very much, during the RPK period from 1979 onward it dealt tactfully with Vietnam, which, although it did not succeed in eliminating the Cambodian resistance, nevertheless dominated Laos and Cambodia. Thai business representatives visited both Vietnam and Cambodia in 1987.

Singapore was, with Thailand, one of the countries most involved in the Cambodian affair. It supplied arms to the FNLPK but did not establish diplomatic relations with the GCKD. With the SRV—and the RPK—Singapore carried out partly open and partly clandestine commerce, through Cambodia and as far as Ho Chi Minh City.

Malaysia and Indonesia (which have problems with their Chinese minorities) felt that the danger came from Peking. Indonesia—the ASEAN country closest to Vietnam—served as intermediary between Hanoi and the GCKD for negotiations on Cambodia. The two countries, unlike their partners, did not want to bleed Vietnam. Malaysia extended diplomatic recognition to the GCKD and provided military training to nationalist guerrillas.

China, co-sponsor with ASEAN of the GCKD, has always feared the total encirclement of its territory by the USSR and its allies; hence its refusal to accept the Vietnamese occupation of Cambodia. Peking supported Democratic Kampuchea in order to prevent it from becoming a satellite of the Soviet bloc. Its intervention in Vietnam in February–March 1979, officially to "teach a lesson" to Vietnam, allowed the Khmer Rouge army to reconstitute itself and to continue its struggle against the *bo doi*. The same was true for the military pressure maintained on the Sino-Vietnamese border. Analyzing Chinese policy in 1986, Sisowath Thomico concluded that, strategically, "more than on Cambodia itself, it is on this current of international disapproval [of Vietnam] that China elaborated its Vietnamese and Soviet policies."[34]

In view of the Khmer Rouge's diplomatic decline, China brought about the tripartite coalition after trying to convince first Sihanouk and then Son Sann to form a bipartite alliance with Pol Pot–Ieng Sary. Peking first voiced the idea of a military settlement of the Khmer-Vietnamese conflict before agreeing to a plan for an international conference within the framework of the United Nations. It supported above all the Khmer Rouge, whom it considered to be the only group capable of opposing the *bo doi* militarily, but it also supplied arms to the nationalists. In another respect, China reestablished commercial relations with Vietnam.

There was thus no convergency among the sponsors—not even among the ASEAN countries—in regard to the Cambodian problem. Divergent political interests prevented them from engaging their full efforts in a common direction. Furthermore, economic relations undertaken with Vietnam placed some of them in an ambiguous situation and reduced their effectiveness.

### The Other Countries

The United States did not intervene directly in the formation of the GCKD but supported ASEAN's diplomatic efforts. After the trauma left by the war in Vietnam, the Americans did not engage themselves militarily in Cambodia; they supplied the resistance with aid that was termed humanitarian.

France, still less partisan, did not recognize the GCKD because the Khmer Rouge belonged to it; Paris received Prince Sihanouk on a personal basis. But each year, France voted in favor of the United Nations' resolution on the withdrawal of foreign troops from Cambodia. Yugoslavia and Romania, although members of the Warsaw Pact, were favorable to the GCKD: the former recognized it, and the latter supported it.

## THE POLITICAL INEFFECTIVENESS AND INDIFFERENCE OF THE CAMBODIAN DIASPORA

Khmers in France, it seems, were more active politically than those in America.

### The Political Movements

Few individuals joined the political movements. In France, where almost forty thousand Khmers live, only several hundred belong to the FUNCIN-PEC or FNLPK. On the one hand, the leaders did not know how (or did not desire?) to recruit talented people to help them; on the other hand, the members could not always be as active as they liked since responsibilities are poorly delegated and clan rivalries inhibit promising structures. Most of them are frustrated and regret not being able to do anything more than lengthen the small list of supporters. Therefore, by belonging to an official movement, they have no more than the right to keep quiet or, at best, to help refugees resolve social difficulties.

The Khmer Rouge lost a number of their allies: several luminaries defected, and most of the progressive intellectuals became inactive. "Our position is difficult; we don't have good press. Because we once supported the Khmer Rouge, the Cambodians consider us their partisans." If their compatriots grant them neither the right to make a mistake nor the chance to evolve, they themselves do nothing to clarify matters. After breaking off support, none of them openly condemned Democratic Kampuchea's regime, not even those who had returned to the country between 1975 and 1978 and escaped the killings. They had participated with faith and patriotic enthusiasm—ill defined but certain—in what they considered to be a social revolution. Today their elan has left them. The rising national feeling among the youth has been broken, and it is the fault of the Khmer Rouge leaders. After this failure, it will probably be a long time before the Khmers can regain such enthusiasm.

The silence of the Khmer Rouge dissidents has caused their compatriots and Westerners to doubt their good faith. Their vagueness conceals various ideas: personal hatred for the leaders, disapproval of the massacres, disappointment at the realization that the important leaders are not changing, and occasionally—but not always—rejection of communism. Their common point is opposition to the principal leaders, Pol Pot and Ieng Sary, but that is not sufficient to make them credible; therefore, even if they wished to do so, they are incapable of undertaking positive action.

*The Associations*

More than one hundred and fifty Khmer associations publishing a bulletin more or less regularly exist in France, approximately sixty of them in the Parisian region: political, cultural, social, and professional associations, their primary justification (with the possible exception of the latter) being each's disagreement with the others. Almost all of them proclaim political preferences. Their members organize receptions—sometimes sumptuous ones— and engage in discussions that generally lead to nothing concrete for the future; orators play with theoretical concepts and ignore the people. A few really engage in social work. Only one has a recognized cultural utility, the Centre de documentation et de recherche sur la civilisation khmère (center for documentation and research on Khmer civilization, or CEDORECK), which publishes a scientific journal and the work of researchers and reprints historical documents.[35] One refugee from another continent attempted to make it known that the Khmer peasantry still exists; at the third conference on Cambodia held in July 1987 at Chulalongkorn University in Bangkok, she even dared to interrupt Khieu Samphan, denying him the right to speak in the name of the Khmer people. But the majority of refugees are out of touch with reality, wrapped in an impenetrable cocoon, and Western journalists remain aloof from the public meetings to which the Khmers invite them in France.

The Khmer New Year, celebrated on three successive Sundays in the Vincennes pagoda (once by the FUNCINPEC, once by the FNLPK, and once by a group of neutral monks, for the monks have also chosen their camps), enjoys a relative success. Some Khmers participate only in these events. The majority no longer see their compatriots or assemble in small groups of friends without getting involved in any cause. Overall, moreover, the celebrations attract more Khmers than the public meetings do. Here is a striking example. On 10 December 1987 there were two meetings in Paris for the defense of human rights: one, under the aegis of Amnesty International, brought together a rostrum focusing exclusively on Cambodia and featuring speeches and debates; the other, in a worldwide perspective and under the patronage of Alain Poher and Claude Malhuret, presented an artistic and cultural program. Khmers poured into the latter, while only twelve attended Amnesty's program. Instead of combining into a vast and constructive movement, the active Cambodian refugees scatter into minuscule rival groups and pass their personal leisure time in merrymaking rather than in the defense of their country. Direct or indirect victims of the Khmer Rouge period, they have drawn no lessons from the past. In the words of Bernard Philippe Groslier, they seem to remain in this state of "post-Angkorian torpor" that returned the country of Angkor "to the most painful mediocrity."[36] Tradition did not allow Cambodians to make effective use of their knowledge, to show initiative and to open up to others; and the leaders have done nothing to change things. Nevertheless, city-dwellers know perfectly well how to conduct their personal affairs. It is not a question of fundamental incompetence—rather of a pitiless indifference to everything outside the family microcosm. Sam Sok—one of the rare Khmers to reflect deeply on his society—explains:

> We are almost always inclined to expect too much from our "leaders." We often give them blank checks, naively thinking that they will give the best of themselves, without ulterior motives, in order to accomplish their missions and duties in the national interest. But the results, alas, have rarely measured up to the long-awaited hopes. We have hopes arising from deep inside ourselves to be led, "enlightened," by responsible leaders, conscious of their duty and their mission. We find only demigods, who care above all for themselves and their private interests. They present no serious and coherent political program nor clearly defined objectives, nothing but empty words and speeches wrapped in an artistic vagueness calculated to dull the mind. . . . In adopting this facile solution, we are giving the impression that national liberation is the business of the resistants and does not concern us in the least. . . .[37]

The majority of the Khmer refugees wait as they watch televised soap operas for a providential solution that would allow them to return to the Cambodia to which they remain attached. They did not mobilize themselves for demonstrations in favor of peace in Cambodia and still less for the undernourished Khmer peasants, denied freedom and dying during the clearing operations in the 1980s. There was no mass action to attract the interest of their fellow citizens in order to move the international community to action, an international community that was used to its blindness, its opportunism, and its refusal to state or even to admit that people were continuing to die arbitrarily in the RPK.

This more-or-less conscious refusal of the Khmers to confront the essential problems is attributable to a cultural blockage. Nevertheless, the refugees' disarray is understandable: they no longer have confidence in any leader. On the popular level, the Khmer Rouge eliminated themselves from consideration. Son Sann's intolerant and feudal behavior brought about the dismantling of his political movement and the discouragement of his partisans. Sihanouk, already contested by the elite during the Sangkum period, refused in 1979 to assume leadership of the nationalist resistance, disappointing many compatriots and causing many declared or potential militants to draw aside. Yet in 1991 he remains the sole person capable of rallying the people, at least in the short run. The presence of the Khmer Rouge in the opposition to Phnom Penh represents an obstacle to any union, even temporary; because of them, the majority of Khmers who should have worked for peace did not support the resistance. No one has the right to say that they are wrong; by the same token, no one stops them from acting in favor of compatriots living in Cambodia.

Faced with this crisis of confidence, former military officers have attempted to create a fourth force in order to rally the opponents of the Communists in general. At least two movements have appeared in the Parisian region. But the painful memory of the republican generals act against these initiators of a fourth force, and, after two or three years of existence, they have made no progress, for want of credibility as much with their compatriots as with foreigners capable of helping them.

In this context, we can better understand the sometimes irritating lack of interest displayed by the generation of those in their forties. The relative consensus of the diaspora on Prince Sihanouk result from a process of elimination rather than enthusiasm: "I'll tell you frankly, I don't like Sihanouk, but he is the one through whom any solution to the Khmer political problem will go. Son Sann's men are too hardheaded; they lack flexibility. Sihanouk can convince people, discuss things. As for the Khmer Rouge . . ."

Very few refugees have thought about the future Khmer society. "We must see that education can't be turned away from its mission and made to turn youth into a passively submissive group," Sam Sok explains. "On the contrary, we should develop the critical spirit and the personal judgment that will facilitate evaluation of the veracity of facts and external influences."[38]

The most qualified to bring about change may be the young people raised abroad and those who, inside the country, have lived through all sorts of misfortunes for eighteen years. The former, to take only the example of youths educated in France, have proven capable of adapting to other habits, of reflecting, and of taking action. But, knowing so little of Cambodia, will they be sufficiently motivated? In terms of the future of those who live in their once-again free country, the latter will certainly have ideas, based on their experience, that exiles would not be able to contest. The adjustment will be made if these exiles do their utmost to evaluate their society in a critical fashion, to examine the historical facts in an objective way, without seeking to revise them, and—only afterward—envisioning the future in cooperation with those who have suffered. Will the leaders of all sorts be able to show as much wisdom as the people who now live in the country?

THE ROLE OF THE MEDIA

In the wake of the Vietnam war and the vast anti-American movement, the masses mobilized throughout the world in favor of the victims of aggression. The generosity and sincerity of a small number of French people cannot cause us to forget the opportunism of many others. The former supporters of the Khmer Rouge, for the most part, initially refused to admit the existence of the massacres and merely followed the current of accusation when foreigners broke silence—without the slightest self-criticism.[39] This does not mean that they recognized the right of the Cambodian people to live in peace. Indeed, very few raised their voices against the abuses committed in the RPK. The "Vietnam syndrome," even if it is different in France, nonetheless exists.[40] The press hardly awakened except to commemorate the painful anniversary of the 1975 Khmer Rouge victory and to make up for its silence by evaluating several years of horror in one fell swoop. There was very little coverage in the news. And how outrageous that the only facts reported were the victories of the *bo doi* along the border and, like a refrain or an alibi, the life of refugees in the camps, with virtually nothing on the accounts of Cambodians who had fled. Moreover, those in charge of the press refused all proposals for articles or stories.[41] Furthermore, the majority of journalists and others who speak or write on Cambodia are often rather ignorant of its history, its inhabitants and their culture, and its social realities, even if they have lived there.[42] Their desire for a "scoop" often causes them to generalize on the basis of a single account, or to accuse refugees of exaggeration as soon as articles prove false. This occurred in 1979. Peasants in distant districts were victims of famine; the press and the humanitarian organizations presented it as a national phenomenon, which proved incorrect. No journalists wondered whether their methods of investigation were responsible.

For their part, from May 1986 through May 1988 the Cambodians were not able to take advantage of the creation of the Human Rights Ministry in Paris, and, if a few reassuring words were spoken from time to time regarding the Cambodian situation, the French government did nothing to draw attention to violations of human rights in the RPK. Amnesty International did not give the subject the emphasis that it deserved, keeping silent for many years. Just as it never denounced the Khmer Rouge's massacres—a fact that it publicly admitted in Paris on 10 December 1987—it waited until September 1986 before asking to visit the RPK's prisons, and until 1987 to denounce them, whereas, according to its representative, it had known of the occurrence of torture since 1982. The above-mentioned reception is revealing (see appendix 12).[43] In light of these problems, a fundamental question arises: did not the placement of persons who are strongly marked politically in the London head office (this was the case for the Cambodia-Laos-Vietnam-Thailand section with Steve Heder, a Marxist who supported the Khmer Rouge regime) constitute an obstacle to the proper functioning of Amnesty International?

Was it also an accident that none of the numerous books written on Cambodia since 1975, by Khmer or French authors, gave rise to wide-ranging debates, broadcast on radio or television?

The RPK ceased to exist on 30 April 1989, a manifest sign of geopolitical changes favorable to Cambodia that emerged in 1988.

# 9  Vietnamese Disengagement
## The Hour of Reckoning

The transformations that are still going on in Eastern Europe make the cohesion of the Soviet-dominated Communist bloc an open question as this book ends in September 1993. Indeed, the Soviet Union's problems caused its president, Mikhail Gorbachev, to turn from regional conflicts and use his rubles to improve conditions in his own country; he no longer wanted to participate in the war effort in Cambodia and even lost interest in the naval base at Cam Ranh Bay (central Vietnam) and thus in the option of a Soviet presence in the China Sea. Hanoi, left without subsidies and faced with destitution—resulting in particular from the Western embargo in force until a diplomatic solution can determine the fate of Cambodia—found itself compelled to withdraw its occupation forces and to allow its protégés in Phnom Penh relative liberty of decision making, symbolized by the fact that the country assumed a less aligned name, the state of Cambodia. The *bo doi* officially left Khmer territory at the end of September 1989.

## THE STATE OF CAMBODIA

Between the *bo doi*'s withdrawal and the signing of the Paris Accords on October 1991, Cambodians experienced two years of political, economic, and social insecurity.

### THE FAILURE OF VIETNAMIZATION

Despite ten years of occupation, the Vietnamese succeeded neither in imposing themselves militarily nor in changing the customs of the Cambodian people; and, paradoxically, despite the undeniable services they rendered, they revived the inhabitants' hostility toward them.

#### Mercenaries in the Service of Phnom Penh

Until September 1989 the Vietnamese officially and actually led and carried out the struggle against the nationalist and Khmer Rouge guerrillas. The

256

Khmers controlled by the Phnom Penh regime showed so little eagerness to join the army that, in order to augment the number of Cambodian combatants, the government was compelled to resort to subterfuge. In 1985 it launched a campaign for recruitment of "policemen," who were sent to the front after six months of military training (hence they were termed *nokorbal prayuth* [combat police]).[1] But this source of enlistment was soon exhausted, and the governmental army never seemed capable of assuring security in the zones that Phnom Penh claimed to control.

The military vacuum became fully evident immediately after the Vietnamese withdrawal in September 1989, when Phnom Penh's troops were unable to contain the advance of the Khmer Rouge and the nationalists, forcing Hanoi to bring back, at least temporarily, some of the *bo doi*. Heng Samrin's troops lacked not equipment but motivation. None wanted to fight, and certainly not against Khmers, whoever they may be. Paid poorly or sometimes not at all, the soldiers ransomed and pillaged, their leaders indifferent to the counterpropaganda that the army's poor behavior represented.

Faced with this lack of enthusiasm for going to the front, Phnom Penh had to call on the Vietnamese to help the governmental army counter Pol Pot's soldiers, who would have overwhelmed it in many areas. In order to deal with the fighting, the government henceforth paid demobilized *bo doi*, quartered outside settlements; according to the people, at the beginning units contained almost as many Khmers as Vietnamese, all dressed in the same fashion and speaking a single language—Khmer. Their number declined after the 23 October 1991 treaty calling for the disarming of 70 percent of each faction. Then it was estimated at around five thousand. Aside from these mercenaries, by the end of 1990 Cambodia no longer had an occupation force—only advisers.

This situation was probably convenient for Hanoi and allowed it to watch over the progress of the fighting. And the leaders of the Cambodian government that bore responsibility for this state of affairs led comfortable lives in a secure capital, far from the dangerous zones and with little concern for the morale and the material needs of the soldiers. The Khmer Rouge's nests (existing or potential ones) around Phnom Penh had been eliminated by the "Works for National Defense." Plan K-5, intended to cut down the forests in the zones bordering Thailand—and responsible for tens of thousands of deaths and many casualties—continued in the northwest until 1990.[2] At that time, people suffering from malaria and those wounded by mine explosions or in combat received care in Phnom Penh, in view of foreigners as well as inhabitants. Therefore, individual Cambodians tried simply to avoid being drafted or levied for clearing; those with adequate means, for example, regularly paid off the recruiting agents.

## The Khmers' Margin for Political Maneuver

Even if restrictions remained, the Khmers had undeniably gained the right to make decisions in purely internal affairs: health, education (plans for a Khmerization of education), religion (official restoration of Buddhism), agriculture (distribution of land to private owners), justice (decisions concerning political prisoners and civil offenders interned in Cambodia), industry (concessions to foreigners), and, to a certain degree, commerce. The granting of visas, previously at the discretion of Vietnamese experts, was henceforth determined by Cambodians alone.

Likewise, many Vietnamese experts returned to their country. Although Vietnamese were said to remain in the principal positions (presidency of the council, ministries of foreign affairs, interior, defense, information, radio), they showed great discretion; they now received their instructions through diplomatic channels, that is, from the Embassy of Vietnam. The special offices of Vietnamese experts, A-50 and A-68 in Phnom Penh, were closed.

The absence of maturity and competence on the part of the Khmer political leaders made full decision-making autonomy difficult to achieve. The qualifier "pro-Vietnamese" to characterize the majority of the state of Cambodia's leaders thus seems less appropriate than that of "dependents" of the Vietnamese in many respects.

The Phnom Penh leaders tried rather to assert themselves metaphorically as Cambodians, yet without giving priority to the national interest. Indeed, their behavior revealed the resurgence of specifically Khmer values: arrogance, a fondness for ostentation and power, contempt for the weak, attention to manipulating the symbols of legitimacy. In this regard, the attitudes (gestures, approach to the peasants, respect for the monks) of Heng Samrin and Hun Sen during the inauguration of pagodas or school buildings (in 1990–1991) revealed a desire to copy the former chief of state, Prince Norodom Sihanouk, then still popular among the population. Buddhism's return to honored status must thus be understood in the context of the Khmer king's traditional role as protector of religion. The search for *khméritude* appeared strongly among the people as well, and the failure of Vietnamization was most evident in education and culture.

## The Affirmation of a Culture

Education, again under the control of Khmers, made a clean sweep of all that was implemented during the previous decade. By the end of 1991 only technical courses continued to be taught partially in Russian (at the Khmer-Soviet Technical Institute) or in Vietnamese (Institute of Commerce), for lack of competent Khmer professors. But at the end of the year all the Soviet experts—military and civilian—left Cambodia. Civil servants were poorly trained in Vietnamese forcibly taught to them for ten years: passive obedience and calculated inertia led most of them to do nothing but mumble their way through the words taught, declaring themselves incapable of making a correct Vietnamese sentence. Since 1989 secondary school students were able to choose English or French as their first foreign language; very few enrolled in Russian or Vietnamese courses, which have become optional languages. Likewise, mathematics lessons no longer dealt with the division of collective goods; instead, there were courses in civics as well as the plan to reinstate the *chbap*, the moral treatises that constituted the basis of traditional education (discussed in chapter 1), in the program of Khmer language and literature. Private classes began to be offered in Phnom Penh. Among them, the Alliance française, opened in September 1990, enjoyed complete success for various reasons, one of the most important being the desire to escape from the Communist orbit. Television broadcast English and French courses; numerous private "schools" provided a parallel training, particularly in English.

In the artistic domain, classical ballet reinstated the canons of the royal ballet; nothing remained of the Vietnamese attempts to give the dances a political connotation, modify the costumes, and eliminate the *sâmpeah kru* (ritual honoring the patron deity of ballet). Ballet dancers and teachers from the 1960s taught children this refined art, accompanied by surviving musicians formerly affiliated with the royal palace; more than one hundred young girls (from eight to sixteen years of age), dressed in the traditional garb for rehearsal, the *sâmpot câng khben*, assiduously attended the courses given at the School of Music.[3]

Now on display everywhere in the cities are the temples of Angkor, in a manner that can almost be described as ostentatious (some establishments may boast several reproductions): on signs outside restaurants and shops of various artisans (photographers, tailors, silk merchants); in offices and homes, they appear in sculptures in copper or paintings, some of which depict the construction of Angkor Wat. When the Khmers fled Angkor because of the Siamese threat, the oral tradition built up a legend describing the construction of this temple, considered the masterpiece of Khmer classicism; it is likely that these paintings reflect the same collective unconscious of the Khmers, concerned as they were about the reconstruction of their country, which they always identify with Angkor Wat. We should remember that Angkor is also a place of pilgrimage for all Cambodians. In 1990, with Angkor too close to the fighting, pilgrims changed their routes and visited the royal pagoda in the former capital of Oudong—it was in ruins, but its great Buddha was still intact. Angkor, Buddhism, and the royalty constitute three powerful forces in the search for Khmer identity.

Long condemned and consigned to the role of political propaganda,

Buddhism is slowly regaining the position that Khmer society would like to see it assume. With the restoration of the monastic communities, the *don chi* (elderly women who serve the monks and look after the upkeep of the monasteries) begin taking up their work again, elderly people follow the holy days, and crowds gather for the great Buddhist celebrations. In the quest for identity, Buddhism—aside from the fact that it represents secure moral values—allows Cambodian Khmers to distinguish themselves from their Vietnamese neighbors, who are either Communists (and thus atheists), Catholics, or followers of the Buddhism known as the Greater Vehicle, different from that of the Lesser Vehicle practiced in Cambodia.

Along with the renewal of Buddhism, popular beliefs in all kinds of supernatural forces, forbidden for fifteen years, vigorously reemerge. Natives of Phnom Penh, previously discreet regarding this kind of activity, carry them out in broad daylight, each family venerating as many as four deities. Some families have even set up ancestral altars, a new development among the Khmers.[4] In the countryside people once again observe the traditional ritual at births. In increasing numbers mediums (known in the cities as *baromey*, a more elegant word than the expression *rup arêak* used in the countryside) travel to Pursat to visit the country's best-known spirit, Neak Ta Khleang Muang. Among other goals, all these practices seek to ward off further miseries like those of the Khmer Rouge regime. The renaissance of Buddhism and the increasing number of altars further indicate the moral distress and the vacuum of reliable sociopolitical values to which people might cling.

In the countryside individualistic practices that had been stifled for fifteen years are reviving. The *krom samaki* (solidarity groups) no longer exist and the private ownership of land is now possible. We must nevertheless weigh this positive cultural balance sheet against demographic factors that are vividly present to Khmers.

### Vietnamese Civilians

Whatever they may be called, settlers or residents, vagabonds or economic refugees, many Vietnamese civilians remain in Cambodia. The Khmers consider their presence to be a major problem. In 1990 Phnom Penh estimated these civilians at eighty thousand, of which twenty thousand were in the capital; the resistance claimed that there were two million of them.[5] They continued to arrive. Although an exact count of their number is impossible (and despite the fact that some of them had to return to Vietnam after the withdrawal of Vietnamese troops) their presence is noticeable. Practicing the same trades as in the 1960s—those of tailor, hairdresser, electrician, mechanic, bricklayer—or owning a stall in one of the capital's great markets, in the center of Phnom Penh, they appear more numerous than they were before 1970. Morever, strong concentrations exist in the peripheral neighborhoods of greater Phnom Penh: Chak Angré and Chbar Ampov (the group living in the Phsar Toch neighborhood has been moved to Km9, that is, nine kilometers north of Phnom Penh). Gathered behind the Cambodian houses and thus not visible from the road, Vietnamese civilians, apparently economic migrants, live in miserable shanties, also found along riverbanks in villages created in 1979. Likewise, Vietnamese prostitutes live in an area located behind the Khmer village of Svay Pak (six kilometers to the north of Phnom Penh), and some fishermen settled not far from there, at Prek Phneou.

At the beginning the government did its best to make people forget about these foreigners, then relegated to the background, but the Khmer people's concern is patent. In particular, it derives from the fact that in 1992 Vietnamese civilians continued to settle in Phnom Penh without anyone, including the government and the United Nations Transitional Authority (UNTAC), controlling their arrival or even knowing their status. If the influx continues, a serious demographic problem could arise, perhaps leading to political, social, and economic difficulties. Although public incidents between Khmers and Vietnamese are rare, tensions exist: "Here, there is no problem between Khmer and Vietnamese civilians; we talk to one another, but we are not friendly. Everyone would be happy to see them leave." In July 1992 eight Vietnamese civilians were killed in Kampot province. As for the assertion that these immigrants constitute so many potential soldiers, it is unverifiable. The same is true for the assertion that demobilized *bo doi* married to Khmer women comprise a fifth column.

If this relative disappearance of Vietnam and the Vietnamese in the leadership of the state of Cambodia gives the Khmers the opportunity to take initiatives, the governmental structures, although sometimes devoid of cohesion, have nevertheless scarcely changed between 1979 and June 1993.

GOVERNMENTAL STRUCTURES

*The Government, the Party and the Front*

Theoretically independent, the governmental and party structures overlapped, a certain number of people belonging to both of them. The influence of the Parti populaire révolutionnaire du Kampuchea (people's revolutionary party of Kampuchea, or PPRK) remained and limited the government's liberalization measures. The third institution, the Front (Front uni national pour la défense et l'édification du Cambodge [united national front for the defense and edification of Cambodia]) concerned itself with all classes of the population (monks, ethnic minorities, unions, women, youth, etc.); it represented the popular masses and, by virtue of this, advised the government but lacked decision-making authority.

Cambodian politicians included in their ranks former Khmer Rouge, such as President Heng Samrin, a peasant before fighting in Pol Pot's army and holder (until 6 April 1992, when Chea Sim replaced him) of a purely formal role that counted for nothing among the people; and Prime Minister Hun Sen, a member of the Communist party[6] and the leading light of the moment, attempted to assert himself domestically as well as on the international level. A good orator, apparently enthusiastic, intelligent, and, at least at the outset, sincere, he enjoyed a certain popularity in 1989 when, partially disengaged from Vietnamese tutelage, he took liberal measures and showed his intent to further the negotiations aimed at bringing peace back to his country. By the end of 1990 the Khmers, disappointed by the pursuit of the war and by the growth of corruption, nonetheless declared: "We are grateful to the Vietnamese and to Hun Sen for saving us from the claws of Pol Pot." In the political apparatus, his liberalism was not unanimously supported: he finds himself the target of the hard-core Communists who united around Chea Sim, another former Khmer Rouge, president of the National Assembly, president of the Front and of the Cambodian state since 6 April 1992, and the person responsible for the arrest, in May–June 1989, of the prime minister's collaborators and their replacement by PPRK strongmen. These changes indicated that the ruling powers lacked real cohesion. In fact, the ministers' freedom of action was all the greater in that they belonged to a sector that was not very "sensitive" and thus not supervised by the Vietnamese advisers; they were nonetheless not secure from an internal purge.

## The Administration, a Poor Relation

An administrative structure existed and could be seen in formal diagrams, but the human vacuum made public offices ineffective. The inadequacy of personnel resulted from the elimination of cadres and technicians by the Khmer Rouge as much as from the conditions offered by the state of Cambodia to its civil servants. Officials from the preceding regimes (Sangkum and the Khmer Republic) refused to take up their former positions, given the salaries offered: in December 1990 an average of 3,000 riels per month, the price of a sack of cement, or $5.00, whereas seven to eight times more was necessary to live modestly.[7] Police and soldiers still received the monthly allocation of rice but other officials now received a sum of money. In late 1991 salaries increased at the same rate as the U.S. dollar, but the standard of living did not similarly improve. The underuse or neglect of some officials caused the overworking of others, and the government found itself in the absurd situation of requesting the assistance of foreign technicians and cadres while there were competent people available in Cambodia. Nevertheless, some officials in charge of services or departments, recruited for their competence and generally not belonging to the party, courageously and honestly worked a demanding schedule, having scarcely the means to purchase basic supplies—pens, for example.

Indeed, since the USSR no longer financed the Vietnamese war in Cambodia, the Khmer government used part of its national budget for the army, officially 40 percent but actually much more. A service as important as education could no longer pay its teachers, who received one month's salary—or sometimes nothing—for the period extending from the beginning of September to the end of November 1990; the same scenario was occurring in 1992. For lack of funds, services under the authority of social action, of agriculture, and of urbanism could make no plans: "We exist, but we have no working budget." In these conditions, working for the national interest and the people's benefit required courage, altruism, and a sense of civic duty (the leaders were not necessarily subject to the same restrictions).

Furthermore, until September 1992 obligations of a political nature regularly distracted officials from their duties. Political courses remained in force, even if many heads of services merely learned their lessons by heart and repeated them "like parrots" to their subordinates. Since the end of 1989 no more has been heard of "returning to the masses," a policy initiated in 1979. For a time the leaders, who feared Sihanouk's popularity, were worried at the prospect of a settlement of the Cambodian conflict carried out under the aegis of the United Nations, followed by general elections. Thus, from November 1990 onward the personnel of the ministries and public administration (with several exceptions) had been sent by half its number on a rotating basis to the provinces to conduct political propaganda that had a single refrain: "Don't vote for Sihanouk; he'll bring back the Khmer Rouge." As a result public services had to do without a part of their already meager staffs, and the leaders lost what little prestige they had.

## An Artificial Economy

Most of the visitors or foreigners working in Phnom Penh declared that the country was experiencing rebirth, that Phnom Penh was animated, and that consumer goods were abundant. All this was true, but what did it really mean?

According to officials, the capital sheltered one million persons, an approximate figure given the absence of statistics in Cambodia; it was in fact a bustling city. Cars, bicycles, and motor bicycles equipped with powerful horns negotiated the streets of the town, proving that some inhabitants were sufficiently well-off to purchase them; likewise, the presence of many jewelers trading in markets and neighboring areas was surprising. In the marketplace vendors displayed—in addition to fish, meat, and local produce—fabrics imported from Thailand, Laos, Malaysia, and other countries, for Khmer cotton fabrics were of poor quality and tended to fade. Shops overflowed with consumer goods (radios and stereo sets) and even luxury commodities while the majority of Khmers hardly had enough to eat. But this trade did not benefit the government in any manner; not a riel went into its coffers. This merchandise entered Cambodia as contraband through Aranhaprathet or the ports of Kah Kong and Kompong Som. The best placed officials (customs officers, policemen, soldiers) deducted a percentage for their own benefit; the government gave free rein to this practice, in which high officials were involved.

Until 1990 Cambodia received significant aid from the Eastern bloc countries; its reduction caused serious problems for the government before the signing of the 23 October 1991 treaty. In 1992 there seemed to be no national economic planning or rational program for exploitation of natural resources. The state, moreover, remained highly dependent on Vietnam and on Chinese compradors in this domain. The coupling of Cambodian and Vietnamese provinces had apparently ended, but according to rumors Phnom Penh paid its war debts to Hanoi in kind: rubber, fish, and particularly wood coming from the overexploited forests of Kratié and Stung Treng. None of the factories functioned at capacity; some had closed down in 1979 for lack of raw materials. Chinese businessmen—former residents of Cambodia or citizens of neighboring countries (Singapore, Hong Kong, or Thailand)—invested a lot of capital in certain sectors. The Chinese of Phnom Penh had moved back into their traditional neighborhoods and renovated abandoned compartments; they had reopened their shops or were about to do so, another positive sign amidst the general anarchy.

The construction industry blossomed in the capital but did not reflect a program intended to benefit the population; it chiefly concerned restoration or enlargement of villas belonging—by virtue of a law passed in 1989 to prevent exiled owners from reclaiming them—either to high officials or indirectly to foreigners who speculated on their own account by reselling them or renting them to private organizations. The Hôtel Cambodiana, completed with capital provided by a firm from Singapore, was managed by a Sino-Khmer from Hong Kong, a former resident of Cambodia. There were even plans to build two more luxury hotels.

The depreciation of the local currency was further evidence of the poor state of the Cambodian economy. The riel—which has undergone several devaluations—served only as "small change" for daily purchases. Apart from necessities, everything was paid for in gold, the Khmers' safe currency—in *dâmloeung* (37.5 grams) or in *chi* (3.7 grams)—or in dollars, the preferred foreign currency that permitted transfers abroad. Furthermore, large quantities of dollars had poured into Cambodia since 1989 without real supervision. In that year the government reopened the Sukhalay hotel in Phnom Penh to accommodate Khmers come from abroad (the United States, Canada, France, etc.) to visit their relatives in Cambodia. Many arrived carrying wads of bills (tens of thousands of dollars each). Financial aid from the diaspora allowed some individuals to avoid destitution. Yet for most of its inhabitants Phnom Penh was a facade of abundance from which they could not benefit.

### The Prisons Maintained

For seven years Cambodians lived in fear of arbitrary arrests. In March 1986 the government promulgated a decree regulating arrests (which henceforth required a warrant), searches of persons, and searches of premises. In October and November 1990 the sentences for approximately twenty political prisoners were reduced. Likewise, jails supervised solely by Vietnamese were closed following the Vietnamese disengagement in September 1989.

Was the problem therefore solved? Individuals whose cases had been judged serious remained on an island near Saigon; the government admitted the existence and operation of prison T-3, located in central Phnom Penh and visible to everyone. Nothing was said of the others, unknown to foreigners, such as Paye Chkaê, located to the south of the stadium, Srah Chak, near the pagoda of the same name and reserved for soldiers, Tuol Sleng (behind the museum of genocide), Prey Sar, in Kandal province, not far from Phnom Penh. The mere mention of these locations still terrified the inhabitants. Nonetheless, since the middle of 1991 many prisoners had gradually been released.

Thus the regime went along, muddling through, its plans for liberalization stymied by the party, by continued fighting, by corruption, and by administrative anarchy. This situation generated abuses and corruption and provoked resentment in a people who had already suffered so much.

A DESTITUTE PEOPLE

The poverty of the Cambodian people is patent in all domains: material, intellectual, and moral.

## The Uncertainty of Daily Life

To visitors' eyes villages appear as in the past—shaded, well kept up, crawling with children. Fields looking much as they did in the 1960s are contained within the one-hectare paddy fields constructed under the Khmer Rouge and then abandoned. The large canals that crisscross them remain as they were, as do some dams, reservoirs, and pumping stations that supply them more or less well. Unused, they have suffered the ravages of time; the canals are filling up with rain water; people fish in them and sometimes plant rice. Four years' hard work by an entire people did not bring a single technical improvement, and the peasants reject these reminders of a painful period.

Rural people are poor. In former times, many of them had set aside a reserve of gold, however small. Confiscated by the Khmer Rouge or spent to buy food since 1979, it is exhausted. Moreover, many peasants complain of cultivating rice paddies smaller than before, high officials having appropriated the lands. Livestock, already insufficient, is subject to theft; the animals are sold in Thailand or Vietnam, to the despair of peasants unable to overcome their difficulties. Because of periodic droughts, the provision of motorized pumps and the installation of small hydraulic works truly adapted to local conditions would be useful; peasants ask for water, but the services concerned lack the money to satisfy them.

The war upset the division of labor: widows are now working the land, in peacetime the domain of men; sometimes children help in the paddies or the fields, delegating their traditional role of watching the oxen to the elderly.

Until 1991 the budgets of peasants as well as townspeople were saddled with several obligatory monthly taxes: a contribution for soldiers leaving for the front and one for those returning; a contribution toward cloth for slogan-bearing banners, and so on.[8] Participation in a war and tolerance of a policy that inhabitants could not support weighed financially and psychologically on everyone. To all these torments were added political meetings, attended by age group and by sex in urban neighborhoods. They were also held in pagodas for the elderly persons who look after them, in the district seats for teachers, and in the places of work for employees of the administration. Women moved freely throughout the entire country; in contrast, men had to show authorization at surveillance stations under pain of immediate conscription into the army. Now these obligations no longer exist.

At Phnom Penh serenity is possible only in the apparatchiks' neighborhood. Once calm and clean, the capital has slid into the third world: dilapidated buildings and dusty, collapsing, and poorly maintained streets that resound with the honking of horns; piles of garbage and stopped-up sewers, despite a real effort in these domains; filthy hospitals that demand payment and where the poor cannot obtain treatment; absence of potable water; insufficient and irregular supply of electricity; a growing gap between poor and nouveaux riches; beggars. After the fall of Pol Pot, peasants moved into Phnom Penh, which had supplies of rice built up by the Khmer Rouge and was the point of arrival for international aid that rarely reached the rural people. For better or worse, one ate in the capital, whereas people starved to death in some villages. As refugees they imported ways of life that were often unsuitable to the city, lodging themselves in empty apartments. "They don't know how to use an apartment," townspeople remark. This makeshift existence, precarious and unclean, added to the demoralization of the most needy, explains the appearance of casual unconcern.

Nevertheless, since the end of 1990 Khmer leaders, Chinese from neighboring countries, and Cambodians of the diaspora are investing in real estate. Some peasants who lived miserably in the capital sold the apartment or house of which they had been declared the owners—sometimes under constraint by high officials. They then returned to the countryside, where they bought a patch of ground if there was any left.

Their extreme poverty forces Cambodians to purchase second-hand clothing, imported by the ton from Singapore and Indonesia. Very concerned about their appearance and unaccustomed to wearing other people's clothing, poor Khmers resign themselves to this practice. Life in Phnom Penh is difficult. Rickshaw drivers—most of whom work seasonally, coming once or twice a year to earn the money to buy foodstuffs—appear to be the privileged ones, despite their tattered clothing: they make a net income five to six times higher than that of an official. Soup and vegetable vendors eat decently. Others, officials or unemployed laborers, have to resort to various expedients.

Since 1979 commerce has been mainly illicit trading. Only those who had a small capital from the beginning profited from it, and the market remained limited because inhabitants did not have the right to possess certain consumer goods, such as motor bicycles, reserved for cadres. Since the liberalizing measures passed in 1989 by the government, these activities experienced a formidable increase: carefully guarded gold (hidden during the Khmer Rouge regime, recovered by some in 1979) and the financial aid provided by the diaspora facilitate transactions of all kinds.

Aside from large-scale traffic developed by apparatchiks' families, by smugglers engaged in the trade since 1979, and by several rich Chinese, trade is mainly petty commerce intended to allow households to survive. Some intellectuals earn their living by transporting merchandise between the border and Phnom Penh in rented trucks. Officials, underpaid, cannot provide the daily rice for their children. If one such is fortunate enough to find a second job—which is indispensable if his wife also works in the public sector at the same inadequate wage—he juggles an overloaded schedule, abandoning his office for part of the day, leading to fatigue and various other problems as well. Sometimes a couple, both of them officials, try to rent out their decent house while they live in a poor man's housing. More generally, the wife obtains daily necessities by improvising as a beautician, learning hairdressing in order to open a salon, or selling imported fabrics in the market; she earns ten times her husband's salary. The initial financing sometimes comes from a relative living abroad.

Indeed, the diaspora plays an important role in the physical survival of the Cambodian people. For individuals too old to participate in commerce, or for those with ridiculously low salaries, the dollars that they receive from abroad serve to buy food in order to eat decently, obtain medical care, clothe themselves, and educate their children. Townspeople without this resource or peasants without rice in the months preceding the harvest have no choice but to beg for food. They are not—with rare exceptions, such as the children who must beg in most of the cities of the third world—professional mendicants but rather starving people (widows, the elderly) who solicit foreigners as well as Khmers whom they confront in shops, in the market, or at home. Elderly people and children search through piles of garbage for objects to sell; one kilogram of scrap iron brings one U.S. dollar. The most desperate of them cut electric or telephone wires from the exchange newly installed by the Australians to sell them in the market. This destitution results as much from the Khmer Rouge regime and the war as it does from the anarchy that affects both the regime and the society.

## A Society in Disintegration

The changes that have taken place in Cambodia during the last twenty years are not only superficial: the community suffered from the general destructuralization applied by the Khmer Rouge, from the lack of freedom under the Vietnamese occupation, and from the egoism and lack of organization of the state of Cambodia.

*The Debasement of Education*     The education that all would like to see their children have—this knowledge that brings respect—was not provided for four years under the Khmer Rouge regime and has been provided only in a mediocre fashion by the state of Cambodia. Officially, the lack of teachers does not permit more than four hours of instruction daily, but the reality is more complex. Everyone complains, on the one hand, of the low quality of personnel who are trained hastily and with inadequate means; and, on the other hand, of the lack of facilities that the inhabitants must pay for. Even in areas where there are enough teachers, they do not work the required four-hour days; in some cases, they teach only eight hours each week, because there are not enough school buildings. Elsewhere, absenteeism produces the same results. The children, in order to obtain the general level—already low—have to take private evening courses that their parents cannot always afford.

After being deprived of all education under Democratic Kampuchea and now hungry for knowledge, young people cannot study as in former times: they have to pay, and dearly, for higher education. In 1991, for example, and at a time when Cambodia urgently needed medical personnel, entrance into the School of Medicine cost three *dâmloeung* of gold ($1,500.00), the diploma of a health officer two more *dâmloeung* ($1,000.00), the physician's diploma three additional *dâmloeung* ($1,500.00)—regardless of the candidate's competence. A year later the bribe increased two- or threefold. This system favors the sons of the regime's privileged few—who often benefit from foreign-sponsored scholarships for education or training—leaving the others (and their families) in anguish about the future. Traditional education, so rigorously taught in peacetime, also involves difficulties.

*Morality and the War*     Young people brought up by their parents submitted, by and large, to the ancestral rules of behavior. From a rigor that was often damaging to individual initiative, they went to the opposite extreme of having no rules at all. Parents, preoccupied by problems of survival, could not devote much time to their children and demanded less of them. Unsupervised boys and girls hung around with street urchins and showed disobedience and sometimes arrogance, according to their elders, who fear a weakening of traditional Khmer moral values. The extreme reserve that has characterized Khmer children is disappearing; they become more hardy and perhaps consequently better equipped to face their future since they learn to show more initiative.

Children educated by the Khmer Rouge—Angkar's children—in their teens or young adulthood in 1990, do not always respect their mothers and fathers (if they are still alive) and sometimes commit violent acts. Those who fought several years in Heng Samrin's armed forces find themselves reduced to idleness; without any great desire to work, they loiter in the streets, the privileged place of the smallest children whose mothers do not have the time to supervise them. The half-days of freedom given to school children favor delinquency.

In theory, children without guardians are supposed to live in orphanages:

these are orphans from the Khmer Rouge period or from the state of Cambodia's regime, the victims of the war or clearing operations. State aid is minimal: less than half a dollar per month per orphan; private organizations and the diaspora contribute considerable amounts.[9] Nurseries house illegitimate children, abandoned at birth by their parents, rich or poor. Social services also assemble juvenile delinquents, penniless adults, and homeless handicapped people in a center reserved for social cases; inadequate budgeting hampers their activities, and delinquency is establishing itself in Phnom Penh. The curfew periodically in force in a capital that is secure from fighting seems intended rather to limit robbery and rape, common-law or political crimes that occur in the provincial capitals as well. To deter robbers, the owners of villas in Phnom Penh have transformed them into bunkers, surrounding them with high walls of corrugated iron and barbed wire and installing alarm systems. These protected villas are grouped in the neighborhoods where the apparatchiks live. Bicycles and motor bicycles are sheltered at night in the more modest houses, and the Chinese take their vehicles inside their compartments.

It is easy to imagine that, in such a context, children constitute, along with the family's daily nourishment, one of the major concerns of parents. How to provide them with a decent education and medical care? How to protect them from delinquency? What does the future hold for them?

In the face of these difficulties, uncertainties, and the disintegration of moral values, society attempts to restructure itself around a certain and permanent element—Buddhism.

*Pagodas without Sanctuaries*    Reestablished in 1989, Buddhism does not receive state assistance. The government gives it no financial or technical aid in the construction or restoration of pagodas, or the reopening of Pali schools. Likewise, the new Buddhist Institute (subordinate, like everything religious in nature, to the Front's religious department) does not have the means to republish its own religious works, in demand throughout the country. Nevertheless, novices crowd into Phnom Penh's seven Pali schools, the largest of which, Wat Moha Montrei, has 180 monks, most of whom are students. Although the pagodas experienced a renewal of activity, they are in no position to fulfill their traditional role of providing refuge to the disinherited; they have no money to feed all the elderly people without means of support or to shelter homeless children. Nevertheless, each pagoda houses about thirty students or scholars (most of whom were orphans) and a few elderly men. Communities are poor and cannot, by themselves, meet all their expenses; monasteries operate with a provisional or uncompleted sanctuary. Yet the fact that a community contributes financially, despite its penury, shows the hope that it places in religion and the confidence that it has in the monks. Khmers assert: "Crime has diminished since the renewal of Buddhism."

The diaspora exercises a fundamental role here also by financing construction of schools and the restoration of pagodas. Since 1979 its support has never been so active and useful. Nevertheless we would be rash to assume that Buddhism could solve everything. The least beneficial social values persist, accentuating the destitution of certain groups.

*Wealth and Prestige*    Traditionally, the strong—those with power or wealth—have influence. The lay community has nothing but contempt for the weak. The difficulties in Phnom Penh do not cause people to behave with kindness. The police engage in racketeering, soldiers in pillage, and the people reject the most unfortunate. Although the rich arrogantly display their wealth, they do nothing for those in need. Even in the suburbs, the several well-to-do families in each village hold the rest of the people in contempt.

Many women—who, it is said, make up 65 to 70 percent of the population—lost their husbands, killed under Pol Pot or in the service of the People's Republic of Kampuchea. Most of them meet with nothing but indifference and disdain: In the words of a widow, "We're poor people, we have no right to speak. They don't help us, they ignore us, they don't see us." Some, particularly those without young children, plunge into the most profitable commercial activities, and, if they succeed, put their widow's status behind them—society accepts their emancipation. Emancipation, moreover, extends to all classes of women; young or adult, they do not hesitate to take up previously forbidden trades (commerce, real estate brokerage), to joke, and to voice their opinions out loud, they who used to operate behind the scenes. For economic reasons, a small (uncounted) number of young girls engage in prostitution, but the prostitutes are primarily Vietnamese nationals.

The shortage of men has led to the revival of polygamy, with several women living in the same enclosure, especially if one of them has an income-producing occupation; moreover, the status of married woman gives her a personal status of which widowhood had deprived her. A policeman or an officer, required to move about, might take wives in two or three different places. For many widows, however, their fate is destitution, and the department of social services can do nothing for them. In 1990 the sum of $2,500.00 would easily provide a visa for a woman who had attracted the attention of a foreigner, allowing her to leave the country; there was no way out for men.

War cripples (from fighting or clearing operations) receive no better treatment. Traditionally in the Khmer milieu, physical mutilation results in severe loss of status; society rejects the handicapped and ranks them among the weak. The state of Cambodia granted them an allowance of 1,500 riels per month, the equivalent of ten kilograms of rice. Too visible and too vociferous in discontent, most of them have been assembled on an island in the Mekong. Those who still live in Phnom Penh beg for their rice in the markets and shops. Although the merchants give them a bit of money in order to calm their anger, the people on the street do not think well of them. Many of the handicapped are young.

As for mendicants—elderly people who are alone, women without the support of husbands—they are severely scolded by those with a decent income: "Let them get a job, they're lazy," say their more comfortable compatriots.

The countryside, it seems, has sheltered its inhabitants from the perversions of the cities. But their urban counterparts in Phnom Penh, powerless to preserve traditional moral values, do not try to understand the distress of the newly poor. Streets bathe in misery, civil servants vegetate, merchants escape unscathed, and the leaders set themselves up in an infantile luxury.

## The Rejection of the Rulers and the Regime's Privileged Few

The political authorities experienced a period of grace, particularly Prime Minister Hun Sen after his liberal attitude and his peaceful intentions, announced in spring of 1989. The people truly believed in him, considering him the man of the hour, although he did not possess the legitimacy of a god-king. He nevertheless would have been able to acquire a psycho-religious legitimacy by proving effective in his efforts to free himself completely from Vietnamese tutelage and to stop the fighting. It is certain that, seeing him as Heaven-sent, the people would have considered him to be a *nêak sil* (sacred person) (or *nêak mean bon* [meritorious person] in the religious sense), having received a sort of mandate from Heaven, all the more easily in that he had just revived Buddhism and had also once again authorized the cults dedicated to the spirits. However, he failed at bringing his plans to completion and at running the affairs of state. He thus lost the confidence that the people had in his status as the Heaven-sent man. One year later questioning, doubt, distrust, and finally discontent prevailed. Having so recently acquired a relative freedom of speech, the people of the cities and the countryside openly criticized the leaders who not only did not keep their promises but also increased the inequalities between themselves and the masses; people attributed the failure of the new policy to the leaders' low intellectual level.

The wealth of these nouveaux riches is shocking in the face of the general misery. Khmers summarize the life-style of their rulers in a short sentence: Three wives, three villas, three cars. This aphorism—incorrect as a generalization—demonstrates, aside from the opulence of a tiny group, the lack of respect on the people's part for leaders unable to give young people the education on which their future depends or to bring peace and a moral guarantee to all in the shadow of Buddhism.

Most of the inhabitants, lacking means to influence the leading group and the apparatchiks, tired of constant pain and suffering, find solace in excesses that accelerate the splitting apart of society.

## To Forget

A powerful desire to live, to forget past and present difficulties, is bursting out in regions not directly affected by the war that continues in some strategic points. The Khmers barely speak of the Khmer Rouge period any more unless a foreigner brings it up; they rather seek to amuse themselves. Phnom Penh offers various forms of escape to all who seek distraction.

For the intellectuals there are no distractions, no physical or psychological tranquility. Realists, given to reflection and preoccupied with the future of their country as well as that of their children, they are compelled to confront problems by hard work in the interest of both. Before Cambodia's political and social stagnation intellectuals remain at a loss.

For the majority of the population, this desire to find their identities once again results in overdeveloped forms of religiosity and social rituals. The aged simply try to find comfort in Buddhism, serving the monks and frequenting pagodas, isles of peacefulness; most homes count more than they did before on the goodwill of deities to right their wrongs; and a marriage ceremony gives rise to celebration, the public portion of which, the meal in a restaurant, assumes a sumptuous character. Loudspeakers broadcast Khmer music without sparing the decibels; the couple, dressed in traditional fashion, is surrounded by one to two hundred persons, each of whom contributes a great sum, the equivalent of twenty days' or one month's work! Behind the form is the desire to amuse oneself for several hours, while displaying a certain social status.

The same collective desire for returning, expressed in the domain of entertainment, probably explains the taste for video, newly arrived in Cambodia. Since 1989 forty companies producing films in the video format have appeared. At first, their primary activity consisted in dubbing foreign films; then they began to produce Khmer films. Hotels, restaurants, shops, and individuals own a monitor, around which clients or neighbors gather to watch Chinese or Indian films—highly regarded—and several local productions featuring Khmer films and theater. Even boats traveling up the Mekong offer passengers a film on video cassette; nothing seems to exist anymore except these images, consumed collectively at all points of social life.

Motorized transport also constitutes a means of escape as well as an affirmation of social status. Some vehicles arrive new in Cambodia; others, stolen in Thailand, are sold as secondhand goods. Often purchased for family trips (with money earned in commerce or received from the diaspora), the motor scooter becomes a source of entertainment at the day's end: with wife and children perched on the machine behind the head of household, the family goes for a drive, following an itinerary that invariably includes the traditional spots such as the royal palace, the independence monument, and the banks of the river.

Women once again pursue stylishness, lost since 1975, and seek to change their look. They want to get new dresses, to have impeccable hands, and to curl their straight hair. Business booms for beauty shops and manicurists, set up in the markets or on the sidewalks.

In contrast, some individuals, unable to endure their living conditions, have fallen into alcoholism. In Phnom Penh, once so concerned to maintain its reputation for aesthetics and moral tone, men stagger about in the street. The maimed drink together in groups.

These different forms of despair contrast with the insouciance of a minority who lead lives of luxury. The high-ranking officials live sumptu-ously in their villas. Their children are gilded youths, taking courses at the university, spending their evenings at surprise parties or on the dance floor of the Hôtel Cambodiana, where they arrive by car, elegantly dressed, very chic.

It is thus society in its entirety that suffers from the war. Seen in its different facets, Phnom Penh resembles a surrealist palette, where the best and the worst exist side by side.

## Mechanism of Social Disaggregation through Corruption

Although it involves no more than a minority of Cambodians, the chain reactions that corruption engendered under the state of Cambodia affect the entire population. It taints the mechanisms of distribution of merchandise, the operation of the public sector, the well-being of the population, and respect for social rules.

Aid supplied to the Phnom Penh regime since 1979 rarely reaches its intended beneficiaries. The misappropriation benefits the professional strata who are indispensable to the functioning of the regime: high-ranking officials, armed forces, police, and cadres, all well fed and cared for in hospitals well provided with equipment and medicines. It is not surprising that the surgeon prefers to operate secretly by night on paying patients rather than treat people free of charge during his daily hours of service: he himself is poorly paid and needs additional salary.

Furthermore, the professional environment leaves something to be desired. Public buildings are required to finance themselves. Sacks of cement are abundant to renovate villas vacated with the departure of the Vietnamese advisers; the leaders and their friends can requisition them, but none can be found to repair an office roof. Consequently, its employees work in a deteriorating hierarchical environment.

In the technical domain, the state no longer provides solid training because universities reject competent but penniless young people and admit some undeserving children of cadres. The country's scientific and economic future thus depends on power-holders who have no other goal but to enrich themselves as fast as possible and as long as the political situation permits.

The display of riches and their advantages by those in high places, moreover, creates an unfavorable impression on a people unaccustomed to abundance for the last two decades and growing more and more convinced that money authorizes all manner of delinquencies that include lack of consideration for the elderly poor and poor table manners.

The network of social rules that has stood the test of centuries is experiencing serious failures, failures that may well be irreversible. Thus a solidly structured society falls apart and reforms itself according to the laws of the jungle.

## The Royalty—A Factor for Social Cohesion?

Until Sihanouk's return in November 1991, the majority of the townspeople, without intellectual training, saw no other solution except to live according to the principle of everyone for himself. A conscious (educated, older urban) minority and many peasants regretted the abandonment of secular values and worried about the society's state of disintegration. After having faith in leaders or events that did not come to pass, uncorrupted intellectuals pondered the means to save their country from disaster. Putting aside political rancor to sift through the former sociopolitical system, they salvaged the only feature that seemed positive for the people—the royalty. In 1990 even convinced opponents of Sihanouk did not hesitate to call for the return of the former monarch, not as an individual but as an institution whose representative he is, an institution that, since Angkor—and despite periods of uncertainty—has provided stability for the country and security for the people: "I hope that Sihanouk comes back, not to be king but to rally the people, to reconstruct society," one of them stated. The common people demanded the prince's return; ever since 1970 they had believed that his removal was the cause of their troubles. However, as a result of the government's efforts to discredit the former chief of state, "people begin to speak ill of Sihanouk, but I am sure that if he returned and conducted an electoral campaign, he'd win them over," a non-monarchist intellectual said. Nobody in the state of Cambodia's government seemed credible and solid in the people's eyes, and for this reason the majority, consciously or not, wanted a return to a form of regime that has already proven itself. Moreover, it was no accident that the former royal city of Oudong was visited by pilgrims who came to offer prayers for peace to the royal Buddha.

In order to avoid quarrels over the semi-elective succession to the throne that exhausted the country for several centuries, the parliamentary monarchy—with the royal power separated from political responsibilities—should be combined with a well-established rule of succession, for example, succession by order of primogeniture.

Without a leader recognized by the people, the Khmers turned to foreigners and asked them for help in various ways.

FOREIGNERS TO THE AID OF CAMBODIA?

Foreigners have been intervening in Cambodia since 1979, first of all by supplying humanitarian aid to the population.

*Humanitarian Aid and Nongovernmental Organizations*

After the fall of Democratic Kampuchea, there were few cadres and technicians in the country. Young illiterates received training in Phnom Penh and then went to study several years—sometimes six—in Vietnam, the Soviet Union, and in the satellite countries; they returned with technical skills. The state of Cambodia should currently benefit from the knowledge in various fields thus acquired. Nevertheless, not all young competent people are utilized since their technical interference might cause problems for those who profit from the existing situation. They are presently unemployed and losing their specific skills, to the great indignation of the population.

Inside Cambodia the nongovernmental organizations (NGOs) increased their activities after 1989. In 1991 more than fifty of them worked there. Their presence comforts the people through the aid that they provided and by the opening to the West that they represent. William Shawcross describes the difficulties encountered in the early 1980s by the international community in helping the Cambodians, particularly the problem of distribution.[10]

Medical assistance seems to suffer from the same inadequacies. Although the government no longer opposes the presence and activities of NGOs, medicines sometimes remain in customs for several weeks, and they reach or remain only rarely at the medical services, not to mention those lost between Saigon and Phnom Penh. Misappropriated, they reappear in the markets. The sick rarely go to hospitals, which have no medicines; theoretically, medical treatment is free of charge, but when patients receive a prescription, they must pay to have it filled. And surgical operations are payable in gold. In these conditions, the inhabitants prefer to consult a traditional healer first and then a village nurse, who are not always qualified to treat their problems. Despite the magnitude of the foreign personnel and means, the people suffer from the absence of decent care, except in several specific areas, such as tuberculosis. This illustrates the weakness of the supervisory powers exercised by NGOs over deployment of the aid.

Humanitarian organizations do not bear the entire responsibility for this partial failure, given the bureaucratic complications and the incomplete cooperation of the government. Nonetheless, anxious to retain their place in this "charity machine" that they put into operation, some of the NGOs tend to accede to officials' wishes without discussion, to say nothing of those that bring declared political support to the regime.[11]

They have, furthermore, serious deficiencies. If some try to understand the needs of the Cambodians and respect their technical knowledge as well as their customs, others engage in activities of little use or positive outcome, to say nothing of NGOs eager to establish themselves so as to be on the spot when the political situation grows stable. For decades, moreover, and in all the countries of the third world, the majority of the "experts," ignorant of much or everything about the countries they visit, particularly local beliefs and traditions, have drawn up inappropriate plans that often end up in filing cabinets, whereas a briefing by persons knowledgeable about the indigenous cultures would give them the basic facts necessary to the successful completion of their work. Further, how can we avoid the sending of truckloads of dollars and the launching of expensive and prestigious projects that scarcely improve the daily lives of the people but on the contrary risk introducing or fostering regrettable practices such as corruption?

On the technical level, therefore, the efforts of NGOs are not always successful. Regarding agriculture, a simple restoration of the means of production would no doubt permit Cambodian peasants to live better lives. The provision of fertilizer, for example, in cooperation with rural workers, produces good results. Indeed, the least that experts can do is to listen to the rice growers, to understand their needs, to take their empirical knowledge into consideration, and then to introduce changes that do not clash with their traditions; otherwise, failure is certain. Here, projects have failed because they have not taken these basics into account, despite the good intentions of their promoters. Indeed, does the shortage of draft animals justify the arbitrary import of foreign oxen and the change in traditional harnessing, the collar-yoke for two oxen? In the hope of improving production, is it really necessary to change the thousand-year-old light plowshare, adapted to Khmer soils and easily transported, for a heavy swing plow? These abortive attempts, and many others as well, have drained the aid budget for a people that still lacks rice. For, in the words of a state of Cambodia insider, apropos of the NGOs: "They reinvent the wheelbarrow, if necessary several times during the same stay."

Education and professional training, for their part, benefit from a notable yet still insufficient Western support. Cambodians appreciate this effort and have great hopes for this aid, which they consider of high priority and urgent for the reconstruction of the country and which they would like to see increase; the basic materials, mainly books, run no risk of misappropriation and resale since they hold little interest for many people. Yet we may allow ourselves to wonder if the Mauger method for learning French is really adapted for the Cambodians.

But the most visibly shocking behavior is that of a number of NGOs who, without consideration for the Cambodian environment, crisscross the capital in off-road vehicles and live in comfortable or even luxurious villas, not to mention some of their women who wear miniskirts at the risk of offending the Khmers. Furthermore, since their contacts with the Khmers are generally limited to the day's work, they remain unaware of the reality of Khmer family and social life. Living apart from the indigenous community, they may involuntarily add to the disarray of the population.

Finally, the same defects characterize the foreign press. For every well-informed journalist, how many representatives of local papers and freelance reporters come to Cambodia with preconceived ideas! And how many write erroneous reports!

Aid to underdeveloped countries requires a realistic vision of things, beginning with consideration for daily concerns. The cistern for treating sewage and the three garbage receptacles provided by the municipality of Paris to Phnom Penh, always in full use, exemplify modest but effective aid. It is these non-prestigious contributions that the country needs most, before it begins campaigns for hygiene and public health that are doomed to failure amid haphazard garbage collection and a disorganized sewer system.

Khmers are placing their hopes in the Westerners, not only for humanitarian aid but also to help them construct the political future of their country.

*The SOS of an Entire People*

Peace and Quickly: at the end of 1990 this leitmotif from the people took precedence over everything else, including the increase of aid and the recognition of any government. Peace for the people living in Cambodia did not mean the signing by the leaders of the Khmer factions of an accord that would not be implemented. They no longer believed in Khmer political parties; they did not trust them and saw their salvation only in foreigners: the United Nations and its enforcement of a political solution.

This wish has been granted by the negotiations begun at the end of 1987, concluded in 1991, and implemented under the aegis of the five permanent members of the Security Council of the United Nations.

## CAMBODIANS FACE TO FACE

Since the Vietnamese began their withdrawal from Cambodia, the different Khmer factions have confronted one another in a struggle for power that exposed their rivalries and personal interests.

### THE PREPARATION FOR AN INTERNATIONAL CONFERENCE

On the political level, the opening of Cambodia to the outside world serves Westerners' plans; under the joint pressure of France and the Association of Southeast Asian Nations, the international community decided to attempt to find a diplomatic solution to the Cambodian problem. Begun informally in December 1987, an initial series of negotiations was completed in July–August 1989 with the meeting of the Paris International Conference on Cambodia (PICC).

The preparatory meetings took place on several levels: bilateral discussions between Sihanouk and Hun Sen, meetings of the four factions, and regional meetings.[12]

*Prince Sihanouk's Goodwill and the Efforts of Hun Sen*

Hun Sen having declared himself ready to meet with Sihanouk, the latter, accompanied by his wife and his son Ranariddh—and with the approval of China—received him at the Hostellerie de la Fère-en-Tardenois (Aisne) from 2 to 4 December 1987; Phnom Penh's prime minister—surrounded by a group of close collaborators—seemed to have good intentions.[13] This was, it was announced, an exploration, undertaken on a private basis and necessarily conducted secretly; Son Sann, Khieu Samphan, and China made the best of a bad situation. The prince nevertheless invited the media and signed, with Hun Sen, a four-point joint communiqué that provided for—among other very general decisions—the possibility of an international conference on Cambodia and another meeting among Khmers in January 1988. The two other parties, the supporters of Son Sann and the Khmer Rouge, were invited to participate.[14] At the end of this second round, Hun Sen appeared before the television audience as young, dynamic, and firm; this was the beginning of international recognition that was to increase with further meetings only to become tarnished three years later.

Returning to the bosom of the Gouvernement de coalition du Kampuchea démocratique (GCKD)—thus of the Khmer Rouge and China—and after referring to Hun Sen as "the valet of the Vietnamese," Sihanouk canceled the January meeting. It seems that the prince was torn between the demands of his Communist partners, the pressures of Westerners to find a solution, and perhaps his own desire to play a personal role. Hun Sen, for his part, received instructions from Hanoi. As for Son Sann, he linked his participation in a dialogue with Phnom Penh to the departure of the *bo doi* from Khmer soil; the Khmer Rouge maintained the same distant attitude. Thus, unless the Chinese and Vietnamese protectors made a gesture, there was no resolution to be seen. Hanoi took the initiative: on 20 January, on the occasion of a second Sihanouk–Hun Sen discussion at Fère-en-Tardenois—preceded by a Sihanouk–Son Sann meeting—Hun Sen announced the intention of the Vietnamese to establish a schedule for the withdrawal of their troops. A first step had been taken, but the coalition wanted to see actions. Furthermore, disagreement persisted on other fundamental points: on the one hand, Hun Sen refused to agree to the simultaneous dismantling of the République populaire du Kampuchea (RPK) and the GCKD as well as the sending of an international peace-keeping force to Cambodia; on the other hand, Sihanouk rejected the dismantling of the Khmer Rouge army.

In a final private attempt—and in order to present himself as an independent interlocutor—Sihanouk then resigned the presidency of the GCKD (30 January 1988) and asked for direct negotiations with Vietnam. Faced with Hanoi's refusal, he resumed his presidency and offered a third meeting to Hun Sen. China expressed its renewed confidence in him.

During this time, the Association of Southeast Asian Nations (ASEAN) attempted to bring about a meeting of the four Khmer factions and succeeded several months later.

### ASEAN and Vietnam Enter the Scene

Indonesia, the ASEAN country closest to Vietnam, launched in August 1987 the idea of a cocktail party or informal meeting (Jakarta informal meeting, or JIM), and Vietnam accepted the invitation. The meeting took place in Bogor (25–28 July 1988), bringing together the representatives of the four Khmer factions (with the exception of Sihanouk, who refused to attend),

Vietnam, Laos, and the six ASEAN countries. The same impediments remained (effective departure of the *bo doi*, dismantling of governments, presence of a UN peace-keeping force, etc.), the Khmer Rouge and Phnom Penh—and through them, China and Vietnam—showing no flexibility whatsoever. Nevertheless, all the Khmer parties had found themselves sitting around the same table, and Vietnam had agreed to come.

For all that, the impasse remained. The Khmer Rouge, showing that they accorded little importance to Hun Sen, sent only a subordinate official to represent them at a meeting—quadripartite—held in Fère-en-Tardenois (5–8 November 1988); Hun Sen thus refused to accept him as an interlocutor and rejected the five-point settlement proposed by Sihanouk.[15] Nevertheless, the protagonists decided to create a quadripartite commission. It met on 22 December in Paris and ended in total disagreement after only several hours of discussion.

Vietnam then announced (6 January 1989) the withdrawal, within the framework of a settlement of the Cambodian problem, of all its troops from Cambodia by the end of September 1989. The informal meeting at Jakarta, known as JIM II, scheduled from 19 January to 21 February, would thus begin in an encouraging context.

But on 25 January the Thai prime minister, Chatichai Choonhavan, received Hun Sen in Bangkok. This realistic invitation on the part of Thailand, which saw in Cambodia a future regional economic partner (the prime minister had, in the weeks preceding this invitation, declared on several occasions his desire to transform Indochina from a battlefield to a marketplace), constituted a de facto recognition of the RPK. The move was not unanimously accepted in Thai political circles, and it provoked the discontent of the GCKD, after which Sihanouk canceled his participation in JIM II. The meeting nevertheless occurred, bringing together the four Khmer factions, but it stopped at the same stumbling blocks.

After these various attempts, any understanding among the Khmers appeared impossible. In this difficult situation, France took over for ASEAN behind the scenes; France had, since mid-1987, announced its intention—accepted by ASEAN—of participating in the settlement of the Khmer conflict.[16]

### France's Diplomacy

France was soon won over to the idea of an international conference on Cambodia, suggested by Sihanouk. The latter officially announced it in Fère-en-Tardenois in December 1987; the declaration issued at JIM II took up the call. Nevertheless, although Paris welcomed the prince as a private individual and as "a friend of France," it did not send representatives to the meetings of Khmer factions or to the regional meetings at Jakarta. But it left no doubt that it would like to participate in an ultimate resolution and that it was counting on Sihanouk to come to that point.

After the failure of JIM II, the French used their influence to convince Sihanouk to resume the pourparlers. He thus met Hun Sen in Jakarta on 2–3 May 1989 and showed flexibility, notably by leaving the question of the UN force to be settled by the future international conference. Optimism reigned abroad. During these discussions, however, Sihanouk represented only the FUNCINPEC, for the GCKD had delegated Son Sann (Council of Ministers from 28 April 1989) to represent it. The discussions that the latter had with Hun Sen revealed deep-rooted disagreement, such that Son Sann declared at the close of the meeting that there was no basis for organizing a Paris international conference on Cambodia as long as the Cambodians did not agree on a quadripartite government.[17]

This ambiguity concerning the mandates of Son Sann and Sihanouk escaped the notice of Westerners. But ASEAN made no mistake about it, being moreover very attentive to the actions of the different Khmer actors: scarcely one month before the meeting of the international conference, scheduled for the end of July 1989, ASEAN expressed its concern about the absence of a political consensus among the Khmer factions.[18] The Quai d'Orsay, more or less aware of the problems, held the conference, despite the probability of failure, which became a certainty after a final quadripartite discussion held in the presence of the French foreign minister, Roland Dumas, at Celle-St-Cloud on 24 July 1989. The factions came to loggerheads about questions of protocol and seemed to forget the primary issue—peace. The PICC, co-chaired by France and Indonesia, opened on 30 July 1989 under inauspicious circumstances.

### The Failure of the Paris International Conference and Its Consequences

Aside from the four Cambodian factions, eighteen countries participated in the first round of discussions (from July 30 to August 1), held at the ministerial level.[19] From the beginning the Hun Sen group and the Khmer Rouge insulted each other. The latter opposed the sending of an exploratory and information-gathering mission to Cambodia and the surrounding countries to work out conditions for a cease-fire, the withdrawal of Vietnamese forces, and the organization of general elections.[20] The members of the mission explored the possibility of traveling throughout Cambodia. Sensitive points to be considered were the villages, where Pol Pot's cadres and soldiers continued to practice terror, and the arms accumulated in caches since the 1980s. To secure the Khmer Rouge's acceptance of the proposal required all the persuasion of China and the flexibility of the secretary general of the United Nations. Sihanouk and the media saw this acceptance as a goodwill gesture on the Khmer Rouge's part, but the latter insisted on the brevity of the UN mission's stay in Cambodia itself—several days. Somehow, few Westerners realized the inadequacy of this mission; the mission's members themselves spoke of its insufficiency.[21] In these conditions, without the effective control of a cease-fire, a genuine settlement of the Khmer conflict would seem illusory despite the optimism of the press, which welcomed a step toward peace.

Many barriers loomed before the bodies composed of Cambodians and foreigners that the conference set up to work during the entire month of August on the principal aspects of a settlement.[22] Until the final day the Khmers discussed the mention of the word "genocide," the presence of Vietnamese settlers, the sharing of power, and the possibility of a UN peace-keeping force. Each camp stuck to its positions. Facing an impasse, Secretary of State James Baker decided that it would not be worthwhile to head the American delegation for the second ministerial round of August 29–31. The final communiqué recorded the failure of the negotiations and announced the suspension of the conference's work.

The Khmers had not learned how to conduct a dialogue or to work toward constructive analysis that could bring the war to a close. During the entire month of August the two nationalist movements demonstrated their inconsistency and their lack of organization in the face of the firmness of the two Communist groups, supported by their respective sponsors, China and Vietnam. The supporters of Son Sann fell into silence. Sihanouk, moving from anger to invective, irritated and disappointed many foreigners who were counting on his skills and political acumen to rally the others. Few understand the importance of his wife, Monique, who attended almost all the meetings; some Khmers assert that certain political forces express themselves through her.

The failure of the PICC resulted from disagreement among the Khmers but also from influence by the Chinese and the Vietnamese, and, it is said, from a lack of cooperation by the United States, which, moreover, was tantamount to an affront to France. Some foreign ministers who flew to France especially for the conference did not understand why France exercised so little influence on its trump card, Sihanouk, and why France had no alternative solution. As for the former monarch, he missed what was then considered to be his last chance; hence the PICC marked the beginning of his international, though temporary, disgrace.

With hope for peace crushed, the Cambodian people continued to suffer from the competition for power among the chiefs and the pressures of regional powers. Arms still arrived from China, the USSR, and probably from the United States. Fighting raged in many districts, where work on the land became more and more hazardous. Guerrillas from all sides recruited people suffering from the war—they even compelled refugees from the Thai camps to return—to their command posts, situated inside Cambodia several miles from the border. Thus, fiefs were formed, a practice to which the Khmer Rouge have had recourse for several years, and which, moreover, has been common in Khmer history. The chiefs thus assured themselves of a certain number of votes in case of elections. Phnom Penh implemented the same practice by moving peasants out of areas visited by the Khmer Rouge at night; they are called "new refugees." The behavior of all parties thus continues in familiar patterns, reflecting a desire for personal power that deprived them of all credibility abroad. The negotiations, dormant for more than four months, resumed in 1990 on the initiative of the UN Security Council's five permanent members.

In the UN General Assembly in autumn 1989 the member states continued to demand "the complete and verifiable withdrawal of Vietnamese forces from Cambodia," thus displaying their skepticism about the merits of Hanoi's declarations regarding the departure of its troops. An American Senator, Stephen Solarz, proposed a provisional administration of Cambodia by the United Nations until the holding of free elections, a plan taken up by the Australian Gareth Evans and endorsed by the four Khmer factions. With this prospect in mind, the five permanent members of the UN Security Council met eight times between January and December 1990.[23] For their part, the Khmers did not succeed in agreeing on anything at all during two other quadripartite meetings, at Jakarta (26–27 February 1990) and Tokyo (4–5 June 1990).[24] In July 1990 President Bush, yielding to American public opinion and to the impatience of the Senate, announced his intention to cease supporting the then GCKD, of which the Khmer Rouge were part, and to negotiate directly with Hanoi concerning the Cambodian problem. The representativeness of the holders of Cambodia's seat at the United Nations was thus called into question. The Cambodian resistance, China, and ASEAN expressed their discontent, while the West, the USSR, and Japan approved. In fact, the Khmer Rouge continued to take part in the negotiations, but they no longer benefited from the supposedly humanitarian aid supplied by the United States to the GCKD.

On 10 September the four Khmer factions, meeting at Jakarta after a good many delays, adopted a UN peace plan and elected a bipartite organ, the Conseil national suprême (supreme national council, or CNS), composed of six delegates from the GCKD and six from Phnom Penh, which would henceforth represent Cambodia at the UN and grant the UN a mandate to administer the country. As always in the Khmer milieu, the struggle for power is bitter, and the representatives of the CNS, which held its first session in Bangkok on 17 September, were not able to agree on a president or on two vice-presidents, and thus on the holding of the seat at the UN. Consequently, Cambodia's seat remained vacant for one year, to the great displeasure of the resistance. The General Assembly approved the UN peace plan, which was endorsed by the foreign powers in Jakarta in November.[25]

In the meantime Americans, Chinese, Soviets, and Vietnamese discussed Cambodia in their bilateral meetings, where it became evident that each of them wanted to pursue negotiations. The final meetings of 1990 did not, however, resolve much of anything. Urged by the two co-presidents of the PICC, Roland Dumas and Ali Alatas, and also by a representative of the UN, the four Khmer factions adopted on 22 December, after two days of debate, the UN's definitive peace plan yet included a note voicing reservations on Phnom Penh's part.

Early in 1991 the negotiations were still blocked by Phnom Penh. French and Indonesian emissaries thus traveled to Hanoi on 1 February 1991 to ask the Vietnamese to bring their Khmer protégés to reason—in vain.

In April talks resumed on the initiative of Thailand and Hun Sen.[26] The United Nations called for a cease-fire, which the belligerents violated on the very day that it became operative, that is, on 1 May. Another unsuccessful meeting was held in Jakarta from 2–4 June 1991. Sihanouk did not attend, but he met Hun Sen in Jakarta and announced an important development, though it did not seem so at the time: his intention to go to Phnom Penh in November 1991 at Hun Sen's invitation. Everything had been decided behind the scenes. Sihanouk would later explain how it happened in a reply to a journalist during the press conference following the PICC's second session on 23 October: in May 1991 the Chinese had told him that, together with the Vietnamese, they had decided to rid themselves of a war that no longer had any meaning and to hand Cambodia over to Sihanouk. Hanoi and Peking had thus buried the hatchet, which led to the normalization of their relations. However, the role of the Khmers was also crucial, and their behavior influenced the train of negotiations.

From that time onward, negotiations accelerated. At Pattaya I (24–26 June), the first meeting of the Conseil national suprême, the Khmer factions agreed on several matters: an unlimited cease-fire, the stopping of arms supply by other countries, the choice of Phnom Penh as CNS headquarters, and the establishment of a CNS secretariat. Nevertheless, it would take another three weeks for the Khmers to meet again in Peking (16–17 July) and to announce, among other decisions, the appointment of Prince Sihanouk as CNS president and the sending of a CNS delegation to the United

Nations; but because all were unable to meet in Phnom Penh, no permanent representative to the UN was named until October 1992. Sihanouk confirmed his intention to return to Phnom Penh in November and to reside in the royal palace, being repaired by France. The five permanent members and the two co-presidents of the PICC endorsed the Peking communiqué on 18–19 June 1991, but Secretary of State James Baker showed his dissatisfaction, fearing a partial settlement caused by modifications of the UN peace plan without the agreement of the four factions, perhaps because of Chinese influence or because some important issues seem to have been decided bilaterally by Sihanouk and Hun Sen, without consulting the other two groups.

During Pattaya conference II (26–28 August), the Khmers defined the status of the future Cambodia as a "liberal democracy"; they endorsed the French proposal to disarm 70 percent of the troops of each faction but did not agree on the method of voting. They would define the method in New York on 19 September as a proportional representation system using the twenty provinces as constituencies; on 20–21 September 1991 it was endorsed, as usual, by the five permanent members.

In order to adapt to these statements the PPRK (that is, the Communist party) held an extraordinary session on 17 October and renamed itself the Parti du peuple cambodgien (people's party of Cambodia, or PPC)—a name that is reminiscent of the first Khmer Communist party formed in 1951, the People's party (Pak Pracheachon). Moreover, Chea Sim, the party hardliner, became the number one leader instead of Heng Samrin, who was never more than a figurehead. The regime announced that it would soon release its political prisoners. Yet two months later people said the jails still held several hundred inmates; Phnom Penh would confirm this assertion, declaring an even higher figure—not counting serious cases, those imprisoned in Hanoi or on an island near Saigon, whom nobody mentions.[27] People, women as well as men, may move freely all over the country and are no longer obliged to attend political meetings. These face-saving changes would ease a reconciliation between Hun Sen and Norodom Sihanouk on the prince's return to Phnom Penh. But the PPC continues to exert a great deal of influence on the structures of state.

### THE PARIS AGREEMENT AND SIHANOUK'S RETURN

The PICC, convened on 23 October, is likely to succeed. In fact, the four Khmer factions and the foreign countries involved signed a treaty that solves, at least on paper, some of the problems. In particular, it defines the prerogatives of the United Nations: direct control of the five main ministries, supervision of the withdrawal of foreign troops and of the implementation of the cease-fire, stopping of arms supply and disarmament of Khmer soldiers, supervision and organization of general elections, and assistance in releasing political prisoners. However, the treaty reveals unsettled questions: the future of existing governmental structures (Phnom Penh and CNS); the effectiveness of disarmament, given the secret caches of arms and munitions. There was no joy in the signing of the agreement; nor would there be in the forthcoming events in Phnom Penh.

## Cheyo Samdech Ov

As the first soldiers of the United Nations' peace-keeping force landed in Phnom Penh, the city feverishly prepared for the long-awaited return of Sihanouk. Numerous teams cleaned or repaired everything along the route that would bring the royal procession from the airport to the palace. The public office signs had been repainted; students swept schools' courtyards and planted grass borders; and the most fortunate of the inhabitants (mainly Chinese) renovated their houses. Thousands of peasants, coming from various provinces of Cambodia, poured into the city to stay with relatives or friends. They wanted to attend the Water Festival and to welcome *Samdech Ov*. On the evenings preceding Sihanouk's return, people wandered about the banks of the Tonle Sap river and admired the illuminated royal palace.

In the capital, the atmosphere resembled that of the "good old days," with people smiling, walking in silence, and looking forward to the celebrations. "Today, arms are locked up, we don't fight any more," said an officer of the Banteay Sleuk barracks. "I'm not afraid of the Khmer Rouge because the people from the United Nations are coming," he added happily. "The war is over; it's true the Khmer Rouge still exist, but *Samdech Ov* is coming back, so they don't frighten me anymore," explained a cyclo driver about forty years of age. Inhabitants living in houses bordering the route from Pochentong airport to the royal palace had a chance of seeing him. The others stayed home. "It's not worth the trouble of going out. They won't let us get near the road. We'll be standing too far away to see *Samdech*." In fact, on 14 November the people lining the ten-kilometer road had all been ordered to come: students, scholars, civil servants, members of associations and, for appearances' sake, a few old women as well. Giant portraits of the prince in his forties, copied from magazine pictures of the 1960s, were stuck on the front of the royal palace, at the airport, and at the main cross streets. The crowd held up welcoming banners and photographs of the portrait. The newly created Association des Chinois du Cambodge participated in the welcoming ceremony, contributing three dragons and an orchestra. Around the royal palace, several bands played traditional songs or melodies composed by Sihanouk in the 1960s. But behind the official line there was a no-man's-land several meters wide guarded by motorcycle police. No one could pass without the official rallying badge. The prince's cool welcome may be explained by the fact that most members of the crowd were young. Waving their flags, they collectively exclaimed "Ah" and unconvincingly yelled "Cheyo Samdech Ov." The presence of Hun Sen—who flew to Peking to return to Phnom Penh with the prince—standing next to Sihanouk was discomforting.[28] In contrast, the onlookers wandering near the palace at dinner time applauded loudly when the royal car passed through the gate.

The so-called popular meeting held two days later in front of the royal palace, presided over by Sihanouk and attended by the regime's dignitaries, was just as carefully organized as the prince's arrival. Sihanouk delivered a speech (in doublespeak), praising the PPC, the state of Cambodia, Their Excellencies Hun Sen, Chea Sim, and Heng Samrin, "true nationalists" who have done so much for the Khmer people. He would continue along these lines during the following days when he traveled through the countryside accompanied by high-ranking officials from Phnom Penh.

During the three-day Water Festival (20–22 November)—a royal ritual through which a ruler confirms and reinforces his power over the people—a relaxed crowd strolled along the riverbanks; policemen smiled; *Samdech* was really back; Khmers felt confident in the future. "We cannot live without *Samdech*," some civil servants said. In the countryside people could move freely when the prince visited them. They lined the road and crowded all around him to touch his hand. One group remained skeptical—the intellectuals, who feared that Sihanouk would become intoxicated by success. Forthcoming events proved them right.

### The Trap?

On 16 November Sihanouk announced an alliance between the PPC and his own party, the FUNCINPEC, now under his son Ranariddh's authority. He declared that Hun Sen's party "will win the elections, it's inevitable, I'll bet on it." He considered himself "the state of Cambodia's guest" and declared that "I shall not interfere in the internal affairs of the PPC or in the government of the state of Cambodia. I strictly respect [the status quo]," which amounts to a disclaimer of any responsibility for the machinations of Phnom Penh's leaders. This was not, however, the view of the population, and, at a meeting the next morning, the cheerleader who leads the young people in repeating phrases for the prince's benefit, was more specific: "*Samdech* is back, not as a guest, but as president of the CNS." The next few days, while touring villages near Phnom Penh, Sihanouk encouraged peasants to vote for Hun Sen as member of parliament; Hun Sen, for his part, urged people to elect Sihanouk as chief of state of Cambodia. People wondered why they should vote for Hun Sen, of whom they wished to be rid; and why did Sihanouk not remain neutral to act as arbitrator, as had been previously agreed? They are convinced that Ranariddh does not decide anything without the agreement or under pressure from his father, including the alliance with the PPC, which will benefit Phnom Penh and its Vietnamese allies.[29]

According to a "reliable source" cited by the press, Hanoi sought this alliance. Hun Sen himself had proposed that the PPC back Sihanouk's candidacy for the presidency, a recommendation already agreed on during the party's extraordinary congress. And the Khmer Rouge, sensing the danger, supposedly tried to prevent it.[30] The PPC and FUNCINPEC strengthened their ties by signing two treaties, one political (20 November) and the other military (25 November).

FUNCINPEC-France had made it clear during a meeting in Paris in November that it was out of the question for FUNCINPEC to sign any agreement with Phnom Penh. They were so surprised that one of the members flew to Bangkok to call on Ranariddh to ask for an explanation. Moreover, Ranariddh did not answer satisfactorily when asked during the luncheon-debate organized on 14 December in Paris. These considerations tend to suggest that Ranariddh was not involved in the above decision. As for Sihanouk, he quickly became disillusioned; as early as 17 November the prince and his wife showed amazement and distress on discovering the daily misery of an orphanage.

In Phnom Penh, after the alliance, the two partners are considering the formation of a bipartite coalition government, as if it were necessary to settle everything before the first CNS meeting at the end of November in Cambodia. After Khieu Samphan was forced to flee from Phnom Penh on the very day of his arrival (27 November) following an anti–Khmer Rouge demonstration, Sihanouk gave up the idea of a bipartite coalition government. The people did not want any outburst of violence. Well before this date, they had declared: "Let the Khmer Rouge come back to Phnom Penh if it means peace."[31] And they reacted angrily and anxiously to the demonstration: "If the Khmer Rouge are angry, they'll refuse to come back, and the war will start up again," say the residents of Phnom Penh, including the poorest of them. "I couldn't sleep at night after the events of the twenty-seventh," a woman adds. And an intellectual explains: "Sihanouk's a clever politician, but he should have allied with Son Sann, a sincere man who is technically qualified. Almost all of Phnom Penh government's officials are incompetent, not even a trace of nationalism; they just want to make money."

They sold their country to the Soviets, then to the Vietnamese, and now to the Thais." After twenty-two years of war the Cambodians have reached a peace agreement, and, frail as it may be, they do not want to see it broken, even if its price is that some Khmer Rouge leaders (except for Pol Pot and his entourage) participate in the CNS and the general elections. The film of the events of 27 November, shown on television twice on 27 and 28 November, is the most impartial evidence of all—it reveals obvious manipulation.[32] After the fact a viewer might well recall the prime minister's repeated declarations that he could not guarantee the Khmer Rouge's safety; at Kandal Stung, he even cried—crocodile tears, some say—while begging forgiveness for being forced to sign the Paris treaty and allowing those responsible for the genocide to return to Phnom Penh.

Undoubtedly, Sihanouk had nothing to do with the demonstration, but he could lead us to think that, in other respects, he had made some secret arrangements with the Phnom Penh regime; hence, the ministry of foreign affairs' communiqué of 19 November, criticizing the reactionary clique responsible for the illegal coup d'état of 18 March 1970 and reinstating the prince in his former position of chief of state, together with President Heng Samrin—an announcement that provoked amused laughter among the unprepared journalists. These statements would be repeated over and over, as if it were necessary to avenge Sihanouk and restore his royal legitimacy to him. Sihanouk described his reinstatement as the legitimate chief of state as an act of justice. According to his followers, this restoration was initially the prince's idea.[33] Son Sann and the Khmer Rouge had no choice but to accept his new status.

Moreover, during a press conference held on 17 November Hun Sen violently and rudely attacked Son Sann, which suggests that, if the Front national de libération du peuple khmer (FNLPK) could be discredited, it and the Khmer Rouge could be marginalized and perhaps excluded from the political settlement. The peasants would not react, but what about the intellectuals? Whatever the prince and his supporters may say, the PPC-FUNCINPEC alliance changes the elements and the balance of the situation, and his restoration as chief of state means either that he considers the CNS to be a supergovernment or that he backs the Phnom Penh regime. In either case, his restoration violates the Paris agreement. Today, almost everyone agrees that settlement must involve the Khmer Rouge to achieve real peace; yet Sihanouk declared on 16 November that he would not object to the exclusion of the Khmer Rouge from the peace settlement; by doing so he undercuts an agreement that took four long years to achieve. The PPC-FUNCINPEC alliance would be little different from that of 1970–1975, when the prince joined Pol Pot and his friends in a bilateral alliance, the Front uni national du Cambodge (FUNC).

After this difficult month, some Khmers fear that Sihanouk may have fallen into a trap or indeed been caught in one of his own making. "The intellectuals have no power, and Sihanouk has no power," complains a member of the government. In the eyes of many townspeople, Sihanouk has lost his "role as the neutral arbiter of Cambodian politics."[34]

### Sihanouk's Preference for Monarchy

Three indicators presage the restoration of the monarchy, provided the situation in Phnom Penh stabilizes. The first is the choice of the royal palace (rather than Chamcar Mon, the prince's former residence) and the celebration of royal rituals, including the Water Festival. The second is the communiqué issued by the ministry of foreign affairs. It refers to "the royal mission" of *Samdech preah* Norodom Sihanouk. Apart from the word "royal," the term *preah* usually indicates sacred objects or people, notably the king. The third can be found in speeches (especially the speech at Kandal Stung on 17 November): Hun Sen declares that he would not oppose the prince's reinstatement on the throne. The prince specifies that Cambodia must accept a system of liberal democracy led by a "President-Monarch" who would reign without ruling. He adds that he would "remain in the country until the four parties agree to reinstate him as king."[35] A sharing of power would not please the prince, and the absolute power of the 1960s no longer exists; the only power not susceptible to being shared is that attached to the quality of kingship, but of a constitutional king reigning only over the royal palace—unless he is given the additional title of Honorary President, who could be consulted in case of disagreement within the CNS or, afterward, the government. In that case, the expression "President-Monarch" would be relevant. In order to emphasize his royal essence, Sihanouk promises a Cambodia wealthy and prosperous as under the monarchy of Angkor (which he mentions twice in the Kandal Stung speech). He addresses the people as "descendants of the race of Angkor" and assures them that Cambodia will return to that period's glory.

What do the Khmers actually gain from this new situation?

### The Public Assets at Auction

Everyone knows of the corruption taking place in the present Cambodia, so reminiscent of the Khmer Republic. This view was prevalent at the end of 1990. Since fall 1991 corruption increased to a large extent, as if the regime's dignitaries wanted to make as much money as possible before the CNS becomes operative in Phnom Penh. Today, they sell the public assets and natural resources without any benefit accruing to the state or the people. Apart from some Khmers living abroad, most of the businessmen are Chinese from Hong Kong, Singapore, and mainly Thailand. If they do not have Khmer nationality (the price of a Khmer identity card is very low nowadays), they use ethnic Chinese of Cambodia as figureheads.

They own an impressive number of villas that they repair before selling or renting. Some high-ranking Khmer officials have kept a few villas each that they rent to NGOs at prohibitive prices ($3,000.00 to $5,000.00 per month). The Chinese have bought courtrooms, factories (some of them as concessions), mechanical workshops, barracks, police stations, ministry buildings, hotels, land, and markets, including the old Phsar O Russey marketplace, which no longer exists and will be replaced by a supermarket.[36] In December 1991 there were rumors about the sale of two hospitals (Hospital of the Monks and Ang Duong Hospital) and even the central prison, T-3, as soon as it could be emptied. Many electric generators have been ceded to Khmers and Vietnamese; at that date the price of kilowatts fluctuated between 200 and 470 riels, and many people were forced to use candles.

Initially the Khmers expressed their disagreement aloud, albeit in a highly critical manner. To whitewash his own role in the sacking of Khieu Samphan's villa on 27 November, Hun Sen has sung the praises of democracy, which, he said, allows popular demonstrations. He has thus given the green light to young people who are dissatisfied for various reasons: the bribes required by officials to enter the university (by late 1991 fifteen *dâmloeung*, that is, 652.5 grams of gold, equivalent to $7,500.00, to register at the School of Medicine, about twice the cost of the previous year's registration); the frustration after the sacking when the students and scholars realized that they had been manipulated for a cause with which they did not agree. Consequently, from 17 to 23 December workers, civil servants, students, and scholars demonstrated against bribery, the selling of offices, factories, and houses. Several ministers (of industry, transport, planning, and health) were involved as well as the manager of a bank and the chairman of a printing house. Demonstrators looted a villa after several civil servants' families were expelled; they threw rocks at police. The army intervened with firearms to restore order. "The order is given to shoot. The green light is on; the government has no choice—it must show that it is in control, or it will collapse," in the words of a senior Cambodian official.[37] The official report listed three deaths; foreigners living in Phnom Penh put the figure at ten; Khmers of the diaspora visiting their relatives at the time claim a higher number. Schools and universities were closed for two weeks. The curfew was reinstated. To calm the youth, Hun Sen dismissed the minister of transport and three subordinates, who were responsible for expelling the villa's residents. The situation remained tense.

Demonstrators may have been manipulated, but by whom? The government's ally, FUNCINPEC does not seem culpable, and the FNLPK lacks the power to intervene; the Khmer Rouge has no reason to interfere since the government's actions work to its advantage. On the whole, the press in neighboring countries and the resident foreigners describe these events as spontaneous.

As a consequence of the current corruption and the sale of public assets, Cambodia is losing part of its natural resources. If the titles to property granted by the state of Cambodia are subject to challenge, what can be said about what is happening to the forests, which is even more alarming?[38] At a meeting held in Phnom Penh on 22 November 1991 some NGOs revealed that about 25 percent of Cambodia's forests have been completely destroyed during the past few years. The giant trees of Stung Treng's forests are shipped to Vietnam, partly as compensation for war debts, partly in fulfillment of the terms of treaties signed between the Phnom Penh and Hanoi governments. The same thing is happening in western Cambodia, where private Thai companies sign agreements with high-ranking Khmer officials (working in ministries and at the presidency of the council) without consulting the foresters, who can do nothing to stop the deforestation of their country. Likewise for the precious stones from Bokeo (northeast). Moreover, one of the most eminent members of the party has been nicknamed "the rubber king." The other parties, too—FUNCINPEC, FNLPK, Khmer Rouge—have all signed contracts with Thai businessmen to exploit the western forest, and the Khmer Rouge has done so for the gem mines in the Pailin region as well.

The situation is no better in regard to fisheries: Cambodia's neighbors threaten the country's reserves by fishing with electric current that kills all living creatures that it touches, big and small alike. A senior official affirms that two species of fish, *trey pruol* and *trey khbâ*, are becoming increasingly rare in the Tonle Sap and Bassac rivers: "The fish cry, the trees cry."

In addition, because the leaders' authority is contested, banditry has reemerged: smugglers, defectors from previous armies' resistance groups, and unpaid soldiers of Phnom Penh as well pillage the villagers, not hesitating to kill them in order to take a few clothes or a pair of oxen that can be sold in Thailand.

To end this intolerable pillage, the Khmers demanded the immediate implementation of the peace plan.

*The United Nations: What Role?*

Since his return, Sihanouk has not said a word in protest of the involvement of the Phnom Penh government in the demonstrations against Khieu Samphan or asked the prime minister to stop the selling of public assets. While the older peasants trust him completely, the younger ones and people living in Phnom Penh question his failure to act since late November. His presence in the capital did not prevent the young people from demonstrating. In short, his return has not changed the anarchy that prevails in Cambodia; the royal order has not been reinstated. The Khmers want the United Nations Transitional Authority in place as soon as possible.

The bureaucratic constraints and the difficulties in collecting funds to finance the UN peace plan have not permitted its immediate implementation. In November 1991 the UN had sent a force of 286 men, the United Nations Advance Mission in Cambodia (UNAMIC), which became the UNTAC, a force of 21,900 men, after the passing of a UN resolution on 28 February 1992. In November 1992 it seems that most of the UN personnel is operational. However the problems have not been solved; Khmers are disappointed because of lack of unity between the four factions, and voices are raised against the way the treaty is being implemented.

In fact, at a political level the CNS could meet in plenary session only in late January 1992 and drew nothing positive from the meetings. Moreover Khmer factions could not agree on their representatives for the UN seat, leaving it vacant until October 1992. Recently the FNLPK congress took place at the Olympic stadium of Phnom Penh; on 20 May 1992 it created the Parti démocratique libéral bouddhique (Buddhist liberal democratic party, or PDLB) to be operative for the election. Although Phnom Penh tried to intimidate the public, about five thousand persons attended. Son Sann, not committed to the Phnom Penh party, is regarded by city dwellers as an exemplar of democracy but his age and the divisions are real handicaps for the FNLPK and the PDLB. In return, Sihanouk is losing popularity in the capital.

Regarding the military aspect, Vietnam expected to withdraw all its troops by June 1992. Phnom Penh asked Hanoi to make a written announcement, in vain. Except for Hun Sen's party, all the factions—including the peasants, the least intrigue-minded of Cambodians—insist that Vietnamese, both soldiers and armed civilians, remain throughout the country. Even UN experts made such a statement.[39] Yasushi Akashi, who headed the UNTAC force, put an end to the polemic by opening the second phase of the peace plan, the disarmament, in effect considering the Vietnamese withdrawal effective. This act gives the Khmer Rouge reason to refuse to be disarmed. "Legally, they are right," say many Khmers who otherwise do

not support their radical policy. Furthermore, who will help UNTAC uncover the major weapons caches of the Khmer Rouge (in the Cardamom
Mountains and in underground tunnels in the north)? The answer is that
no one will, for fear of retaliation after UNTAC's departure. The cease-fire
is not at hand. The fighting still going on between Khmer Rouge and Phnom
Penh soldiers in order to gain territory before the election illustrates the
situation.

For eight months Khmer opponents have complained that Phnom Penh's
party alone continues to lead the country, whose main ministries should be
controlled by UNTAC. Apart from the delay quoted above, there are other
impediments. Phnom Penh has always balked at this clause and Sihanouk
adheres to the regime's policy. Thai journalists report that the "Cambodian
chief of state, Norodom Sihanouk, and Hun Sen have indicated that they do
not see a major administrative role for the UN in the ministries."[40] It is a
question of money, for a UN regime would mean the end of illegal transactions; and it may be a question also of Vietnamese influence: Hanoi does
not favor UNTAC's presence for domestic reasons, namely the possibility
that Saigon might use the presence of the UN to escape from the yoke of
the north. Facing strong criticism from many quarters, in July 1992 Yasushi
Akashi decided that UNTAC would control the five key ministries but it
never came about. In the meantime Phnom Penh has shifted security
matters from the ministry of interior to the new ministry of national
security, in order to keep them out of the control of UNTAC. And the CNS,
the only legal institution, does not have the power to assume its role, left to
Phnom Penh's discretion.

On a humanitarian level the conditions for repatriation of Khmers who
live in border camps have not been fulfilled. Previously it had been decided
to give each family (four to five persons) two hectares of arable land. In fact,
to remove the mines from the Khmer countryside was impossible because
they litter the soil everywhere and because some factions continue to put
down still more of them. Only the road connecting the border to Battambang (which is also a commercial road for Thai businessmen) has been
cleared. In addition to a year's supply of food, the returnees may choose
among four options: to wait until arable land becomes available; to accept a
plot of land and a kit to build a house on it; to take a professional tool kit; or
to choose the option of money ($50.00 per adult and $25.00 per child).[41]
What will they do once they have eaten the rice and spent the money: starve
in the country or beg in the city?

As for the general election of May 1993, what kind of confidence can
Khmers have in it? Political murders in Phnom Penh and disappearances of
opponents in the countryside limit the freedom of action.[42] Moreover, the

election law allows many Vietnamese settlers—who continue to arrive in Cambodia "as the waters of the Mekong flow," that is, ceaselessly—to vote and forces Khmers living abroad to fly to Phnom Penh to get registered on electoral lists;[43] a Khmer identity card costs between $35.00 and $50.00 ($250.00 for Thai businessmen).[44] This law alarms the entire population and reinforces the Khmer Rouge leadership in their desire to ignore the Paris Treaty. To part of the people the Khmer Rouge now appear as true patriots who are the only ones capable of defending the sovereignty of Cambodia. Last but not least, who will protect peasants from political pressures by the most powerful groups, namely Khmer Rouge and Phnom Penh? In this context, fair and free elections may appear fictitious. Some Khmers living in France contest the legitimacy of the electoral lists.

Sihanouk's illness, forcing him to retire in Peking, is not really alarming for Cambodian politics. In fact many Khmers living abroad or inside Cambodia agree that the prince does not fulfill his charge as president of the CNS and allows UNTAC to decide in his stead. Wherever his residence, it will not change anything so long as he remains officially the president of the CNS. His retirement from all political activities would accelerate the disorder of civil war sure to burst out violently after UN departure with or without Sihanouk's participation in the new regime.

Heedless of the delicate complexity of the Khmer problem, knowing very little of Khmer mentality, the international community is also trapped by the enormous promises written into the treaty. Its members believed that a huge amount of dollars would replace a lack of rigor in the implementation of the peace accord and that a clean solution would emerge quickly, allowing all participants to gain international credibility. But we are seeing the outline of its failure, even though locally UNTAC's blue helmets work heartily and successfully. At all events, the UN presence will result in dramatic consequences, for the Khmer people and the Khmer Rouge—saved by China and Thailand—seem to be the beneficiaries of the situation. The nationalists—no longer supported by Sihanouk (who arranged the FUNCINPEC–PPC alliance) are no match for Phnom Penh's profiteers, the Khmer Rouge utopists, the Chinese businessmen of Southeast Asia, the annexationist neighbors. Except for a few, the Khmer people who are now part of the third world do not receive much—some receive nothing at all—of the manna that pours into their war-ravaged and miserable country. The UN peace plan may even have worsened the social situation by favoring the displacement of peasants, by enlarging the gap between poor and rich, and by giving great scope to corruption and particularly to prostitution. In the short term the partition of Cambodia between Thailand and Vietnam—though unofficial—seems certain and also reminiscent of the situation in

1863 when the French installed their protectorate and between them Vietnam and Siam reigned over divided Cambodia. Today they must reckon with the Khmer Rouge, at least for some time. The three protagonists stationed in their respective areas might let Phnom Penh remain a showplace capital of a fictitious state maneuvered by the neighboring countries, before they share it or fight for it.

Was it worth spending two billion dollars to come to this?

# Epilogue:
# The Unforeseeable Future

As I write this, in December 1993, UNTAC is progressively withdrawing. With enthusiasm and trust in the future, Cambodians have elected a majority of FUNCINPEC candidates to the Constituent Assembly and in so doing have shown their attachment to royal power and to its representative, Norodom Sihanouk. On September 1993 the Constituent Assembly adopted a constitution establishing a real parliamentary monarchy, separating political powers and royal prerogatives. Once again Sihanouk was enthroned (on 24 September 1993), and he is likely to play the role of arbitrator in bringing about the national reconciliation. This achievement might prove difficult, as some Westerners want to interfere despite the fact that they neither perceive nor understand Asian ways of thought and still refuse to allow the participation of any Khmer Rouge in the government, whatever the consequences for the people. In the face of international pressure and internal uncertainties—among them the reluctance of the Khmer Rouge's hard core to work with the other parties and the continued but diminished presence of the Thais and Vietnamese—will the new government gain enough freedom to build a neutral and totally independent Cambodia?

The country needs generous and strong leaders to establish and maintain peace. Without it there will be no demining and therefore no safe rice fields for cultivation; fear, hunger, threats, and more casualties and deaths will continue. Will all the sufferings endured by the Cambodians for more than twenty years at last give way to happiness and peaceful life? Will lassitude and anxiety yield to the smile that the sculptors of Angkor have immortalized? Will peasants' hollow cheeks fill out again? Cambodians have not lost their dignity; all speak hopefully of the national reconciliation, including the participation of the Khmer Rouge in government (except for Pol Pot,

Ieng Sary, Ta Mok, and Nuon Chea), which now seems near at hand. People remember happily the daily life under Sangkum's regime, and their eyes light up when they speak of *Samdech Ov*, of his supporters, and of the educated people. They are convinced that these leaders will know how to bring forth a Cambodian rebirth, as in the past, and how to maintain social order and peace and to allow normal daily existence. But there is a difficult task ahead for politicians, so exposed to foreign pressure and so ready to break into factions.

The sun is setting. A gentle breeze stirs the leaves of a tamarind tree and brushes the cheek of a crouching, happy old man; an old, toothless face lets forth a jet of red-stained saliva and a mother gently rocks her baby in a *krâma*; healthy children play silent games . . . A little farther on, men are engaged in endless palavering, girls pound rice, and a group of young men wander through the village . . . In the distance the music of a country orchestra drowns the recitations of the monks. In the cities people walk along the riverbank. Here is Cambodia in peacetime, and so the Khmers remember it while thinking of the future.

# APPENDIXES

# APPENDIX 1: CHRONOLOGY

| | |
|---|---|
| Early 3rd to mid-6th century | Empire of Funan. |
| Mid-6th to late 7th century | Chenla. |
| 802–1431 | Angkor. |
| Mid-15th to mid-19th century | Post-Angkorian period; Internal conflicts; absorption by Annam of lower Cambodia (Kampuchea Krom); Siamese and Vietnamese tutelage over Cambodia and occupation of its territory by the two neighbors. |
| 1853 and 1856 | Requests by King Ang Duong for an alliance with the French emperor. |
| 1863 | Establishment of French protectorate over Cambodia. |
| 1884 | New Franco-Khmer convention stipulating a stricter application of the protectorate; France's assumption of all powers. |
| 1907 | Return by Bangkok (at insistence of France) of Battambang and Siem Reap provinces, occupied for more than a century, to Cambodia. |
| 1925 (?) | Assassination by Cambodians of the French resident of Kompong Chhnang, Bardez. |
| 1930 | Creation of the Indochinese Communist party, 3 February. |
| 1934 | First rallying of young Khmers in the Association des anciens élèves du lycée Sisowath. |
| 1936 | Founding of *Nagara Vatta* newspaper. |
| | Revolt of the Lycée Sisowath students, 5 May. |
| 1941 | Occupation of French Indochina by Japanese forces. |
| | Coronation of Norodom Sihanouk as king of Cambodia, 25 April. |
| 1942 | *Révolte des ombrelles*, 20 July. |
| Mid-1940s | Birth of the *issarak* movement. |
| 1945 | Creation in Paris of the Fraternité khmère by Prince Youtevong, in January. |
| | Japanese takeover of all command positions in Cambodia, in March. |
| | Surrender of Japanese forces, 16 August. |
| 1946 | Founding in Paris of the Association des étudiants |

khmers (AEK). Dissolved by the French government on 9 February 1953, it reappeared on 26 November 1956 under the name Union des étudiants khmers (UEK).

Proclamation of the Democratic Republic of Vietnam in the north, in March.

Birth of the two first Khmer political parties, the Democratic party and the Liberal party, in March and April.

France's recognition of the internal autonomy of Cambodia, 1 July.

Cambodia's first elections based on universal suffrage.

1947 Following the Treaty of Tokyo, retrocession of Siem Reap and Battambang provinces, occupied by the Siamese since 1941.

Passing of the constitution of the Kingdom of Cambodia, 6 April.

1949 Treaty restoring *de jure* independence to Cambodia within the French Union, in January.

Late 1940s to
early 1950s The future Khmer Rouge leaders' studies in Paris.

1951 Creation of the first autonomous Khmer Communist movement, the Parti révolutionnaire du peuple cambodgien, which would later become the Communist party.

1952 Royal crusade for independence, announced 5 June.

1953 Cambodia's recovery of complete independence, 9 November.

1954 Geneva Accords on French Indochina, 21 July. The International Control Commission (ICC) is set up in Cambodia.

Operation *Samakki*, to drive from western Cambodia all remaining Vietminh soldiers, in October.

1955 Cambodian acceptance of American aid.

Abdication of Norodom Sihanouk in favor of his father, Norodom Suramarit, 3 March.

Creation in April by Prince Sihanouk of the Sangkum Reastr Niyum movement, victorious in the elections of 11 September. Beginning of the Sangkum era.

First national congress, in December.

1956 Founding of the Khmer *serei* movement by Son Ngoc Thanh.

1959 Birth of Jeunesse socialiste royale khmère (JSRK), 5 September.

1960 After the death of King Suramarit, election of Norodom Sihanouk as chief of state, 14 June.

Creation of the National Liberation Front of South Vietnam (NLF), 20 December.

1961   Rupture of diplomatic relations with Thailand, 20 October.

1962   Election of Hou Yuon and Khieu Samphan on the Sangkum list.

Decision of the International Court of Justice at The Hague stipulating that the Preah Vihear temple, occupied by the Thais, belongs to Cambodia, 15 June.

1963   Presence of Saloth Sar (Pol Pot) and Ieng Sary in the maquis.

Rupture of diplomatic relations with South Vietnam, 27 August.

Rejection of American aid, 10 November.

1964   American–South Vietnamese aggressions against Cambodian villages along the Vietnamese border.

Creation in Phnom Penh of the Association d'amitié khméro-chinoise (dissolved on 1 September 1967 by Sihanouk).

Sacking of the American and British embassies in Phnom Penh, 11 March.

1965   Creation by left-wing students in Phnom Penh of the Association générale des étudiants khmers (AGEK), 17 January (dissolved by Sihanouk in 1967).

Rupture of diplomatic relations with the United States, 3 May.

Signature of a military pact with China, allowing, notably, the Viet Cong to station troops in Cambodian territory and to be supplied with arms through Cambodia, 25 November.

1966   Beginning of the Chinese Cultural Revolution, 18 April.

Gain by the right of a majority of seats in the legislative elections, 11 September; ministerial portfolios for Khieu Samphan, Hou Yuon, and Hu Nim.

Formation by Sihanouk of countergovernment to balance the rightist government in office, in November.

1967   First return of some Khmer Communists from exile in Hanoi to Cambodia (process continuing until January 1979), where they join forces with the Khmer Rouge guerrillas.

Rebellion of Samlaut peasants, 2 April. Hou Yuon and Khieu Samphan, accused of being the instigators, take to the maquis on 24 April.

Recognition of Cambodia's borders by the NLF and the Democratic Republic of Vietnam (DRV), May and June.

Change of diplomatic representation of the DRV at Phnom Penh to embassy status, 30 June. Installation of a permanent representation for the NLF in Phnom Penh.

1968   Revolt of the northeastern hill tribes.

1969   Secret American bombings of Vietnamese Communist sanctuaries in Cambodian territory.

Opening of a gambling casino in Phnom Penh, in January.

The diplomatic representation of the NLF is raised to embassy status, 9 May.

Phnom Penh resumes diplomatic relations with Washington, 22 May.

Expulsion of the ICC, in December.

Last national congress, 27–29 December. Sihanouk is relegated to the minority.

1970  Departure of Sihanouk for France, 6 January.

Organization of anti-Vietnamese demonstrations in the border province of Svay Rieng, 8 March, at the request of Sihanouk. Sack of NLF and DRV embassies by inhabitants of Phnom Penh, 11–16 March.

Military coup, 18 March. Lon Nol takes power, his government immediately recognized by Washington. Sihanouk, deposed while abroad, moves to Peking.

Sihanouk's formation 23 March in Peking of the Front uni national du Cambodge (FUNC), which links him to the future Khmer Rouge leaders. He calls upon the Khmer people to take up arms.

Massacre by Khmer soldiers of Vietnamese civilians living in Cambodia, during April.

Summit of Indochinese peoples held at Canton, 24–26 April.

First American military air intervention under the Khmer Republic, 30 April; it would last two months.

Phnom Penh's resumption of diplomatic relations with Bangkok and Saigon, in May.

Sihanouk's announcement of the composition of the FUNC as well as of the Gouvernement royal d'union nationale du Cambodge (GRUNC) to represent it, 5 May.

Proclamation of the Khmer Republic, 9 October.

1971  Shelling of Pochentong airport by the Vietnamese Communists, in January.

Lon Nol is afflicted with hemiplegia.

Creation of a FUNC committee in Paris.

1972  Assumption of leadership over the Khmer Rouge armed forces by the Saloth Sar (Pol Pot) group.

Promulgation of the constitution of the Khmer Republic, 10 May.

Assumption of Lon Nol to presidency of the republic, 4 June.

1973  Closing of the Cambodian pavilion at the Cité universitaire, Paris, 7–8 January.

Signature of the Paris Accords on Vietnam, 27 January.

Resumption of American bombings in Cambodia, lasting from February until mid-June.

Visit by Sihanouk and some close associates to Cambodian zones controlled by the Khmer Rouge, in March and April.

1974 In Phnom Penh, death of two government officials, one of them the minister of education, at hands of angry students.

1975 Closing of the United States Embassy in Phnom Penh, 12 April, and recognition of the GRUNC by the French government.

Entrance of the Khmer Rouge into Phnom Penh, 17 April, and order for evacuation of city by all residents, including invalids. Expulsion of all diplomats and de facto rupture of diplomatic relations with France. Massacres begin on this day (and continue during the entire duration of the regime). The population learns that it must follow the orders of Angkar, the "organization," invisible but omnipresent and all-powerful. Confirmation several days later of Sihanouk as chief of state.

Entrance of NLF and DRV troops into Saigon, 30 April.

Permission from the Khmer Rouge for Sihanouk's return to Cambodia, in December.

1976 Change of name from Cambodia to Democratic Kampuchea, and promulgation of a new constitution, 5 January.

Death of Chou En-lai, 8 January.

Formation in Paris of the Association générale des Khmers à l'étranger (AGKE), favorable to Son Sann, in January.

Resignation of Sihanouk and dissolution of the FUNC and GRUNC, in April. Formation of the first government of Democratic Kampuchea.

Following plots against the regime, the first purges of Khmer Rouge cadres and soldiers (in north; purges would continue in 1977 and 1978 in the other regions, with the exception of the southwest, from which elements led by Ta Mok and loyal to Pol Pot would gradually extend their control over the entire country).

Death of Mao Tse-tung, 9 September.

1977 Intense border fighting between Khmer Rouge and Vietnamese, beginning in the spring (and continuing until the general Vietnamese offensive of 25 December 1978).

Speech by Pol Pot revealing Angkar to be the political bureau of the central committee of the Khmer Communist party, 30 September.

Hanoi's rupture of diplomatic relations with Phnom Penh, 31 December.

1978 Escape of Heng Samrin, future head of the République populaire du Kampuchea (RPK), to Vietnam, in May, amid purges after the discovery of plot against the regime fomented by Khmer Rouge cadres and soldiers of the eastern zone (where massacre of the people, accused of complicity with the plotters and with Vietnam, continues until early 1979).

Membership of Vietnam in Conseil d'aide économique mutuelle (des pays d'Europe de l'Est [Comecon]), 29 June.

Cancellation of Chinese aid to Vietnam (already reduced since 1973), 3 July.

Announcement by Hanoi of formation of the Front d'union nationale pour le salut du Kampuchea (FUNSK), 3 December, to be led by Heng Samrin, a Khmer Rouge defector opposed to Pol Pot.

Beginning of general offensive by the Vietnamese, with the help of FUNSK troops, 25 December.

1979   At the request of the Chinese, departure of Norodom Sihanouk for Peking, 6 January, and then for New York, to the General Assembly of the United Nations Organization, where he pleads Cambodia's cause against the Vietnamese invasion.

Expulsion of Khmer Rouge by the Vietnamese army, 7 January, and installation of Heng Samrin at the head of the country, which assumes the name of République populaire du Kampuchea.

Signature of a treaty of friendship and cooperation between the RPK and Vietnam, in February.

Signature of a treaty of friendship and cooperation between the RPK and Laos, in March.

Mass flight of Cambodians to the Thai border, during the spring.

Opening in Phnom Penh of the first political prison, in July.

Arrival of the routed Khmer Rouge army at the Thai border, in October. The leaders set up their headquarters at Phnom Malay in Cambodian territory. The opening in Thailand of Sa Kaeo, the first settlement center, and then of Khao I Dang to shelter Cambodian refugees from all sides.

Founding by Son Sann of the Front national de libération du peuple khmer (FNLPK), 9 October.

The UN General Assembly's first resolution demanding the withdrawal of foreign troops from Cambodia (a vote renewed each year), 14 November. Democratic Kampuchea retains its seat.

1980   Establishment of a land-bridge on the Khmer-Thai border under the aegis of UNICEF in order to supply rice to Cambodians living inside Cambodia.

Many refugees continue to arrive at the Thai border.

1981   Norodom Sihanouk's creation in March of the Front uni national pour un Cambodge indépendant, neutre, pacifique, et coopératif (FUNCINPEC).

Signing in Singapore of general agreement among the Khmer Rouge, the FNLPK, and the FUNCINPEC concerning the formation of a government opposed to the RPK, 4 September.

The Khmer Rouge announce the dissolution of Pol Pot's Communist party of Kampuchea, in December.

1982 Formation in Kuala Lumpur of the Gouvernement de coalition du Kampuchea démocratique (GCKD), 22 June.

Release by Phnom Penh during autumn of memoranda legalizing settlement of Vietnamese civilians in Cambodia.

1983 Start of Phnom Penh's "works for national defense"; levies of peasants and then city dwellers; erection of a barrier-wall along the border to isolate Cambodia from Laos and Thailand.

1985 Capture by the Vietnamese army and Phnom Penh's forces of all resistance sanctuaries.

First internal problems of the FNLPK.

1986 Eight-point proposal by the GCKD for a political settlement of the Cambodian problem, 7 March.

1987 Creation of the Association des Vietnamiens du Cambodge.

Sihanouk's announcememt in May of one-year departure from presidency of the GCKD.

Withdrawal of Hun Sen in late December from foreign ministry in favor of Hor Nam Hong.

First Sihanouk–Hun Sen discussions at Fère-en-Tardenois, 2–4 December.

1988 Second Sihanouk–Hun Sen meeting at St-Germain-en-Laye, 20–21 January; acceptance by Phnom Penh of multipartite principle.

Sihanouk's resignation of the presidency of the GCKD, 30 January.

Sihanouk's proposal for direct negotiation with the Vietnamese, 2 February (which Hanoi refuses).

Sihanouk's resumption of presidency of the GCKD, 16 February.

New resignation by Sihanouk from the GCKD, 10 July.

Meeting of the Khmer factions in Jakarta (Jakarta informal meeting or JIM I), 25–28 July.

Sino-Soviet discussions on Cambodia in Peking, 28 August.

Sihanouk–Son Sann–Hun Sen meeting at Fère-en-Tardenois, 5–8 November; creation of a quadripartite working commission.

Sihanouk's five-point proposal, 27 November.

Sihanouk–Khieu Samphan meeting at Fère-en-Tardenois, 14 December.

In Paris, first (and last) meeting of the quadripartite working commission, 21–22 December.

1989 Sino-Vietnamese discussions in Peking, 14–20 January.

Sihanouk's resumption of the presidency of the GCKD, 12 February.

Meeting of the four Khmer factions at Bogor (Jakarta), termed JIM II, 19–21 February.

Liberal measures by Phnom-Penh begun in spring: official restoration of Buddhism, private property in land, relative freedom of commerce and movement.

Change of name from the People's Republic of Kampuchea to the State of Cambodia, 30 April.

Meetings at Jakarta between Hun Sen and Sihanouk and between Hun Sen and Son Sann, 2–3 May.

Sino-Soviet discussions in Peking, 15–18 May.

Arrest in Phnom Penh of liberals in the government and administration, during May and June.

Announcement of political support for the regime from nongovernmental organizations (NGOs) in Phnom Penh, June and November.

Meeting in Celle-St-Cloud of the four Khmer factions in the presence of the French foreign minister, 24 July.

Paris International Conference on Cambodia (PICC), 30 July–31 August.

Sino-Vietnamese discussions in Paris, on the sidelines of the international conference, in August.

Resignation of Sihanouk from the presidency of FUNCINPEC, 27 August, and appointment of Monique Izzi (Sihanouk's wife) and General Nhiek Tioulong to replace him.

Official withdrawal of all Vietnamese troops and advisors from Cambodia, 26 September.

In western Cambodia, victories for the resistance movements opposed to Phnom Penh, during autumn.

Suggestion from American Senator Stephen Solarz of United Nations' provisional administration for Cambodia, in October. This plan, taken up in late November by Australia, is termed the "Evans plan."

Establishment of curfew (9 P.M.) in Phnom Penh, 30 October.

1990 First meeting, in Paris, of the five permanent members of the UN Security Council (Big Five) to discuss the Cambodian problem, 15–16 January.

Second meeting of Big Five in New York, 11–12 February.

Meeting of the four Khmer factions in Jakarta, 26–27 February.

Third meeting of Big Five in Paris, 12–13 March.

Fourth meeting of Big Five in New York, 25–26 May.

Purges in the Phnom Penh government, in May and June.

Meeting of the four Khmer factions in Tokyo, 4–5 June. Hun Sen and Sihanouk sign an appeal for a cease-fire (not carried out).

Franco-Indonesian talks on Cambodia held in Paris, 12 June.

Fifth meeting of Big Five in Paris, 16–17 July.

The United States' announcement of intention to discontinue diplomatic support to the GCKD, 18 July.

American-Vietnamese discussions on Cambodia in New York, 6 August.

Resumption of diplomatic relations between Peking and Jakarta.

Sixth meeting of Big Five in New York, 27–28 August.

Creation in Jakarta of a Conseil national suprême (CNS) bringing together the representatives of the four Cambodian factions, 10 September.

First meeting—aborted—of the CNS in Bangkok, 17 September.

Visit of General Giap to Peking, 19 September.

Secret contacts between Peking and Phnom Penh, during September.

Official opening of the Alliance française in Phnom Penh, 30 September.

Normalization of diplomatic relations between China and Singapore, 3 October.

Death of Le Duc Tho, a key figure in the Vietnamese Communist party, 13 October.

Seventh meeting of Big Five in New York, 15–16 October.

Franco-Indonesian discussions on Cambodia in Paris, 30 October.

Declaration by UN General Assembly of Cambodia's vacant seat, in October.

American-Vietnamese discussions in New York.

International meeting on Cambodia held in Jakarta, 9–11 November, including Big Five, Indonesia, Australia, Canada, India, Japan, Laos, Malaysia, and a UN representative.

Eighth meeting of Big Five in Paris, 23–25 November.

Meeting of the four Khmer factions in Paris, 21–22 December, in the presence of the French foreign minister, his Indonesian counterpart, and a representative of the UN. Acceptance of a UN peace plan, with assorted reservations on Phnom Penh's part.

1991 Trip to Hanoi, 1 February, by representatives from France and Indonesia, co-presidents of the PICC, urging Vietnam to use its influence to sway Phnom Penh.

Meeting of the four Khmer factions in Bangkok, 20 April.

Cease-fire among four Cambodian parties, 1 May.

Meeting of the Khmer factions in Jakarta, 2–4 June, with Sihanouk present but not participating (and announcing intention to return to Phnom Penh in November 1991).

First meeting of the Khmer factions' CNS at Pattaya (Pattaya I), and decision to set up CNS's headquarters in Phnom Penh, 24–26 June.

Informal meeting of the Khmer factions in Peking; Sihanouk is named president of the CNS, 16–17 July.

Meeting of Big Five in Peking, 18–19 July.

Official visit by Hun Sen to Peking, 22–24 July.

Second meeting of CNS in Pattaya (Pattaya II), 26–28 August.

Meeting of the Khmer factions in New York, 19 September.

Meeting of Big Five in New York, 20–21 September.

Presence of CNS in UN General Assembly, 29 September. With the Khmers unable to agree on a candidate, the Cambodian seat is declared vacant. It is to be occupied by a temporary president in October 1992 and then by a permanent representative in fall 1993.

Change from Parti populaire révolutionnaire du Kampuchea (PPRK) to Parti du peuple cambodgien (PPC); replacement of Heng Samrin by Chea Sim as its president, 17 October.

Signing of the Paris Treaty on Cambodia, 23 October.

Arrival of UN peacekeeping forces as part of UN preparatory mission in Cambodia, 12 November.

Sihanouk's return to Phnom Penh, 14 November.

Meeting of People's Congress in front of royal palace, Phnom Penh, and Sihanouk's announcement of FUNCINPEC-PPC alliance, 16 November; the signing of two bilateral treaties: political (20 November) and military (25 November).

Statement by Hor Nam Hong reinstating Sihanouk as head of state of Cambodia while maintaining Heng Samrin in similar duties, 20 November.

Water Festival, with Sihanouk presiding, 20–22 November.

Demonstration against the return of Khieu Samphan (who leaves Phnom Penh the same day); sack of the Khmer Rouge's villa, 27 November.

Meeting of CNS in Pattaya, 3 December.

Demonstrations in Phnom Penh against corruption and the sale of public property, involving several deaths, 17–23 December.

1992    Start of politically motivated assassinations in Phnom Penh, during January.

Nomination of Yasushi Akashi to head the United Nations Transitional Authority in Cambodia (UNTAC), 9 January.

First plenary meeting of CNS in Phnom Penh, 26 January (of many meetings to follow).

Creation of UNTAC following proposal by Boutros Boutros-Ghali, 28 February. Arrival of first contingents, 2 March.

First serious fighting between Khmer Rouge and Phnom Penh troops after signing of the Paris Treaty, during late February.

Yasushi Akashi's arrival in Phnom Penh and assumption of duties, 15 March.

First repatriation of refugees living in camps along the Thai border, 30 March.

Replacement of Heng Samrin by Chea Sim as Cambodian head of state, 6 April.

Visit of CNS members to China, 7 April.

Visit by Boutros-Ghali to Cambodia, 18 April.

Cambodia's participation—in seat that had been vacant since 1979—in the meeting of nonaligned countries in Bali, 14–15 May.

FNLPK congress in Phnom Penh and, to prepare for elections, creation of the Parti démocratique libéral bouddhique (PDLB), 20 May.

Rising tension between China and Vietnam over the Spratly Islands, during June.

First application of disarmament, the second phase of the peace plan, 13 June.

Tokyo conference on the reconstruction of Cambodia, 22 June.

Appearance of the *Cambodia Times*, the first English-language Khmer newspaper, 13 July.

Massacre of eight Vietnamese civilians by unidentified Khmer soldiers, 23 July.

UNTAC's first registration of political parties for the elections of May 1993, 17 August.

Official release of all political prisoners, during September.

Illness of Sihanouk and visit to Peking for treatment, 1 October.

Start of electoral registration of Khmers, 6 October.

Khmer Rouge refusal to participate in elections (refusal reconfirmed 23 January 1993), 12 October.

Ultimatum by the UN Security Council to the Khmer Rouge with 15 November deadline to complete implementation of disarmanent, 13 October.

Settlement of Cambodia's debt to International Monetary Fund (65 million francs) by France and Japan, in November (following their settlement of two-thirds of Vietnam's debt, 19 August).

International meeting on Cambodia held in Peking, 7 November, including Big Five, Indonesia, Australia, Japan, Thailand, and Sihanouk and CNS representatives.

Visit to Phnom Penh by Roland Dumas, French minister of foreign affairs, 8 November.

First repatriation of Cambodian refugees from Vietnam, 16 November.

Loan by Asian Development Bank of 67.7 million francs to Cambodia for reconstruction, 26 November.

Economic sanctions by UN Security Council against Khmer Rouge, 30 November. Thailand's refusal to freeze Khmer Rouge assets.

Criticism of UNTAC from Sihanouk in Peking, during December (ended by Yasushi Akashi's visit to Peking 8 January 1993).

Attacks by Khmer Rouge in Battambang against UNTAC barracks and villages under their control, 13–14 December.

1993 Spread of banditry and unrest throughout Cambodia and decreasing confidence of inhabitants in UNTAC.

Embargo against export of Cambodian timber, 1 January.

Decision by Ranariddh to leave Phnom Penh, for security reasons, 5 January (he will return for electoral campaign).

Sihanouk's announcement of candidacy for April presidential elections, with UN approval, 8 January (the vote, postponed from April to May, will not take place).

Trip by Thai minister of foreign affairs, Squadron Leader Prasong Soonsiri, to Peking for meeting with Sihanouk, 18 January.

Offensive by Cambodia against Khmer Rouge in several provinces, 25 January.

Meeting by CNS in Peking, 28 January, to set constituent elections for 23–27 May, a date confirmed by the UN Security Council on 8 March.

Signing of agreement by Cambodia, Laos, Thailand, and Vietnam to continue work of Mekong committee, 5 February.

Decision by CNS on 10 February to ban the export of precious stones (not carried out).

First appearance of French-language periodical *Le Mékong*, 11 February.

Visit by François Mitterrand on 9–12 February to Vietnam and then Cambodia, where he meets Sihanouk, come for the occasion from Peking (to which he returns a week later).

Resignation of Gérard Porcell from UNTAC, citing his inability to control the key ministries and stressing UNTAC's lack of compliance with the Paris Accords, 26 February.

National congress of Cambodian women in Phnom Penh, 5–8 March.

Massacre of Vietnamese civilians in the great lake area of Siem Reap province, 10 March, and departure of others for Vietnam or the frontier (they will begin to return in July); other acts against Vietnamese occurring in Phnom Penh and the provinces.

Closing of site 2, last refugee camp on Khmer-Thai border, 30 March.

Visit by Boutros-Ghali to Phnom Penh and meeting with Sihanouk, 7–8 April.

Unannounced departure from Phnom Penh of Khmer Rouge representatives on CNS, 13 April, leaving Son Sann as sole leader of factions opposed to Phnom Penh party to remain in the capital.

Sihanouk's departure for Peking, 14 April.

Series of attempts by Khmer Rouge to sabotage the elections, during April and May: reported deaths in the provinces of a dozen PDLB members; attacks on UN soldiers' posts.

Publication of manifesto by committee of one hundred Khmer refugees in France, to condemn the failure of the Paris Accords, 30 April.

Peace march from Siem Reap to Phnom Penh, organized by Buddhist monks, 4–21 May.

Bombing of Chinese UNTAC troops' headquarters by Khmer Rouge, 4–5 May.

Meeting of CNS in Peking, 6 May, without Khmer Rouge representatives.

Discussion by UN Security Council, 17 May, of sanctions against Khmer Rouge to prevent sabotage of elections.

Sihanouk's return to Phnom Penh, 22 May.

Constituent elections, 23–27 May; turnout of about 90 percent of the population to decide among twenty parties. Results announced 11 June by UNTAC: 58 seats to FUNCINPEC, 51 to PPC, 10 to PDLB, and 1 to MOULINAKA; results contested by PPC but recognized by the UN Security Council, 15 June.

Partial withdrawal of UNTAC team in June, to be complete by 28 August.

In violation of the Paris Accords, creation by Sihanouk on 3 June of Gouvernement national du Cambodge (GNC), recognized by Hanoi, and dissolution of state of Cambodia.

Dissolution of GNC announced by Sihanouk, 4 June, and positive reaction from United States, Britain, and Australia.

Announcement by Khmer Rouge of willingness to participate in quadripartite government led by Sihanouk, 8 June.

Formation by three majority parties of Forces armées nationales cambodgiennes (FANC), 9 June.

Secession of eastern provinces, led by Sihanouk's son Norodom Chakrapong and PPC leaders, 10 June; asylum in Vietnam is denied to Chakrapong, 15 June, and he returns to Phnom Penh two days later.

Alliance of FUNCINPEC and PDLP in Assemblée nationale, 11 June.

First session of Constituent Assembly, 14 June, to vote "full special powers" to Sihanouk and declare illegal the coup d'état of 18 March 1970.

Announcement by Sihanouk, 16 June, of government's formation for 24 June, after negotiations by FUNCINPEC and PPC: Hun Sen and Ranariddh to be joint prime ministers and to head FANC, Son Sann to be president of Constituent Assembly.

Letter from Khieu Samphan to Sihanouk, 24 June, demanding his return to Phnom Penh as a private citizen heading a private party; meeting in Phnom Penh of two Khmer Rouge leaders with military head of UNTAC.

Change of country's name to Cambodia (*Kampuchea*, in Khmer), 29 June, with resumption of its flag and national hymn (stripped of references to royalty).

Revision of regional economic agreements announced by new finance minister, primarily concerning export of timber and precious stones, 1 July.

Visit by French defense minister, François Léotard, to Cambodia, 5 July.

Occupation of frontier temple of Preah Vihear by Khmer Rouge, 7 July.

Meeting in Phnom Penh, 13 July, of Sihanouk and Ranariddh with Khieu Samphan, who demands the inclusion of Khmer Rouge in the army and as advisors to the government; cancellation of planned discussions on the subject following American pressure, denounced by Sihanouk (19 July) and by ASEAN (24 July).

Departure of Sihanouk for Peking, then Pyong Yang, 15 July.

Visit by Ranariddh and Hun Sen to Thailand, 12–15 August, and reception by prime minister, Chuan Likpai, and visit by Ranariddh and his wife to king and queen; during same month, visit by Ranariddh and Hun Sen to Laos.

Round of discussions for 22–25 August proposed by Khieu Samphan, 16 August.

Delegation from U.S. Senate received by Chea Sim, 18 August.

Son Sann received, 19 August, by Thai foreign affairs minister, Prasong Soonsiri; he approves of Khmer Rouge demand to be advisors to Cambodian government.

Hostilities between Khmer Rouge and FANC, during August; capture of base of Phnom Chhat by FANC, 20 August.

Trip by Ranariddh and Hun Sen to Vietnam, 23–25 August, to resolve issues of Cambodian frontiers and Vietnamese settlers (unsuccessful).

Extension by UN Security Council, 27 August, of UNTAC's mandate up to final installation of Phnom Penh government; departure of last UNTAC soldiers set for 15 November.

Agreement by Phnom Penh government, 27 August, to Ranariddh's demand for restoration of constitutional monarchy.

Delegation to Pyong Yang, 30 August, led by Son Sann, Ranariddh, and Hun Sen to meet Sihanouk to give him projected constitution.

Surrender of 500 Khmer Rouge soldiers announced in *The Nation*.

Proposal to Khmer Rouge by Sihanouk for cease-fire, 1 September, and for discussions following promulgation of the new constitution.

Consensus by Ranariddh and Hun Sen on adoption of constitutional monarchy, 3 September, rejected by Sihanouk the following day.

Second international conference on reconstruction of Cambodia, 8–9 September in Paris; leading the Cambodian delegation is finance minister, Sam Rainsy.

Clashes between soldiers of the government and of the Khmer Rouge throughout August and September. Defection among the Khmer Rouge (estimated at two thousand by UNTAC); some undergo training before enlistment in the government army.

Adoption by the Constituent Assembly of a constitution installing the parliamentary monarchy, 21 September. On 24 September, Sihanouk, back from Peking, signs the new constitution, which begins, "We, the Cambodian people." That same day he is enthroned for the second time and names his son Ranariddh first prime minister and Hun Sen second prime minister.

Signing of a memorandum by FUNCINPEC and PPC, 25 September, to extend the political agreement signed by the two parties on 20 September 1991.

Departure of the head of UNTAC, Yasushi Akashi, from Cambodia, 29 September.

Reception of Khieu Samphan, who has come to communicate the Khmer Rouge's approval of the restoration of the monarchy and the new constitution, by Sihanouk in Peking, 1 October.

Sihanouk has a tumor removed from his colon, 7 October. The Chinese doctors find his condition satisfactory.

Election of Chea Sim as president of the National Assembly, replacing Son Sann, 25 October.

The last blue helmets (from France) leave Cambodia, 14 November.

Planning of the national reconciliation, with the probable future reintegration of the Khmer Rouge (except for its four main leaders, Pol Pot, Ieng Sary, Ta Mok, and Nuon Chea). This reintegration, which the majority of Cambodians support, is currently under joint study by the various parties (end December).

# APPENDIX 2: TERRITORIES TAKEN FROM CAMBODIA BY FRANCE, 1870–1914

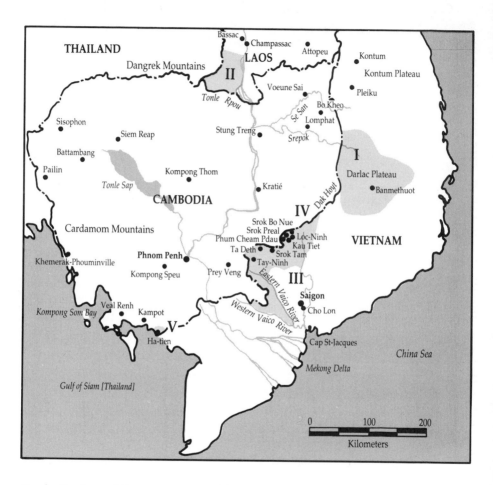

Cambodian losses following successive delimitations:

   I   Territory of Stung Treng linked to Annam (Darlac)
  II  Cambodian Muongs linked to the kingdom of Bassac
 III  Cambodian territories linked to Cochin China in 1870 and 1872
 IV  Cambodian territories linked in 1893 to Cochin China (Cuu-an, Tranh-an, Minh-Ngai, Loc-Ninh, Phuoc-la)
  V  Territory linked to Cochin China in 1914.

Redrawn from Sarin Chhak, *Les Frontières du Cambodge* (Paris: Dalloz, 1966).

# APPENDIX 3: THE CAMBODIAN ISLANDS: THE BRÉVIÉ LINE

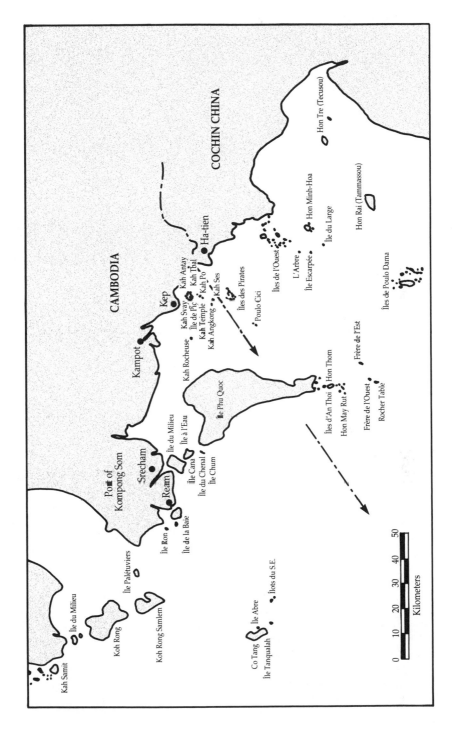

Redrawn from Sarin Chhak, *Les Frontières du Cambodge* (Paris: Dalloz, 1966).

# APPENDIX 4: CREATION OF THE FRATERNITÉ KHMÈRE

Cambodian Association
FRATERNITÉ KHMÈRE
Rue Georges de Porto-Riche
Paris XIVe/Tel.: GOB.72.07

The Cambodian workers and infantrymen who came in 1940 to fight and work in France have endured five years of war under extremely difficult material and moral conditions.

In addition to being far from our native country, and all kinds of difficulties inherent to war, there were other hardships, the most difficult of which was not due to material causes.

In order to help these nationals, we hereby found, under the name "FRATERNITÉ KHMÈRE," an association with the purpose of bringing moral and material aid to Cambodians living in France, maintaining fraternal bonds among them, organizing appropriate festivals and celebrations to create the traditional and familial atmosphere indispensable to their physical and moral well-being, and increasing and managing their contacts with French circles. To accomplish these aims, "FRATERNITÉ KHMÈRE" places in operation a program that includes:

(a) the creation of a semimonthly newsletter in Cambodian to be sent to all the Cambodian infantry and workers' camps to give them news of France and Cambodia;

(b) visits by representatives of "FRATERNITÉ KHMÈRE" to the different camps for Cambodian workers and infantrymen in Paris and outside of Paris;

(c) invitations sent by "FRATERNITÉ KHMÈRE" to Cambodian infantrymen and workers inviting them to spend some time with their compatriots living in Paris;

(d) periodic meetings of Cambodian nationals.

In addition to this program, there are also folkloric programs and other initiatives tending to interest Cambodian nationals in French artistic, cultural, and family life.

"FRATERNITÉ KHMÈRE" calls upon all people of goodwill to help in the realization of these goals.[1]

The President,
FRATERNITÉ KHMÈRE

---

[1]Non-Cambodian nationals are admitted with the status of benefactors with an annual membership fee payable in cash or kind of a minimum value of 5,000 francs, and with the status of supporters with an annual membership fee of 120 francs and an optional, unspecified cash contribution.

Send your requests for membership to the president: Prince SISOWATH YOUTEVONG / 2, rue Georges de Porto-Riche / Paris XIVe.

Les travailleurs et les tirailleurs cambodgiens venus en 1940 pour combattre et travailler en France ont subi cinq années de guerre dans des conditions matérielles et morales particulièrement pénibles.

A l'éloignement du pays natal, aux difficultés de toutes sortes inhérentes à la guerre, s'ajoutent d'autres souffrances dont la plus grave n'est pas due aux causes matérielles.

Pour venir en aide à ces ressortissants, il est fondé, sous la dénomination de " *FRATERNITÉ KHMÈRE* ", une association dont le but est d'apporter une assistance morale et matérielle aux Cambodgiens résidant en France, de conserver entre eux les liens fraternels, d'organiser des fêtes et des manifestations propres à créer une ambiance traditionnelle et familiale indispensable à leur santé physique et morale, de multiplier et de diriger leurs contacts avec les milieux français.

Pour cela, la " *FRATERNITÉ KHMÈRE* " met à exécution un programme comportant :

*a)* la création d'une feuille bimensuelle en langue cambodgienne, envoyée dans tous les camps de travailleurs et de tirailleurs cambodgiens pour leur donner des nouvelles de la France et du Cambodge.

*b)* les visites par les envoyés de la " *FRATERNITÉ KHMÈRE* " dans les différents camps de travailleurs et de tirailleurs cambodgiens à Paris et hors de Paris.

*c)* les invitations adressées par la " *FRATERNITÉ KHMÈRE* " aux tirailleurs et aux travailleurs cambodgiens à venir séjourner quelque temps auprès de leurs compatriotes résidant à Paris.

*d)* des réunions périodiques entre les ressortissants cambodgiens.

A ce programme s'ajoutent des manifestations folkloriques et d'autres initiatives tendant à intéresser les ressortissants cambodgiens à la vie artistique, culturelle et familiale française.

La " *FRATERNITÉ KHMÈRE* " fait appel à toutes les bonnes volontés pour aider à la réalisation de ses buts (1).

LE PRÉSIDENT,

---

(1) **Les non-ressortissants cambodgiens** sont admis à titre de **membres bienfaiteurs** avec une cotisation annuelle en espèce ou en nature d'une valeur minimum de 5.000 francs, et à titre de **membres sympathisants** avec une cotisation annuelle de 120 francs et facultativement un apport numéraire non déterminé.
Adresser la demande d'admission au Président : Le Prince SISOWATH YOUTÉVONG, 2, rue Georges de Porto-Riche, PARIS-XIV°.

---

Source: AOM Paris, Indo NF, carton 405, dossier 3471

# APPENDIX 5: APPROXIMATE ZONAL BOUNDARIES UNDER THE KHMER ROUGE

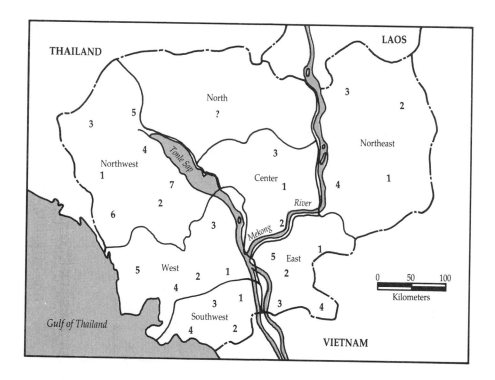

The solid lines show the approximate layout of zonal boundaries. The numbers correspond to the *Dâmbân* and thus relate to former provinces whose boundaries are poorly known. They were integrated into a general classification going from one to an unspecified number, a classification of which I have only fragments. The Kratié autonomous zone, the Stung Trâng autonomous sector (Kompong Cham province), and the special zone, created between 1970 and 1975, were abolished at the end of 1975.

# APPENDIX 6: JOINT DECLARATION OF CAMBODIANS ON THE EVE OF DEPARTURE FOR DEMOCRATIC KAMPUCHEA

We—students, trainees, officials, soldiers, former "forced refugees" expatriated to the United States, Canada, and Europe in the context of the U.S. war of aggression against our country—are going to return this very week to our dear native land, Democratic Kampuchea.

To return to one's country is something "self-evident," not to say normal or natural. But in the situation in which vile campaigns of calumny are orchestrated against our country and our people, and when we ourselves are exposed to multiple pressures, we are determined, by means of this joint declaration, to express before international public opinion, devoted to peace and justice, the reasons for our decision to return as well as our profound indignation and our condemnation of these denigratory campaigns and pressures.

Our decision was not dictated by any pressure whatsoever. Nor was it made in blind ignorance but after mature reflection, based on knowledge of authentic accomplishments in all realms—political, economic, social—accomplishments that were realized in the new society of Democratic Kampuchea, notably after the total liberation of 17 April 1975.

Indeed, it is almost superfluous to restate it: the prodigious and immense present accomplishments of our people, achieved with such sublime fervor, not only explain the enthusiasm and the haste of the Cambodians to go and make their contributions, but are also, for humanity, which has always been on the side of Kampuchea's people in their difficult hours, so many sources of profound pride, admiration, and joy.

But the American imperialists and their accomplices harbor a base rancor against our people, who inflicted a humiliating defeat on them by forcing them to retreat from Kampuchea in disgrace. This is why they are conducting, with their apparatus for propaganda and slander, an entire campaign of calumny tending systematically to obscure this glorious situation in Kampuchea.

This smear campaign seeks to convince public opinion that there are "terrible things" in Kampuchea, "crimes," "massacres . . ."; the ardor, the

323

enthusiasm, of the population in fields that are in full metamorphosis is presented as "forced labor" in "camps" under the bayonet; the authorities of the present popular power are compared to the worst "dictators" with epithets such as "intransigent sectarianism" if not "primitive, brutal conceptions," etc.

How can the success obtained by our people in all fields be explained if there were so many "hundred of thousands of massacres"?

How can it be believed that such a people, who so obstinately fought all the injustices, all the inequalities, all the tribulations, could once in power institute or tolerate the same evils?

Some of us, who were embarked on boats by force by reactionary generals on the day of liberation, taken to the United States, and confined in real camps, have directly experienced and suffered from these smear campaigns, and even from personal threats.

Some of us are also among those who were confined in refugee camps in Thailand. We know too well how the imperialist propaganda machine fabricates news. People are paid to give accounts of things that never happened; pictures are faked.

Thus, this whole campaign of denigration expresses once again a profound contempt, a serious affront by its authors to the people of Kampuchea as well as to the public opinion of the whole world, devoted to peace and justice.

It is not difficult to penetrate the dark intentions of the authors of this slanderous campaign: they desire at any price to have their crimes against our people forgotten as soon as possible; at the same time, they seek by all possible means to prevent our people from rebuilding its country. As a recent example, these defenders of "freedom," the American imperialists, in cowardly fashion bombed the city of Siem Reap, with approximately fifty people dead or wounded, and naturally their apparatuses for propaganda and slander attempt to distort and conceal these events.

It cannot be denied that the American imperialists and their accomplices want to subjugate our people. Their smear campaigns seek to isolate it politically, to misrepresent the successes won by our people, and to denigrate its just cause, which is also the cause of all peoples devoted to independence, peace, and justice. But facts are very tenacious, and words can do nothing to alter them.

Moved by a deep feeling of brotherhood and of great national union, and knowing that the immense destruction suffered by our country requires not merely passive pride and formal membership but rather resolution and efforts, we take the liberty of launching an appeal to all of our compatriots in foreign countries to return as quickly as possible to Democratic Kampuchea in order to bring our contributions to the restoration of the national economy, the construction of the new society, and the defence of the country.

We are convinced that public opinion, devoted to independence, peace, and justice, in the United States and Canada and Europe will not give any credence to this entire slanderous campaign on the part of the American imperialists and their accomplices, who still use their apparatuses of propaganda and slander to conceal their neocolonial actions against the innocent nations and peoples in the world.

Paris, 23 May 1976
The Undersigned*

*[127 persons signed this document, including: 77 soldiers (army, air force, and especially navy); 10 students and teachers; 5 rice growers; 5 engineers and members of related professions; 8 persons of various professions; 13 children; 9 housewives. Not a word has been changed from the original text (in French, translated here into English).]

# APPENDIX 7: PROPOSAL BY A GROUP OF CAMBODIANS IN THE CONTEXT OF THE KHMER-VIETNAMESE CONFLICT (PARIS, 31/12/77)

Whereas on the morrow of the Indochinese revolutionaries' victory of 1975, one hoped for a lasting peace in this part of the world that has for so many years been in torment, whereas the victory by the ideology invoking the people should place itself over above the one that it opposed, that was a source of exploitation, poverty, and want, the present situation demonstrates that the passions of another epoch have not, alas, been divested of their aftereffects; on the contrary, at present a historical resurgence is gaining force: the drive to the south, long pursued by Vietnam, tends to produce in the minds of some a self-defensive attitude provoking xenophobic reactions, and in minds of others a superiority complex that manifests itself in an imperialistic and annexationist illusion.

In this context, the recovery and maintenance of historical antagonisms in the narrow framework of nationalism only tarnish the image of socialism and undercut the third world people's confidence in this route to social progress.

In other respects, the withdrawal of an imperialist power from this region of Southeast Asia unfortunately leaves the way open for other local imperialisms and neoimperialisms, whose so-called ideologies underpin expansionist designs, thus plunging entire populations into new sufferings and new calamities.

Consequently, we—a group of Cambodians living in Paris—united in a special meeting, have adopted the following resolutions:

1.   We launch an urgent appeal to the two parties involved to put an end to their hostilities by means of: the total withdrawal of Vietnamese troops from Khmer territory, as delimited in its de facto and de jure borders by Vietnam in June 1967 and April 1970; the establishment of frank and friendly negotiations based on mutual respect and affection.

2.   We ask the government of the Soviet Union and the People's Republic of China to use their influence to put an end to this distressing situation and to guarantee the territorial integrity of the two countries.

3.   We launch an appeal to the peoples of the entire world, devoted to justice and peace, so that they will bring their support and their guarantee to the principles of peaceful coexistence throughout all of Southeast Asia.

4. We denounce and condemn imperialism and neoimperialism in all their forms.

5. We address an appeal to the present leadership of Democratic Kampuchea to renounce its suicidal policy of totalitarian dictatorship based on terror, fanaticism, and sectarianism, and make good that of national Reconciliation, Unity, and Reconstruction on the new and sound basis of a true Democracy, the sole guarantee of our survival.

6. We appeal for Union of all the Khmers who have taken refuge abroad to fight against any regime of oppression and repression that leads Cambodia to rapid extinction.

Paris, 4 January 1978

A representative of the group:
M. Kong Rithy
9, place du président Mithouard
Paris 75007

# APPENDIX 8: CORRESPONDENCE
# WITH KHIEU SAMPHAN

Concerning the past:

> Q: Khmer Rouge leaders have never been willing to admit the massacres committed from 1975 to 1979. In 1979, they merely acknowledged committing several errors, something that they tend to deny today; there is thus a reversal. This attitude is not likely to reassure the Khmers, or for that matter to reassure international opinion either. . . . Consequently: Are you prepared to reconsider the past and admit the excessive character of your revolution? If you persist in denial, how can you explain, among other things, the existence of Tuol Sleng, linked directly to the foreign ministry?
>
> A: First of all, let me remind [you] that we, the party of Democratic Kampuchea, consider it our duty not to focus on the past during the entire duration of our present resistance struggle against the latest aggressors, the Vietnamese aggressors. The reason for this is, as you know, that the past constitutes a very controversial question at the moment, thus extremely delicate, and any diagnosis on this subject greatly risks provoking sterile debates within the Kampuchean nation as well as within the international community, which would be harmful to the national and international support that we need so much in our struggle. I thus believe that, in the interest of our struggle, which is, so to speak, a common struggle of all those in the world who are on the side of peace, fairness, and respect for international law in the relations between states, we should rather concentrate all our attention, all our energy, on the present and the future. As for the past, history will take it upon itself to illuminate it, for only with the perspective of time will each event assume its true context and consequently, its real importance.

On the present and future: My questions dealt with, among other things, the concept of a *Khmer race*; the repeated attacks by Khmer Rouge soldiers against the soldiers of their two partners in the GCKD (FNLPK and FUNCINPEC); the necessity of unifying the Khmer armed forces after the departure of Vietnamese troops; the lack of popular support for the Khmer Rouge as reported by refugees; the dropping of intellectuals (the regime's prominent individuals and the generation in their forties); reconciliation at the level of political parties and more generally at that of the population (amnesty law).

Khieu Samphan stated:

> Concerning the questions that you ask regarding the present and future of my country, I would prefer to give you a global response intended to clarify several important points that can help you to grasp more firmly the nature, the context, and the scope of our national struggle all at once.

Following this came a historical evocation of Vietnamese objectives in Cambodia and the actions of the GCKD. Among other pearls:

> I would first like to emphasize that the positive and the negative sides of any human action are like two sides of the same coin, and that as the saying goes, "to err is human." The important thing is to see if the errors were committed deliberately or if they were the unexpected result of an effort born of good faith.
>
> In brief, we have always been faithful to our people and to our country. We have always fought for our national dignity. We were able to spare our Kampuchea the sad fate of Laos, which has already become a territorial dependency of Vietnam. But our people on the whole know that we are patriots devoted heart and soul to Kampuchea.

In conclusion:

> Such is my point of view on the situation in Kampuchea and the fundamental considerations that inspire our policy of great national union in the present and the future. The principle having been propounded, each question will be settled in its time based on this principle and in conformity with the concrete situation.

These excerpts are taken from the author's correspondence with Khieu Samphan on 26 August and 2 October 1986 and his responses on 24 October 1986.

# APPENDIX 9: PRINCIPAL POLITICAL PRISONS UNDER THE RPK

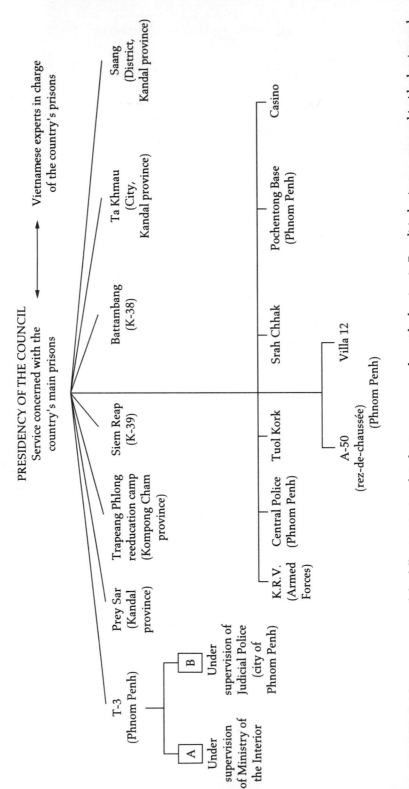

PRESIDENCY OF THE COUNCIL

Service concerned with the country's main prisons ←→ Vietnamese experts in charge of the country's prisons

T-3 (Phnom Penh)

A — Under supervision of Ministry of the Interior

B — Under supervision of Judicial Police (city of Phnom Penh)

Prey Sar (Kandal province)

Trapeang Phlong reeducation camp (Kompong Cham province)

Siem Reap (K-39)

Battambang (K-38)

Ta Khmau (City, Kandal province)

Saang (District, Kandal province)

K.R.V. (Armed Forces)

Central Police (Phnom Penh)

Tuol Kork

Srah Chhak

Pochentong Base (Phnom Penh)

Casino

A-50 (rez-de-chaussée) (Phnom Penh)

Villa 12

Note: T-3 was for the incarceration of the following: in A, political prisoners arrested outside the city; in B, political prisoners arrested inside the city, and criminals. In Phnom Penh, more than 25,000 prisoners entered prisons between 1980 and 1984. The main prisons, as shown in this diagram, were located in Phnom Penh, Battambang, Phnom Penh, and the contiguous province of Kandal. The prisons named

# APPENDIX 10: MEMORANDA LEGALIZING
# THE SETTLEMENT OF VIETNAMESE CIVILIANS
# IN CAMBODIA

Kampuchean People's Revolutionary Party
Central Committee

No. 240 S.R.M. Ch.

Phnom Penh, 13 September 1982

Memorandum

Guide for the application of decision no. 142 S.R.M. Ch. of 7 May 1982, issued from the central committee of the People's Revolutionary party of Cambodia, for solving the problems of Vietnamese nationals who have come to settle and work in Cambodia.

In order to apply correctly the seven points and measures stipulated in decision no. 142 S.R.M. Ch. of 7 May 1982, issued from the central committee of the party, the Secretariat would like to provide a guideline for all relevant levels and sections to permit a good understanding of the following essential points:

1. The application of this departmental memorandum has the goal of reinforcing the bonds of special friendship and fighting solidarity between Cambodia and Vietnam, and of creating conditions favorable to the improvement of relations between the Cambodian people and Vietnamese nationals living in Cambodia so that they may improve each day. This memorandum also has the goal of associating Vietnamese nationals living in Cambodia with the two revolutionary tasks, that is, the defense and the territorial construction of our Cambodia.

2. This memorandum resolves only urgent problems and, among these, protects the lives of Vietnamese nationals who honestly exercise their trade and assures them a certain stability. It represents a step toward the settlement of border passage between the two countries and toward the elimination of bad individuals mixed with the mass of Vietnamese nationals. This

[The two memos in this appendix have been loosely translated, since the use of jargon in the Khmer text precludes a literal translation.]

memorandum does not take up essential long-range problems such as immigrant status, the citizenship of Vietnamese nationals in Cambodia, and the problem of the Khmer-Vietnamese border, which the central committee and the Council of Ministers will resolve through decisions that will be published subsequently.

3. The settlement of the problems of Vietnamese currently living in Cambodia is complex and can, moreover, facilitate the enemy's task of carrying out psychological warfare aiming at separating the two peoples. Consequently, all the levels and sections concerned should strive to act with the greatest rigor and attention. First of all, the cadres must clearly understand the meaning of this work and devote themselves to the indestructible spirit of solidarity between Cambodia and Vietnam. Next, we must pay particular attention to instilling this spirit in the Cambodian population and in Vietnamese nationals wherever they have settled in Cambodia. We must eliminate the narrow nationalist spirit among the Cambodian population as well as among the Vietnamese population. Through this educational work, following after firmly taking the situation in hand, we will divide Vietnamese nationals into different categories, and we will analyze all the measures and define all the appropriate forms of organization.

4. This is one of the aspects of propaganda work to which all institutions (levels and sections) should devote considerable effort to carrying out actively. During the development of this process, they should diligently consult Vietnamese experts and seek out those Vietnamese nationals on whom they can rely in their work and whom they consider capable of propagating it. In places where a great many Vietnamese have settled, we can request the aid of Vietnamese experts and rely on their support to enlighten us and guide us in the work of educating Vietnamese nationals.

5. During the period of application of this memorandum 142 S.R.M. Ch., which began following its signing on 7 May 1982, reports should be sent to the central committee on a regular basis and in a definitive and timely fashion so that the central committee can draw lessons from them and be able to take additional measures.

For the Secretariat of the Central Committee
People's Revolutionary Party of Cambodia

Stamp
Signed: Say Phuthang

Cc.: Ministries
    Services and departments of the central committee
    Provincial administrative party committees
    Presidents of the provincial and municipal people's revolutionary
        committees

Council of Ministers

No. 38 SR

People's Republic of Kampuchea

Independence, Peace, Liberty, Happiness

Phnom Penh, 9 October 1983

Memorandum

To the Honorable:

Comrade Ministers, Comrade Presidents of national institutions subordinate to the central committee, Comrade Presidents of people's revolutionary committees of all provinces and municipalities.

The secretariat of the central committee of the Cambodian People's Revolutionary party issued on 7 May 1982 memorandum no. 142 concerning measures to be taken in regard to Vietnamese civilians coming to settle and work in Cambodia. The secretariat of the central committee also issued on 13 September 1982 a notice to facilitate the application of the above-named memorandum. The present Council of Ministers reminds all ministers and all the provinces and municipalities that the directives contained in the memorandum of the secretariat of the central committee concerning Vietnamese civilians coming to settle in Cambodia are to be literally applied.

Cambodia and Vietnam are two bordering, friendly countries whose peoples have had relations for many generations. Their geopolitical situation and history have welded the two peoples together in the cause of the resistance struggle against the common enemy to defend and construct their nations.

Before 1969, there were approximately 500,000 Vietnamese civilians living in Cambodia. They practiced various trades such as rice grower, fisherman, saltmaker, artisan, and petty merchant. They respected the laws in force in Cambodia as well as the Khmers' customs; they contributed to the revolutionary struggle of the Khmer people, who accepted, supported and helped them.

Under the Lon Nol and Pol Pot regimes and because of the unfriendly policy of these groups, Vietnamese living in Cambodia endured the same fate as Cambodians. They were tortured, executed, or repatriated to Vietnam. Very few survived. After the total liberation of Cambodia, Vietnamese brothers returned to live and work in Cambodia.

In order to consolidate and develop the friendship and fighting solidarity between the peoples of the two countries, Cambodia and Vietnam; in order to ensure the political security and the social order, all the departments and institutions of state under the authority of the central committee and the people's revolutionary committees in all provinces and municipalities should fully understand the following principles and measures relating to Vietnamese civilians coming to reside and make their living in Cambodia.

1. Concerning Vietnamese civilians who previously lived in Cambodia and including those survivors of tortures and massacres by former regimes who have been helped and hidden by the Cambodian population or repatriated to Vietnam and have returned to live and work honestly in Cambodia, the government and the population of Cambodia bring them aid and support and create favorable conditions for their rapid integration in order to stabilize their lives.

2. As for Vietnamese civilians arriving in Cambodia just after the country's liberation, who are settled, who contribute to the restoration and the development of the economy as farmers, woodcutters, fishermen, saltmakers, craftsmen, etc., and who have good relations with the local population and the local authorities, the public authorities of the province, cities, districts, regions, and communes will create conditions useful for their settlement and for the practice of their trades.

3. Concerning Vietnamese nationals who are traitors to the revolution or who participate in illegal activities in the course of their work, violating the law, our authorities and the nearby Vietnamese services such as the [committee for the] organization of Vietnamese troops and [the committee of] Vietnamese experts must take concerted action to pass appropriate measures and render appropriate judgments.

4. As for Vietnamese civilians who have friends or close relatives who want them to come to Cambodia to settle or visit their families, the competent services in Cambodia and Vietnam should authorize them to do so.

5. Concerning the border provinces, the governments of the two countries will issue common instructions for a long-term application, permitting provinces of Cambodia to discuss with Vietnamese border provinces the facilities to be given for dossiers for changes of abode for civilians of the two countries who desire to move to the border communes to earn their living there in an honest fashion. This will take place within an atmosphere of equality, friendship, and mutual interest and with reciprocal respect in order to ensure social order and political security under the supervision of the public powers of the districts and communes of the two sides.

6. Considering the nature and the duties of the present Cambodian revolution, it is necessary to create the conditions that will enable the entire Vietnamese population to receive an appropriate status quickly in order to facilitate work in all fields: education, sustenance, and the Vietnamese popular movements united to serve the two strategic goals of the revolution in our country.

7. Increase supervisory measures of all kinds at each point of crossing; strictly forbid people to come and go illegally.

The services and public institutions under the supervision of the central committee, and all the provinces and municipalities must apply these measures and rules with determination. In order to apply these measures, attention must be paid to the following points:

a. The application of this memorandum must tend to increase the spirit of special friendship and Khmer-Vietnamese fighting solidarity, ceaselessly to create conditions favorable to the relations between the Cambodian people and Vietnamese civilians living in Cambodia, between the rallying movements of the Vietnamese of Cambodia so that they actively participate in the two revolutionary tasks, that is, the defense and construction of our country.

b. This memorandum resolves only a part of the problems concerning the future, viz., the durability of the installation of Vietnamese civilians living honestly in Cambodia, and the elimination of bad elements who hide themselves among the Vietnamese population of Cambodia; and it constitutes a step toward the settlement of the problem of border crossings between the two countries. This memorandum does not resolve basic, long-term problems such as measures concerning nationals with Vietnamese citizenship in Cambodia or that of the crossing of the Khmer-Vietnamese border. However, for all these problems, the central committee and the presidency of the council will issue various memoranda to resolve them later.

c. The solution to the problem of Vietnamese civilians living in Cambodia is very timely and appropriate, but it is very complex. And it is easy for the enemy to foment discord and fear through psychological warfare dividing the two peoples. The central, provincial, and municipal administrations will proceed with care and make all necessary arrangements.

To begin with, action must be taken so that the cadres understand this work and get it thoroughly into their minds, so that they clearly grasp the spirit of staunch Khmer-Vietnamese national solidarity. Next, in the places where there are Vietnamese civilians, they must conscientiously conduct educational work among the Cambodian population as well as among Vietnamese civilians; they must attempt to vanquish manifestations emanating from a narrow nationalism among the Cambodian population as well as among Vietnamese civilians. Through this educational work, they must clearly grasp the nature of the division of the Vietnamese people into categories and try to develop the appropriate measures and forms of organization for administering and educating Vietnamese civilians.

d. This constitutes a part of the work of the popular masses and of the central, provincial, and municipal administrations that must supervise the application of the rules. During this process, clear discussions must be held with the Vietnamese experts, and Vietnamese civilians belonging to the cell [of the Vietnamese Communist party] must be sought out so that they may be used for support in mobilizing popular Vietnamese movements. We can count on the Vietnamese experts for helping us to guide, educate, and explain matters to the Vietnamese civilians wherever they have settled.

e. This memorandum is in force from the day of its signing.

During its period of application, if the central administration, the state institutions, and the provincial and municipal administrations encounter difficulties or any points whatsoever of disagreement or imperfection or any obstacle of any kind, they should quickly report them to the Council of Ministers so that the latter can draw conclusions and issue new instructions for the future. The central departments and the provincial and municipal administrations should regularly prepare a report to the Council of Ministers in order to inform that body of the development of the application of this memorandum.

For the Council of Ministers,

The President,

Seal
Signature of Chan Si

# APPENDIX 11: PROPOSAL BY THE COALITION GOVERNMENT OF DEMOCRATIC KAMPUCHEA FOR A POLITICAL SETTLEMENT OF THE KAMPUCHEAN PROBLEM

This proposal is inspired by the sincere desire of the Kampuchean people and of the CGDK [GCKD] to find a political solution to the Kampuchean problem, and it is based on the relevant resolutions of the United Nations adopted in the course of the last seven consecutive years and on the declaration of the international conference on Kampuchea in 1981.

1. The tripartite Coalition Government of Democratic Kampuchea (CGDK) calls upon the government of the Socialist Republic of Vietnam to enter into negotiations with it in view of discussing the process for the withdrawal of Vietnamese troops from Kampuchea. We do not demand that the Socialist Republic of Vietnam withdraw all of its forces from Kampuchea at once. We accept the withdrawal of Vietnamese forces in two phases in a predetermined period.

Other countries may, in accordance with their judgment, participate in the negotiations for helping to find a political solution to the problem of Kampuchea.

2. After the accord on the process of withdrawal of Vietnamese troops from Kampuchea, there will be a cease-fire in order to permit Vietnam to withdraw its forces in conformity with this accord.

3. The withdrawal of Vietnamese troops and the cease-fire should be directly supervised by a group of UN observers.

4. After the first phase of the withdrawal of Vietnamese troops, Heng Samrin and his faction will enter into negotiations with the tripartite Coalition Government of Democratic Kampuchea in order to form a quadripartite coalition government of Kampuchea, with Samdech Norodom Sihanouk as president and his excellency Son Sann as prime minister, in conformity with the spirit of great national union and national reconciliation such that each of the four parties will have the same rights as political forces in the national community.

5. The quadripartite coalition government of Kampuchea will hold free elections under the supervision of a team of UN observers.

6.  Kampuchea will become an independent country, united in its territorial integrity, with a liberal-democratic regime, peaceful, neutral and nonaligned, with no base for foreign troops on its territory. The neutrality of Kampuchea will be guaranteed by the UN, with the presence of its observation team on the ground during the first two or three years.

7.  Kampuchea gladly welcomes the aid of all the countries of the West as well as the East, and that of neutral and nonaligned countries, for the reconstruction of the country.

8.  Concerning the Socialist Republic of Vietnam, independent Kampuchea, united in its territorial integrity, peaceful, neutral, and nonaligned, is prepared to sign a treaty of nonaggression and peaceful coexistence and to establish for all time commercial and economic relations between the two countries.

The above-stated proposal is made in the interest of the peace of Kampuchea as well as that of peace and security in the region of Southeast Asia and the Asian-Pacific region.

Peking, 17 March 1986

Signed:

Khieu Samphan        Samdech Norodom Sihanouk        Son Sann
Vice-President of                    President of              Prime Minister of CGDK
Democratic Kampuchea        Democratic Kampuchea
in charge of foreign affairs

# APPENDIX 12: AMNESTY INTERNATIONAL MEETING ON CAMBODIA, 10 DECEMBER 1987 IN PARIS—EXCERPTS

*The Amnesty representative*: "I will content myself with a short historical account dealing with questions of a methodological nature."
Regarding the Khmer Rouge period:

> Why did Amnesty remain silent from 1975 to 1979? I believe that there are three important factors involved, which do not, of course, excuse Amnesty's silence but can help explain it. They are:
> 1. The fact that, in 1975, the research department was still underdeveloped. There were three researchers working on all of Asia.

*Author's commentary*: Even if there had been but a single researcher for Asia, it is evident that Cambodia should have held his attention.

> 2. At the time, there were practically no research trips; that is, the department's researchers very, very rarely went out in the field. . . . Above all, they worked on "secondary sources."

*Commentary*: The secondary source consisting of Father Ponchaud's book, from the beginning of 1977, which contained firsthand accounts, was not taken into consideration.

> 3. The third aspect that I think must be considered, is an aspect that we may call ideological. In the months and the years that followed the Laotian, Cambodian, and Vietnamese revolutions, there was, in international public opinion, a very, very favorable prejudice, be it toward the Vietnamese revolution or the Cambodian revolution, that granted the benefit of the doubt to the young Indochinese revolutions. Consequently, the people who worked in London and who did not go on the spot—and thus who did not have the possibility of interviewing refugees—were dependent on the vision that the Cambodian specialists had. These specialists on Cambodia were very often favorable to the regime that established itself on the seventeenth of April 1975.

*Commentary*: Amnesty International thus favored ideological arguments at the expense of reliable secondary sources.

Concerning the present period:

> For six or seven years rather significant resources have been de-
> voted to research. . . . Thus, all the areas that were left blank in the
> past are in the process of being filled in. . . . By 1984, Amnesty had
> been receiving regular information on the human rights situation
> in Cambodia. . . . From 1984 onward, a researcher was recruited, a
> specialist on Cambodia. . . . The first methodological problem that
> we came up against was the question of how to obtain information . . .
> either by going directly to Cambodia or by going to Thailand. To go
> to Cambodia was forbidden us after 1984. It thus has not been possi-
> ble to go into the field to conduct an investigation on human rights.

*Commentary*: This statement is not accurate. Amnesty asked for the first time to go to Phnom Penh in September 1986.

The following portion provided technical data on the camps along the Khmer-Thai border and on the methodology for interviewing former pris-oners, for sifting through the local press, and for using secondary sources that "Amnesty does not use on a high-priority basis."

Concerning the construction of the border wall for which the Vietnamese armed forces requisitioned Cambodian civilians, who were forced to clear malaria-infested and mined forests, a project that caused tens of thousands of deaths:

> *Question (from the audience):* At the time of the Khmer Rouge
> massacres through 1979, Amnesty said nothing, Amnesty did noth-
> ing. Christophe Peschoux had the honesty to admit it. Now Am-
> nesty is launching a campaign on Cambodia; fine, better late than
> never. . . . The problem is the bamboo wall. Nothing was said about
> the first massacre, all right; we're presently working with people
> who are being tortured, very good, but you're still not talking
> about—and I have Amnesty campaign documents to support this
> that were distributed to all the groups in June 1986—there's still
> nothing on the bamboo wall, that is, on the genocide that goes on.
> To make such a monstrous mistake once is already serious, but
> twice is beyond my comprehension.
> *Answer*: I think that the problem of the bamboo wall is no mis-
> take at all; we are perfectly well aware of what is happening. But . . .
> Amnesty functions under a mandate, a mandate with a limited
> scope that concerns itself primarily with the arrest and detention of

individuals for reasons that are either political, religious, philosophical, ethnic, linguistic, or arise from other problems. As for the bamboo wall, we got information about it from the beginning and from various sources; we are perfectly well aware of it. We looked for ways to bend the mandate to allow the inclusion of this matter; and in accordance with Amnesty's mandate, the only possibility of working this problem, of developing it, and of defining a certain number of acts was to succeed in finding people who had been arrested, detained, tortured, or executed [*sic*] for refusing to report for forced labor. The problem of forced labor in Cambodia is not punitive and individual; that is to say, a person is not sent to the Cambodian border, to work on a wall, to plant mines as a punishment. It is a measure that was decided upon at the national level, and practically all Cambodians have gone there. In other words, it is a measure similar to a draft, a military conscription, and you know very well that in these cases Amnesty cannot intervene. We tried to obtain information on individuals who had been arrested and detained for refusing. . . . We have not succeeded in finding a single case.

*Commentary*: In other words, if Cambodians have the misfortune of being killed en masse and within the framework of the regime's laws, this event does not concern Amnesty.

In these conditions, a question arises: is it useful to maintain the organization with its present mandate?

# APPENDIX 13: MOUVEMENT DES ÉTUDIANTS POUR L'INDÉPENDANCE, LA LIBERTÉ, ET LA DÉMOCRATIE (MEILD)

Resolution:

- Having learned through the media of Phnom Penh that SAMDECH has rallied to the Phnom Penh regime, and that He will soon assume a High Position offered by the stated Power,
- In view of the fact that the "Phnom Penh government" is established by and for the Foreigner,
- Observing that the KPRP is only an emanation of the Vietnamese Communist Party,
- In view of the fact that the present regime, incompetent, corrupt, rotten, and unpopular, is on the point of collapse,
- In view of the fact that SAMDECH is the only Khmer Personality capable of achieving national CONSENSUS AFTER THE RETREAT IN 1990 of the FAV [Vietnamese armed forces], and is credible in the international domain for obtaining the international Cooperation necessary for the reconstruction of CAMBODIA,

The MEILD CONGRESS, meeting in extraordinary session, at the University of Phnom Penh on this SUNDAY, 3 JANUARY 1988, unanimously

- begs SAMDECH most affectionately to reconsider his decision to collaborate with the Power in Phnom Penh,
- begs SAMDECH instantly to continue the FIGHT by Force and by Political and Diplomatic Means against the Occupier and his servants until the total and unconditional withdrawal of the FAV [Vietnamese armed forces] and the Proconsuls of the Vietnamese protectorate,
- begs SAMDECH most respectfully never to agree to implicitly legitimize the present regime by meeting with its representatives in betrayal of national interests, while the FAV [Vietnamese armed forces] are on Cambodian soil,
- begs SAMDECH with insistence to demand that Vietnam agree to carry on negotiations directly with Himself, perhaps accompanied by the Phnom Penh authorities, in order to determine the schedule for withdrawal of its troops under appropriate international supervision by 1990 at the latest, as it has formally promised to do,

asks all its members in a brotherly fashion to enlarge and consolidate THEIR SACRED UNION in the COMMON STRUGGLE with OUR BROTHER expatriates and guerrillas until the achievement of NATIONAL INDEPENDENCE and the realization of OUR IDEALS OF LIBERTY AND DEMOCRACY.

Phnom Penh
3 January 1988

# Notes

INTRODUCTION

1. Cambodia and Kampuchea are, respectively, English and Khmer pronunciations of the same word.

2. On Tree Day, 6 July 1965, the director of the Forestry Department, Tan Kim Huon, put forward a figure of 73.8 percent, including sparsely wooded areas.

3. Discovery of hydraulic networks by Bernard Philippe Groslier, visible on aerial photographs. Among others, see Groslier, "Pour une géographie historique du Cambodge," *Cahiers d'outremer*, no. 104 (1973): 337–379.

4. In November of each year (until 1969), when the waters of the Tonle Sap returned to their normal north-south flow, the Water Festival took place in Phnom Penh. During its three days, magnificent canoe races were held among teams from all the country's provinces.

5. Jacques Migozzi, *Cambodge: faits et problèmes de population* (Paris: C.N.R.S., 1973), 44.

## PART 1.  PEACEFUL CAMBODIA

The epigraph, from Aragon's *The Gypsy*, reads: "In those days I was credulous / A single word was a biding promise / And I would think that all the bluebells / Could be passionflowers."

### 1.  A CONSERVATIVE SOCIETY

1. Since the administrative reorganization undertaken by the French at the beginning of the twentieth century, the *srok* is the equivalent of the French district. For peasants *srok* still means native place.

2. Migozzi gives the percentage of rural inhabitants as 87.4 (*Cambodge*, 228).

3. All quoted material otherwise unattributed (in this and later chapters) comes from the author's private interviews with witnesses who asked not to be named; unless otherwise identified all translations are the author's.

4. In the northwest and southeast, the only regions where mechanized cultivation was practiced, the soil was under continuous cultivation so as to produce two or three crops per year and the land belonged to large-scale owners.

5. One individual without any possessions and newly arrived at a camp in Thailand was told to choose several essential items that would be purchased for him. His choice—"socks." He had just been accepted for immigration to France, where he could not arrive with his feet bare inside his shoes.

6. *Charet khmer* (Khmer mentality) (Paris: Cedoreck, 1984); first published as *Kuk noyobay* (Political prison) (Phnom Penh: Apsara Press, 1971).

7. Some of these treaties have been translated into French by Thay Sok, "Traités de morale des Cambodgiens, du XIVe au XIXe siècles" (Thèse pour le doctorat d'université, Paris, 1964). Most of the excerpts from the treatises given below come from this thesis. The January–March 1967 issue of *Études cambodgiennes* referred to the translation into French of a *chbap*, *Morale aux jeunes filles*, written at the end of the nineteenth century or the beginning of the twentieth. The editor added: "This code will perhaps make young modern girls who attend lycées laugh. . . . Nonetheless, despite an extraordinary change in external behavior, this ancient morality is still the one that mothers teach their daughters and that the latter adapt to new conditions." See also the joint studies by Saveros Pou and Philip Jenner appearing in *Bulletin de l'École française d'Extrême-Orient* (1975, 1976, 1977, 1978, 1979, 1981), and the education given to apprentice monks in country schools: the *chbap* are part of the program. See also Meas Yang, "Le bouddhisme au Cambodge," *Études orientales*, no. 6 (1978): 46–47; and the work of Try Sengly, "Le bouddhisme dans la société khmère contemporaine" (Mémoire de l'École pratique des hautes études, section sciences religieuses, Paris, 1986).

8. Son Soubert states, in "The Historical Dimensions of the Present Conflict in Cambodia," in *Buddhism and the Future of Cambodia* (Rithisen Camp, Thailand: Khmer Buddhist Research Center, 1986), 10–17, that France neglected traditional education but established a parallel system of French education, which he says illustrates the alienation of the population by the French. As the Archives d'outremer (hereafter AOM) at Aix-en-Provence demonstrate, this statement is inaccurate. See for example the annual reports of the French residents, who were in charge of the provinces: in the section dealing with education, the most numerous schools are the Khmer pagoda schools. On the technical level, the Khmers have, since 1974, criticized the system; I discuss the subject in chapter 2.

9. Excerpted from *Revue de l'instituteur,* no. 1–2 (1954), reproduced in *Recueil de traductions: thèmes* (Phnom Penh, 1957), 11–12.

10. Pou Choti, "Le cambodgien d'hier et d'aujourd'hui: essai sur les conflits de génération au Cambodge" (Mémoire de 2e année, École technique d'outremer du Havre, 1965), 9.

11. Robert Lemaignen, Léopold Senghor, and Sisowath Youtevong, *La Communauté impériale française* (Paris: Alsatia, 1945), 128.

12. Under the aegis of Jean Delvert, then headmaster of the French lycée Descartes, a "khmer" section was opened, and individuals as eminent as Madeleine Giteau taught Cambodian history and civilization there. Several others did the same in Khmer lycées. Moreover, the Université royale des beaux-arts was set up to study the archeology, ethnology, and history of Cambodia; French instructors, knowing the country, took students to remote villages. In the lycées Khmers gradually replaced the French in teaching history even before the decision to "khmerize" education. Using books written by the French, they were supposed to inculcate in their students notions of Khmer history; the benefit seems to have been minimal.

13. In the refugees' language, the "third country" is the country of definitive resettlement, the country of transit or second country being Thailand (or for some, Vietnam).

14. Sok Vanny, "Réflexion sur la khméritude," *Asie du sud-est et monde insulindien: Cambodge II,* 15, no. 1–4 (1984): 141–144.

15. Sam Sok, *La Future Société khmère* (Maisons-Alfort, 1981), esp. 13.

16. Tith Huon, "Problème de l'assainissement dans la fonction publique cambodgienne" (Thèse pour le doctorat en sciences administratives, Université de Paris II, 1976), 159.

17. It is known that the Khmer kings periodically rewrote history. See the various versions of the *Royal Chronicles* and particularly the analysis of Mak Phoeun, *Chroniques royales du Cambodge de 1594 à 1677: traduction française avec comparaisons des différentes versions et introduction* (Paris: École française d'Extrême-Orient, 1981). See also Prince Sihanouk's attempt to rehabilitate King Norodom, particularly *Rois de Kampuchea: Ang Duong, Norodom, N. Sihanouk;* it does not mention Kings Sisowath and Monivong, who do not belong to the Norodom branch but reigned for a total of thirty-seven years. Today, for political reasons, some Khmers holding scientific degrees and some of Sihanouk's relatives challenge the article by A. G. Haudricourt (which, however, they have not read) wherein the author definitively classifies Vietnamese in the Mon-Khmer language family. This article, "De l'origine des tons en vietnamien," *Journal asiatique,* no. 242 (1954): 69–82, is considered authoritative throughout the entire world; in it Haudricourt confirms the hypotheses of the first linguists with decisive arguments on phonological relevancy and phonetic change.

18. On this point, see the work of Charles Meyer, *Derrière le sourire khmer* (Paris: Plon, 1971).

19. Jacques Brunet discusses appearance in "Règles de courtoisie chez les khmers," *Asie du sud-est et monde insulindien: Cambodge I*, 13, no. 1–4 (1982): 13–21.

20. Pou Choti, "Le cambodgien," 17.

21. Lemaignen et al., *Communauté impériale française*, 127.

22. Sam Sok, *Future Société khmère*, 13.

23. Letter of 23 March 1987 to the author; original emphasis.

24. "L'ingratitude du crocodile," a tale summarized by Chim Sunli in the *Revue de l'amitié franco-khmère* (Service français d'Information du Cambodge), no. 39 (1955): 24.

25. Sok Vanny, "Réflexion sur la khméritude," 144.

26. *Mandarin* is a Chinese word adopted by the Khmers as *montrey*, to designate a high official.

27. Interview granted to the author on 3 February 1987, in Paris. Sim Var died on 12 October 1989.

28. Buddhist tradition expects the faithful to behave in a more pious manner one day per week; these days occur on the eighth and fifteenth days of the rising moon and on the eighth and fifteenth days of the declining moon.

29. Forest gathering was conducted by highland Khmers and by the Pear, a minority speaking a Mon-Khmer language and inhabiting the foothills.

30. For popular religion see Ang Choulean, *Les Êtres surnaturels dans la religion populaire khmère* (Paris: Cedoreck, 1986).

31. AOM Aix-en-Provence, Amiraux 10 321.

32. AOM Aix-en-Provence, Gougal 20.1.17, dossier 26 918 and Gougal 1885, dossier 7 814; AOM Paris, Indo AOO 29, carton 2 and Indo AF carton 26 D A 71, dossier 18.

33. AOM Aix-en-Provence, Amiraux 11 738, letter dated 13 May 1875.

34. Tith Huon, "Problème," 125.

35. The posts for Khmers only were those of exchange agent; consignee for boats and maritime agent; intelligence agent and private policeman; immigration and emigration agent; placement agent; licensed dealer for firms buying and selling various products; arms and munitions dealer; maker or seller of wireless receivers or of spare parts for them; printer; barber (owner or employee); secondhand dealer or moneylender; coastal or river pilot; jeweler or goldsmith (owner or employee); driver of taxis or transport vehicles; docker; owner or operator of lumber concern; grain dealer; salt merchant.

36. At the time ten riels equaled one franc at the official rate; one kilogram of rice cost one riel.

37. This magical conception did not limit itself to goods; the Khmers willingly attribute what they cannot understand to supernatural powers. A widespread legend in Cambodia credits the construction of the archeological ensemble of Angkor to the gods.

38. Say Bory, "L'administration rurale au Cambodge et ses projets de réforme" (Thèse pour le doctorat en sciences administratives, Université de Paris II, 1974), 27. See in particular the author's original second part, which represents an excellent contribution to the study of Khmer society.

39. The account of these movements is painstakingly reported in two illustrated monthly journals headed by Prince Sihanouk at the time: *Sangkum* and particularly *Kambuja*.

40. In Cambodian common law, the king is the owner of the soil; those who exploit it have usufructuary rights to it.

41. Jacques Népote, *Parenté et organisation sociale dans le Cambodge moderne et contemporain: quelques aspects et quelques applications des modèles les régissant* (Geneva: Olizane, 1992); Marie Alexandrine Martin, *Les Khmers daeum, "Khmers de l'origine": société montagnarde et exploitation de la forêt; de l'écologie à l'histoire* (forthcoming).

42. Sok Vanny, "Réflexion sur la khméritude," 143.

43. Here and in the rest of the text, I refer to *clan* not in its ethnological sense but in its figurative connotation of a small closed group of persons with common ideas and tastes.

44. "Le lien de filiation au Cambodge," in *Lieux de l'enfance*, no. 11 (1987): 59–75.

45. Ibid., 7.

46. *Notes cambodgiennes: au coeur du pays khmer* (1921), 2d ed. (Paris: Cedoreck, 1983), 131.

47. AOM Aix-en-Provence, Amiraux 10 300, letter from the governor general dated 27 August 1885.

## 2. THE COLONIAL HERITAGE

1. The name *Vietnam* was established in 1802; the capital of the kingdom was in Hue. When France began its colonial rule in 1859 it divided the region into several entities: the protectorates of Cambodia, Laos, Tonkin, and Annam as well as the colony of Cochin China (Mekong delta, formerly the property of the Cambodian crown), certain of whose provinces both Vietnam and Cambodia claimed. At the time of decolonization Vietnam received the whole of Cochin China. (On Cochin China, see pp. 39–44.) The Cambodians still use the name *Kampuchea Krom* for the Mekong delta provinces.

2. Adémar Leclère, *Histoire du Cambodge*, 2d ed. (1914; Phnom Penh: Nokor Thom, 1974), 459. "Four-Arms" designates Phnom Penh, site of the confluence of four rivers: the Upper Mekong, the Lower Mekong, the Tonle Sap, and the Bassac.

French administrators and researchers studied certain periods or aspects of the protectorate. For the researchers, see Pierre Lamant, "Les prémices des relations politiques entre le Cambodge et la France vers le milieu du XIX siècle," *Revue française d'histoire d'outremer* 72, no. 267 (1985): 167–198; Alain Forest, *Le Cambodge et la colonisation française: histoire d'une colonisation sans heurts (1897–1920)* (Paris: L'Harmattan, 1980). For another source, the colonial archives and political correspondence filed at the Quai d'Orsay contain a great deal of information. To this day only a single Khmer, Sarin Chhak, has studied this crucial period in the history of his country.

3. These events are mentioned in Leclère, *Histoire du Cambodge*, 499 ff.; and David P. Chandler, *A History of Cambodia* (Boulder, Colo.: Westview Press, 1983), 123–133.

4. Jean Moura, *Le Royaume du Cambodge* (Paris: Ernest Leroux, 1883), 2:131. The six provinces in question were Saigon, Bien-hoa, Mi-tho, Vinh-long, Chau-doc, Ha-tien.

5. Letter of de Montigny to the minister of foreign affairs, 8 May 1857, Archives du ministère des affaires étrangères (hereafter AAE), Paris, correspondance politique, Siam, 417.

6. The letter from Ang Duong to Napoleon III, dated 25 November 1856, was read in part by Princess Yukanthor to the Assembly of the French Union during the meeting on 19 May 1949 dealing with the status of Cochin China (Assemblée de l'union française, *Annales*, no. 1 [1949]: 515). For details of the relations between Ang Duong and France see Lamant, "Les prémices."

7. Letter from the comte de Chasseloup-Laubat to the minister of the navy, 7 May 1862, Paris AAE, correspondance politique, Siam II, 322–324.

8. Letter from Admiral de la Grandière to the French consul at Bangkok, 26 August 1863, Paris AAE, correspondance politique, Siam II, 390–391.

9. Communication from Ong Phra Norodom Maha Uparat to His Excellency Chow Phya Kalahome, 15 August 1863, Paris AAE, correspondance politique, Siam II, 407–408.

10. Mak Phoeun and Po Dharma, "La première intervention militaire vietnamienne au Cambodge (1658–1659)," *Bulletin de l'École française d'Extrême-Orient* 73 (1984): 285–318.

11. Leclère, *Histoire du Cambodge*, 495.

12. Letter dated 29 April 1867; original emphasis. This document and the two others cited may be found in AOM under AF A30 (12), carton 11.

13. Letter from the minister of the navy and colonies to the minister of foreign affairs, 8 January 1865, Paris AAE, correspondance politique, Siam II, 93; original emphasis.

14. Leclère, *Histoire du Cambodge*, 498.

15. *Les Écoles d'art de l'Indochine* (Hanoi: Gouvernement général de l'Indochine, 1937), 6, 8.

16. AOM, Gougal 21 740, letter from the resident superior of Cambodia to the French resident at Stung Treng, 1905. For details on the administrative reforms see Forest, *Le Cambodge et la colonisation française*.

17. In this context the slavery consisted of corvée, unpaid labor due from subjects to their sovereign.

18. AOM, Aix-en-Provence, Résuper, F(03) 153, rapport d'ensemble année 1888. In 1936 it was the minister of the navy and colonies who was concerned: "It is my strong conviction that the indigenous populations are presently subjected to a fiscal regime that is too severe" (AOM, Paris, Indo NF dossier 639, carton 55, letter of 12 August 1936 to the governor general of Indochina). A detailed account of these taxes and duties is given in Forest, *Le Cambodge et la colonisation française*, 191–232.

19. AOM, Amiraux, 10 236, report from the governor general of Cochin China to the minister of the navy and colonies, 15 April 1882.

20. AOM Aix-en-Provence, Résuper, F(03) 105, 1922, quarterly reports by the resident superior.

21. In 1908, forty-five years after the establishment of the protectorate, for all of Cambodia the following personnel were in service: Europeans—one departmental head, nine professors (two of whom were temporary), eight schoolmistresses (five temporary), one master on duty; non-Europeans—forty schoolmasters (sixteen in Phnom Penh and twenty-four in the provinces), including thirty-three Khmers, six Annamese, and one naturalized Frenchman (AOM Aix-en-Provence, Résuper, F(03) 94, annual reports).

22. In 1935–36 the renovated pagoda schools had 25,166 regular students and the Franco-indigenous primary schools had around 1,000. There was only one French primary school in Phnom Penh, the École Norodom, and no lycée in the provinces. Professional education was at a very reduced level (fewer than 150 students). In 1884 a proposal to create industrial and agricultural schools, an intelligent project aimed at improving the well-being of the population, was made by a man named Pelletier (the proposal was not pursued). The only higher establishment was the École supérieure d'application, which became the École supérieure de Pali, a part of the famous Institut bouddhique de Phnom Penh.

23. Ministère de l'Information, "L'oeuvre de la France en Indochine: l'enseignement," *Notes documentaires et études* série coloniale 13, no. 108 (1945).

24. AOM, Aix-en-Provence, Résuper, F(03)95, rapports généraux, and F(03)103; Annuaires statistiques de l'Indochine, vol. 12, 1947–1948, Haut commissariat de France en Indochine: see tables on 14, 20. Since Ho Chi Minh had proclaimed the Democratic Republic of Vietnam in the north in 1945, France was concentrating its efforts on Annam and especially on Cochin China, which had become key for maintaining its presence in this new territorial ensemble henceforth called Vietnam.

25. AOM, Aix-en-Provence, 3E9 (1).

26. Maurice Guichard, "Hévéa: aménagements des plantations en Indochine" (Mémoire de l'École pratique coloniale du Havre, 1953), 2.

27. AOM, Paris, A50 NF 202, carton 181, letter of 8 October 1917.

28. This situation has changed little. In 1970 the French were above all

familiar with the Phnom Penh–Sihanoukville and the Phnom Penh–Kep routes, which led to the sea, and the road to Kirirom, a low-altitude pine tract equipped as a spa.

29. Sarin Chhak, *Les Frontières du Cambodge* (Paris: Dalloz, 1966); Chhak has carefully studied the French overseas archives, and his analysis of this source largely inspires the following considerations.

30. Report by Commander Alleyron of 22 June 1866, quoted by Sarin Chhak, ibid., 1:66 ff.

31. Ibid., 72, 77, 83.

32. Ibid., 121.

33. I am quoting the official French translation, which differs from the Cambodian text. I shall discuss the Khmer text and translation more thoroughly elsewhere, and here I note only errors concerning the territorial claims. The term "province," used in the translation, is inappropriate for translating the word *srok*, which was probably mentioned in either its former sense, "locality, native region," or as the equivalent of district. Since Saigon was part of Dong-nay province, it may concern two different *srok*. I include the *srok* of Bassac and Moat Chruk, which appear in the Khmer text but were missing from the French translation; I omit the words "or Ha-tien" that are not in the Khmer text. Cô-Trol (Kah Tral) and Trelach are the Cambodian names for the islands of Phu-Quoc and Poulo Condore.

34. Assemblée de l'union française, *Annales*, no. 1 (1949): 305 ff.

35. Regarding the question of Kampuchea Krom–Cochin China, see the debates in the Assembly of the French Union during March, April, and May 1949 (Assemblée de l'union française, *Annales*, no. 1 [1949]: 255–542); reports of debates in the French National Assembly for March, May, and June 1949; those of the Senate (then Conseil de la République) for May 1949 (ibid., 1252 ff.).

36. Author's personal interview with Norodom Sihanouk, 20 November 1986, Roissy-en-France.

### 3. THE BIRTH OF NATIONALISM

1. Etymologically, *issarak* comes from the Pali *issara* (the master, he who has the power). Alain Daniel thinks that another meaning given by the official Khmer dictionary, "he who strolls about freely," explains the translation "Free Khmers." Since this translation leads to confusion with Khmer *serei*, which literally means "Free Khmers," I designate the groups as Khmer *issarak* and Khmer *serei*, just as the Khmers do. These expressions refer both to the movements and to their partisans.

2. Author's interview with Keng Vannsak on 12 November 1982, Montmorency.

3. Published in *Moulkhmer* (October 1987): 14, 21.

4. *Le Peuple khmer lutte pour l'indépendance et la paix* (Service

d'information du gouvernement de la résistance khmère, reissued by Agence d'information de la république démocratique du Vietnam, 1954).

5. AOM, Paris, NF, carton 3933, dossier 32488; AOM, Aix-en-Provence, Gougal, F(03)119. Students' accounts here (as in later chapters) are excerpts from testimonies.

6. Chandler, *A History of Cambodia*, 169.

7. Pierre Lamant, "Le Cambodge et la décolonisation de l'Indochine: les caractères particuliers du nationalisme khmer de 1936 à 1945," in *Les Chemins de la décolonisation de l'empire colonial français* (Paris: Centre national de la recherche scientifique, 1986), 189–199.

8. Boun Chan Mul, *Charet khmer* (Khmer mentality), 2d ed. (Paris: Cedoreck, 1984); first published as *Kuk noyobay* (Political prisons) (Phnom Penh: Apsara Press, 1971).

9. Author's interview with Sim Var, 28 January 1987, Paris.

10. As chapter 7 explains, Saloth Sar was known as Bang Pot in the maquis (during the 1960s and probably also the 1950s), then as Pol Pot under the Democratic Kampuchea regime.

11. Cambodians follow Theravada Buddhism, also known as the Lesser Vehicle; it comprises two sects: the Mohanikay, to which the majority of the population belongs, and the Thomayuth, to which the royal family and some high-ranking officials belong.

12. Interview with Sim Var, 28 January 1987.

13. The Liberal party and the Democratic party seem to have been formed during the same month, even though the French give February and March 1946 for the former and April 1947 for the latter. See Pierre Lamant, "Les partis politiques et les mouvements de résistance khmère vus par les services de renseignements français (1945–1952)," *Guerres mondiales et conflits contemporains*, no. 148 (1987): 79–96.

14. Interview with Sim Var, 28 January 1987.

15. The government of the Constituent Assembly included Sisowath Youtevong (vice-president and interior); Chhean Vâm (education); Prak Sarinn (health); Sisowath Watchayavong (justice); Son Sann (finance); Pen Samel (economy); Huy Kanthoul (propaganda and information); Ouk Touch (supply); Van Chheu (public worship, religious education, and fine arts); Penn Nouth (state). The composition of this government and the following ones, given by Cambodians, has been verified and sometimes supplemented from Philippe Preschez, *Essai sur la démocratie au Cambodge*, série C, recherche no. 4 (Paris: Centre d'Études des relations internationales, 1961).

16. Norodom Sihanouk, *Souvenirs doux et amers* (Paris: Hachette, 1981), 148.

17. The first Democratic government in the National Assembly included Chhean Vâm (presidency of the council, and education); Son Sann (vice-presidency, economic relations, finances and planning); Meakh Kon

(finances); Huy Mong (defense); Yut Sann (interior); Yem Sambaur (interior, deputy to the police); Sonn Mam (health); Pitou de Monteiro (justice); Thonn Ouk (information); Ith Seam (communications, industry, provisioning); Huy Kanthoul (public worship, fine arts, social action); Son Voeunsai (public works). The two counselors, Penn Nouth and Prince Monipong, declined to serve.

18. The parties represented were the Democratic party, the Liberal party, the Progressive party (Norodom Montana), the Khmer Renovation party (military men Nhiek Tioulong and Lon Nol), the National Rectification party (Yem Sambaur), the People's party (Sam Nhean), the National Union party (Khim Tit), the Party of the Victorious Northeast (Mao Chay).

19. Fifty-four seats compared to eighteen for the Liberals, two for Khmer Renovation, four for the Party of the Victorious Northeast (a newcomer), none for National Rectification, the Progressives, the People's party, and two other recently formed parties, the National Union party and the independents.

20. The last Democratic government in the National Assembly included Huy Kanthoul (presidency and social action); Khuon Nay (vice-presidency, justice, and public worship); Duon Sam An (finance); Sok Chhong (economy); Son Voeunsai (defense and interior); Sonn Mam (public health and foreign affairs); Pach Chhoeun (information); Entaravong (public health and communications); Thonn Ouk (education, youth, and fine arts).

21. In this regard see Serge Thion and Jean-Claude Pomonti, *Des courtisans aux partisans: la crise cambodgienne* (Paris: Gallimard, 1971).

22. Intervention by Sok Chhong during the 3 March 1949 session (*Annales de l'Assemblée de l'union française* 1 [1949]: 115).

23. It was in this establishment and in another private school, Chamroeun Vichea, that the future Khmer Rouge leaders taught for many years; see chapter 5.

24. Union des nationalistes khmers, "Samdech Norodom Sihanouk répond à ses détracteurs," *Bulletin d'information de l'Union des nationalistes khmers*, special issue (April 1986).

4. SIHANOUK'S POLITICS: A FRAGILE EQUILIBRIUM

1. This legend tells of the murder of a king who decided to test his gardener by pretending to steal some cucumbers of which he was very fond and for which he had assigned care to the gardener. The latter, mistaking his sovereign for a thief, killed him and was in turn anointed king by the people.

2. Say Bory, "L'administration rurale," 24. In the text, parenthetical page numbers for subsequent quotations from Say Bory refer to this work.

3. Ros Chantrabot, "La république khmère et l'Asie du sud-est après son écroulement" (Diplôme de l'École des hautes études en sciences sociales, 1978), esp. 13.

4. Tep Chhieu Kheng, "Notre jeunesse (JSRK)," *Sangkum* (August 1965): 30–31. Son Sann's speech, which closed a JSRK cadre training session on 3 July 1967, exhorted the young people to civic responsibility and to "the necessity of continuous and sustained work" but explained nothing.

5. Norodom Sihanouk, "Étude corrective de la constitution du Cambodge octroyée par le roi en 1947," *France-Asie* 11, no. 108 (1955): 659, 661.

6. The measures led one author to write that Cambodia was under a regime of "semidirect democracy" or was a "semidemocracy" (Preschez, *Essai*, 6, 75).

7. Ros Chantrabot, "La république khmère," 13.

8. Journalist Bernard Hamel published a paper on this subject with photographs provided by Phnom Penh's ministry of information: "Le surprenant parcours du prince Sihanouk," *Historia*, no. 391 (1979): 88–98.

9. At the end of the 1960s this pattern obtained in Trapeang Chheu Tatrav (Russey Chrum valley, Kah Kong province). The mayor, who came from the plain, carried out a lucrative traffic in local forest products with the Chinese of his native village. The peasants who collected the products had no recourse and were thoroughly fleeced. Further south, at Thmar Bang, the subprefect and the local merchant were the law.

10. Tith Huon, "Problème," 112. In the text, parenthetical page numbers for subsequent quotations from Tith Huon refer to this work.

11. In Southeast Asia a Chinese merchant's house often consists of a succession of rooms separated by simple partitions that the visitor passes through in linear fashion; the French call this unique construction a *compartiment* (compartment).

12. Author's interview with Sim Var, 28 January 1987, Paris.

13. Meyer, *Derrière le sourire khmer*, 179.

14. For details of the scandals caused by corruption, see the tables in Tith Huon, "Problème," 43–46, 63–65, 69–73.

15. Two comparative tables of the monthly *Sangkum* (no. 13 [July 1966]: 39) show the state of the health and sanitation situation in 1955 and afterward. I cite only statistics for 1955 (first figure) and 1965 (second figure): hospitals, 16/36; health centers, 0/6; dispensaries, 3/13; infirmaries, 100/385; maternity centers, 60/518; number of beds, 2,445/4,650; physicians, 77/326; pharmacists, 4/37; dentists, 3/15; male and female nurses, 630/2,137; midwives, 52/206; rural midwives, 73/598; sanitary agents (health officers), 0/299.

16. Author's interview with Chhay Han Cheng (former minister of health), 6 March 1987, Paris.

17. The experience in Spean Khda village (or, as some officials named the village, Thmar Bang) typified these desertions: the teacher and nurse did not last one year, and the employee assigned to meteorological records was absent about six months out of twelve. Further north, the dispensary at Russey Chrum, opened in 1967, was in service only the day of its inauguration by Prince Sihanouk.

18. Kao Kan, "Les relations sino-cambodgiennes (1963–1970)" (Thèse pour le doctorat en études politiques, Paris, École pratique des hautes études 6e section, 1973), 197.

19. To give an idea of such modifications, here are the published official figures for 1954 and 1964, respectively: public primary schools, 982/2,227; public primary school students, 130,628/362,704; Khmer primary teachers, 30/52; high schools, 7/85; high school students, 3,813/56,933; Khmer high school teachers, 1/17; technical schools, 5/10; technical students, 334/3,814; Khmer technical teachers, 0/7; faculties or higher schools, 2/37; higher school students, 347/4,763; Khmer higher school teachers, 19/124 (the figure for 1963). The figures for pagoda schools come from the *Bulletin de statistiques scolaires: l'évolution de l'enseignement au Cambodge* (Phnom Penh: Ministère de l'éducation nationale et des beaux-arts, 1965).

20. These data are recorded in a balance sheet presented by the journal *Kambuja*, no. 8 (May 1965): 72–73.

21. Concerning the development of education, its Khmerization, and the literacy campaign, see the articles by the then minister of education, Vann Molyvann, in the journal *Sangkum*, particularly the issues of July and September 1967 and July and October 1969. For the people's university see S. C., "L'université populaire," *Kambuja*, no. 16 (July 1966).

22. "L'éducation nationale sous l'ancien régime," *Cambodge nouveau* (June 1970): 38.

23. Hu Nim, "Les services publics économiques au Cambodge" (Thèse pour le doctorat en droit, Phnom Penh, 1965), 262, 266.

24. For more details on growing rice see Jean Delvert, *Le Paysan cambodgien* (Paris–The Hague: Mouton, 1961).

25. Author's interview with Norodom Sihanouk, 20 November 1986, Roissy-en-France.

26. Author's interview with Keat Chhon, 2 February 1987, Paris.

27. Rémy Prud'homme, *L'Économie du Cambodge* (Paris: Presses universitaires de France, 1969), 88.

28. Interview with Prince Sihanouk, 20 November 1986.

29. "Rapport de Sahachivini Tip Mam sur la situation de la main-d'oeuvre," *Sangkum*, no. 25 (August 1967): 7.

30. Author's interview with Prince Sihanouk, 8 December 1986, Roissy-en-France.

31. The silk-cotton tree (*Malvaceae* family) is abundant in Africa and has at its base large abutting aerial roots that extend and crawl along the ground. The tree that flourishes at Angkor (*Datiscaceae* family) also has such structures and crawling roots; for this reason the French in Cambodia incorrectly called it *fromager* (silk-cotton tree).

32. In 1969 a French couple teaching at the Siam Reap lycée—on the Angkor road—had not yet visited the temples after three months' residence but had spent several weekends at Sihanoukville, five hundred kilometers away.

33. Interview with Prince Sihanouk, 20 November 1986.

34. Supplement to *Réalités cambodgiennes,* 12 September 1969.

35. Kao Kan, "Les relations sino-cambodgiennes," 282.

36. One of these intermediaries was Monique Sihanouk's mother, called "the witch of the doorway to Chamcar Mon palace."

37. Ros Chantrabot, "La république khmère," 25–26.

38. Kao Kan, "Les relations sino-cambodgiennes," 3–28.

39. Ibid., 32.

40. Excerpts from Norodom Sihanouk's speeches, respectively: "Very Serious, Very Grave Warning to the American-South Vietnamese," Phnom Penh, 15 February 1964; "Important Press conference at Kep-sur-Mer," 16 February 1964; "Inauguration of School Buildings at Phum Tuol Kruos, Khemarak-Phouminville," 24 February 1964.

41. The journal *Études cambodgiennes,* no. 4 (October–December 1964): 11, mentions "a protocol agreement on terms according to which the People's Republic of China grants to Cambodia very considerable and completely unconditional new military aid."

42. Kao Kan, "Les relations sino-cambodgiennes," 141. The author states that these two articles summarize an account of the military protocol signed on 25 November 1965 between China and Cambodia, printed in "Kung-fei shen-tou chien-pu-chai shu-yao" (Essential account of the penetration of Cambodia by the Chinese Communists), *Feiching yüeh-pao* (Communist questions monthly) 12, no. 10 (30 November 1969): 347.

43. The change resulted from pressure by American intellectuals, who prevented their government from destroying civil installations in North Vietnam with their giant bombers, which (with a few exceptions) carried out raids against military objectives; they were in use on a large scale and indiscriminately in Cambodia. The Americans thus lost the war for psychological reasons.

44. *Sangkum,* no. 46 (May 1969): 26.


5. HARBINGERS OF CHANGE

1. When the association became the UEK, the Khmer title of its bulletin was first *Sahaphiep Nisset* (students' union), then *Sahaphiep Nisset Khmer* (Khmer students' union, or UEK).

2. Association des étudiants khmers, *Bulletin,* no. 11 (January 1951): 5.

3. Author's interview with Keng Vannsak, 10 November 1982, Montmorency.

4. Ibid. Hou Yuon, who was part of the Khmer Rouge team, was killed in 1975 because he disapproved of the evacuation of Phnom Penh. Phung Ton, on a mission to France in April 1975, returned in December 1975 to his family in Cambodia and was killed by his Khmer Rouge comrades. His widow is believed to have survived the regime.

5. The UEK asked to be officially represented at this festival as part of the delegation assembled by Phnom Penh. The daily newspaper *La Dépêche* (19 July 1962) reported the prince's refusal, emphasizing that the UEK, "led by a group of Marxist students, is opposed to the community of overseas Khmers loyal to the ideals of Sangkum."

6. During the 1961–1962 academic year the UEK sent representatives to the world festival of Youth and Students for Peace and Friendship at Helsinki, to the seventh meeting of organizations belonging to the World Federation of Democratic Youth at Warsaw, to the seventh congress of the International Union of Students at Leningrad, to the tenth Festival de Lille organized by the UNEF. See the 28-page report of UEK activities for 1961–1962.

7. Union des étudiants khmers, *Bulletin* (1965): 1.

8. Ibid., no. 3 (May 1958): 18. This motion, drawn up on 5 March 1958, carried an endorsement at the end of the text: "The assembly of Khmer students and residents voted unanimously in favor of this appeal, after having considered the motions and letters from students of Montpellier, Switzerland, and Belgium."

9. In Cambodian, Laotian, and Siamese *yuon* is the usual term designating the Vietnamese. The Vietnamese have not had a good press in these countries for a long time, and to name them is to speak of the long-standing enemy. But the term does not "literally mean savage," as Nayan Chanda asserts in *Brother Enemy: The War after the War; A History of Indochina since the Fall of Saigon* (New York: Harcourt Brace Jovanovich, 1986), 52; cf. the definition given in the official Khmer dictionary, *Vacananukram Khmaer* (Phnom Penh: Buddhist Institute, 1968), 955. After the Geneva Accords many townspeople recognized the names Vietnam, Vietminh, and Vietcong. The peasants had contact with the Vietminh during the *issarak* interlude but continued to use the term *yuon* to designate inhabitants of Vietnam in general, without the pejorative connotation that Khmer politicians and foreigners impute to it.

10. Union des étudiants khmers, "L'abandon d'Angkor par les Khmers," *Bulletin* (June 1964): 31. *Thnot*, which means sugar palm tree, is a pseudonym.

11. Author's interview with Norodom Sihanouk, 20 November 1986, Roissy-en-France.

12. He was the second in command at the first refugee camp, known as camp 204, which appeared on the Khmer-Thai border to the north of Aranhaprathet in 1979. His swindling was soon recognized; Thai authorities conducted a cleanup operation and closed the camp. André Ouk Thol disappeared.

13. See in particular *Sangkum*'s issues of March, April, August, and October 1969.

14. Interview with Prince Sihanouk, 20 November 1986.

15. Meyer, *Derrière le sourire khmer*, 183.

16. *Études cambodgiennes*, no. 8 (October–December 1966): 4.

17. Interview with Prince Sihanouk, 20 November 1986.

18. Meyer, *Derrière le sourire khmer*, 184.

19. Recall that the JSRK was a youth movement created by Prince Sihanouk to support Sangkum. The statement that the peasants rose "against land grabbing by an officially sponsored youth group" (Nayan Chanda, *Brother Enemy*, 63) incorrectly imputes responsibility for the revolt to members of the JSRK.

20. Kao Kan, "Les relations sino-cambodgiennes," 347.

21. Meyer, *Derrière le sourire khmer*, 303; see its detailed explanation of these three historically important days.


PART 2.  CAMBODIA IN AGONY

The first epigraph, from Brassens's "Mourir pour des idées" (To die for an idea), reads: "If all it took were a few mass murders / To finally change everything, settle everything / Since so many times so many heads have fallen / By now we'd have achieved heaven on earth / But the Golden Age is forever in the future / The gods are always thirsty, never have enough / And it is death, death always renewed."

The lines from Apollinaire's work *Le guetteur mélancolique* (The melancholy watcher) read: "Sunsets will never win over the dawn / Let us wonder at the evenings, let us live the mornings / Let us despise what will not change, like stone and gold / Springs that will go dry."


6.  DISASTERS OF THE REPUBLICAN PERIOD

1. Meyer, *Derrière le sourire khmer*, 305.

2. Ros Chantrabot, "La république khmère," 50.

3. Many commentators claim that the French provoked anti-Vietnamese feeling among the Khmers. In his 1978 thesis, "Cambodia before the French: Politics in a Tributary Kingdom, 1794–1848," David P. Chandler, who has examined Khmer, Siamese, Vietnamese, and other sources, demonstrates the power and extent of this enmity among the Cambodian population from the beginning of the nineteenth century—antedating French influence in the region.

4. Meyer, *Derrière le sourire khmer*, 314.

5. Only male descendants of King Ang Duong could ascend the Khmer throne. In 1955 Sihanouk abdicated in favor of his father, Suramarit. At the latter's death there was no successor, and the queen mother Kossomak became the guardian of the vacated throne.

6. Inhabitants of remote regions, such as certain communes in the Cardamom Mountains that had never seen the prince, remained indifferent

to the announcement of his removal. Three things were important to them, and they did not suspect that these were threatened—peace, fallow fields, and the family.

7. In *Brother Enemy* Nayan Chanda writes (121): "The March 1970 coup d'état in Phnom Penh against Prince Sihanouk, and the American invasion of Cambodia that followed, finally removed the last barriers." It is appropriate to add that for many years Cambodian borders had been violated by B-52s as well as by Vietnamese artillery, and that the first invasion after the coup and the appeal launched from Peking by Prince Sihanouk was that of the Vietcong in March 1970.

8. The decisions made in Washington concerning Cambodia and the responsibilities of the president and his adviser are related in detail in William Shawcross, *Sideshow: Kissinger, Nixon, and the Destruction of Cambodia* (New York: Simon and Schuster, 1979). No teak trees grow in Cambodia, and the beautiful species decorating the streets was *koki* (*Hopea odorata*), from which the bark was removed to make, notably, a medicine for treating toothaches, and a replacement for the areca nut in betel-leaf masticatories (ibid., 184).

9. Kao Kan, "Les relations sino-cambodgiennes," 144.

10. Author's interview with Sim Var, 28 January 1987, Paris.

11. The Chams are the descendants of the survivors of the Champa empire—located in the center of the present Vietnam, absorbed by the latter from the thirteenth to sixteenth centuries—joined by the arrival of Malayans and other members of the same linguistic family. The Chams are linguistically distinguished by their membership in the Malayo-Polynesian family, while the Khmers belong to the Mon-Khmer family. Thus, to include them all in a "Mon-Khmer-Malayo-Polynesian" group, or to consider the question of the assimilation of the notion of race to that of linguistic family, would be absurd.

12. *Le Néo-Khmérisme*, revised edition (Phnom Penh [1972?]).

13. Ros Chantrabot, "Aperçu chronologique," in *La République khmère, an IV* (Paris, 1974), 5. In the text, parenthetical page numbers for subsequent quotations from Ros Chantrabot refer to this short work.

14. *Revue de l'armée*, no. 5 (February 1971): 23.

15. I am grateful to Charles Meyer for calling my attention to this point.

16. Ros Chantrabot, "La république khmère," 97.

17. Author's interview with Son Sann, 11 June 1987, Paris.

18. *Pékin Information*, 30 March 1970, 21.

19. *Pékin Information*, 18 May 1970, 11.

20. *Pékin Information*, 30 March 1970, 13.

21. *Pékin Information*, 11 May 1970, 3–5.

22. *Revue de l'armée*, no. 6 (September 1971): 15.

23. Ith Sarin, *Poor Cambodia* (Phnom Penh, 1973); for a translation from the Khmer, see Nguon Kami, "Pauvre Cambodge," *Asie du sud-est et monde insulindien: Cambodge II* 15, no. 1–4 (1984): 201–233.

24. Étienne Manac'h, *Mémoires d'Extrême-Asie*, vol. 2, *La Chine* (Paris: Fayard, 1980), 112–113.

25. One way to predict the future in Cambodia, *cak kompi* consists of placing a needle randomly between the pages of a book of prognostications, the *kompi*. The *kru* (master) who directs the seance reads the page designated by the needle, and the text serves as the prediction. All Khmers know and talk about these predictions.

26. *Put Tumneay* (Paris: Cedoreck, 1982), esp. 11.

27. Charles Meyer gives an entire series of other baneful signs that Sihanouk revealed; they dealt more specifically with him (Meyer, *Derrière le sourire khmer*, 91–96).

28. A special edition by the GRUNC mission in France (13 December 1974) assembled the declarations from FUNC and GRUNC (Paris and Peking), the speech by Chau Seng at the cremation of a student who had been killed, and a text mentioning the support of various FUNC branches in France and noting the accounts of many foreign associations.

29. On 15 November 1991 Paris resumed diplomatic relations with Phnom Penh at the level of the Khmer factions' Conseil national suprême (see chapter 9), which will probably allow the repairing and reopening of the Pavillon du Cambodge.

7. THE KHMER ROUGE GENOCIDE

1. Data in chapters 7 and 8 derive from official documents, mainly from accounts collected between 1978 and 1986 from Cambodian refugees newly arrived at the Khmer-Thai border: peasants, technicians, intellectuals, politicians, and others; for reasons of security these individuals did not want to be identified. For relevant political data, see Serge Thion and Ben Kiernan, *Khmers rouges! matériaux pour l'histoire du communisme au Cambodge* (Paris: J. E. Hallier–Albin Michel, 1981); Élisabeth Becker, *Les Larmes du Cambodge: histoire d'un autogénocide* (Paris: Presses de la Cité, 1988); Stephen R. Heder, "Kampuchea's Armed Struggle: The Origins of an Independent Revolution," *Bulletin of Concerned Asian Scholars* 11, no. 1 (1979): 2–24; Nayan Chanda, *Brother Enemy*.

2. Nicolas Martin, interview with Prince Sihanouk, 13 December 1986, Roissy-en-France.

3. Hou Yuon, "La paysannerie du Cambodge et ses projets de modernisation" (Thèse pour le doctorat en droit et sciences économiques, Université de Paris, 1955).

4. Hu Nim, "Les services publics."

5. Pol Pot and Ieng Sary's membership in the PCF cannot be established beyond doubt.

6. The Khmer *krom*, even though they are entirely Khmer, are at home nowhere: despised and mistreated by the Vietnamese on their territory; mistrusted by the Khmers of Cambodia, who suspect them of connivance with the Vietnamese.

7. Author's interview with Keng Vannsak, 10 December 1982, Montmorency.

8. See Nayan Chanda, *Brother Enemy*, 12; Yves Lacoste, *Contre les anti-tiers-mondistes et contre certains tiers-mondistes* (Paris: La Découverte, 1985), 23; François Ponchaud, introduction to *Le Mur de bambou: le Cambodge après Pol Pot*, by Esméralda Luciolli (Paris: Régine Deforges–Médecins sans frontières, 1988), 16; William Shawcross, *The Quality of Mercy* (Glasgow: William Collins Sons, 1985), 336.

9. Khieu Samphan, "L'économie du Cambodge et ses problèmes d'industrialisation" (Thèse pour le doctorat en droit et sciences économiques, Université de Paris, 1959).

10. Reported by *Le Monde* on 6 April 1975.

11. The *krâma* is a sort of multi-purpose scarf used to carry things, protect against the sun, and so forth. In polite urban society the different verbs "to eat" depend on whom the speaker is addressing: the king, monks, someone who is owed respect, an equal, or an intimate. In remote villages only two verbs existed: *hop*, a polite term, is the root word—forgotten in the towns—for *mohop* (dish of food); and *si*, an informal term reserved on the plains for animals.

12. Montagut is a brand of French knitwear very popular among urban Khmers, who would ask French friends to bring Montagut knits from Paris for them.

13. Nhang Sonnthic, "La chute de Phnom Penh telle que je l'ai vue," in *Cambodge 1987: annuaire cambodgien de documentation politique* (1988): 130–156; emphasis added.

14. Regarding agriculture, see Marie Alexandrine Martin, "La riziculture et la maîtrise de l'eau dans le Kampuchea démocratique," *Études rurales*, no. 83 (1981): 7–44.

15. See the contribution by botanist Pauline Dy Phon, "Les végétaux dans l'alimentation khmère en temps normal et en période de disette," *Asie du sud-est et monde insulindien: Cambodge I*, 13, no. 1–4 (1982): 155–169.

16. French authors have published accounts of Khmer life between 1975 and 1978: François Ponchaud, *Cambodge, année zéro* (Paris: Julliard, 1977); Bernard Hamel, *De sang et de larmes* (Paris: Albin Michel, 1977). Refugees, including a French woman, have given their personal testimony: Pin Yathay, *L'Utopie meurtrière: un rescapé du génocide cambodgien témoigne* (Paris: Laffont, 1980); Jacques Eng Hoa, *Le Vent sauvage de Eng Hoa* (Paris: Ramsey, 1984); Molyda Szymusiak, *Les Pierres crieront: une enfance cambodgienne, 1975–1980* (Paris: La Découverte, 1984); Laurence Picq, *Au delà du ciel: cinq ans chez les khmers rouges* (Paris: Barrault, 1984); Boun Sokha, *Cambodge: la massue de l'Angkar* (Paris: Atelier Marcel Jullian, 1979); Y Phandara, *Retour à Phnom Penh: le Cambodge du génocide à la colonisation; témoignage* (Paris: Métailié, 1982).

17. Apsara, "Les enfants du Kampuchea démocratique," *Asie du sud-est et monde insulindien: Cambodge I*, 13, no. 1–4 (1982): 192.

18. "Paroles d'élèves," *La Chronique d'Amnesty International*, no. 11 (September 1987): 21.

19. Illustrating this point are the films shot in Siem Reap and Battambang provinces in 1983 and deposited at the then permanent diplomatic mission of Democratic Kampuchea at UNESCO, Paris.

20. Ponchaud, *Cambodge, année zéro*.

21. Marie Alexandrine Martin, "La politique alimentaire des Khmers rouges," *Études rurales*, no. 99–100 (1985): 347–365.

22. GRUNC mission in Paris, *Bulletin d'information* (1 August 1975), 8.

23. This feeling emerges clearly in the film made by Yugoslav filmmakers in spring 1978 and shown on Antenne 2.

24. Marie Alexandrine Martin, "L'industrie dans le Kampuchea démocratique," *Études rurales* nos. 89–91 (1983): 77–110.

25. The five others—Lon Nol, Cheng Eng, In Tam, Son Ngoc Thanh, and Sosthène Fernandez, commander-in-chief of the republican forces—fled abroad.

26. The Khmer-Islamic community numbered seventy thousand in 1970. Nayan Chanda's assertion that "many thousands" of Chams who had taken refuge in Cambodia after the absorption of their country, Champa, by Vietnam "were eventually killed by the Pol Pot regime for their Islamic faith" (Nayan Chanda, *Brother Enemy*, 49) is not entirely correct. Aside from the fact that they had become more numerous, a small part of their number escaped from Democratic Kampuchea's purges, even though some Khmers have slipped in among the Chams as a means of gaining acceptance by Malaysia. The various Cham communities in the West publish a newsletter.

27. Becker, *Les Larmes du Cambodge*, 261–264.

28. See this French woman's account of her stay in Picq, *Au delà du ciel*.

29. On this question, see Marie Alexandrine Martin, "Les écoles techniques de Phnom Penh: la dramatique épopée du massif des Cardamomes," *Asie du sud-est et monde insulindien: Hommage à Georges Condominas* 12, no. 1–4 (1980): 113–126.

30. Nouth Narang and Nguon Kami, prime movers behind the Centre de documentation et de recherche sur la civilisation khmère (center of documentation and research on Khmer civilization, or Cedoreck), prepared the manifesto agreed upon by other neutral students.

31. Without precise information, the press (never averse to morbidity) has increased an already catastrophic balance sheet. The American Department of State gives a range of 1.2 million to 1.8 million deaths during the short reign of the Khmer Rouge. Demographer Ea Meng Try uses the minimum figure for his calculations, to arrive at an estimate of 1 to 1.2 million deaths.

32. In appendix 8, see the stereotyped response (in doublespeak) given by Khieu Samphan on 24 October 1986 to my written questions of August and October 1986.

33. Mentioned in press communiqué by minister of foreign affairs of Democratic Kampuchea, 11 November 1977.

34. Interview by comrade Pol Pot, secretary of the Khmer Communist party, prime minister of Democratic Kampuchea, to the delegation of Yugoslav journalists visiting Democratic Kampuchea, Phnom Penh, 17 March 1978 (in fact they traveled to a few places within Cambodia, but the communiqué was issued in the capital).

35. Some of this new vocabulary has been examined by Laurence Picq, "De la réforme linguistique et de l'usage des mots chez les khmers rouges," *Asie du sud-est et monde insulindien: Cambodge II*, 15, no. 1–4 (1984): 351–357.

36. "Nouvelles du Kampuchea démocratique," broadcast from Phnom Penh by the Voix du Kampuchea démocratique, June 1977.

37. The Vietnamese did not arrive in this region, to the west of Maung, until April, which explains why such massacres occurred at this time.

38. *Le Livre noir: faits et preuves des actes d'agression et d'annexion du Vietnam contre le Kampuchea* (Paris: Éditions du Centenaire, 1979); originally published in Phnom Penh by the ministry of foreign affairs in September 1978.

## 8. THE VIETNAMESE OCCUPATION AND THE RESISTANCE

1. Regarding these repatriations in southwestern Cambodia see Marie Alexandrine Martin, "Migrations et répartition de la population dans l'ouest cambodgien communisé," *Hérodote*, no. 49 (1988): 114–138.

2. Van Saren and the self-proclaimed Prince Suryavong, whose real name is André Ouk Thol, were trafficking at the expense of the refugees in camp 204.

3. *Indochina Report*, no. 3 (July–September 1985); issue is entitled "The Military Occupation of Kampuchea."

4. Shawcross, *Quality of Mercy*.

5. Ibid., 224.

6. For details on the distribution of aid see Marie Alexandrine Martin, "Les réfugiés cambodgiens: raison de leur exil, tragédie, et aspirations actuelles," in *Les Réfugiés originaires de l'Asie du sud-est: monographies* (Paris: Documentation française, 1984), 2:82–85.

7. Luciolli, *Mur de bambou*, 64.

8. Ibid., 81.

9. See Marie Alexandrine Martin, "Cambodge: une nouvelle colonie d'exploitation," *Politique internationale* (Winter 1985): 177–193; Jacques Broyelle, "Le Cambodge emmuré," *Le Spectacle du Monde* (March 1987): 40–42.

10. Luciolli, *Mur de bambou*, 120.

11. Ibid., 121, 128, 125.

12. The projects are reminiscent of the conscription of Cambodian workers by the Nguyen court in 1820 to dig the Vien Te canal, which was to isolate the rest of the country from the southern Khmer provinces occupied by the Vietnamese; these murderous levies provoked a rebellion (Chandler, "Cambodia Before the French," 101).

13. Le Duc Anh, "The VPA and Its Lofty International Duty in Friendly Cambodia," *Tap Chi Quan Doi Nhan Dan* (December 1984).

14. Luciolli, *Mur de bambou*, 130.

15. At the time, there were nine jails in Phnom Penh and three major ones in the contiguous province of Kandal. Four of the jails were under the exclusive control of the Vietnamese: a building at Tuol Kork, one at the Pochentong base, villa 12, and the ground floors of villas where the Vietnamese experts from Bureau A-50 in charge of Phnom Penh worked (between the Independence monument and the Chamcar Mon State House); some of the Vietnamese experts of A-50, in charge of the jails, lived in the Raja Hotel. The ministry of the interior ran other jails: part of T-3, Srah Chak, the former casino, the police headquarters, a building located between the market and the airport of Pochentong, known as KRV under the Khmer Republic, and Prey Sar in Kandal, near the Phnom Penh neighborhood of Stung Mean Chey. The city of Phnom Penh, under the control of the judicial police, directly administered another part of T-3. The ministry of defense was in charge of other jails (Ta Khmau and Saang in Kandal).

16. The accounts were published in *Kampuchea: After the Worst* (New York: Lawyers Committee for Human Rights, 1985). To my knowledge, this committee of jurists was the first organization to ask Phnom Penh for a visa—which was refused—to visit the jails. The ICRC, on the spot, asked in vain in the early 1980s for access to the detention centers. Amnesty International waited until the end of 1986 and in 1987 published *Kampuchea: tortures et emprisonnements politiques*.

17. See the accounts in Marie Alexandrine Martin, "Vietnamized Cambodia. A Silent Ethnocide," *Indochina Report*, no. 7 (July–September 1986). These refugee accounts do not contradict the report by a Canadian specialist: H. B. Schiefer, "Study of the Possible Use of Chemical Warfare Agents in Southeast Asia" (Saskatchewan University, 1982).

18. "Whether it was Hanoi's deliberate policy to settle Vietnamese in Cambodia, as its opponents charged . . ." (Nayan Chanda, *Brother Enemy*, 376).

19. This figure comes from the single serious demographic study available on the Sangkum regime's Cambodia: Migozzi, *Cambodge*, 44. The newspapers included *Far Eastern Economic Review*, 26 May 1983; *Focus*, 3 April 1984; *Le Monde*, 6 May 1983; *International Herald Tribune*, 27 June 1983; *Études internationales* 15, no. 2 (1984); all the newspapers from Southeast Asia, including the two English-language Thai papers, the *Bangkok Post* and *The National Review*; and, in addition, Marie Alexandrine

Martin, in *Politique internationale* (Winter 1984). As early as 1835 a Khmer who was a prisoner of the Siamese mentioned demographic colonization of the capital: "His account of Phnom Penh at this time contains many vivid details. In some way, it had become a Vietnamese city . . . about 800 Vietnamese merchants and dependents had been brought in" (Chandler, "Cambodia Before the French," 128).

20. On 1 January 1986 Leopold Gratz, the Austrian minister of foreign affairs, succeeded Willibald Pahr as the president of the International Conference on Kampuchea, held in New York in July 1981.

21. The French term *ethnocide* often designates the physical extermination of ethnic groups studied by anthropologists and, in this sense, does not differ from the *génocide*, which I prefer. *Ethnocide* here describes the phenomenon of destruction of a culture; the first to use the term in this sense was Georges Condominas (*L'Exotique est quotidien* [Paris: Plon, 1965], 469). To describe this phenomenon Anglo-Saxons use the expression "cultural genocide," which I consider a barbarism. I discuss the policy further in "Vietnamized Cambodia." In *A History of Cambodia*, Chandler describes an analogous phenomenon occurring in the nineteenth century: on the Vietnamization of Cambodia, see 123–133.

22. Lack of means nevertheless prevents all the children who live in the border settlements from attending school.

23. *La Solidarité Kampuchea-Vietnam* (Phnom Penh: Commission de Propagande et d'éducation, 1982), 5.

24. *La République populaire du Kampuchea au seuil de sa 6e année* (Hanoi: Le Courrier du Vietnam, 1983), 34.

25. Here is an example of the transformation of a Khmer dance, *apsara*, by changing the words (mixing old with new words, in the following order). Old words: "Today my heart is full of joy [*twice*] / I watch the flowers grow in the garden"; new words: "This seventh day of January seventy-nine / Is for me like a day when they ring all / the bells and all the gongs throughout the country. / The national art of Kampuchea / has no equal in any other [national] history in the world"; revised version of old words: "The flowers fall from the sky. / My heart is full of undying love."

26. *National Geographic Magazine*, May 1982, 577.

27. See "The Military Occupation of Kampuchea," 10. There Angkor Wat is called Angkor Toch, according to the peasant tradition; Srah Srang, not named, is the "armored vehicle brigade based behind Angkor Toch."

28. The holding centers (Sakeo, Khao I Dang, Kap Cheung, Kamput II) were opened under the control of Thai military officers after the fall of the Khmer Rouge regime; they are all closed today. Unlike the refugees who arrived between 1975 and 1978 and were placed under the supervision of the ministry of the interior, Khmers in these centers were without facilities to request political asylum from a third country.

29. The account of this reversal is given by Sihanouk himself in *Prisonnier des khmers rouges*, 342–345, 365–370.

30. Sihanouk wrote three letters to Prime Minister Pham Van Dong, expressing his desire to return to Cambodia as a private citizen. He received no response; worse still, the second and third letters were returned to him unopened.

31. See Sisowath Thomico, "Norodom Sihanouk and the Khmer Factions," *Indochina Report*, no. 9 (1986), and the reactions it provoked: Sihanouk's response, "A Passion for Cambodia: Norodom Sihanouk and the Khmer Factions—A Reply," *Indochina Report* (October–September 1987); letters and telegrams from various FUNCINPEC members.

32. This battle was part of the 1984–1985 dry-season offensive. The seizure of Khmer Rouge strongholds by Vietnamese and Heng Samrin's troops was arduous. The Sihanoukists resisted the heavy fire of the Vietnamese and withdrew only when faced with encirclement; FNLPK troops hardly fought at all, at least not in the northwest.

33. Ros Chantrabot, "La république khmère," 103.

34. Sisowath Thomico, "Quelle solution pour le Cambodge?" In *Cambodge 1986: annuaire cambodgien de documentation politique*, 2:21 (Neuilly-sur-Marne: Centre de documentation cambodgienne contemporaine, 1987).

35. By the end of the 1980s CEDORECK abandoned its publishing and reprinting activities and became a simple documentation center. In 1993 it ceased to exist in Paris, but it is still well established in Phnom Penh.

36. Groslier, "Pour une géographie historique du Cambodge," 350.

37. Sam Sok, "Cambodge: quel avenir?" In *Cambodge 1986: annuaire cambodgien de documentation politique*, 1:5, 7 (Neuilly-sur-Marne: Centre de documentation cambodgienne contemporaine, 1987).

38. Sam Sok, *Future Société khmère*, 18.

39. The only self-criticism was the opportune remorse expressed by Jean Lacouture in *Survive le peuple cambodgien!* (Paris: Le Seuil, 1978), when the Khmer Rouge were being defeated by the Vietnamese. An academician devoted a thesis to a left-wing daily: J. N. Darde, *Le Ministère de la vérité: histoire d'un génocide dans le journal "Humanité"* (Paris: Le Seuil, 1984).

40. Only two French researchers, who were favorable to the SRV and had supported the Vietnamese people's struggle in the 1960s and 1970s, have, on their return from a trip to Vietnam in 1980, given an accurate view of the situation in this country: Pierre Brocheux and Daniel Emery, "Le Vietnam exsangue," *Le Monde diplomatique* (March 1980). Each then became persona non grata for several years.

41. *Le Monde; Le Monde diplomatique; Le Matin.*

42. Errors and distortions of historical facts were pointed out to authors and journalists, but no corrections were forthcoming. Cambodians protested to *France-Soir*, TF-1, and A-2. Chantal Lescanne undertook multiple interventions with many newspapers, various radio stations, TF-1, and A-2. Esméralda Luciolli reestablished several truths with the publishing house L'Harmattan. I myself pointed out gross factual errors to France-Inter, *Le*

*Monde diplomatique, L'Express,* and *Le Nouvel Observateur.* But none of us was able to obtain satisfaction. Two Khmers won a libel suit against *L'Express* for erroneous representation of facts.

43. *Kampuchea: tortures et emprisonnements politiques* (Paris: Amnesty International, 1987).

## 9. VIETNAMESE DISENGAGEMENT: THE HOUR OF RECKONING

1. To avoid conscription, many men preferred to enlist and soon found themselves on the way to the battlefields. At Phnom Penh, the colors of clothing distinguish several categories of police: greenish for the national police; navy blue for the municipal police; brown for the *nokorbal prayuth.*

2. This K-5—which could mobilize all classes of the population—included five important points for clearing: one in Kah Kong, one in Pursat, and three in Battambang, at Ampil Pram Daeum (the most difficult), Pailin, and Sisophon. The army museum displays photographs of K-5, presenting it as one of the regime's glorious achievements. In 1990 those wounded in combat or in clearing operations continued to come: those under the authority of the ministry of the interior, the *nokorbal prayuth,* went to the Calmette hospital, while true soldiers coming from the front went to hospitals reserved for them, such as Preah Khet Mealea. Month by month, they added to the number of the handicapped.

The last plan to date, K-6, went into action in 1989 at Muk Kampul, in Kandal province, approximately thirty kilometers north of Phnom Penh, where the levied civilians cut down the forest.

3. Since children attend classes only on a part-time basis, they have time for three and one-half hours of daily dance courses.

4. The altar to the guardian spirit of the household, *preah phum,* is set up outside many houses. Offerings to the pillar god and those to the *mrenh kongviel,* who watch over young children, are prominently displayed. The construction of a house or the addition of a wing call for an inauguration ritual. Concerning the ancestral altars that the Vietnamese set up to honor their ancestors, the ritual may, paradoxically, have appealed to some Khmers as a dependable means of safeguarding their identities. But this is only a hypothesis. What is certain is that people perceive it as a means of protecting themselves from misfortunes.

5. One estimate of their numbers comes from the tract calling for the demonstration on 5 January 1991.

6. The Communist party, known as the PPRK, was renamed Pak Pracheachon (people's party) on 17 November 1991.

7. By way of comparison, in December 1990 the two basic components of the Cambodian diet—rice and fish—cost, respectively, one hundred and fifty riels and four hundred riels per kilogram.

8. Moreover, the monthly tax of eighty riels for a stall in the market

actually reached nearly four hundred riels if one includes the daily racketeering by police. These figures are for December 1990.

9. In spring 1993 the two orphanages that were open (a third closed in 1983) sheltered 303 children and adolescents—boys and girls—including young beggars brought in from the streets.

10. Shawcross, *Quality of Mercy*.

11. "Motion concernant le Cambodge en vue du sommet européen de Madrid le 26 juin 1989," signed by three Belgian nongovernmental organizations; the response of the two nationalist movements, "Lettre adressée aux ministres des Affaires étrangères de la Communauté économique européenne," 3 July 1989. New intervention on 6 November 1989 by eighty-five nongovernmental organizations, represented by Oxfam's director.

12. The chronology of the preparatory meetings mentioned in the text is as follows: 2–4 December 1987, Sihanouk–Hun Sen, Fère-en-Tardenois (department of Aisne); 20–21 January 1988, Sihanouk–Hun Sen, St-Germain-en-Laye; 25–28 July 1988, Jakarta informal meeting I (hereafter JIM), bringing together the four Khmer factions, ASEAN, Laos, and Vietnam; 5–8 November 1988, Sihanouk–Hun Sen–Son Sann, Fère-en-Tardenois; 14 December 1988, quadripartite meeting, Paris; 16–18 February 1989, quadripartite meeting, Jakarta before JIM II on 19–21 February; 2–3 May 1989, Hun Sen–Sihanouk, and Hun Sen–Son Sann, Jakarta; 24 July 1989, the four Khmer factions and the French foreign minister, Celle-St-Cloud.

13. See the telex sent by Hun Sen to Ranariddh in December 1987, stipulating that there should be no preliminary conditions so that the two parties could directly discuss all questions of common interest in order to implement national reconciliation and resolve the Cambodian problem in a peaceful fashion (*Bangkok Post*, 12 March 1988).

14. An excerpt from the communiqué appeared in *Le Monde*, 5 December 1987. In September 1987 Hun Sen announced that he agreed to hold discussions with Khieu Samphan, the nominal head of the Khmer Rouge.

15. At Fère-en-Tardenois Sihanouk proposed a precise schedule for the withdrawal of Vietnamese troops and the termination of military aid to the four factions; the simultaneous dismantling of the RPK and the GCKD; internationally supervised elections; the formation of a quadripartite provisional government and national army; the sending of a UN peacekeeping mission.

16. *Le Quotidien*, 6 August 1987.

17. Reports on the discussions were in the *Bulletin du FNLPK* (June–July 1989): 16, 24.

18. *Far Eastern Economic Review*, 20 July 1989.

19. Participants included the five permanent members of the UN Security Council, the six ASEAN countries, Vietnam, Australia, Canada, India, Japan, Laos, and Zimbabwe as a representative of the nonaligned countries.

20. The Khmer Rouge position was reported in *Le Monde,* 8 August 1989.

21. *Bangkok Post,* 12 August 1989.

22. The conference set up four institutions: a commission to determine the modalities of a cease-fire and the creation of an international supervisory mechanism; a commission to examine the means for preserving the independence, sovereignty, territorial integrity, and neutrality of Cambodia; a commission to study the eventual return of exiles and a plan for the reconstruction of Cambodia; an ad hoc commission to make preparations for national reconciliation, the creation of a provisional quadripartite authority presided over by Sihanouk, and the organization of free elections.

23. These were, respectively, 15–16 January in Paris; 11–12 February in New York; 12–13 March in Paris; 25–26 May in New York; 16–17 July in Paris; 27–28 August and 15–16 October in New York. During their meetings on 23–25 November in Paris, the UN peace plan, which had been endorsed in the meantime by the foreign powers (the five permanent members, Indonesia, Australia, Canada, India, Japan, Laos, and Malaysia), underwent a final modification before being presented to the Khmers, meeting in Paris on 20–21 December.

24. The Khmer Rouge slammed the door during the interfactional meetings in Tokyo. Hun Sen and Sihanouk signed a cease-fire agreement that engaged only themselves and was thus invalid.

25. The foreign powers met from 9 November to 11 November 1990 and included the five permanent members of the UN Security Council, along with Indonesia, Australia, Canada, Japan, Malaysia, India, and Laos.

26. On 26 April 1991 and at Hun Sen's initiative, the four factions met in Bangkok in the presence of the Thai prime minister, Anand Panyarachun; on 28 April Anand received Hun Sen, for what proved to be a useless interview as Bangkok refused to connect the cease-fire to the end of arms supply to the Khmer Rouge.

27. While visiting Kandal Stung with Sihanouk, Hun Sen declared on 17 November 1991 that the ICRC would not be allowed to visit two groups of prisoners (number unknown) still in jail: in the first group were people who had plotted against the prime minister; in the second were bandits and smugglers who attacked the people and who could, Hun Sen added, be considered terrorists. At the end of December the official press agency, Sarpordarmean Kampuchea, mentioned 1,260 prisoners. The regime was to release 290 persons on 15 January 1992. The jails supervised by Vietnamese (villa 12, A-50, KRV, Tuol Kork) were closed in 1989 when the *bo doi* withdrew.

28. There were about as many state of Cambodia flags (white Angkor Wat temple on blue and red stripes) as Conseil national suprême flags (white map of Cambodia on a blue background). To welcome Sihanouk properly, Phnom Penh rented (from a Thai newspaper) the white 1963 Chevrolet

Impala convertible in which Miss Universe had traveled in 1990. A French transport plane (a Transal) went to Bangkok to get it.

29. Two stories, neither confirmed, circulate about the PPC-FUNCINPEC alliance. According to a diplomatic source, Hun Sen confronted the two princes with a fait accompli by announcing an alliance arranged unilaterally by Phnom Penh. Ranariddh, believing that his father had decided without consulting him, did not react, and vice versa. The other story suggests that it was jointly settled by Hun Sen and Sihanouk a few months before the latter returned, and that this was the price that the prince had to pay in order to be reinstated as Cambodia's legitimate chief of state.

30. *Le Monde,* 30 June–1 July 1991: "The Vietnamese want the 'transition period to be as short as possible' and think that 'the best situation' would be an electoral alliance between Prince Sihanouk and Mr. Hun Sen." The maneuvers by Hun Sen and the Khmer Rouge were reported in *Le Monde,* 18 October and 7 November 1991.

31. According to rumors, Sihanouk became angry and prevented another anti–Son Sann demonstration from taking place. For reactions of Cambodians see the *Bangkok Post,* 27 August 1991.

32. Khmers who visited Cambodia brought a copy of this film back to Paris; it was shown in the Cambodian community there.

33. The day after the communiqué appeared, Sihanouk gave an explanation: Heng Samrin would remain president of the state of Cambodia with himself as president "of all Cambodia" (including territories occupied by the resistance); his statement may have referred to a gradual reduction of Heng Samrin's role. Sihanouk delivered a similar speech at the inaugural session of the Water Festival on November 20; see also "Sihanouk: Happy Justice and Pride Restored," *The Nation,* 22 November 1991. His followers' views appeared in *The Nation* and *Bangkok Post,* 22 November 1991.

34. *SPK,* 13 November 1991 (daily bulletin issued in Phnom Penh).

35. *Bangkok Post* and *The Nation,* 26 November 1991.

36. To compensate for civil servants' low salaries in the early 1980s, the government had given them land that they could cultivate to feed their families, either directly or by selling the produce. Some were forced to give up these lands to unscrupulous high officials, in exchange for ridiculously low sums of money or even nothing at all.

37. *The Nation,* 24 January 1991.

38. Khmers living abroad contest these property titles, obtained as they were from a government they do not recognize and through illicit gifts, contrary to all applicable laws. Bangkok's officials have warned Thai businessmen that the situation is unclear and that risky ventures should be avoided (*The Nation,* 27 November 1991). See M. A. Martin, "L'État des forêts cambodgiennes," Colloque International de phytogéographie tropicale, Paris, 6–8 juillet 1993 (forthcoming in *Actes du Colloque*).

39. *Bangkok Post,* 13 March 1992.

40. *The Nation* and *Bangkok Post,* 17 December 1991.

41. "Refugees," published by the United Nations High Commission for Refugees, July 1992, 25.

42. Political murders started in Phnom Penh in January 1992. They stopped in the capital, because of the arrival of UNTAC's numerous blue helmets. But in the countryside opponents still die or disappear. FNLPK has declared the loss of twenty-three members.

43. "United Nations Electoral Law for the Conduct of a Free and Fair Election of a Constituent Assembly for Cambodia," 1992. Witnesses report that UNTAC is taking all kinds of precautions to reduce electoral fraud, at least in Phnom Penh; measures in the countryside could not be confirmed.

44. *Bangkok Post,* 1 June 1992.

# Bibliography

ARCHIVES

Archives nationales: Archives d'outremer (AOM), Paris and Aix-en-Province; Archives diplomatiques, ministère des affaires étrangères (AAE)

UNPUBLISHED MATERIALS

Brunet, Jacques. "La musique et les chants dans le mariage cambodgien." Thèse pour le doctorat en ethnologie, Université de Paris VII, 1974.

Central Intelligence Agency. "Kampuchea: A Demographic Catastrophe." Research paper, May 1980. Washington, D.C.

Chandler, David P. "Cambodia before the French: Politics in a Tributary Kingdom, 1794–1848." Ph.D. thesis, University of Michigan, Ann Arbor, 1978.

Daniel, Alain. "Étude d'un fragment du Ram-Ker dit par un conteur cambodgien." Thèse pour le doctorat en études indiennes, Université de Paris III, 1982.

Dupaigne, Bernard. "Les maîtres du fer et du feu: étude de la métallurgie du fer chez les *kouy* du nord du Cambodge, dans le context historique et ethnographique de l'ensemble khmer." Thèse pour le doctorat ès lettres et sciences humaines, École des hautes études en sciences sociales, Paris, 1987.

Ellul, Jean. "Le coutumier rituel des chasseurs d'éléphants de l'ouest du Cambodge." Thèse pour le doctorat en ethnologie, École des hautes études en sciences sociales, Paris, 1987.

Fontanel, Jean. "Ratanakiri: étude du milieu naturel d'une région frontière du Cambodge." Thèse pour le doctorat en géographie, Université de Grenoble, 1967.

Goulin, Christian. "Phnom Penh: étude géographique urbaine." Thèse pour le doctorat en géographie, Université de Strasbourg, 1965.

Guichard, Maurice. "Hévéa: aménagements des plantations en Indochine." Mémoire de l'École pratique coloniale du Havre, 1953.

Hebihara, May. "Svay: A Khmer Village in Cambodia." Ph.D. thesis, University of Michigan, Ann Arbor, 1971.

Hou Yuon. "La paysannerie du Cambodge et ses projets de modernisation." Thèse pour le doctorat en droit et sciences économiques, Université de Paris, 1955.

Hu Nim. "Les services publics économiques au Cambodge." Thèse pour le doctorat en droit, Phnom Penh, 1965.

Kao Kan. "Les relations sino-cambodgiennes (1963–1970)." Thèse pour le doctorat en études politiques, École pratique des hautes études, VIe section, 1973.

Khieu Samphan. "L'économie du Cambodge et ses problèmes d'industrialisation." Thèse pour le doctorat en droit et sciences économiques, Université de Paris, 1959.

Khin Sok. "Le Cambodge entre le Siam et le Vietnam." Thèse pour le doctorat d'état ès lettres et sciences humaines, École des hautes études en sciences sociales, Paris, 1987.

Pou Choti. "Le cambodgien d'hier et d'aujourd'hui: essai sur les conflits de génération." Mémoire de 2e année, École technique d'outremer du Havre, 1965.

Ros Chantrabot. "La république khmère et l'Asie du sud-est après son écroulement." Diplôme de l'École des hautes études en sciences sociales, Paris, 1978.

Say Bory. "L'administration rurale au Cambodge et ses projets de réforme." Thèse pour le doctorat en sciences administratives, Université de Paris II, 1974.

Schiefer, H. B. "Study of the Possible Use of Chemical Warfare Agents in Southeast Asia." Saskatchewan University, 1982.

Thay Sok. "Traités de morale des Cambodgiens, du XIVe au XIXe siècles." Thèse pour le doctorat d'université, Paris, 1964.

Tith Huon. "Problème de l'assainissement dans la fonction publique cambodgienne." Thèse pour le doctorat en sciences administratives, Université de Paris II, 1976.

Try Sengly. "Le bouddhisme dans la société khmère contemporaine." Mémoire de l'École pratique des hautes études section sciences religieuses, 1986.

## PUBLISHED MATERIALS

### PERIODICALS

*ASEMI (Asie du sud-est et monde insulindien)*. 1982, 1984, Paris.

Assemblée de l'union française. *Annales*. 1949–1953, Versailles.

Assemblée nationale. *Comptes rendus des débats*, 1949, Paris.

Association des étudiants khmers. *Bulletin*. 1946–1953, Paris.

*Cambodge nouveau* [formerly *Kambuja*]. 1970, Phnom Penh.

Conseil de la république. *Comptes rendus des débats*, 1949, Paris.

*Études cambodgiennes*. 1964–1967, Phnom Penh.

*Kambuja*. 1965–1966, Phnom Penh.

*FNLPK Bulletin*. 1979–1989, Paris.

*Moulkhmer*. 1987–1988, Paris.

*Nagara Vatta*. 1936–1942, Phnom Penh.

*Pracheatipatey*. 1940s, Phnom Penh.

*Réalités cambodgiennes*. 1969, Phnom Penh.

*Revue de l'armée* and *Chadomuk*. 1971–1973, Phnom Penh.

*Revue de l'Instituteur*. 1954, Phnom Penh.

*Sangkum*. 1965–1969, Phnom Penh.

*Seksa khmer*. 1980–1987, Paris.

Union des étudiants khmers [formerly Association des étudiants khmers]. *Bulletin*. 1956–1960s, Paris.

Union des nationalistes khmers. *Bulletin d'information*. 1986, Phnom Penh.

BOOKS AND ARTICLES

Ang Choulean. *Les Êtres surnaturels dans la religion populaire khmère.* Paris: Cedoreck, 1986.

Aymonnier, Étienne. *Le Cambodge.* 3 vols. Paris: Leroux, 1900–1904.

Becker, Élisabeth. *Les Larmes du Cambodge: l'histoire d'un autogénocide.* Paris: Presses de la Cité, 1988.

Bhattacharya, Kamalesvar. *Les Religions brahmaniques dans l'ancien Cambodge d'après l'épigraphie et l'iconographie.* École française d'Extrême-Orient, Publication no. 49. Paris, 1961.

Bizot, François. *Le Figuier à cinq branches: recherche sur le bouddhisme khmer.* Publication de l'École française d'Extrême-Orient, no. 107. Paris, 1976.

Boulbet, Jean. *Le Phnom Kulen et sa région.* École française d'Extrême-Orient, collection de textes et documents sur l'Indochine, no. 12. Paris, 1979.

Boun Chan Mul. *Charet khmer* (Khmer mentality). 1971. Paris: Cedoreck, 1984.

Boun Sokha. *Cambodge: la massue de l'Angkar.* Paris: Atelier Marcel Jullian, 1979.

Broyelle, Jacques. "Le Cambodge emmuré." *Le Spectacle du Monde* (March 1987): 40–42.

Brunet, Jacques. "Règles de courtoisie chez les khmers." *Asie du sud-est et monde insulindien: Cambodge I,* 13, no. 1–4 (1982): 13–21.

Centre de documentation cambodgienne contemporaine. *Cambodge 1986: annuaire cambodgien de documentation politique.* Neuilly-sur-Marne, 1987.

———. *Cambodge 1987: annuaire cambodgien de documentation politique.* Neuilly-sur-Marne, 1988.

Chanda, Nayan. *Brother Enemy: The War after the War; A History of Indochina since the Fall of Saigon.* New York: Harcourt Brace Jovanovich, 1986.

Chandler, David P. *A History of Cambodia.* Boulder, Colo.: Westview Press, 1983.

Chim, Sunly. "L'ingratitude du crocodile." *Revue de l'amitié franco-khmère,* no. 39 (1955): 24.

Coedès, George. *Les Peuples de la péninsule indochinoise.* Paris: Dunod, 1962.

———. *Les États hindouisés d'Indochine et d'Indonésie.* Paris: De Boccard, 1964.

Decrop, Véronique. *Voyage dans les rêves des enfants de la frontière.* Paris: Hervas, 1988.

Delvert, Jean. *Le Paysan cambodgien.* Paris-The Hague, 1961.

———. *Le Cambodge.* Paris: Presses universitaires de France, 1983.

Dy Phon, Pauline. "Les végétaux dans l'alimentation khmère en temps normal et en période de disette." *Asie du sud-est et monde insulindien: Cambodge I,* 13, no. 1–4 (1982): 155–169.

Ea Meng Try. "Kampuchea: A Country Adrift." *Population and Development Review* 7, no. 2 (1981): 209–228.

*Les Écoles d'art de l'Indochine.* Hanoi: Gouvernement général de l'Indochine, 1937.

Eng Hoa, Jacques. *Le Vent sauvage de Eng Hoa.* Paris: Ramsay, 1984.

Forest, Alain. *Le Cambodge et la colonisation française: histoire d'une colonisation sans heurts (1897–1920).* Paris: L'Harmattan, 1980.

Giteau, Madeleine. *Histoire d'Angkor.* Paris: Presses universitaires de France, 1974.

———. *Angkor: un peuple, un art.* Paris: Bibliothèque des Arts, 1976.

Groslier, Bernard Philippe. *Angkor: hommes et pierres.* Paris: Arthaud, 1965.

———. "Pour une géographie historique du Cambodge." *Cahiers d'outremer,* no. 104 (1973): 337–379.

Groslier, George. *Recherches sur les Cambodgiens.* Paris: Challamel, 1921.

Hamel, Bernard. *De sang et de larmes.* Paris: Albin Michel, 1977.

———. "Le surprenant parcours du prince Sihanouk." *Historia,* no. 391 (1979): 88–98.

Haudricourt, André G. "De l'origine des tons en vietnamien." *Journal asiatique,* no. 242 (1954): 69–82.

Heder, Stephen R. "Kampuchea's Armed Struggle: The Origins of an Independent Revolution." *Bulletin of Concerned Asian Scholars* 11, no. 1 (1979): 2–24.

Hun Sen. *Dap chnam damnaeur Kampuchea* (Ten years in the history of Kampuchea). Phnom Penh, 1989.

Khing Hoc Dy. *Contes et légendes du pays khmer.* Paris: Sudestasie, 1989.

Khing Hoc Dy and Khing Jacqueline. "Les recommandations de Kram Ngoy." *Mon-Khmer Studies* 7 (1978): 141–181.

Kiernan, Ben, and Chanta Boua, eds. *Peasants and Politics in Kampuchea, 1942– 1981.* London: Zed Press, 1982.

Lacoste, Yves. *Contre les anti-tiers-mondistes et contre certains tiers-mondistes.* Paris: La Découverte, 1985.

Lamant, Pierre. "Le Cambodge et la décolonisation de l'Indochine: le caractère particulier du nationalisme khmer de 1936 à 1945." In *Les Chemins de la décolonisation de l'empire colonial français.* Paris: Centre national de la recherche scientifique, 1986.

———. "Les prémices des relations politiques entre le Cambodge et la France vers le milieu du XIXe siècle." *Revue française d'histoire d'outremer* 72, no. 267 (1985): 167–198.

———. "Les partis politiques et les mouvements de résistance khmère vus par les services de renseignements français (1945–1952)." *Guerres mondiales et conflits contemporains,* no. 148 (1987): 79–96.

Lawyers Committee for Human Rights. *Kampuchea: After the Worst.* New York, 1985.

Leclère, Adémar. *Histoire du Cambodge.* 1914. 2d ed. Phnom Penh: Nokor Thom, 1974.

———. *Fêtes civiles et religieuses.* Paris: Imprimerie nationale, 1917.

Le Duc Anh. "The VPA and Its Lofty International Duty in Friendly Cambodia." *Tap Chi Quan Doi Nhan Dan* (December 1984).

Lemaignen, Robert, Léopold Senghor, and Sisowath Youtevong. *La Communauté impériale française.* Paris: Alsatia, 1945.

*Le Livre noir: faits et preuves des actes d'agression et d'annexion du Vietnam contre le Kampuchea.* Paris: Éditions du Centenaire, 1979.

Luciolli, Esméralda. *Le Mur de bambou: le Cambodge après Pol Pot.* Paris: Régine Deforges–Médecins sans frontières, 1988.

Mak Phoeun. *Chroniques royales du Cambodge de 1594 à 1677: traduction française avec comparaisons des différentes versions et introduction.* Publication de l'École française d'Extrême-Orient, collection de textes et documents sur l'Indochine, no. 13. Paris, 1981.

Mak Phoeun and Po Dharma. "La première intervention militaire vietnamienne au Cambodge (1658–1659)." *Bulletin de l'École française d'Extrême-Orient* 73 (1984): 285–318.

Manac'h, Étienne. *Mémoires d'Extrême-Asie.* Vol. 2, *La Chine.* Paris: Fayard, 1980.

Martel, G. *Lovea, village des environs d'Angkor*. Publication de l'École française d'Extrême-Orient, no. 98. Paris, 1974.

Martin, Marie Alexandrine. "Les écoles techniques de Phnom Penh: la dramatique épopée du massif des Cardamomes." *Asie du sud-est et monde insulindien: Cambodge I*, 12, no. 1–4 (1980): 113–126.

———. "La riziculture et la maîtrise de l'eau dans le Kampuchea démocratique." *Études rurales*, no. 83 (1981): 7–44.

———. "L'industrie dans le Kampuchea démocratique." *Études rurales*, no. 89–91 (1983): 77–110.

———. "Les réfugiés cambodgiens: raison de leur exil, tragédie, et aspirations actuelles." In *Les Réfugiés originaires de l'Asie du sud-est: monographies*, 2:52–105. Paris: Documentation française, 1984.

———. "La politique alimentaire des khmers rouges." *Études rurales*, no. 99–100 (1985): 347–365.

———. "Cambodge: une nouvelle colonie d'exploitation." *Politique internationale* (Winter 1985): 177–193.

———. "Vietnamized Cambodia: A Silent Ethnocide." *Indochina Report*, no. 7 (July–September 1986).

———. "Les savoirs naturalistes dans l'ouest cambodgien." *Seksa khmer*, no. 8–9 (1986): 77–188.

———. "Migrations et répartition de la population dans l'ouest cambodgien communisé." *Hérodote*, no. 49 (1988): 114–138.

———. *Les Khmers daeum, "Khmers de l'origine": société montagnarde et exploitation de la forêt; de l'écologie à l'histoire*. Paris, forthcoming.

Martini, François, and Solange Bernard. *Contes populaires du Cambodge*. Paris: Maisonneuve, 1946.

Matras-Troubetzkoy, Jacqueline. *Un village en forêt: l'essartage chez les Brou du Cambodge*. Paris: Selaf, 1983.

Meas Yang. "Le bouddhisme au Cambodge." *Études orientales*, no. 6 (1978).

Meyer, Charles. *Derrière le sourire khmer*. Paris: Plon, 1971.

Migozzi, Jacques. *Cambodge: faits et problèmes de population*. Paris: C.N.R.S., 1973.

Ministère de l'information. "L'oeuvre de la France en Indochine: l'enseignement." Notes documentaires et études, série coloniale 18, no. 108. Paris, 1945.

Moura, Jean. *Le Royaume du Cambodge*. 2 vols. Paris: Ernest Leroux, 1883.

Népote, Jacques. "Le lien de filiation au Cambodge." *Lieux de l'enfance*, no. 11 (1987): 59–75.

———. *Parenté et organisation sociale dans le Cambodge moderne et contemporain: quelques aspects et quelques applications aux modèles les régissant*. Geneva: Olizane, 1992.

Ngeth Sim. *Le cri du Cambodge martyr*. Caen: Acasea, 1988.

Nhang Sonnthic. "La chute de Phnom Penh telle que je l'ai vue." In *Cambodge 1987: annuaire cambodgien de documentation politique*, 2:130–156. Paris: Centre de documentation cambodgienne contemporaine, 1988.

Norodom Sihanouk. *Rois de Kampuchea: Ang Duong, Norodom, N. Sihanouk*. Phnom Penh, 1957.

———. *Souvenirs doux et amers*. Paris: Hachette, 1981.

———. *Prisonnier des Khmers rouges*. Paris: Hachette, 1986.

Pannetier, A. *Notes cambodgiennes: au coeur du pays khmer*. 1921. 2d ed. Paris: Cedoreck, 1983.

Pavie, Auguste. *Mission Pavie*. Vols. 1, 2. Paris: Leroux, 1901–1904.

Pelliot, Paul. *Mémoires sur les coutumes du Cambodge de Tcheou Ta-Kouan*. Paris: Maisonneuve, 1951.

Picq, Laurence. *Au-delà du ciel: cinq ans chez les khmers rouges*. Paris: Barrault, 1984.

———. "De la réforme linguistique et de l'usage des mots chez les khmers rouges." *Asie du sud-est et monde insulindien: Cambodge II*, 15, no. 1–4 (1984): 351–357.

Pin Yathay. *L'Utopie meurtrière: un rescapé du génocide cambodgien témoigne*. Paris: Laffont, 1980.

Ponchaud, François. *Cambodge, année zéro*. Paris: Julliard, 1977.

———. Introduction to *Le Mur de bambou: le Cambodge après Pol Pot*, by Esméralda Luciolli. Paris: Régine Deforges–Médecins sans frontières, 1988.

Porée-Maspero, Éveline. *Étude sur les rites agraires des Cambodgiens*. 3 vols. Paris–The Hague: Mouton, 1962–1969.

Pou, Saveros. *Études sur le Ramakerti (XVIe–XVIIe siècles)*. Publication de l'École française d'Extrême-Orient, nos. 110, 111, 117. Paris, 1977–1979.

Pou, Saveros, and Philip N. Jenner. "Les *cpāp'* ou 'codes de conduite' khmers, 1: *Cpāp' Kerti kāl*." *Bulletin de l'École française d'Extrême-Orient* 62 (1975): 369 –394.

———. "Les *cpāp'* ou 'codes de conduite' khmers, 2: *Cpāp' prus*." *Bulletin de l'École française d'Extrême-Orient* 63 (1976): 313–350.

———. "Les *cpāp'* ou 'codes de conduite' khmers, 3: *Cpāp' kūn cau*." *Bulletin de l'École française d'Extrême-Orient* 64 (1977): 167–215.

———. "Les *cpāp'* ou 'codes de conduite' khmers, 4: *Cpāp' rājaneti* ou *cpāp' brah rājasambhār*." *Bulletin de l'École française d'Extrême-Orient* 65 (1978): 361–402.

———. "Les *cpāp'* ou 'codes de conduite' khmers, 5: *Cpāp' kram*." *Bulletin de l'École française d'Extrême-Orient* 66 (1979): 129–160.

———. "Les *cpāp'* ou 'codes de conduite' khmers, 6: *Cpāp' trī neti*." *Bulletin de l'École française d'Extrême-Orient* 69 (1981): 135–193.

Preschez, Philippe. *Essai sur la démocratie au Cambodge*. Série C, recherche no. 4. Paris: Centre d'Études des relations internationales, 1961.

Prud'homme, Rémy. *L'Économie du Cambodge*. Paris: Presses universitaires de France, 1969.

*Put Tumneay*. 1970. 2d ed. Paris: Cedoreck, 1982.

Regaud, Nicolas. *Le Cambodge dans la tourmente: le troisième conflit indochinois*. Paris: L'Harmattan, 1992.

*Le Roman cambodgien du lièvre*. Paris: Cedoreck, 1985.

Ros Chantrabot. "Aperçu chronologique." *La République khmère, an IV* (1974): 1 –21.

Sahai, Sahachhinand. *Les Institutions politiques et l'organisation administrative du Cambodge ancien (VIe–XIIIe siècles)*. Publication de l'École française d'Extrême-Orient, no. 85. Paris, 1970.

Sam Sok. *La Future Société khmère*. Maisons-Alfort, 1981.

———. "Cambodge: quel avenir?" In *Cambodge 1986: annuaire cambodgien de documentation politique*, 1:3–12. Neuilly-sur-Marne: Centre de documentation cambodgienne contemporaine, 1987.

Sarin Chhak. *Les Frontières du Cambodge*. Paris: Dalloz, 1966.

Shawcross, William. *Sideshow: Kissinger, Nixon, and the Destruction of Cambodia*. New York: Simon and Schuster, 1979.

——. *The Quality of Mercy*. Glasgow: William Collins Sons, 1985.

Sihanouk, Norodom. *Statut de Sangkum Reastr Niyum*. Phnom Penh: Ministère de l'Information, 1955.

Sisowath Thomico. "Quelle solution pour le Cambodge?" In *Cambodge 1986: annuaire cambodgien de documentation politique*, 2:13–41. Neuilly-sur-Marne: Centre de documentation cambodgienne contemporaine, 1987.

Sok Vanny. "Réflexion sur la khméritude." *Asie du sud-est et monde insulindien: Cambodge II*, 15, nos. 1–4 (1984): 141–144.

Szymusiak, Molyda. *Les Pierres crieront: une enfance cambodgienne, 1975–1980*. Paris: La Découverte, 1984.

Thierry, Solange. *Le Cambodge des contes*. Paris: L'Harmattan, 1985.

——. *Les Khmers*. Paris: Seuil, 1964.

Thion, Serge, and Ben Kiernan. *Khmers rouges! matériaux pour l'histoire du communisme au Cambodge*. Paris: J. E. Hallier–Albin Michel, 1981.

Thion, Serge, and Jean-Claude Pomonti. *Des courtisans aux partisans: la crise cambodgienne*. Paris: Gallimard, 1971.

*Vacananukram Khmaer*. Phnom Penh: Buddhist Institute, 1986.

Vickery, Michael. *Kampuchea: Politics, Economics, and Society*. London: Pinter-Reiner, 1986.

Y Phandara. *Retour à Phnom Penh: le Cambodge du génocide à la colonisation; témoignage*. Paris: Métailié, 1982.

# Index

Compositor: ComCom
Text: 10/13 Aldus
Display: Aldus
Printer: Haddon Craftsmen
Binder: Haddon Craftsmen